# RIVER IN A
# DRY LAND

# RIVER IN A DRY LAND

## A Prairie Passage

Trevor Herriot

Published in 2001 by
Stoddart Publishing Co. Limited
895 Don Mills Road, 400-2 Park Centre, Toronto, Canada M3C 1W3

First published in hardcover in 2000 by Stoddart Publishing Co. Limited

**www.stoddartpub.com**

To order Stoddart books please contact General Distribution Services
Tel. (416) 213-1919     Fax (416) 213-1917
Email cservice@genpub.com

10   9   8   7   6   5   4   3   2   1

**National Library of Canada Cataloguing in Publication Data**

Herriot, Trevor
River in a dry land: a Prairie passage
Includes bibliographical references and index.

ISBN 0-7737-3271-3 (bound). — ISBN 0-7737-6241-8 (pbk.)

1. Herriot, Trevor.   2. Herriot Family.   3. Farm life — Qu'Appelle River Valley
(Sask. And Man.) — Description and travel.   4. Farm life — Saskatchewan.
5. Qu'Appelle River Valley (Sask. And Man.) — Description and travel.
6. Qu'Appelle River Valley (Sask. And Man.) — History.
7. Qu'Appelle River Valley (Sask. And Man.) — Biography. I. Title.

FC3545.Q36Z49   2000       971.24'403'092       C00-931352-4
F1074.Q34H47   2000

Cover design: Angel Guerra
Cover illustration: "River Bend," by Brian Hoxha,
a drypoint print with watercolour
Maps and text illustrations: Trevor Herriot
Text design, typesetting and grass icon: Kinetics Design & Illustration

Excerpts from "Telling the Holy" by Scott Russell Sanders reprinted by
permission of *Orion* (Winter 1993), 195 Main Street, Great Barrington, MA 01230.
Excerpt from *Silton Seasons* by R.D. Symons reprinted by permission of the
Estate of R.D. Symons. Excerpt from "Arctic Dreams" by Barry Lopez reprinted
by permission of Sterling Lord Literistics.

THE CANADA COUNCIL | LE CONSEIL DES ARTS
FOR THE ARTS | DU CANADA
SINCE 1957 | DEPUIS 1957

*We acknowledge for their financial support of our publishing program the Canada Council, the Ontario Arts Council,
and the Government of Canada through the Book Publishing Industry Development Program (BPIDP).*

Printed and bound in Canada

*For Karen*

*And a man shall be as an hiding place from the wind,*

*and a covert from the tempest;*

*as rivers of water in a dry place,*

*as the shadow of a great rock in a weary land.*

*— Isaiah 32:2*

# CONTENTS

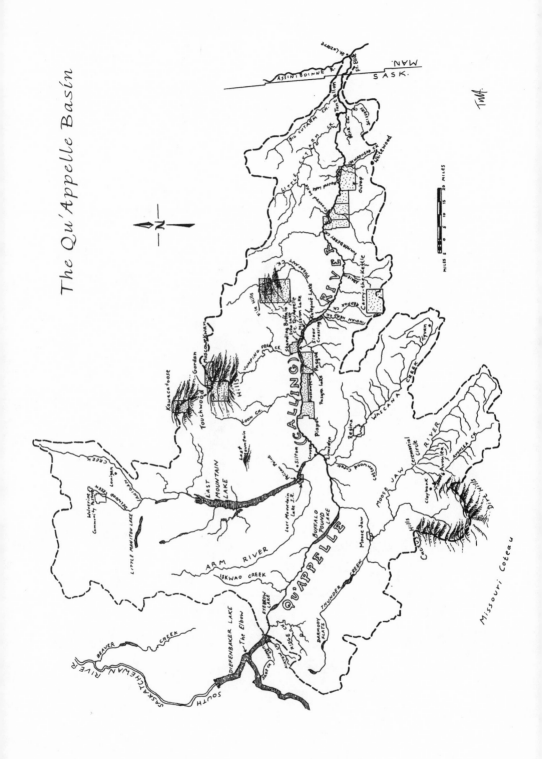

The Qu'Appelle Basin

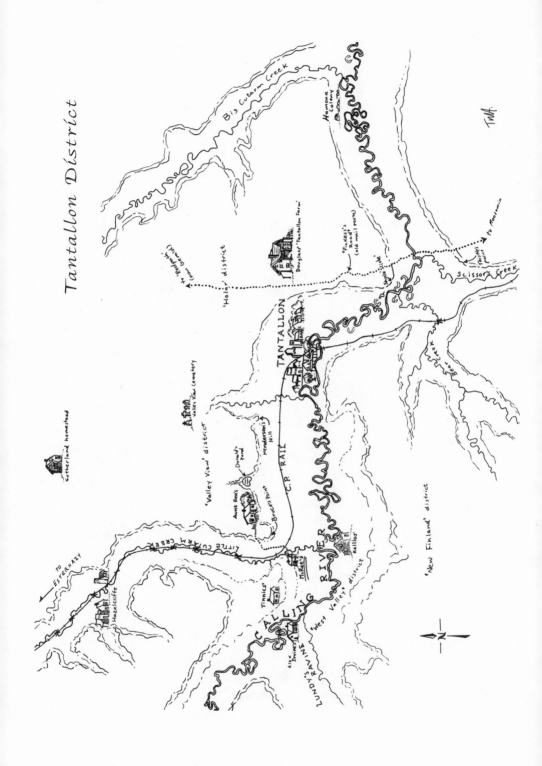

Tantallon District

# RIVER OF VOICES

*GRASS ENCIRCLING, A SHIFTING CURTAIN OF GREEN that parts with each step along the bottomland. The blue, remote and radiant beyond the wavering rim of grass. Warm. There are sweet fragrances and a hand leading, holding. Then the grass falls away at the edge of a cut meadow, and on the horizon hills appear — round, shaggy, humpbacked. On the meadow, people stand beneath and around a long, low canopy open to the wind. Ruddy-faced men in baggy pants and suspenders smoke pipes in the shade of broad-brimmed hats. Beside tables that seem endless, women stand hip to hip, and between their gingham and paisley-printed backsides come glimpses of cut flowers, jams and jellies, pies, loaves of bread, bunches of carrots, squashes, tomatoes. No hand now, only the warmth of the women under the canopy and the garden-row scent of marigolds and petunias.*

This fragment of memory from days I spent as a child in the eastern Qu'Appelle Valley has been surfacing in my dreams for fifteen years now — the time I have lived in this city. First, and most vividly, as an unsolicited daydream at my desk, when I was supposed to be writing equipment test procedures for the office job that has supported me and my family all these years. Its intensity surprised me that first time. I still have the gold-coloured inter-office mail form on which I scribbled down the images while they were burning bright in my mind.

I recognized the place at once as the tallgrass bottomland on the west side of the village of Tantallon, which lies in the valley a few miles upstream of the wooded bend where the Qu'Appelle River leaves Saskatchewan and, just inside Manitoba, spills into the Assiniboine. In the dream I am, to the best of my reckoning, four years old, and I am walking through grasses, perhaps big bluestem and green needle grass, holding my father's hand. We lived in Tantallon for part of 1961 and 1962, and though we visited frequently thereafter and attended more fairs, I am convinced that this memory comes from the late summer or early fall of 1962.

In the opening of the dream I cannot see beyond the immediate wall of grass, which at that time of year would have been well over my head. Somehow this did not scare me, although I was a fearful boy, terrified of large dogs and the bats that flickered their shadows on the ceiling of our home by the river. I walk through the fairgrounds like a ghost in my own memories and then wake up feeling a warmth, a security that comes from my father's hand, the embrace of the grass, and the smells of vegetables, flowers, and pies under the canopy. Such feelings, and those associated with my other memories of the eastern Qu'Appelle, nourish me now as an adult, and keep me in mind of home, where the valley and my origins once converged.

Feelings of nostalgia — and my dream is nothing if it is not nostalgia in its original sense, a yearning for home — are not to be trusted, we are told. Nostalgia creates mythologies that cover up the reality of our past as individuals and as a culture. Undeniably, those of us who live west of the 100th meridian have been using nostalgia to construct a romance fiction out of our history. The virtuous plains settler and plains culture are something of a lie, of course, and the best of our literature has done much to expose it. Still, there is no denying the power of nostalgia. A people who fall easily under its spell are living in exile from something — a life or a home that they or their ancestors forsook.

It is exile that interests me. We of the colonizing European races on the Great Plains have passed through a succession of exiles: most recently, from the farms and towns of our childhood; before that, from the homestead-subsistence lives of our immigrant grandparents; before that, from the landscape and culture of the old country. Predating all these displacements is the deeper, older exile that set us onto a trail of looking for the next fertile valley, a better home, a richer life. This first exile, summarized in the Eden myth, is the one that drew us apart from the rest of the Creation and its wildness, turning us into farmers and God into an absentee landlord.

If nostalgia works strongly upon our modern sensibilities it is because we are yearning, not so much for "home," whatever that may be, as for the time when we were still on speaking terms with our landscapes. The sharpest pangs of wistfulness we feel are the intimations of a former communion with a meadow, a valley, a stand of trees, a river — the land that knew us. Something in our blood remembers, yearns hopelessly for lost lifeways and the time when we were native and kin to the soil, the water, the creatures, and the plants. Hopelessly or not, prairie people continue to dream of a cultural bargain that would allow us to live well and long in a dry land. Getting there from here would require, among other revolutions, a willingness to make actual, hand-and-foot contact with the land, to accumulate an intimate knowledge of local lives and ecologies, and to tell and retell the right stories. An unlikely journey, perhaps, but the right kind of nostalgia, a selective yearning that remembers our failures and imagines our possibilities, would be enough inspiration to allow us to embark. Hope resides in a better nostalgia — one that leads not to sentimental fraud but to reconciliation and atonement; one that sounds within our hearts an ethic that has nothing to do with the claims we stake upon the prairie and everything to do with the claims the prairie stakes upon us.

THE LAST TIME the dream came to me was a week ago. That night I had been out playing basketball. It was early November, the beginning of the season during which I will sometimes go out to an old gymnasium, late in the evening, to pretend I am sixteen again and huff and sweat alongside other pretenders. The ball would not drop for me that night and I went to bed afterwards, replaying in my mind back-door lay-ups and fast-breaks. The next morning I dragged myself to the office late. I was aching from post-basketball trauma, but the real problem was lack of sleep. Karen had been out in the middle of the night at a birth.

I suppose there are men married to midwives and birth attendants who become used to the late-night bedside telephone conversations. "Yes . . . good. No, that's the mucous plug, uh-huh, it's supposed to fall out. Call me back when the contractions are too strong for you to sleep." They are almost always too strong for *me* to sleep. I am a light sleeper, and so when someone next to me is whispering phrases that include "cervix" and "perineum," I am awake and waiting for a progress report before I can close my eyes again. Sleep came more slowly than usual after the phone calls had finally stopped and Karen had left to attend the birth. Pregnant herself with our fourth child, Karen was nauseated and tired most of the time. She was attending a simple hospital birth where she would act as labour support for the couple, but in my fitful sleep I began to imagine other scenarios, all variations on the birth of our last child, Sage, five years ago.

It was the same time of the year, late fall. A freezing rain had glazed the city with ice. Karen was swaying in the dark of the living room, taking each contraction stoically and passing through what we thought was early labour. But then, as she was braiding her hair before the mirror, she started making throaty, guttural sounds — the kind of noises that I had heard her make before, in the final five minutes of birth, when all the life in her gathers up to bear the child forth. Other signs of advanced labour came forth and then, just as we were putting on coats, the baby's crown appeared. It was too late and the streets were too slippery to risk a dash for the hospital, so Karen stood in our kitchen, her coat still on, and pushed a daughter out into my arms.

Recalling the drama and beauty of that surprising birth — and mingling it with the unknown births of the night and of a night the following spring when I would again watch Karen bear a child into our home — I eventually fell back asleep.

Then the alarm. I bolted upright and saw that Karen was back in bed, asleep after the night's work. Birth was still with me, hovering in the darkness of the bedroom, but there was something else: marigolds, petunias, and an abiding warmth. I closed my eyes and saw the grass, the fairgrounds, and the distant valley hills, ponderous as dragons sleeping. No images of the river; it never appears in the dream. But afterwards, for the remainder of that day, as I sat before the computer screen or listened to someone expound on the corporation's new strategic initiative, the river invaded my thoughts, winding in and out of view in silver elliptic lengths across the broad plain of my longing.

SOMEONE — who, I cannot recall — once said that all human longing is a longing for mother. Or was it a longing for home? For me it almost amounts to the same thing anyway. The eastern Qu'Appelle is my mother's country *and* my mother country. My mother was born there on a farm just upstream of Tantallon more than seventy years ago. The Tantallon area is part of the deepest, most heavily wooded, and in some ways the wildest portion of the valley.

If a true valley is a lowland between ranges of hills or mountains that protrude above the surrounding elevation, then the Qu'Appelle is less a valley than a great groove set into the level plain. To geologists it is a classic post-glacial meltwater channel — an alluvial trench one mile wide and from 100 to 450 feet deep, running roughly west to east 250 miles across Saskatchewan from its origins just east of the Elbow of the South Saskatchewan River. To the First Peoples, it is God's country. It might have been that for us too, had we taken Isaiah at his word, for the valley has long been exalted, the hills were made low beneath the first push of Pleistocene ice, and every field and pasture proclaims that "all flesh is grass."

The Qu'Appelle country brackets the northeastern limits of North America's Great Plains, the high and dry lands stretching across the continent's rain-shadowed interior. Wherever annual evaporation exceeds annual precipitation in this region, prairie holds sway. The glaciated peneplain that gathers water for the Qu'Appelle receives on average less than sixteen inches of precipitation a year. During the hottest months, however, when the spear grass grows brittle and the hills take on their gold and khaki summer dress, the sun will pull as much as thirty inches of surface water from the valley's lakes. A river in a dry land, the Qu'Appelle has been known in drought years to vanish along part of its length, leaving behind a muddy stream bed and disgruntled muskrats. But there are wet years too, like the summer of '96 when I travelled the basin's length and breadth, from the valley's start near Ridge Creek in the west to its confluence with the Assiniboine at St. Lazare, Manitoba, and from the Dirt Hills uplands in the south to the head of Lanigan Creek in the north. That year the rain seemed to fall every day, keeping the hills as green as the Appalachians, pushing the river beyond its banks and out across its floodplain, and filling the creeks and sloughs with sticklebacks, leopard frogs, gadwall, and wigeon.

The valley itself, a relatively moist corridor of prairie aspiring to be woodland, is a refuge from the arid domain above, a hiding place from the unceasing wind. It appears to the traveller as a wandering line of returnings, a shelter you leave and rejoin and leave again. If you were to zigzag your way across the basin's 20,000 square miles, you would experience the sunken landscapes of the Qu'Appelle and its tributaries as a dramatic intaglio of remnant wildness, a network of the old grass and buffalo world etched into the ground of your journey. Each time you dropped down into a valley or coulee, the shift from cropland to grassland would arrest your senses, dulled from the flat monotony of wheat fields above, embracing you again in velvety slopes, curves, shadows — the rondo of mixed-grass prairie.

At Tantallon, the valley shows its downstream affinities with the eastern and northern hardwood forests. White birch, American elm, Manitoba maple, aspen poplar, green ash, nannyberry, and bur oak cover all the north-facing slopes and much of the south-facing ones. Plants from the eastern tallgrass prairie mingle with mixed-grass species on the hilltops and in the forest openings. Upstream at Crooked Lake, less than forty miles away, this eastern influence has all but disappeared — the last bur oaks have dropped off and the south-facing hills are half bare. The westernmost patches of tallgrasses such as big bluestem are another fifty miles or so upstream at Katepwe Lake, not far from places where cactus species begin to dominate amid the shorter grasses. Continuing upstream, passing three more lakes, dozens of tributaries, and an ever-widening valley floor, the trees on the shady, north-facing slopes become smaller and scarcer, until upstream of Buffalo Pound Lake the valley is a shallow, broad range of prairie hills shouldering a flat bottomland: native grasses on the uplands, tame grasses on the bottoms. Along the valley's length, the fertile bottomland has been sown to grains and hay. Only small remnants of native floodplain habitat remain. The hills on either side, however, form a long margin of interwoven native prairie and woodland, continuous save for roads and other interruptions. Throughout, there are farms and ranches, lakeside resorts, and a half-dozen small towns and villages, Tantallon being the easternmost of these.

AFTER THE YEAR we lived in Tantallon, we moved north of the valley a few miles to Esterhazy, a larger town along one of the Qu'Appelle's tributaries, the Little Cutarm Creek. From there, visiting on weekends, we stayed in touch with the valley, with life in the village and on my relatives' farms nearby. Our time in Tantallon was spent by the river in a rambling old house my grandfather had bought. He did not like living there, preferred the quiet of the country, and so we shared the house with my great-aunt and -uncle. Three storeys, high ceilings, a verandah sweeping round the side and front — it was a magnificent edifice in our eyes. We called it the Mansion. There were large elms and maples growing on the rough lawn between the Mansion and the riverbank. I remember running in their shade, clambering along their limbs, looking out from leaves to the east where our driveway turned onto the road and the bridge at the south side of town. Across the river were wilder trees: birch, poplar, and oak in a wall of dark green that formed the southern slopes of the valley. In my recollection, this was the unpeopled place: a wildness anchored by the river to my world of climbing trees, Mansion, and village.

Around a bend in the river and within earshot was a swimming hole where my older cousins and their friends spent a good portion of each summer. As soon as the river calmed down and warmed up in spring, they would dive for an afternoon, working to clear the bottom of snags, freshwater mussels, and other items that might gash their feet. Then it was a matter of setting up the diving board, using planks and pilings liberated from the village lumberyard. The river was theirs from June to August, a place to be naked and tribal and almost wild, to plunge into the danger and mischief of boyhood. When the water was high enough they would launch themselves in yodelling, limb-flapping dives from the concrete archways of the bridge by the Mansion. There would be days when their voices echoed from the high banks across our lawn and onto the verandah.

THE QU'APPELLE is a river of voices. The name — French for "what calls?" — is a rough translation of the original Cree words for the river and refers to stories from the oral tradition that have been reinvented over the years by a succession of missionaries, fur traders, and poets. If the valley has any fame beyond Saskatchewan, it stems from the shamelessly romantic treatment of the Qu'Appelle story given by the Métis poet Pauline Johnson. Johnson had a brief but successful (for a poet) career at the end of the nineteenth century, reciting her ballads and lyrics in concert halls across Canada and in England. She appeared on stage in full Pocahontas regalia, feeding white audiences the tincture of post-colonial romanticism they craved. In rollicking Victorian verse — the kind that puts "thees" and "thines" into the mouths of every ardent character — her poems served up bittersweet, heroic tales of the wronged savage and lost innocence in the New World. She was Canada's most popular poet in her day, and two of her poems — "The Legend of the Qu'Appelle" and "The Song My Paddle Sings" — still appear in Canadian school texts. And we, the white inheritors of racial guilt, still accept generalizations — simulations of the Shaman, the Indian Princess, the Vanishing Native, the Lazy Indian — in place of the real, living tribal people of the late twentieth century on the Great Plains.

The irony of any effort to understand the original stories of a place in the New World is that the accounts were translated and recorded most often by missionaries — the men whose ordained vocation it was to turn the aboriginal peoples away from their lore and beliefs. Pauline Johnson based her version of the Qu'Appelle legend on a story she heard from Father Hugonard of the Lebret Mission in the valley. In "The Legend of the Qu'Appelle," the voices of the Qu'Appelle are the cries of a phantom, an "Indian maid"; at her death she calls out for her lover who is far away across one of the valley lakes, paddling his way home. These lines show the lovelorn brave giving his account of the events the day he hurried back to see his "queen."

*When suddenly from out the shadowed shore,*
*I heard a voice speak tenderly my name.*

*"Who calls?" I answered; no reply; and long*
*I stilled my paddle blade and listened. Then*
*Above the night wind's melancholy song*
*I heard distinctly that strange voice again —*
*A woman's voice, that through the twilight came*
*Like to a soul unborn — a song unsung.*

*I leaned and listened — yes, she spoke my name,*
*And then I answered in the quaint French tongue,*
*"Qu'Appelle? Qu'Appelle?" No answer, and the night*
*Seemed stiller for the sound, till round me fell*
*The far-off echoes from the far-off height —*
*"Qu'Appelle?" my voice came back, "Qu'Appelle?"*

Our multilingual narrator then rushes ahead to the camp, where he finds that his betrothed has died during the night. Sorrow overtakes him, yet he finds consolation in learning that she called his name twice just before her death, at the exact hour he heard the voice.

There may be instances when this sort of lore-tampering is harmless poeticizing and not a real threat to the way a culture regards its place in the landscape. In this case, however, the ersatz legend seems to have added at least a layer to the cataracts that prevent us from seeing the real mystery and myth of a river that calls. Given the possibility that the river's name and its stories of origin might in some way inform our relationship with the ecologies of this northeastern stretch of the Great Plains, the accounts that predate Pauline Johnson's melodrama are worth a second look.

One version of the naming story was passed on to Oblate missionaries by a great Cree chief and medicine man named Loud Voice.[1] He ascribed the Cree name for the river, Kahtapwao Sepe (What Is Calling? River), to an incident years before when two groups of people, one from the north and one from the south, met at the river. Unable to cross, the people traded news by standing on their respective shores and shouting back and forth to one another.

Though this version too has been interpreted by missionaries, the simple story appeals to me for its image of the river as a place for people to gather and communicate. That it was told to the missionaries by a man named for his voice makes it all the more compelling.

An earlier account of the river's naming comes from James Austin Dickinson, a surveyor-naturalist on the 1858 Assiniboine and Saskatchewan Exploring Expedition. In July, the month the saskatoon berries ripen and the spear grass sets seed, Dickinson and his men paddled downstream from the Anglican mission on Mission Lake (just east of today's Fort Qu'Appelle) to the outflow of the Qu'Appelle into the Assiniboine at Fort Ellice. At the end of his week-long journey, Dickinson encountered an old Cree hunter who knew the valley well and the names of all its tributaries. The man was in his seventies, which places his birth well into the previous century when the valley and the northeastern Great Plains were still the undisputed domain of the Cree and the Assiniboine nations. Picking up a charred stick and scribbling on the floorboards of Fort Ellice, the hunter drew for Dickinson a detailed map of the lower Qu'Appelle Valley, showing the contours of the 110 miles of valley and 270 miles of river the surveyor had just travelled. Dickinson was amazed and said in his report that the hunter's map showed "every little creek so accurately that I easily recognized them."[2]

The first time I read Dickinson's report, I had a certain creek in mind. When I realized he was explaining the names of all the downstream tributaries in order, I skimmed forward to find the original name for the creek that runs past my old schoolyard on the edge of Esterhazy and then several miles down to the Qu'Appelle at what was once my grandfather's farm. We knew it by two names that were used interchangeably, depending on whether one favoured immigrant or indigenous history. To many people it was and is the Kaposvar Creek, named after a place in Hungary, the old country for most Esterhazy settlers. To others, especially those down where it enters the Qu'Appelle, it has always been the Little Cutarm Creek, which is a rough translation of the Cree name cited by Dickinson: Kiskipittonawe Sepesis.

There is something about the way Cree words sound that matches the breath and music of this region — a resonance with other native voices, the sound of a prairie snowstorm, of birdsong over short grass.

*Kiss-ki-pitt-a-now-way see-pi-siss.* If I say it the way my teacher, an elder from Piapot, spoke in the introductory Plains Cree class I once took — softly, through the teeth, with the mouth just barely open — the k's and p's make small, sharp tones like pebbles clacking together, while the s's create a sibilance, a hissing that comes from the force that stirs the grass, that makes all of us, Cree and English alike, speak through clenched teeth. *Kaposvar* is a word that sounds native in a river valley somewhere north of Hungary's Meosek Mountains; it belongs to the Little Cutarm only as a footnote in settler history.

A landform as vast and dramatic as the Qu'Appelle would have been known by a succession of names and stories over the ten thousand years of tribes travelling across and along its length. All but the most recent are lost. At the Moose Bay burial mound overlooking the Qu'Appelle at Crooked Lake, the bones, potsherds, and projectile points are mute on the subject. Archaeology fails us here. We cannot sift from the soil the place names spoken by a people who buried loved ones on the valley rim a thousand years ago. As for the names listed by Dickinson, their appeal and power endure with the people who first formed their syllables. The Plains Cree remain the dominant First Nation of the region and are anything but a vanquished people.

Cree and mixed-blood people live in my neighbourhood, and their children play with my children. Home might be a reserve in the valley, but now they live in the city and work in banks, on construction crews, in restaurants. The First Peoples are here, making claims and much else: headlines, powerful music, political bargains, community, astonishing art, court dockets, more of themselves. They endure and thrive despite racism and cultural repression, despite the horrific legacy of residential schools, despite the statistics of unemployment, prostitution, alcoholism, child abuse, and suicide, and despite the loss of self-respect that comes with dependency on white government.

In early spring, at the outflow of Katepwe Lake, I see young men from the reserves standing in the river, aiming arrows at buffalo fish; in summer while I am looking for hawk nests, I meet families out picking saskatoon berries. Yes, they drive half-tons and wear hats and shirts marked by the logos of shoe manufacturers, but they are at home here, in this city and in this same valley where their ancestors left offerings, dug breadroot, and impounded buffalo. For me, this adaptability and sustained tenancy lends their names for the Qu'Appelle and its tributaries — the Cree names documented by Dickinson — a validity that no other names can claim.

The river itself, according to Dickinson's hunter, is known as Katepwie Sepe. Here is its naming story, as taken down by the Queen's surveyor 140 years ago:

> *A solitary Indian was coming down the river in his canoe many summers ago, when one day he heard a loud voice calling to him; he stopped and listened and again heard the same voice as before. He shouted in reply, but there was no answer. He searched everywhere around, but could not find the tracks of anyone. So from that time forth, it was named the "Who Calls River."*[3]

There is always the problem of translation from Cree to English — the hunter's words were interpreted by the chief factor at Fort Ellice — and from oral context to the absence of context when such a story appears on the page. But there is no questioning the authority of a man who has travelled and hunted buffalo in the valley for a lifetime, who draws maps in charcoal and hangs a name on every lake, every ephemeral stream and creek.

The earliest written record of the river's name came a half century before Dickinson. In 1804, a young white trader for the North West Company, Daniel Williams Harmon, made a trip that took him to the upper Qu'Appelle, where, in his words, "a White Man was never before known to come." Without describing the person who told him the name of the river, Harmon begins his journal entry for March 11 with a different spelling of the same name recorded by Dickinson, attached to a similar but not identical story of origin:

> March 11, Sunday. Ca-ta-buy-se-ps *or the River that Calls, so named by the Natives, who imagine a Spirit is constantly going up and down the River, and its voice they say they often hear, but it resembles the cry of a human being.*[4]

Harmon's version contains the basic myth line of the river that calls out to people, but expresses it in the present tense — "its voice they say *they often hear"* something that the more recent versions lack. The other accounts describe the river's call not as a current reality but as a story from the past. This change in tense has set me to wondering whether, by the time Dickinson passed through the valley (fifty-four years after Harmon), the people had already stopped hearing some of the voices in their landscape.

Viewed this way, Pauline Johnson's poem, another half century later, completes the transition of what we have done with the river's call: originally an enduring and present communication between landscape and dwellers, then a respected story of ancestors, and finally a quaint legend that is of some comfort to the colonial myth-makers who would have us believe that the Indians have been conquered.

Since Daniel Harmon's visit to the valley, the First Peoples of the Qu'Appelle have been coming to terms with a culture whose trail is marked not by stories or deference to the order indwelling in wildness but by agrarian settlement, complex machinery, fossil fuels, and the alien values these imply. Along the way, although the descendants of the nineteenth-century Cree namers have survived, much has been lost. The world of the plains hunter-gatherer, where people once heard rivers call, is gone and cannot be retrieved. Most of us have no way to re-enter the myth-wisdom of that cosmos.

When I go now to sit along the banks of the Qu'Appelle River, the only calls that strike my ear come from the kingfishers, the bobolinks, and a dozen other birds of the riverside. Lacking the hunter-gatherer's flow between self and environment, we are unable to hear the Creation in the same way as Dickinson's map-drawing hunter. Even so, something in me wants to believe that our deafness is not incurable; that, in learning new ways to listen to and communicate with our home landscapes, we may be able to head off ecological catastrophe and find deliverance.

Although it is clear that we have done much to reduce our conversation with the land to a monologue of demands and plunder, and although we do not have the myth-mind of the original listeners, we do have other faculties — the will, imagination, thought, emotion, and memory of modern man. With these we can again listen and respond to a mountain or a river. At least this is how I explain certain moments of insight or disclosure, when the distance between myself and the river vanishes, bearing the voice of Kahtapwao Sepe into my awareness and apprehension of the land.

IF I WERE to describe the experience of these moments in the Qu'Appelle country, I would begin by saying that each impression remains with me, in vibration or consonance, like a scrap of verse that echoes, remembered and reimagined, in my mind.

The dream of the fair eventually led me to find a place in the valley. For five winters and five summers now we have made our weekend trips to seventy acres of spear-grass ridges and poplar-filled coulees. From the porch we can see down the full length of Katepwe Lake, the last and deepest in the string of the four Calling Lakes, each besieged by the cottages of too many others who are responding in their own way to the river's call. The mile of valley between our porch and the nearest subdivision is buffer enough: for the family of long-eared owls that nested in Balsam Coulee and hunted above Mole Meadow (we are namers too); for the brooding ruffed grouse who held her ground while I cut trail two paces away; and for the hazel that blooms in whorls of fuchsia so small and yet so startling against the grey of April in the woods.

And, other times, in the coulees and on hilltops: a fawn hunkered down in green needle grass; a black and white warbler singing in the breath of dawn every day of the summer, gradually making his way down Grouse Coulee, until August arrived and his song, unrequited, lifted faintly one last time from the end of the coulee; discovering the old trail down the west side; losing a kite and finding a yellow lady's slipper instead; making love one morning in a patch of sarsaparilla and violets; the afternoon my daughter pointed out to me the precise snowberry bush beneath which she saw a smooth green snake last year.

And the moment I realized, at the government archives office, that these seventy acres belonged first to a Métis family, who on June 8, 1883, received a patent for the land. Alexander Fisher, Alexander the Elder, said the homestead file. Whether he lost the land or let it go during the

Métis resistance in 1885, the records do not show. Just the same, the message came through loud and clear: there are other claims upon this land.

And the radiance of a mixed-blood woman I saw at a music festival in the park named after a queen who never saw, much less dreamed of, this place. I looked at her shamelessly — long, auburn hair gathered up in loose strands above her neck. Wide-set eyes almost black. The tops of her cheeks were freckled and they pressed against her lower eyelashes when she faced the sun. There were flower patterns embroidered on her dress and in her hair a single gaillardia blossom, the "blanket flower," a native prairie flower that inspired beadwork and blanket designs. The broad circle of her face, the arch of her nose, and the set of her eyes and cheekbones have been in people here since the glaciers retreated; but her fair skin and auburn hair and her freckles recalled another northern race more recently arrived. If I stared, it was in the way any man stares — to possess something of a woman's beauty — but it was also in astonishment at seeing manifest a romantic construct I have fallen for, despite my better judgment: the notion of the Métis people as a superior plains race, an embodiment of the best in the native and the new. We can, if we will let ourselves, dream of a prairie culture where categories and blood do not matter so much. Beyond our knowing how, we might then at least recognize that the original wildness and the indigenous breath of a country find their way into our lives, into more than the meander of rivers and the ecologies of grass, trees, soil, and water, inhabiting a woman's grace, a child's voice, a song, a painting.

And swimming with my children at Katepwe Beach in the valley. My attention taken for a moment by the accusing message on a T-shirt worn by a nine-year-old Cree boy standing in the lake shallows. It read, "INDIAN HOLOCAUST — 1492–1992." The shock tactic worked: I stared. A white man's conscience had been tweaked, but instead of the usual wash of liberal guilt, I found myself thinking about Loud Voice's story and wondering if the waters the boy's family and my family were standing in might still reconcile us; if Kahtapwao Sepe might still be a place to call to one another from opposing shores. City people across from rural people, indigenous across from immigrant. We could meet

on the banks of the Calling River to float our differences, our griev-
ances, and our hopes upon its waves, to call out our diversity and our
fears, and then listen for echoes from the far shore.

These varied revelations of the Calling River cross the membrane of my
consciousness in a dialogue that, for lack of any other correlative, I could
call prayer. Prayer in the sense of communicating with the Other, something outside the self and the daily round of things.

The line between vocation and invocation blurs when I watch mists
lift at sunrise over Donald's Pond; when the cut of wing against air
wakes me on a hilltop beneath shadows of turkey vultures so near I can
make out the bristles on their bare red skulls; when the pinched end of
a roll-your-own cigarette or the amber-red of tea in a cup brings my
grandfather to mind; when a thousand frogs and salamanders escort me
to the rim of the Little Cutarm on a road that runs with three days of
rain; or when, having eviscerated our catch at the riverside, I carry the
heart of a big northern pike in my hand to show the children, and
doubting my senses I see and feel it throb, pressing upward from my
palm, rhythmically with the hunger for life that dwells in a predatory
fish in midsummer. And we stare in awkward reverential silence,
regretting death, remembering our own hearts and hungers.

And I wonder whether the river is calling or I am replying. Perhaps
it does not matter.

*Part One*

# THE
# DIRT HILLS

*"I*F THERE IS MAGIC *on this planet, it is contained in water."*

— LOREN EISLEY, THE IMMENSE JOURNEY

*Chapter One*

## LINES ON THE CIRCLE

IT IS EARLY APRIL. The land laid bare is forty shades of dirty straw yellow to dun grey. An elm tree east of me, longing for colour, reaches up and snags a piece of sky. I have seen this before: turn to the wind, fold wings once, twice, and then sing. Sing the wild notes a mountain bluebird always sings on a day like this. Softly, to the hillside.

The sound hangs in the air like spindrift over the great swell of prairie combing the northeastern shores of the Missouri Coteau. These are the Dirt Hills near Avonlea, Saskatchewan. No mountains here for the bluebird and me; only an elevation from the prairie's flatness sudden enough to arouse a sense of altitude and expansiveness in anyone who looks out from the crest. Seven hundred feet below me swings the level floor of farmland hinged at the horizon and overarched by the vaulting sky.

I turn to face the bluebird downslope from me where a trough of snow waters a rag-tag band of elm and ash trees. Beside my left shin is an oblong boulder spattered orange and black with lichens. A museum archaeologist once told me the names of each lichen on this rock, and how they can be used in dating ancient campsites on the plains. I wrote the Latin binomials down in a notebook and now all I remember of them is *Xanthoria*. The name suited the grandeur of the place. Such rocks are called erratics because they arrived here on paths and schedules we do not completely understand, riding the continental ice sheets that shaped this land more than twelve thousand years ago. This erratic became less so sometime during the past thousand years, when a clan of ancient hunters, mindful of the spirit of the place, the stars, or some event worth marking, aligned it within a large circle of smaller stones. Looking out beyond the central boulder I see a ring of stones at a thirty-foot radius from me. I raise my eyes above the arc of stones to the prairie's far circumference beneath the sky. A thought falls away from me, fissile and heavy as shale: these people, the men and women who arranged the granite and limestone into this ceremonial circle, did not choose this place at random. They knew that here they could celebrate within sight of a generous sweep of their range. They reckoned the position of this hilltop within the whole landscape and — as surely as they knew the stories of their grandfathers — they knew where its waters flowed.

IF THE SURFACE of the land has axis points, this is one of them. The Dirt Hills are halfway between the natural borders of the Great Plains at this latitude: the Rocky Mountains in the west and the Red River in the east. They stand at the edge of the Missouri Coteau, a rolling brim of upland that rises against the southwestern reaches of the Qu'Appelle River basin.

Sweeping south and west from here in a massive horseshoe open to the north, the hills are made of bedrock that was stacked up like tiles by a thrust of the last glacier to pass this way. A small creek originates from within the embrace of the hills and runs out the opening to join the Qu'Appelle by way of the Moose Jaw River. This particular promontory at the tip of the horseshoe's eastern arm is 2,800 feet above sea level — the highest point in the Qu'Appelle watershed. Here you look out as from a crow's nest upon the southern shoals of the basin. There is no better place to stand and stare and pitch yourself into the lay of this land.

By the mid-nineteenth century, white explorers were hearing of the Dirt Hills as a place where the people of the northern grasslands gathered in ceremony and dance, merging their lives with the life of their country. The journals of Henry Youle Hind mention a July afternoon in 1858 when he and his imperially appointed expedition of surveyors, engineers, and voyageurs paused on the plains just west of the spot where Cottonwood Creek joins the Qu'Appelle River. From there, looking south across the intervening forty miles of grass, Hind saw what could only have been this range of hills: "We caught a glimpse of the blue outline of the Grand Coteau, with a treeless plain between us and the nearest part which is called the 'Dancing Point of the Grand Coteau'; and has long been distinguished for the 'medicine ceremonies' which are celebrated there." Modern readers are left wanting more details, perhaps a story his mixed-blood[5] guides told him of the hills; but Hind was a geologist, not an ethnographer. Any more than this brief citation would have exceeded the requirements of his colonial mission.

Facing north toward the pathway of Hind's exploration, I can see across a large piece of the prairie domain that empties into the Qu'Appelle. Beyond the Moose Jaw River, past towns named Drinkwater and Briercrest, the level land runs to the edge of the earth where the city of Regina floats on its lake bed of clay like a shiny new boat. Behind me on the far side of the hills, water runs west and south into the Coteau's internal drainage basins. In front of me all the land I see drains into the Qu'Appelle. This ceremonial circle — this Dancing Point of the Grand Coteau — is an inscription on the heel of the foot of the entire watershed.

We are both, the bluebird and I, newcomers to this monumental landscape. In the 1920s, settlers near Regina saw the first mountain bluebirds arrive in the region. An arresting sight those first bluebirds must have been to a farmer working the grey fields of spring. Imagine the even greater surprise of the Indian people who saw the first European, Anthony Henday, trekking across the northernmost tip of the Qu'Appelle basin 170 years earlier. The bluebirds, finding hospitality in the prairie's fresh growth of fence posts and poplar bluffs, accommodated themselves well to the unfamiliar landscape and thrived. The Europeans, accommodating the land to suit themselves, eventually settled by creating an alien, and some would say provisional, hospitality. The bluebird tribe has come to belong here in a matter of eighty years. My tribe, 250 years after Henday's visit, is still working at it.

Leaving the ceremonial circle, I walk north across a rancher's fence to another hill pasture. There are tipi rings here. I've seen them before, but now they elude me like a constellation when the sky turns. I stand

and peer into my memory of where they should be. Finally, a bargain arrives between the sunlight and the grama grass shadows, casting fieldstones into sharp relief. In the flickering of a moment, the pasture resolves itself into an assembly of stone circles. From this vantage point I can see several tipi rings and a burial mound that was looted long ago by amateur archaeologists or grave robbers. Here a hunting people — the people of the prairie — once camped, prepared meals, prayed, made music, boasted, laughed, danced, made love, and honoured their dead. The day they moved on to follow the buffalo or travel to winter camp, the women pulled up the tent skins, leaving behind the stone anchors and creating these rings of granite and gneiss. Circles on a circular land.

Looking out again from the elliptic contours of this pasture to the distant flatland of the Qu'Appelle watershed, I am jarred by the dissonance of its squares and straight lines. I want to turn and walk away from the vista, away from the hatchwork lain across the land below, away from the boundaries that say nothing of wholeness and much of alienation, abuse, and loss. The familiar litany runs through my thoughts: small farms lost to large; country people lost to the city; youth lost to despair; organic matter lost to cultivation; native pastures lost to subsidy programs; wilderness lost to greed; wild species lost to pesticides and the plough.

Some creatures have adapted to the new geometry on the landscape and survived. Many dwell along the borders, in easements, rights-of-way, and ditches, where the grass is left alone and some diversity persists. Pragmatic conservationists are now at the important task of protecting these last allowances of almost wild habitat. But these marginalia to our ledgered landscape — we call them wildlife corridors — have not changed the ancient order of life here. We must not think that wild plants and animals have embraced our linear landscaping and abandoned their bond to the circle. Antenaria flowers may grow along the railroad, but they still mark their place on the land with rings of white bloom. Hawks will hunt the roadways from utility poles, but when they head skyward they festoon the sun with spirals. Bluebirds thrive along fencelines and readily accept the nest boxes people construct for them. But inside the box the bluebird always builds a circle of grass to shelter new life.

The evolved creation of the prairie remembers the circles. Builds

them, honours them, broods over them, sweeps across them in tribute
to the self-sustaining integrity of the land. Living and dying within the
rhythm of circles has worked here for more than ten thousand years.
The Cree, Assiniboine, Saulteaux, Dakota, Atsina, and their ancestors —
the ancient ones whom we know only by the chert they shaped and the
stone rings they left — succeeded as prairie people in part because they
kept faith with the wholeness of circles.

The first dwellers of the prairie addressed themselves to an original
wholeness when they came to the Dirt Hills. I come here to convince
myself that we have not yet erased all vestiges of that organic unity, that
we may still take counsel from the circle.

The unbroken arc has, at one time or another, entered the cosmolo-
gies of all religions, all civilizations east and west. My own culture at its
forgotten core recognizes too that life sustains itself in a circle of wholeness. There is a harmonic in the English language that runs from the
circle to the ideal of beauty through the words *wheel*, *whole*, and *health*. It
goes like this: a circle is a wheel, a wheel is a whole — the two words
echo one another. *Whole* comes from the Old English *hal*, and *hal* is the
root of *heal* and *health*. Beauty, by the standards of nature and any sane
culture, is nothing more and nothing less than health, wholeness.
Robinson Jeffers, a West Coast poet, bypassed all this etymology and
said it as a simple truth: "The greatest beauty is organic wholeness."

Standing here, my vision pulled along lines that run to the hundred-
mile sweep of horizon, there is no avoiding another voice of the western
part of this continent and what he had to say about lines, circle, and
man on the prairie. In *Wolf Willow*, Wallace Stegner described the
Northern Great Plains as "a country of geometry" where a "Euclidean
perfection abides." It is a land, said Stegner, that has made man "a challenging upright thing, as sudden as an exclamation mark, as enigmatic
as a question mark."

This April afternoon, Stegner's words arrive on a warm, arid wind
that blows across the Coteau from the western plains, where the human
question stands exposed in a land that is even higher and drier than this
hilltop. The prairie's circle can be an inhospitable place. A month ago, if
I had been the upright thing punctuating this summit of the Dirt Hills,
my exclamations and questioning would not have withstood the wind
chill. Even now, as I look out over the drawn and quartered flatland

from my seven-hundred-foot-high perch, I feel the urge to run downhill along a rivulet that will lead me to a creek that will lead me to the bottomland low in the Moose Jaw River bound for the Qu'Appelle. Away from the high and dry, down to the low and moist. Although I can't altogether blame Stegner for this impulse, there has always been something unsettling about that image of man as a punctuation mark on the prairie. Something that disturbs us in our provisional comfort, that threatens to disabuse us of the bivouac culture we have contrived as shelter against the elements.

I lean back to bathe my eyes in light from the April sky. The world is rounding toward its yearly increase. Toward crocus bloom, high water, a flush of green, birdsong. Toward the indivisible whirl of whelping, flowing, brooding, waking, spawning, hatching, birthing, hooting, howling, singing, sprouting, budding, and blossom. Sometime participant, full-time spectator to this round of things, I will take my family out to our acreage in the valley above Katepwe Lake, and we will look for owl nests and plant potatoes.

And our long shadows will mark the same questions brought to the prairie first by our immigrant ancestors — questions of civilization and belonging in this landscape. In my mind, these questions have always been up here exposed to the sun on the high plateaus and uplands. The answers, I have come to believe, are down in the bottomlands, the coulees, the ravines, and valleys, where running water calls us to its side.

THE SUN PULLS WEST and I walk deeper into the hills. On a plateau covered by last year's spear grass and overlooking a gully filled with poplar and ash trees, I come across another kind of circle. It is a newer one, for someone has raised above it a dome-shaped cage of poplar saplings, and at its centre is a small ring of stones enclosing ashes from a recent fire. A red flag of cloth remains from the last ritual performed here. I am told that red signifies, to the Lakota people, the south, direction of warmth, hope, and the goodness of the earth. Seeing that flag, I allow a small hope to settle into my mind, slowly, cautiously. *Somebody still comes here to sweat and pray.* The circle remains, awaits our attendance and apprenticeship. The tools and ethics we have applied in this landscape are failing. We have others — permaculture, plant ecology, habitat restoration, sustainable communities, tolerance, forbearance, stewardship — that could help us honour the wholeness here and create new boundaries that encompass and unearth the ancient integrity beneath the divisions we have so hastily imposed.

I turn and face the distant scene again. The earth has shifted to a different angle, drawing a soft, grey light from the sky. The lines shrug off their shadows and recede; fields between the lines merge with one another. The soil is bare now. The primeval grass is gone. The margins and pathways of our toil have faded, and upon the horizon of possibility there looms a fresh landscape, a prairie formed by wildness and the care of its human dwellers.

*Chapter Two*

# BOUNDARIES

*I AM BOUND to the earth by a web of stories, just as I am bound to the creation by the very substance and rhythms of my flesh. By keeping the stories fresh, I keep the places themselves alive in my imagination. Living in me, borne in mind, these places make up the landscape on which I stand with familiarity and pleasure, the landscape over which I walk even when my feet are still.*

— SCOTT RUSSELL SANDERS, "TELLING THE HOLY"

CREATION IS ENOUGH and not enough. It always needs tinkering. A seventy-acre patch of fescue/spear grass upland and poplar/ash lowland, in the Qu'Appelle Valley near Katepwe Lake, tolerates my family and me on weekends. To us the place is sanctuary. To the fox, raccoons, hare, grouse, chickadees, and deer, we are an annoyance, at best a curiosity and potential leavers of food. To the hills, grass, and trees, we are beyond notice, beneath their scale of interest.

The year we bought the place, we named the woods, draws, and meadows, widened the deer trails running down two major wooded draws, and cut a short pathway across the west meadow: Mole Meadow, the children named it, after the pocket gophers who were there before us. The second year, we moved an old farmhouse onto Mole Meadow, thereby creating the sharpest boundary between ourselves and the wilder world beyond. The next year, we tilled a plot and planted cucumbers, potatoes, strawberries, and raspberries. Now, I am scheming to catch the spring run-off in a pond at the bottom of the property, where three deep draws converge.

The qualms I experience each time I make a new boundary or pathway on the land come, I suppose, from the wilderness philosophy that aspires to remove man from the landscape. In a culture where Creation is always either a whore or a virgin and almost never a mother, our attempts at "saving the earth" have created a bizarre nature mythos expressed in everything from "Man has come to the forest, Bambi" to the self-loathing extremes of the deep ecology movement.

Wilderness may be "the preservation of the world," but the valley where I take my family on weekends is no fastness of nature untouched by man. It never was. The Cree, Assiniboine, and Saulteaux have fished its lakes, killed its buffalo, burned its grass, gathered its sage, and dug its breadroot since time out of memory. Boundaries recognized by a hunter-gatherer are different from those recognized by a weekend naturalist, or a peasant-farmer, or a wheat-producer, or a factory-owner. The quality of such boundaries defining human enterprise, and their alignment with the lines of Creation, say much about a culture's long-term viability.

The Dirt Hills, like any place of long human occupancy suddenly overtaken by a civilization bent on acquiring wealth, has seen its lines of culture and economy redrawn with each successive generation. By rummaging through the middens of local history, I turned up traces of that succession of boundaries and its accompanying descent of myth. On a piece of land at the foot of the hills, out over the north face, a mile or more away from the ceremonial circle, the trail begins and ends.

Downslope: walk away from the stone rings, through a steep-edged coulee with poplar protecting enough moisture for the coming summer still held in coarse-grained snow banked above last year's mouldering leaves, out onto the broken, ridged, fluted, folding, eroding exposures of soft Cretaceous bedrock along parapets above holes in sandstone structures that re-emerge fifty feet below as caves, down a face of mud-stone ornamented with rubber rabbitbrush and contoured by wind and water, the prairie's sculptors, into ice-cream sundae heaps, and then out upon the grassy flats to stride past a succession of salt-loving forbs, cacti, and ground-plum, arriving finally, unaccountably, at a wall made of brick.

The bricks belong to the end of the story, but the beginning is here too, beneath the wall, where invisible footpaths once marked the original prairie sod.

*The aspiration of aboriginal people throughout the world has been to achieve a congruent relationship with the land, to fit well in it. To achieve occasionally a state of high harmony or reverberation. The dream of this transcendent congruency included the evolution of a hunting and gathering relationship with the earth, in which a mutual regard was understood to prevail; but it also meant a conservation of the stories that bind the people into the land.*

— BARRY LOPEZ, *ARCTIC DREAMS*

IT WAS 1941. Sam McWilliams sat in the shadows of another time. He sat alone in his house remembering when the ranch belonged to his father, Thomas. Where the bricks are now there once were cattle, corrals, and the new rangeland on their doorstep. He remembered the day the plant was built, and he remembered a hot afternoon in 1886 when he and his sister Jennie went with their father to the hills for the first time. And he remembered the handfuls of white clay they dug out of the hillsides. He remembered hearing as an eleven-year-old the sound of the prairie sod tearing before the ploughshares, the smell of the Poitras children who lived in a sod-roof shanty, and, in the early years, the hunted look of the Sioux taking refuge in the hills.

Whether they were the ancestors of the Lakota Sioux, the Nakota (Assiniboine), or the Atsina (Gros Ventre) is anyone's guess, but there was once a people who lived on the Northern Great Plains in a large area roughly centring on the Missouri Coteau. They lived in the Dirt Hills and by the categories of modern archaeology they have been granted a further association with this region.

Archaeologists distinguish the succession of ancient cultures by developing a lineage of technologies among the only artifacts that do not decompose in the soil: stone tools and pottery. When someone unearths a site with artifacts that are distinctive from any others within the known chronology of cultures, archaeologists date the new materials, name the cultural/technological complex that made them, and then place the new people on a time line next to the peoples that preceded, coexisted with, and superseded them. The Avonlea people were named for the "type site," or locality, in which this specific style of projectile point was first located in October of 1956, in the Avonlea Creek Valley, just east of the Dirt Hills. They appear to have dominated the Northern Great Plains from roughly AD 250 to 850 in a region covering much of southern Alberta and Saskatchewan, northern Montana, and parts of southwestern Manitoba and northern Wyoming.

Archaeology has sandwiched the Avonlea people between the preceding complexes called Pelican Lake and Sandy Creek and the later complexes called Plains Side-notched and Prairie Side-notched. Another technological complex called Besant, named after the type site west of Moose Jaw, was contemporary with Avonlea. In fact, the Besant people and the Avonlea people may have been one culture using different tools in different applications. No one knows for certain.

Avonlea points are often found in the creek and river valleys around the Dirt Hills. They are delicate flakes of locally obtained chalcedony or quartzite. Some pieces have finely serrated blade edges and are so small and thin — the average weight of an Avonlea point is 0.68 grams — that they look more like jewellery than something to kill with. The illusion falls away when you see one hafted onto a straight branch of snowberry with goose feather fletching on the other end. Avonlea points were made for arrows and are thought to be the first to appear anywhere on the Great Plains.

With bow and arrow, the people of the plains thrived. Its accuracy allowed them to use the coulees between hills as natural corrals. Before long, the new tool had spread throughout the plains and to tribes living along the great rivers in the east and in the woodland edges to the north.

AVONLEA arrowheads have been found at buffalo jumps, pounds, and traps in the Dirt Hills area and at other kill sites across the northern plains from Alberta's Head-Smashed-In to Gull Lake, near the Great Sand Hills. On the glaciated terrain of this region, the cliffs, escarpments, and steep-sided coulees required for such hunting methods are usually found in glacio-fluvial valleys and meltwater channels, where rivers and springs would also have provided the people with abundant water for preparing the meat and hides.

This immediate bond to landscape established the limits of plains life for thousands of years. The first people to dwell in and around the Dirt Hills made boundaries and pathways that suited their place within Creation. Buffalo trails, and therefore the trails of the people, connected hills to plains to river valleys within a shifting web of borders aligned with and expressing the limits of local economy.

This is the congruency of hunter-gatherers. Agreement between lines of economy and lines of nature informed their ethics, dreams, and narratives. The congruency was maintained or aspired to in this third kind of boundary, the lines of myth. With stories, the Avonlea people corralled the holy, or perhaps more accurately, the truth behind the holy, pulling its power and mystery into their lives, and binding themselves to the prairie's landscapes, the boundaries of coulee, hill, river valley, plains.

Starvation or grief, prosperity or joy all fit within the boundaries of narrative gathered, ritualized, and passed on along the trails of their movement over the land. The truths of what is worthy of respect, how much is too much, where the holy resides, what sustains life, these they bore with them in narrative vessels, the songs and stories that told the flower, grass, rock, and sky lives of their country.

Bruce Chatwin, who followed in *The Songlines* the myth-laden pathways of the Australian Aborigines, has proposed that language, myth, and song come from the meanderings of our restless forebears. The songline is an invisible line on the land from one mythic landmark to the next, and the singer follows it, telling stories and singing couplets that match the cadence of walking. Each Australian songliner, practising what is now recognized as the world's oldest surviving religion, retraces the trail of the ancestral creature to which he is bound by birth. With a narrative from the originating times, the songliner people keep the land alive. "An unsung land," says Chatwin, "is a dead land."

Referring to our nomadic origins as hunters and pastoralists, Chatwin suggests that we all became singers, makers of myths, as we travelled the landscape marking, circumscribing, our territories. Like birds, wolves, or Aborigines, we sing our landscapes into being. Song, story, and poetry come from this celebration of pathways and boundaries. For most of our tenure as a species, human children have been jostled to sleep by the movement, cadence, and song of their mothers marking the land on foot along such lines, such alignments of economy and Creation. Chatwin refers to modern vestiges of this urge to recreate the world in movement over land. The journey myth is still central to our literature, and we still have poets who prefer to walk while they write.

For this landscape and its early people, the people of Avonlea and Besant tools, it is easy to imagine narrative boundaries of home based upon their own particular antiphony between man and Creation. By hearing the prairie world named and storied at trailside, the children of the Dirt Hills would have learned their place within the boundaries. An infant, peering out beyond its sling or backboard, watching the hills or creeks of the Coteau roll by, would have been enveloped in the language and song of grassland: the metallic trill of the lark bunting, the rasp of the grasshopper, the boom of the prairie chicken. From within this trailside acoustic would come the mother's voice, a counterpart above the plainsong, set to a bipedal rhythm, naming and telling plants, creatures, and landforms into being.

*Once a young woman out digging breadroot laid her infant down on a tuft of grass to lighten her load while she worked. When she had collected all the tubers she could carry, she returned to the tuft but could not find the child anywhere. She called and searched for her young one in vain. As she passed once more by the place she had left the child, she saw something move in the grass, something fluttering like a cradle blanket in the breeze. She ran to the spot but only flushed a bird into the air. The bird circled on quivering wings and cried out in the tremulous voice of the child, and it was then that the mother knew that her baby had left her in the form of a familiar prairie bird. She watched and called to her child as the bird flew across the prairie and away. It disappeared over the hills still crying in tones the young mother*

had grown to love, in the mournful utterance we have come to know as the
song of the upland sandpiper.

Passed on from mother to child at breadroot digging time or when
the eerie call of the upland sandpiper comes on the wind, and strung
together with a hundred other stories, songs, names, and dances that
each animate a range of hills, a patch of red soil in a creek bed, a sandstone outcropping, a type of grass, or a prairie animal, such a story is
a point along a wandering, ground-truthing myth-line within a web
of myth-lines that form and inform the pathways and boundaries of
human agency in a region, aligning economic borders with the natural
limits of the land.

The name Dirt Hills is itself an echo from the time when landmarks
had mythic origins. The Lakota Sioux name for the hills was Shunka
Chesela, or "Dog Shit Hills." Settlers changed it to Dog Dirt and then
simply Dirt Hills, burying the Lakota name and any story of its origins.
To explain the reference to dog dung, local historians have pointed to
the abundance of coyote droppings in the hills, where the wild canine is
common to this day. Possible, I suppose, though coyote scat appears on
every prairie prominence. A flight of hawks and owls two springs ago
stopped me long enough to discover another way of relating this name
to the hills, and to imagine the Lakota telling stories of the landform's
origins as they walked past on the plains below or danced upon its ceremonial summit at midsummer gatherings.

I was returning home at dusk along roads through stubble fields
bare of the snow that would soon push the Moose Jaw River beyond its
banks. It had been a winter of heavy snow, and now, in the failing light,
the land shone dark and wet as afterbirth. With the hills twenty miles
behind me, I stopped the car to get out and watch two rough-legged
hawks quartering low to the ground, hunting for voles; then a red-tailed
hawk, and deeper into the field two and then three short-eared owls
flapping high and teetering like strange giant moths. On power poles
ahead, two more rough-leggeds. I swirled around with my binoculars,
watching the spectacle for several minutes. When the birds moved on
north, I returned to the road and the car. I could see the hills as I turned
to open the car door. In the silence, there came a soft hiss from the
thawing soil on the other side of the ditch, like breathing. I paused and
looked back at the hills lying heavy and dark on the horizon. Like dog

shit — yes, I thought, the whole range of hills, a great, ropy pile of earth, is a giant coprolite excreted from a colossal dog in some ancient genesis time. *Here the first dog stopped to empty his bowels upon the grassland. In this way the Dog Shit Hills came to be.*

*The dominant question was how cultures and environment could be modified and this fundamental question was personified in the Métis. To observers at that time it seemed the choices were clear cut. The mixed bloods could become nomads of the woods and the plains or they could become as Europeans and be governed by the pen and the plough. The Métis chose neither one, but pulled both ways incessantly and sought a compromise between European and Indian ways; between paganism and Christianity; between hunting and agriculture.*

— D. BRUCE SEALEY AND ANTOINE S. LUSSIER,
*THE MÉTIS: CANADA'S FORGOTTEN PEOPLE*

SAM MCWILLIAMS REMEMBERED the half-breeds. They were the same as the wandering Sioux people who stopped by the ranch from time to time, but different. The "breeds" were more talkative, more inclined to joke or try to barter with father — an axe for a pig or a willow basket for a pound of butter. A superstitious and religious bunch, though. They would be talking of windigoes one minute and St. Joseph the next. Good, generous people, hard working, but you had to watch them around tools. It's just a short ride up into the hills where you can still see their graves and broken-down chimneys.

In 1941, McWilliams wrote: "There was a Métis family that lived three miles southeast of the ranch. The eldest boy, Lipsey Poitras, 17 or 18 years of age, had a rifle. The two younger boys had to make do with bows and arrows. Lipsey's mother had tanned the skin of a mule deer's head and left the ears on. Whenever Lipsey went deer hunting, he took this deer skin along and when he sighted a deer, he would put this over his head and when he got near the deer, he would get down on his knees and was able to get very close to them."[6]

Before the McWilliamses arrived in 1886, several Métis families had already come and gone. They came from the Red River settlements in the late 1860s, during the first dispersion of the Métis across the North-West. In those years, hundreds of Métis were leaving their homes at Pembina, St. Francis Xavier, and White Horse Plain to be nearer the buffalo, which were each year farther to the west, and to put distance between themselves and the new white settlers who, by their political and numerical strength, as well as by outright persecution, were becoming a threat to the Métis way of life. As many as twenty families moved into the Dirt Hills. They came as early as 1865, and lived by hunting buffalo, trading pemmican, and freighting. Seven years later, most of these people had either left or died from smallpox. One name survives from that time, a pemmican trader named Kississaway Tanner.

There is a place, a knoll on the east slopes of the Dirt Hills, where Tanner may have lived, along with his wife and children and other *hivernants* (another name for the Métis, meaning "the winterers"). I have not yet seen the remains of the settlement, but it is said to include, in the language of archaeology, five "sub-areas" with cellar depressions and "other surface features." Below the surface, in 1986, archaeologists found building foundations, refuse pits, and chimney mounds.

When I go to the hills now I sometimes think of Tanner and the twenty Métis families; of the reasons they came in the 1860s and the reasons they did not stay for long. I imagine Kississaway Tanner leading a small caravan of Red River carts west from Pembina, a caravan unlike those of past buffalo hunts in which parties of up to a thousand Métis in two hundred or more carts would make the trek to the Grand Coteau where the great herds fed in the hills and watered in the creeks and sloughs. Was it ten, twenty, or thirty carts carrying all that belonged to the Tanners and the nameless families who joined them, who agreed one day that the Red River settlements had become colonies of a civilization that would not grant quarter to a people who lived by the hunt? To stay was to grub in the soil for a living, starve when the crops failed, and give up the ways of the people. And so Tanner and the others headed for the Coteau, nearer the buffalo and into the country where the Métis marked some of their greatest moments as a nation.

After several days travelling west on their first trek with no planned return, Tanner's people would have finally seen the blue outline of the Dirt Hills rising up on the horizon. More than a welcome sign that they would soon be leaving the flatland to shelter in the draws and ridges of the Coteau, the sight would have also called to mind one of those legendary moments, the Battle of the Grand Coteau in July 1851.

Historians have not been able to pinpoint the site of this encounter between the Lakota and a Métis caravan — it was somewhere south of present-day Estevan, likely just over the international border — but Tanner and his people would have known the place well, as the ground upon which sixty-seven Métis hunters, including thirteen-year-old Gabriel Dumont, defeated more than two thousand Lakota warriors and thereby secured the right of the Métis to travel and hunt the Coteau in peace. Tanner himself might have been at the battle, as a young man or boy watching Pierre Flacon, captain of the hunt and national poet of the Métis, who commandeered the Métis forces as they withstood the Lakota attack from rifle pits dug outside their circled caravan. When the gunfire subsided after a day and half of fighting, the Lakota leader came forward, suing for peace, and promised to allow the Métis safe passage thereafter in the Coteau. The defence of Batoche has since eclipsed this moment in history, but in 1865 the Battle of the Grand Coteau still held its place alongside Seven Oaks as an early assertion of Métis nationhood.

Arriving at the Dirt Hills, Tanner and the Métis would have been attracted to the shelter of its eastern face and to the essentials of game, wood, and water near at hand. A freighting trail, running 250 miles from Wood Mountain in the southwest to Fort Qu'Appelle in the northeast, passed by the foot of the hills a mile and a half west of where the town of Avonlea now stands. With a hide and pemmican trading post at Fort Qu'Appelle only a week's drive along this trail, and fair buffalo hunting nearby, the Dirt Hills would have seemed as good a place as any to stop and build a shack for the winter.

Satisfied with their lives as *hivernants*, they stayed, raised families, hunted, trapped, and traded. Their pathways suspended them between the life of the indigenous hunter-gatherer and the commercial life of the trading forts. Warmed by Hudson's Bay cloth and tea paid for in the hide and flesh of the prairie's last wild buffalo, the Dirt Hills Métis spent long winters by the fire in drafty, smoke-filled, flea-ridden cabins, mending clothes, telling stories, and dancing to a wild fiddle music that matched the blend in their own blood. Thus, the boundaries of the Dirt Hills economy shifted one notch off the local and ecological by the distance of a trade that — although it still afforded mere subsistence to its resident population — was dictated now by the principle of maximizing profit for a remote industry and a European culture, a culture that had long ago abandoned its mythology of congruency in favour of a mythology that offered the world and its materials as the means to private accumulation of riches. Before long, the buffalo became harder to find each year and the Dirt Hills *hivernants* succumbed to starvation and disease. With them died the last ethical and cultural boundaries that maintained some agreement between the limits of the economy and the limits of the land.

Tanner and his people knew the names and stories of the prairie well — not as the Cree or Lakota had, but more so than any of us today. The breadroot and the upland sandpiper were as plentiful as ever in the 1860s; Métis grandmothers may have told stories about them, and about other creatures, the mischief of coyote, or the words a meadowlark says to the wind — *peesteh-atchewusson*. But there would also have been stories about a virgin birth, a man who spoke wisdom to fishermen, healed the sick, and fed the hungry.

These stories suited their faith in a Christian god who had acquired pagan tendencies and therefore had not abandoned the earth — a god who had given them the buffalo, music, myth, and dance, a god who had delivered them from the Lakota at Grand Coteau. It was, I believe, this adept mingling of mythologies that, despite their ties to a mercantile, extractive industry, kept the Métis culture that much closer to a life within locally established and ecologically affirmed boundaries. Such a life has not been seen in the region since.

*Thomas McWilliams came west with a greed for gold or some paying material.*

— Avonlea Historical Committee,
*Arrowheads to Wheatfields*

A FRIEND ONCE TOLD ME that native prairie breaking under the plough sounds something like a scream muted by distance. Sam McWilliams would have been able to testify to the romantic content of such a description. He was there on the plains north of the Dirt Hills in the 1880s when his father, Tom, first broke the land. Sam was not yet tall enough to see above the backs of the oxen but he was out on the prairie with a team, drawing a small harrow over the seed that his father was tossing into the furrows by hand. In 1885 the crop was fair on their meagre acreage. The next year a drought reclaimed the land. The soil was baked so hard in places that it would not take a walking plough. Anything that sprouted was dried on the stem by ten days of blowtorch wind in July.

Still, Thomas McWilliams had no thought of giving up and returning east with his wife and six children. He stood on his fields of shrivelled grain and looked south thirty miles to a thin blue smear of hills lying on the horizon like a shirt dropped on the floor of the world. Something he saw, a shadow or suggestion of contrast, made him borrow the station agent's telescope to get a better look at those hills. He squinted through the glass at what appeared to be wooded draws — potential firewood — but it was the large patches of white that caught Tom McWilliams's eye and convinced him that a trip to these Dirt Hills might be profitable.

After an initial visit to the hills to cut firewood, Tom returned with neighbours and two of his children, Sam and Jennie, to pick saskatoon berries for the winter. All the berries were shrivelled — it was hard to say whether they had been scorched by the sun or a recent fire that had passed through — but Tom found something else on that day that was worth gathering. The white patches he had seen earlier turned out to be large outcroppings of a pale clay bedrock. When the McWilliamses returned home from the Dirt Hills they took with them samples of the clay to ship back east for testing.

Before long, Tom received word that his clay was "equal if not superior to the clays of Bristol, England" and would make fine refractory ceramic or bricks. He wasted no time in filing a homestead claim on the half section (320 acres) of land containing the best deposits. The dream of a clay-brick factory would have to wait a bit, but there was much work to do building a home at the foot of the hills, setting up cattle ranching, proving up the homestead. Over the next several years, Tom gathered the money and support required to start a brick-firing business. In the meantime, word got out that there were minerals of undetermined potential in the Dirt Hills, virtually on the doorstep of one of the North-West's boomingest boomtowns, Moose Jaw. The *Moose Jaw Times* did what any frontier newspaper would do, given the chance to print a headline containing those two words that never fail to lift the spirits of a colonial people: "mineral deposits." In a February 1, 1895, editorial that sounds like something out of Leacock's *Sunshine Sketches*, the editor of the *Times* tried valiantly to foment a claims rush or at least some civic optimism about the capacity of this new land to produce wealth at the turn of a shovel.

> *Mr. McWilliams had no difficulty locating his unbounded treasure. He is patiently awaiting developments on the part of the Dominion Government or some other strong company to produce the money bags with interest.*
>
> *As a disinterested party let me call your attention as an analyst and experienced mineralogist for many years. In this capacity I am fully convinced of there being an unlimited quantity of wealth in these adjacent hills if only properly developed. To give you an idea of the rich properties they contain the compass will not work in this region. The rich quarter is thirty miles southeast of Moose Jaw lying ten miles south of the Soo Line. There are enormous veins of bituminous coal, some twelve feet wide. This quality of coal which is generally known as petroleum shale, yields 150 gallons of crude petroleum to the ton, while samples of iron, copper, magnesia, antimony and other minerals are even visible with the naked eye, so that it astounds the beholder at first sight, particularly if you be familiar with mineral resources. These hills are one of the chief points of interest to all classes of visitors.*

The "unlimited quantity of wealth" was never "properly developed" and so few visitors of any class bothered with the Dirt Hills or its white mud until 1914, when Tom McWilliams and a small group of Moose Jaw businessmen opened up a full-scale firebrick factory on the McWilliamses' land under the name Saskatchewan Clay Products. In the early years, the factory produced several varieties of face bricks and insulating bricks. The new industry soon gave rise to a company town, named Claybank, just north of the factory. In its heyday, Claybank residents could get a haircut, buy a slab of bacon, and play a game of pool all on Main Street. Today, Claybank is a smattering of houses separated by large gaps where a community of factory workers once lived.

The official history of the factory at Claybank measures its success by the distance the ceramics and bricks travelled. The bricks were used in Quebec City's Château Frontenac, and minesweepers and corvettes in the Canadian navy lined their boilers with Claybank ceramics. The bricks were used locally too, in towns and farms nearby. Moose Jaw's downtown remains to this day distinctive and graceful for its buildings made of brick from the local clay, buildings such as the old Capitol Theatre and the Bellamy Block. Courthouses and grand farmhouses here and there throughout southern Saskatchewan glow with the orange-yellow brick fired from a sandy mud that once formed the bed of primordial rivers. It is these buildings, the edifices made from materials ancient and near at hand, that have me wondering if the Dirt Hills brick operation was not something rarely seen on this continent: an extractive industry that, at least for the first few decades of its life, added to the well-being of the local economy without causing extensive damage to the local ecology.

By the 1950s, the globalizing postwar economy had gathered the Claybank brick factory into the wider boundaries of international trade. The company was taken over by A.P. Green Refractories of Ontario. For the next thirty years, products made of clay dug out of the Dirt Hills were shipped across the country and into the United States and South America. In June of 1989 A.P. Green closed the doors of the Claybank plant, citing the usual reasons absentee owners cite at the closure of a local industry: the technology was outmoded, inefficient, and incapable of competing in today's global marketplace.

The old beehive kilns still work, could still be used to make native clay bricks in a region that imports virtually all its building materials. Instead, the Claybank brick factory has become a historic site with guided tours and untapped heritage interpretation potential. The tours, conducted by retired factory workers, are simple and unassuming. There are no multimedia exhibits, no gift shops, no visitors' centres. At least not yet. People are planning, looking at the old brick walls at the foot of the Dirt Hills and wondering if they have another kind of mine, another way to attract "all classes of visitors," another way to make the hills say *money* instead of *grass* or *buffalo* or *home*.

The McWilliamses and the others who first mined this area by shovel and plough were no worse or better than any other home- steaders on the Great Plains. They came with little, expecting much. They worked hard, lived in virtue, lived in sin, and populated the area with a society that has succeeded and failed by two sides of the same colonizing measure: an attachment to an elsewhere, which, over time, has delivered a life of wealth and comfort with one hand while taking away community and wholeness with the other.

The only boundaries that mattered were the ones drawn by sur- veyors and others expanded by technology. Section lines, townships, and road allowances made neat squares where there once had been con- tours of land and water. More damaging have been the boundaries overcome and then writ larger by the latest offerings of agri-science and engineering. These lines hardly appear on landscape, although we mark them, measure ourselves against them every day. Each time a new machine or technique makes agricultural production and export easier, we move further away from the material constraints that have in the past conserved communities of soil, plants, animals, and people together in something approaching a dynamic balance. Each leap — from growing grazers to growing grain, from animal power to gasoline, from small tractor to large, from local trade to distant, from small farms to large — has widened the misalignment between the boundaries that determine how much our labour will produce and how much the land can bear. We have bulldozed the limits of what one farmer could accomplish with the help of a few good animals and neighbours and, in so doing, ren- dered superfluous the pathways connecting household to household and household to the land; the pathways, worn by feet and honoured by stories, forming a network of interdependencies we have sometimes called culture.[7]

*As we walk our own ground, on foot or in mind, we need to be able to recite stories about hills and trees and animals, stories that root us in this place and that keep it alive. The sounds we make, the patterns we draw, the plots we trace may be as native to the land as deer trails or bird songs. The more fully we belong to our place, the more likely that*

*our place will survive without damage. We cannot create myth from*
*scratch, but we can recover or fashion stories that will help us to see*
*where we are, how others have lived here, how we ourselves should live.*

— SCOTT RUSSELL SANDERS, "TELLING THE HOLY"

ON WHAT REMAINS of the mixed-grass prairie, the breadroot plant can
still be found here and there in places like the Dirt Hills, where the
regimen of soil and sun suits it nature. Few people know its name, however; even fewer its stories or its flavour. The upland sandpiper, once a
tremendously abundant bird of the northern plains, is increasingly rare.
It will not nest in wheat fields, though it will tolerate hayland. The settlers, who knew it better than prairie people today, called it prairie
snipe, pasture plover, or prairie dove, and used it for target practice.
Its habit of perching on fence posts apparently made it ideal for sighting
in a .22.

Aldo Leopold had a particular affection for the upland sandpiper.
In *A Sand County Almanac*,[8] he wrote of its long migration from the
Argentine pampas and of its near extinction from market gunning at
the turn of the century, when plover-on-toast came into fashion. Though
it has recovered from the days of armed and hungry homesteaders, the
upland sandpiper remains an uncommon bird. Uncommon, but also
unnamed and unstoried by the people who live in its midst. When I am
lucky enough to hear its long, whistling cry, the voice of the lost child,
rising and falling above a pasture speckled with Herefords, I remember
the breadroot diggers and wonder if a species dwindles and disappears
because it has lost its habitat or because we have lost its stories.

Without the stories of alignment, the ligaments of culture that bind
economic boundaries to ecological ones, turning space into place and
land into home, we are blundering toward Yeats's apocalypse: "Things
fall apart; the centre cannot hold." Whatever else we forsake in the land
— small farms, wilderness, habitat, species, community — is merely a
playing out, a dénouement to this primary loss of myth.

The possibility of forming a local culture and sound economy in this
region begins with a renewal of myth-lines, made by artists, scientists,
songwriters, and engineers, that will rea*lig*n and re*lig*ament our labour
and lives. It is the truly re*lig*ious work of finding the *lig* in our ob*lig*ation
to home, for that is the root meaning of *religious*, "the ties that bind." A

religious painting might bind the viewer to the view by placing him, unsentimentally and responsibly, within the landscape. A religious agronomy might bind the eater to the grower by finding ways to allow them to live near one another. A religious song might bind the singer to the territory sung into life by celebrating what is holy and wholesome in that relationship. A religious engineering, working within the limits of renewable and locally available energy, might bind us all to the wind and the sun.

Religion is not a word to be used in polite company these days. It has become so obviously a force of misalignment and estrangement in our communities that the original meaning of the term is gone. People still feel the tug of the immutable, however, and so now the talk is of "spirituality." Men and women sit on hillsides, touch rocks, and walk the prairie looking for personal encounters with the spirit of a place or a generalized "spirit of nature." And they come away, when the afternoon is over, convinced they have or have not had a revelation equal to the ones enjoyed by their favourite authors.

Mystical experience is real — it may arrive unbidden on a crowded downtown street or in the solitude of trees — but it does not come easily, or by mere exertion of will. I may never be a mystic by thought and hard work, but by these I can become a heretic. And heresy, I believe, is just what our irreligious religions need. Heresy crosses lines drawn by dogma, making new ties that bind, that restore the ligaments of our contact with the holy. Heresies are heterogeneous. They blend traditions promiscuously, join the native to the new, and blur the lines between elements commonly held to be discrete.

The heresy we need here, in the Dirt Hills and throughout the Northern Great Plains, would blur the lines between what is good for the economy and what is good for the land, between a love of god and a love of wildness, between ourselves and the hills, the deer, the bread-root, and the song of the upland sandpiper.

Think again of Lipsey Poitras, hunting with the ears of a mule deer on his head, stalking his next meal through a poplar-filled draw high in the hills. By measure of years of tenure and wealth, the Métis may seem the least successful of the peoples who have lived in this region. As a standard of heresy, however, the mixed-blood culture is the best model we have. A heretic retains the ability to choose, and the people of

Kississaway Tanner chose their tools, technics, ethics, and beliefs freely from among the traditions of their ancestors. They chose, further, to reject the colonizing culture that overtook their homeland along the Red River. They moved out west and, from heresy and heterogeneity, formed a new culture here that, given half a chance, may have been able to coexist with a much wilder prairie than the one we have today.

THINKING OF THE MÉTIS in this light brings me round again to the hope of finding answers down in the prairie bottomlands. In my mind, the possibility of a valid prairie culture has much to do with rivers. The Métis began as river people. Their founding fathers were paddlers on the great rivers at the interior of this continent. When, later, they formed villages, they had the good sense to gather along a prairie river: the North and South Saskatchewan, the Red, the Assiniboine, the Qu'Appelle. Their farm and village lots were organized along the riverfront, with shared grazing lands out back and the wild commons beyond. Even their boundaries of ownership paid tribute to the river and recognized it as the natural gathering place of their communal life, connecting household to household by the sustaining flow of a prairie waterway.

Great heresies start down by the riverside. There we can begin the religious exercise of snaring through the myths of our art and science what is healing and holy in this land; there, through stories, we can store and restore, steer, and stake our claims; and there we can locate the source of what might realign and religament our culture with good boundaries and pathways.

Let us sew ears upon our deerstalkers and head down to the river.

## Chapter Three

# THE WAYS OF WATER

ON THE EDGE OF HIGH terraces overlooking certain prairie rivers, there are mounds recessed into the earth. In these low-roofed domes, the Avonlea people once buried their dead, facing the water that gave them life. By rivers, the early prairie people lived and died. By rivers, they hunted, navigated, and took shelter from the elements. By rivers, they collected berries, gathered herbs, firewood, and stone. By rivers, they bathed and washed. By rivers, they made earthen vessels.

The potsherds left behind by the Avonlea people are identifiable by a distinctive pattern of spiralling lines. The lines are actually parallel troughs and ridges that run on an angle across the pot, imparting to the surface a pleasant, rhythmic pattern of shadow. Archaeologists have named this pattern "channelling," an apt term, for it looks like the channelled undulations on a sandy riverbed or beach.

Lines to the well, lines to the river have always drawn the limits of life in an arid environment. Water is the ultimate maker of maps on the Great Plains, and the watershed is a natural circumscription of our local responsibilities. The watershed, if we will allow it, can still organize our interests, measure our competency, and command our allegiance. As the circumference of our lifeways and the margin of our interdependencies with the world beyond, the watershed can move us toward the life of the dweller, toward an answer to the question mark in the circle, toward a new geography of home.

In the dry interior of this continent, water and the forms it takes in shedding over the landscape determine where life flourishes. Its quality and quantity separate a desert from a prairie from a meadow from a forest from a bog from a marsh. The water we share is a visible sign of the interconnectedness of all living things. We draw sustenance, blessing, and rebirth from a common well. As the delineation of our intercourse with and responsibility to the land, no natural geography is more compelling and true than the watershed.

The lines made by water are what we have in mind when we say that natural contours are sinuous, never straight. Look at a map of a watershed. The border between it and the neighbouring watershed, as well as the path of the rivers and creeks it contains, draw pleasing, abstract patterns that, neither random nor arbitrary, make elegant sense of the landscape's agreement with gravity.

The words we use to describe a watershed — *headwater, branch, watercourse, divide, current, tributary, source* — bring to mind their secondary role as metaphors of human organization and movement. The language seems to recognize what we have forgotten: that culture and nature converge where water meets the land. Carl Sauer, essayist and geographer, has speculated that one of the characteristics that distinguish humans, the domesticated primates, from their wilder ancestors is an affinity for water. Citing a study by Sir Alistair Hardy, Sauer suggests that we may have had "an ancestral habitat in water as well as on land," and that "the symmetry and grace of the human body" may be traced to an era when we were all spending much more time foraging in rivers, estuaries, and oceans.[9]

We are drawn to what American writer Ann Zwinger has called rivertime, to lives we may have once had, nourished by, immersed within, the river's "constant communion of change."[10] Children make rivers in springtime with curbside watersheds; in summer, given half a chance, they will lose an afternoon in a creek's ankle-wetting depths. Poets and songwriters evoke the river's ancient appeal, usually without ever getting their feet wet. The river, like other archetypes of landscape — the sea, the road, the forest, the mountain — enriches a lyric with metaphor and mystery. I have sat and listened to folksingers and counted the number of songs that mention rivers, streams, or creeks. The record-holder is an urban songwriter from the West Coast, a man whose songs are about community and relationships between lovers or friends or father and son. Although not one of his pieces was "environmental" or oriented toward the wild, rivers, creeks, and streams appeared in six of the eleven songs he performed.

I HAVE ALWAYS BEEN FASCINATED by those maps that show the assumed ranges of North American Indian nations before contact with Europeans furnished the motive, guns, and horses required to wage territorial campaigns. Keeping rivers and divides in mind as you look at the territories of these early dwellers, you can see that watersheds and human cultures at one time shared many borders on this continent. The overlap is particularly clear in mountainous regions, but even on the Great Plains, major divides between watersheds sometimes coincided with territorial lines.

Archaeologists speculate that in the 1600s, the grasslands of what is now southern Saskatchewan fell to the Atsina people (Gros Ventre) in the west and the Assiniboine people in the east. The border was roughly the divide between the South Saskatchewan River basin and the Qu'Appelle/Assiniboine River basin. At the mid point along this border was a neutral zone respected by all. This no-man's land, which according to the earliest records was a sanctuary for buffalo and other game, surrounded the Elbow of the South Saskatchewan, including the summit of land in the Aiktow Valley that separates the Elbow from the source of the Qu'Appelle a few miles east.

By the mid-1800s, the Plains Cree had joined the Assiniboine in the east, and the Blackfoot had replaced the Atsina in the west and southwest. The Saulteaux (Plains Ojibway) had moved from the forest edge out onto the eastern plains drained by the Assiniboine basin, roughly from the Red River to the juncture of the Qu'Appelle and Assiniboine Rivers at Fort Ellice (near St. Lazare, Manitoba), the eastern extremity of the Qu'Appelle basin. The Assiniboine people ranged over most of the Qu'Appelle basin and the Souris basin to the southeast, both of which send their water to the Assiniboine River on its way to the Red River at Fort Garry (Winnipeg).

The Cree, allies of the Assiniboine, moved freely through all these regions and had extended their territory north and west to include much of the land draining into the Saskatchewan River. The border between the Blackfoot and Cree now ran in a line from Fort Edmonton southeast all the way to the juncture of the Yellowstone and Missouri Rivers at Fort Union (near Williston, North Dakota). At the centre of this line, however, was the sacred ground at the Elbow, still the pivot point of the border and still neutral.

The Plains Cree and Blackfoot regularly travelled into one another's territories, to raid a camp or wage war, but they acknowledged the neutrality of the watershed boundary at the Elbow, realizing that in crossing it they were leaving their home landscape and entering the territory of their enemies.

In September 1857, Captain John Palliser's overland expedition crossed the western extremity of the Qu'Appelle watershed and arrived on the banks of the South Saskatchewan River, just above the Elbow. After a brief side trip into the Aiktow Valley interconnecting east to the headwaters of the Qu'Appelle, the expedition turned south. Palliser then proceeded along the valley of the South Saskatchewan River until his Métis guides, most of whom had Cree blood, became nervous and reluctant to continue. They had passed through the neutral ground and were heading deeper into the land of the Blackfoot, where they knew they would be regarded as hostile trespassers. Palliser's journal says that his proposal to continue south and west along the river "was met with universal alarm among the men, who thought that they had done wonders already." Near the site of today's Riverhurst ferry crossing, they turned north.

The power of that watershed divide at the Elbow meant something to the first people of this area, and it may still signify something to their descendants today. In the 1960s, the provincial and federal governments sponsored a massive irrigation and hydroelectric project that breached the divide and formed an artificial link between the river systems. A large dam was built across the South Saskatchewan River just below the Elbow, creating Lake Diefenbaker and flooding the entire Aiktow Valley, a portion of the upper Qu'Appelle Valley, and the summit that separated the two watersheds. Now, bold achievement, water can be periodically diverted from the reservoir through a control dam and into the Qu'Appelle system.

Despite modern engineering and its desecrations, the Qu'Appelle watershed retains its power to link, divide, and extend the ranges of the creatures of the Northern Great Plains. The valley itself is a 260-mile-long belt that weaves together the dry southwestern ecologies of the mid-continental prairie and the moist ecologies of the northern and eastern parkland and forests. Bur oak trees and big bluestem grass, outliers from the tallgrass country of the Assiniboine and Red River valleys, reach their westward extremities along the hills of the Qu'Appelle, where they are at times within view of typical western plants, such as blue grama grass and thorny buffaloberry.

The birds are equally inclined to mingle east and west in the valley. I have seen a pair of eastern bluebirds fluttering along a hilltop fence while rock wrens and Say's phoebes sang from the ruins of an old fieldstone barn in the bottom of a nearby coulee. One bird that is characteristic of the Qu'Appelle, the rufous-sided towhee, breeds in good numbers all along the valley's length, though it is almost never seen on the adjacent plains. In 1996, science officially recognized what the towhees have always known: the rufous-sided is actually two birds, the spotted towhee in the west and the eastern towhee in the east. The ranges of these two species meet in the middle of the Qu'Appelle Valley, east of the Fishing Lakes, where you can sometimes hear them singing their distinctive songs across a coulee from one another.

Though we are not as faithful to the valley as the towhees and pay scant attention to the boundaries created by rivers, water on the prairie still has an ability to gather us and shape our lives. The Qu'Appelle watershed contains eight large natural lakes: seven spaced throughout the valley and Last Mountain or "Long" Lake on the plains to the north. Since 1900, more than six thousand cottages have been built along the shores of these lakes, which, despite cheap gasoline and good highways leading to northern resorts, have not lost their appeal for the throng of cottagers and campers who each weekend abandon urban homes throughout the basin and head to "the Lake." Loving the lakes has had its ecological costs: the pike and walleye are getting harder to find;

loons and other waterbirds that once bred on the lakes are all but gone; sewage from cottages has not helped the water quality in a system that is already overloaded with nutrients; and every time someone builds the summer home of his dreams on undeveloped beach land, we lose another piece of critical shoreline habitat.

In spite of these inroads, the Qu'Appelle lakes retain a fair mix of wildlife and continue to be the primary place where people who live in the region encounter, admittedly on compromised terms, the local remnants of the wild: a hummingbird at the feeder, walleye in the pan, an osprey fishing from a power pole, a posy of crocuses in spring. For the children of Regina, Moose Jaw, Melville, and fifty other towns, summertime trips to a valley lake remain a part of living and growing up in this corner of the Great Plains. On the July 1st long weekend, Katepwe Beach becomes one of the most populated communities in the valley. The lake is full of boats, the cottage subdivisions are bristling with cars from the city, and the beach wears a multicoloured lacquer of sunbathers. Head down the valley a mile east of the lake, however, and you will be alone but for the farmer mowing hayfields and the Métis fisherman dangling a line into the river.

PART OF WHAT DRAWS ME to a place like the Dirt Hills is water. As dry as the land might appear from the top of the ceremonial circle, I know that if I walk north and downslope along a certain coulee I will eventually come to a small seep of water flowing out of the hillside. Barely a trickle, it feeds a microecology of wetness amid the sere world of sandstone cliffs and prairie grass.

Discovering this spring was one of those gratuitous encounters in nature when a moment's attention transfigures the simple and unremarkable — a few shrivelled leaf stalks — into the shards of a relict wildness. It was one of the last days of November. A good friend, Rob Wright, had asked me to join him for an overnight deer hunt in the Dirt Hills. Rob is a plant ecologist whose tramps over prairie landscapes are fired by a passion for grassland and a boyish delight in seeing what might be over the next rise. We were walking at nightfall up a gully to find a place to bed down. Just as I was beginning to wonder how far Rob's legs were intending to go, we came across a spot where we could see the sparkle of water and feel the crunch of ice underfoot. A spring.

There was enough moonlight to see by and so we paused to identify some of the vegetation. I listened as Rob named the place into existence with what sounded like a canticle to the flora of a wet, saline prairie: *Distichlis stricta, Glaux maritima, Suaeda depressa*. Alkali grass, sea milk-wort, Western sea-blite, among a bed of unnamed mosses and sedges. It is the strangeness, the sudden change in plant community, that appeals in a place like this. On that night, what brought the transition most remarkably to mind was the grace and testimony of a small clump of ferns. *Cystopteris fragilis*, the fragile fern. Its fronds, curled and brown from the frost, were no larger than my hand. I crouched to regard the passing beauty of a fragile fern on a prairie hillside. There, at one of the southern tributary's sheltered headwaters, an effusion of primitive plants expressed faith in the permanence of things below, of the integrity that underlies the Dirt Hills and all the land bound to the Qu'Appelle River.

When I think of places like this throughout the watershed, where an ancient, wilder symmetry emerges into the daylight, I realize that many of them occur at the meeting of land and water. A set of terraced beaver ponds on the valley slopes fed by spring water; a small slough surrounded by willows in a pasture of fescue grass; a swimming hole at a bend in the river passing through a village; the nesting islands at the end of a lake — all fragile ecotones, as vulnerable as any relationship that communicates the wholeness between two opposites.

At the level of the watershed, this duality evokes a sexual geography. The masculine prairie plateau, high and dry, with harsh geometry exposed to the heat of the sun, gathers energy and sheds water fertile with the milt of ancient soils. The feminine rivers, creeks, valleys, and coulees remain curvilinear and cool down in the shadows, as they receive and distribute the water that nourishes all. The two conjoin in the valley, where silt from the prairie swirls its burden of mineral and nutrient within the waters of the river.

The primary threats to the Qu'Appelle watershed's ecological health occur at this intercourse of soil and water. Agricultural run-off, siltation, pollution, damming, and channelization: these changes are threats because they fragment the wholeness of the watershed and increase the influence of one element (upland towns and farms) at the expense of another (lowland waterways and communities). The Qu'Appelle Valley has the bearing of an ancient and enduring landscape. But we are deluded by our short time. The valley is young in geological terms, its union of water and land still fresh and vulnerable. Attending to this bond, and finding our role within it, is our responsibility if we aspire to belong to this landscape.

THE PATHWAYS OF WATER on the land form a sound basis for beginning a discussion of the lines a local culture shares with the wild — the boundaries of the bioregion. The discussion should eventually arrive, however, at a map that honours the ancient and recent pathways of the people who have seen themselves as belonging to the place.

Before we consigned ourselves to automobiles on asphalt and gravel, this land was criss-crossed by the meanderings of people on foot, on horseback, on carts and wagons. They found their way over it and discovered limits that bear some relation to the spirit, economy, and ecology of the place — a string of lakes, the distance an ox-cart will travel in a day, a storied plateau where no one hunts. Some pathways remain — the wagon-ruts of Métis buffalo hunters cut deep into the prairie sod — and remind us of the geo*graphic* interlacings of a cultural network that once formed a semi-permeable membrane between human beings and the wild.

For that is what a successful culture must be, of course: a membrane, marked by the local imprint of creation, through which we conduct a healthy interchange with the wild. A lithograph or *geo*graph, if you will, imprinted by the self-organizing networks of the land and made up of our stories, our beliefs, our pathways, our economies, and our work.

Networks within networks persist in the land, though they have been weakened by our efforts to transcend them, live beyond them. A watershed forms a network; a couple of longtailed weasels and a population of path-making meadow voles form a network; the infinitely intertwined mycellia of fungi within the substrate of an aspen and ash coulee form a network; and the microbes that surround us and populate us form indispensable networks that keep the wildness near and within.

These cultures succeed because of their mutuality. An ecosystem is dynamic, always in flux, but its characteristic interaction, interdependence, and co-operation provide an inherently stable mutuality over many generations. The modern state, with its marketplace run on individualism and competition, cannot manage for even a single generation this kind of self-organizing sustainability.

The mutuality of the wild works because it settles a good balance between the needs and limits of the individual and the needs and limits of the whole. To be a healthy individual in a healthy population, a prey species such as the meadow vole needs to live within the limits of (that is, not overgraze) its habitat. Its predator, the longtailed weasel, is limited by its own hunting skills and the state of the vole population. The weasel meets its individual needs by eating voles and meets the needs of the ecosystem (and therefore itself, the grass, and the voles) by keeping the voles from eating themselves out of a home.

It is impossible to explain such intricacy without diminishing it. An ecosystem is an organic, living thing. It flows from life to life within livingness. To talk of voles and weasels is to hugely oversimplify an intricate set of self-regulating exchanges.

Maybe it is enough to look at the river turning slow and steady in the valley bottom, and learn something about boundaries, pathways, and permanence. The channel carved by the Qu'Appelle moves imperceptibly at the pace of geological time, but it is always walking across the valley floor from one wall to the other, meandering, eroding, changing, and not changing. The river makes new boundaries, leaves old pathways (its oxbows and dry channels), and says to the valley and the land above that its waters came with the last glacier and will leave with the next one. It is possible to imagine a human culture that recognizes sensible boundaries, leaves beautiful pathways, and speaks the language of a prairie river to the world beyond.

I WALK DOWN the northern slope of the Dirt Hills, past the elm the bluebird has abandoned and into a fold between two ridges that will take me back to the road and my car. These north-facing draws shelter a thick growth of ash and poplar, but I find a deer trail that seems to be heading my way. My legs are pleasantly rubbery by the time I have descended the full elevation and spilled out onto the open palm of prairie that holds the ridges in repose, like fingers on an outstretched hand.

At the car, I step upon weeds and alien grasses. I look back over my shoulder to see if I can still make out the ceremonial circle. I find it readily, one far hilltop among many, but distinct with its stone necklace and boulder crown. Then a shadow rises over the crest of the hill and just as quickly drops behind. I stare, trying to pull it into view again. A moment later it sweeps across the circle and pulls up to hover a few feet above the boulder. A young golden eagle, the first I've seen this spring. It spirals up into the sky until finally it is lost to the colour of distance.

*Part Two*

# LOST
# HEADWATERS

ONE NIGHT I MET AN ELDERLY WOMAN *while I was walking the beach along the cottage subdivision named after the great rock. She had expensive gemstones on her fingers and her hair was a shade of yellow. There was moonlight, and a bug zapper crackled nearby. We spoke in tones that are used in funeral chapels. She told me a story about her father.*

*He grew up on a farm east of the Elbow at the turn of the century. As a boy he would walk the two miles to the rock and spend an afternoon climbing its sides and probing its fractures. Often he would sit in the shade on its north flank and fall asleep facing the River That Turns. In his thirteenth or fourteenth summer a dream came to him as he slept at the rock. He was sinking down through the depths of a great river that was not a river. Eventually he arrived at the bottom. When he looked around he saw the valley, its trees, hills, and grass all under water. He searched the valley for the rock and found in its place a pile of rubble. He picked up a piece of the rock. It sparkled with feldspar and as he turned it over, it became a giant luminous eye. He dropped it in terror and tried to swim to the surface, but his feet had lodged between large shards of stone, holding him fast to the valley bottom.*

*That was the last summer he went to the rock. On the day the cairn was unveiled, he told his daughter of the dream.*

*Chapter Four*

## EQUALITY OF ORIGIN

RAIN AGAIN. I am watching it fall upon the surface of a reservoir that floats pleasure craft above the ancestral buffalo range at the upper Qu'Appelle Valley. Rain upon river is a wild grace. This engineered flood is its opposite: as tame a product of our cupidity as a golf course.

Somewhere in front of me beneath the grey captive waters rests the height of land from which the Qu'Appelle River once trickled out its life onto the prairie. There were days when this piece of valley brimmed with herds beyond counting. The original, originating landscape — the essence of the place ordained by Creation, celebrated by ritual and story — was lost to tides of colonialism that are just now ebbing.

I can sit here on the beach, pondering, grieving the loss. I can try to reckon the span of what we forsook in this place, but I cannot recover the mystery of what this first length of valley once meant to the Calling River and its people.

DURING THE LAST PHASE of the Wisconsin glaciation, approximately 13,500 years ago, a lobe of melting ice paused north of the Elbow of the South Saskatchewan River. For fifty, one hundred, perhaps five hundred years, glacial lakes draining massive amounts of meltwater from the north and south joined in a fork at the Elbow that sent the combined flow sharply eastward. The torrent of debris-filled waters cut easily into the glacial till east of the Elbow and, in so doing, carved the valley of the upper Qu'Appelle. As the ice-dam melted back north, the South Saskatchewan River resumed its original course northward, but continued to spill over into the Qu'Appelle system at high water. Since then, centuries of snowmelt and rain have brought material from the uplands into the lowlands of the valley, filling it to a level that is only half its original post-glacial depth. A low summit developed over time in the bottom of the old meltwater channel at a place roughly fourteen miles east of the Elbow. This elevated land within the valley divided springs flowing west to the South Saskatchewan River from those flowing east. The eastern springs formed the ambivalent headwaters of the Qu'Appelle. Ambivalent because the inosculation between the two river systems continued, now diminished to a small stream that could flow in either direction, depending on water levels at the Elbow. This stream with the strange power to reverse its flow was called Aiktow by the Cree — the River That Turns.

DAVID THOMPSON, eighteenth-century explorer and cartographer, drew the first map of Rupert's Land to show the connection between the Elbow and the Qu'Appelle headwaters. He named the turning stream Heart River. Thompson may have translated this from a name used by the Blackfoot, whom he often travelled with and who knew the Elbow region well as a neutral ground between themselves and the Cree. Whatever the source, the name suits a river that circulates its lifeblood between two major arteries at the core of the Northern Great Plains.

A turning river, a low divide with perennial streams flowing out of sand dunes on either side, and a no-man's land between nations all in a shallow, broad valley: these features drew the wild creatures of the plains in concentrations that beggared description. Palliser had this to say of the area: "We were now in the heart of the buffalo country. This region may be called a buffalo preserve . . . The whole region as far as the eye could reach was covered in buffalo bands varying from hundreds to thousands. So vast were the herds that I began to have serious apprehension for my horses, as the grass was eaten to the earth."[11] Reading reports like this, you cast your vain imaginings into the vanished country where you want to stand with the Irish captain on the high banks of the South Saskatchewan and watch the herds crossing at the ancient buffalo ford just above the Elbow. It was one of the only places the buffalo crossed the South Branch. The herds came from the west in season, crossed at the ford, and then fanned out across the upper Qu'Appelle Valley. There they would graze sedges at the springs and wallow in the bogs and marshes along the Aiktow and the source of the Qu'Appelle.

I was told once by a man who held great affection for the country around the Elbow that when the Canadian Pacific Railway moved its line above the north rim of the upper Qu'Appelle and Aiktow Valleys, evidence of ancient buffalo hunts appeared routinely wherever the workers would excavate. Teeth, bones, and skulls tumbled to the surface in some places like rocks behind a plough. One day when he was out walking over the soil exposed during construction, he came across a few charred buffalo bones jutting out from the sand. He checked a larger area and probed carefully with a shovel. Wherever his shovel entered the sand it scraped against bone. He had found a pile of bones from a hunt of unknown antiquity, most likely a kill site where there would be other artifacts, but he left the place undisturbed and did not return. People who live near the Elbow will tell you such stories of what they have seen and left in the soil, of coming across the evidence of absent hunters and then walking on, empty-handed.

The Elbow was one of those distinctive thumbprints of creation on the face of the earth where hunting peoples gather. All bioregions have such places. A range of hills that shelters deer, a coastal delta favoured by snow geese, a bay where the belukha come to mate. The animals, climate, and land forms characterize the life of a sanctuary like the Elbow, but any landscape receives its spirit from the repeated attention and ceremonies of people over an accumulation of seasons beyond reckoning.

A story of long occupancy is a story of chipped stone. If I could paddle upstream in the history of this river and arrive at the headwaters in 1905 or another year when the grass first felt the plough, I would know, as the settlers must have known, the abiding presence of the ones who had dwelt on the land before, because I would bump the toe of my boot against their kitchen tools, heft them in my hands and turn them over, astonished that this one is stained, that another still has its leather thong. And I would imagine heat from the last hands, the hands that dropped these implements not long ago.

Finding arrowheads on a prairie farm is a commonplace event, but some regions — landscapes, like this one, consistently inhabited by aboriginal peoples — have yielded more than others. Every established farm near the Elbow seems to have its own cache of arrowheads stowed in drawers and glass cases. If not, they have turned the lot over to the local museum.

At the Fred J. Hill Museum in Riverhurst, a wagon-wheel fenceline draws you into the building. The day I visited, a pair of Say's phoebes sat upon the wagon rims. I was surprised to see them in the middle of town, but not surprised to see they had chosen the museum as a nesting site. This poised and serene bird, a distinctively western flycatcher that carries the burnt sienna of canyon rock on its belly, has taken to nesting in the rafters and eaves of old buildings. Its affection for abandoned homesteads is surpassed only by the museum collector's.

Inside the museum, among a collection that includes buffalo coats, a full set of Métis buckskin vest and chaps, a badger skull, and other miscellany of our inroads, lay some elegant and ancient pieces of lithic art. They are spear points labelled "Yuma," 8,000-year-old blades, the tools of daily life from a time when we were all working with stone and trying to keep the fire going.

In his journal, Thoreau calls arrowheads stone fruit and says "each one yields me a thought." Such crafted things never fail to astonish. Light strikes the chipped surface of the chalcedony, penetrates the thin, translucent edges, and casts shadows at the rims of each dished crescent where a flake of stone, by its absence, calls to mind the skill of the one who removed it. I stared at the Yuma points, thinking about the pull between what has been chipped away and what remains, and I wondered at hands, fleshed and sinewed as my own, that made something so undiminished, so complete that they might as easily have turned out the tail of a fish or talon of a hawk.

Other articles have been placed in no particular order on the museum tables: a stone hammer still lashed with a leather thong to its wooden handle, scrapers found at Gilroy, a stone pipe, a pestle, chert knives from Eyebrow Lake, a smooth shaft of soft stone hewn into a hoof and dew claws at one end. The tools of first dwellers, so randomly displayed in local museums, refract one's view of plains history. Next to butter churns and Hudson's Bay Company trade rifles, the flint-knapped points appear to be part of the same jumble sale peddling the leftovers of miscellaneous failed civilizations.

The truth, however, is arranged in the soil, in the layered midden of a successful way of life finally interrupted by the butter churn and rifle people. I thought about this record of human tenure and the possibility of distortion in our regard for the succession of lifeways, when I learned the story of a local artifact hunter named Houghton. Living and farming near the upper Qu'Appelle Valley twelve miles east of the Elbow, Houghton hunted for arrowheads whenever he had a chance. Once, he was digging in the sediment of an old lake and found charred soil three feet below the surface: a fire pit. Houghton began finding stone points, fragments, and other artifacts, enough to fill one pail and part of another. A man who has measured out in buckets the habitation of a Paleolithic people has learned something about his own people's tenuous grasp upon the soil, about the difference between history that comes from three feet underground and history that comes from china cabinets.

On the heels of Palliser came Henry Youle Hind and the next official expedition to run the yardsticks of empire across the origins of the Qu'Appelle watershed. Hind, an English geologist who was in some ways more broad-minded than most colonial explorers, had been charged with the task of exploring the region "lying to the west of Lake Winnipeg and Red River, and embraced (or nearly so) between the river Saskatchewan and Assiniboine." Hind was dispatched with orders from the colonial government in Upper Canada to "procure all the information in your power respecting the Geology, Natural History, Topography, and Meteorology of the region."[12]

The expedition, consisting of four "gentlemen," twelve Iroquois paddlers, and a guide, headed west from Toronto on April 29, 1858.[13] Over the next seven months, they surveyed and probed and collected whatever the landscape would yield to them. They measured coal deposits, graded soil and timber for the possibility of settlement, recorded rainfall and the temperatures of air and water, measured the discharge of rivers and the depths of lakes, and collected everything from Devonian fossils to Lakota peace pipes.

By July 17, the expedition had reached the Qu'Appelle Mission, founded a year earlier on the land between Echo and Mission lakes where Fort Qu'Appelle now stands. There, Cree hunters told Hind of the Qu'Appelle's source more than one hundred miles farther west. The Indians said that Hind could follow the river valley in that direction to its source just a short distance east of the Elbow. They told him that this region, where the valley became shallower toward the headwaters of Kahtapwao Sepe, was the hunting grounds of the Sandy Hills Cree. They also mentioned that in years of flood, the entire valley floor, just under a mile in width, was filled by a swift river. Only six years before, they said, water flowed east from the Elbow "as a mountain torrent through the short distance of twelve miles which separates [the head-waters] from the South Branch of the Saskatchewan."[14] The legendary Aiktow River had turned.

The nearer Hind and his men came to the upper Qu'Appelle Valley the more they fell beneath its powerful influence. Five days out from the Qu'Appelle Mission, the guides paused to look south from a rise above Cottonwood Creek, west of today's town of Lumsden. They spotted three fires burning on the plains toward the Coteau's Dirt Hills. It was a sign of some sort, likely from Cree or Assiniboine hunters. A few days later they learned that the Cree had set the fires, in part to divert a massive herd of buffalo streaming south and east from the Qu'Appelle's headwaters. The distance from the headwaters to the plains where the fires were set is more than seventy miles. The buffalo had forded the South Branch at the crossing above the Elbow and were now advancing east toward the region south of Hind's expedition. When the herds came to the burnt prairie they would turn south to feed on the Coteau, where they could be hunted by the Cree before moving on through to the lands of the Lakota people.

Ponder the scale of this operation long enough and you will come to see that the Plains Cree and other prairie people drew their lifeways from their hold upon vast tracts of land. The long distance from the Elbow to the Dirt Hills, which would have been almost featureless land-scape to European eyes, was a familiar neighbourhood to the Cree. Storied places, as near to mind as your grandfather's hay pasture, blazed with the marks of myth and memory on pathways in a home-land large enough to accommodate a ranging, indigenous life alongside herds that roamed the interior of the continent.

As Hind resumed his march westward along the valley he began to see more small groups of Cree camped on the hilltops. One morning, at Buffalo Pound Lake, he encountered three different encampments — people heading south to meet the buffalo in the Coteau. The Cree, hospitable to a fault, shared their breakfast of "pounded meat and bone marrow fat" with Hind. They told him that Chief Mistickoos, a respected leader of the Plains Cree, was camped at the Sandy Hills of the upper Qu'Appelle. There, the Indians said, they would find Mistickoos and the Sandy Hill Cree capturing buffalo in a pound.

From Buffalo Pound Lake to the headwaters, Hind and his men were never far from a camp of Cree people. As they passed west of the lake, they started to see fresh buffalo bones and carcasses, some attended by wolves. On the morning of July 27, having sated himself the night before on the generosity of the Cree, Hind saw buffalo. The herds were streaming in single file south out of the valley toward the Coteau. That night he camped with another small group of Cree at "Sand Hill Lake" (Eyebrow Lake) in the valley.

After a supper of fresh buffalo with the Cree at Eyebrow Lake, Hind listened as his hosts told him about the large herds that had passed through the area only days before. They discussed the creeks that form part of the source of the Qu'Appelle and the small ponds that sent water both west to the Elbow and east into the Qu'Appelle. And once again, Hind was told that Mistickoos and the main band of the Cree would receive him upstream at the Sandy Hills where the Qu'Appelle begins. Where the source was found, and lost, in a single day.

Questions, to which I have little hope of finding answers, come with me whenever I am out upon the unploughed remnants of this land. *Was there a way of keeping the unfenced prairie, the buffalo, the wolf? Were it not for the Dominion Lands Act and herd law,[15] would we have arrived at a half-wild prairie economy based on a mixture of indigenous and imported grazers? What if we had allowed the Indians to become tribes of modern pastoral people ranging herds domestic and wild over the entire Great Plains?*

On an evening walk across a community pasture, such questions will rise up from my footsteps like grasshoppers, each interrogating the boundaries between my boots and the insect, leaf, and moisture they displace. Any answers I contrive only last until the next time I cross barbed wire or trip on tines of a harrow lurking in the grass.

One question in particular keeps coming back: *When did we turn away from integrity in our relationship with wildness here? When did our civilization forsake an opportunity for renewal and engagement with the spirit of the New World?* The path of alienation runs back through Pizarro, Cortes, the Age of Exploration, the Spanish Inquisition, St. Augustine, and finally to the dawn of agriculture, but it is possible to narrow the question to the boundaries of a bioregion, to discover the place in one's own landscape where the path forked and one's forebears took the road most travelled. Such inquiry is a chance to reappraise our choices in the watershed and to plan better paths from here on.

Lately I have come to believe that if the turn in this region occurred at any one decisive moment, it happened on July 29, 1858, at the headwaters of the Qu'Appelle, the day Hind was escorted by sixty Cree horsemen into the precincts of Mistickoos. The encounter between these two men was a climax in the history of the Calling River — one that reverberates more than 140 years later in all that we assume and allow in living here.

This is not to say that Hind could have been other than himself or that another would not have come along to enact the moment in colonial destiny that was his. Our culture is our culture and our history is our history. Still, I cannot help speculating on the opportunity that presented itself to Hind. What if he had been moved in a moment of grace to a different regard for all that he found at the upper reaches of the valley? The scales might have fallen from his eyes and he might have seen the place as it was: the buffalo-wallowing, -shitting, -killing ground, the ground of origins, the font of all that made the great valley a place of endless returnings and ceremony and life. In the shade of poplars at springs dammed by beaver and flowing over sand hills grassed with *Koeleria*, Hind and his men might have lingered. Upon hallowed ground, embraced by the tolerance and welcome of the Cree, Hind would have in time come to a new respect for the plains. He might even have made a real discovery — distinct from what he was to later pass off as discoveries. He might have learned that the life of the

Cree, and of the bioregion itself, was valid and good, not requiring improvement but only our respect and forbearance.

This miracle did not happen, and we are not surprised. As broad-minded as Hind may have seemed in his day — he spoke out against the effects of smallpox and the fur trade upon the Indians of the region — he was, finally, as opaque as any European who blundered upon privilege in the New World. He met the Cree at the Sandy Hills and saw only a vagrant people living a degraded life in a harsh land. The Cree, showing remarkable restraint, did not slit the throats of the intruders. They withstood the arrival of this foreign mission with courage, dignity, and no doubt some concern for what would follow on its heels.

According to Hind's account,[16] Mistickoos and several of his men held council with Hind for seven hours in a large tipi. They gave him a place of honour and treated him with respect. A black stone pipe was passed from hand to hand around the circle. Mistickoos and each of his councillors spoke in turn. They addressed Hind directly and told him of their concern for their people and their homeland. They raised, in Hind's words, "strong objections against the Hudson's Bay Company encroaching upon the prairies and driving away the buffalo." They would tolerate posts on the periphery of their country, they said, but did not want to see the plains invaded by white culture.

Hind summarized in one sentence what he took to be the gist of these lengthy presentations: "They generally commenced with the creation, giving a short history of that event in most general terms, and after *a few flourishes about equality of origin*, descended suddenly to buffalo, half-breeds, the Hudson's Bay Company, tobacco, and rum." [my italics] In this summary and elsewhere between the lines of Hind's description of this meeting, I hear a mild impatience with this customary manner of speaking, the unspoken disdain of the civilized for the uncivilized. There sat Hind in a smoky lodge, fidgeting in his tweed jacket and riding boots next to men who a few hours earlier were revelling in the gore of a buffalo pound. He was a Christian servant of the Empire and was not about to be taken in by the "flourishes" of these bare-chested orators. Hind knew that the God of Abraham created the earth and that any interest that God might take in the matter of adding the plains to the Crown would fall clearly on the side of the Christians, who were, after all, bringing the light of the Holy Trinity to these unredeemed pagans. To Hind, all this stuff about Creation and origins was meaningless preamble, superstition, at best the rhetoric of primitive politicians.

I would like to have heard and understood those flourishes of "equality of origin" as they were spoken in the vernacular within that tent. Did they declare how the Cree viewed their place in wildness? Or was it something about their rights as original people? Even now, our consideration for what was lost in this story is damaged by the cliché we have created of the Indian chief beginning his speech by sweeping his arms over the landscape while making ponderous statements about the Great Spirit. Passed on through a translator and then through Hind's own disregard for the claims of aboriginal people, the little we have to go on leaves much for speculation.

It is possible that the preamble, reiterated as the context of all other remarks made by Mistickoos and his councillors, was much more than convention. It was, I believe, a vessel without which the words of each speaker would only spill out upon the ground, unanswered and undignified. The schism in Hind's own culture between Creation and human enterprise — between boundaries of economy and boundaries of the holy — rendered him insensible to such unity of message and context. He had nothing to contain this information within and so heard only the pleading of the soon-to-be disenfranchised.

Unlike Hind, Mistickoos has not spoken to us across the intervening 140 years. We are left to guess what might have been the thoughts of the Plains Cree chief on that day. Mistickoos had just impounded 250 buffalo for his people in a valley that would, he hoped, continue to nourish his Sandy Hill Cree into the future. Still, this white man in his tent was worrisome. The prairie delivered Hind unto Mistickoos as an emissary of the same disease-ridden people who had been chasing away the buffalo and invading the edges of the plains for generations. Mistickoos was not about to ask favours, but he and his councillors wanted to convince Hind of their legitimate and holy bond to their home. They would present their concerns openly and within an understanding of what they knew of Creation and their place within it. Any man of integrity would then see the rightness of an indigenous life on the plains. Surely this man who measured hills and handled stones would return to his leaders and recommend tolerance and preservation?

Hind was destined to be a historic disappointment. Before the council met with Hind, the chief's son had taken him out to see the remains of the recent buffalo pound. The Englishman was reviled. To Hind, it was "a sight most horrible and disgusting. . . . dreadful and sickening." The Cree looked upon the abattoir and saw the whole drama of their lives amid wildness: the blade-in-the-belly that is hunger, the fearful tumult of the hunt, the exultation of the feast — all affirmed within the pound's tableau of gore and bone. Hind saw "reckless and wasteful savages" and wrote in his notes that "man in his savage, untutored, and heathen state shows both in deed and expression how little he is superior to the noble beasts he so wantonly and cruelly destroys."[17]

This gets at the heart of the matter. Here we have the basis for Hind's executive recommendations of what would be required to deal with the Indians and make the plains safe for settlement. These Indians, who in their stories, economy, and religion placed themselves within the menagerie of the wild prairie, would need redemption from their degraded state. At the end of the expedition, Hind returned east and wrote reports. In one appendix he speaks of "evangelizing the heathen Indians," who, he recommends, "must be induced to relinquish their wandering habits of life and settle down." The way of the cross and the way of the hoe would save the people of the plains from themselves and from the depredations of the fur trade. He vilifies the fur economy as a destabilizing force that kept the Cree wild and reluctant to settle and become Christian.[18] Within the next two decades, Hind's civilization provided more inducement than even he envisioned. By 1880, the buffalo were gone. The sons and daughters of Mistickoos were on reserves posing for photographs in potato fields, churches, and schools.

In his reports, Hind also speculated on the prospects of damming and diverting water from the Elbow of the South Saskatchewan River to flood the Qu'Appelle Valley and provide a navigable west-east waterway between Fort Garry (Winnipeg) and the Rockies. As he sat in a tipi in the Aiktow Valley — deaf to the cosmology of the Sandy Hill Cree being recreated speaker after speaker — Hind was daydreaming of a flood that would destroy the land most sacred to his hosts. In 1958, exactly one hundred years after the Hind expedition, Canada's first Saskatchewan-born prime minister announced a scheme to build dams at the Elbow. John Diefenbaker's project would not achieve Hind's entire design — the great valley would not be flooded along its length — but a huge reservoir created at the Elbow would flood the valley of the River That Turns, the summit, and the upper Qu'Appelle. The summit separating the two watersheds, the sandhill springs forming the origins of the Qu'Appelle and Aiktow rivers, the ancient hunting grounds of the Cree, and the land where Hind sat in council with Mistickoos all disappeared under water in the 1960s. The story of all that we renounced in taking the trail blazed by Henry Youle Hind is the story of an ancient prairie shrine lost to the waters of that same engineered flood.

## Chapter Five

# THESE ARE THE SHARDS

THERE IS A ROMANCE IN MAPS and map-making that has me at times wishing I had studied geography instead of poetry and novels. Then I realize that the appeal comes from literature itself, from what such writers as Hugh Brody, Barry Lopez, and others have had to say about maps. Passages about geomorphology in a novel like Michael Ondaatje's *English Patient* will linger in my thoughts for days. At one point Almasy, the main character, nearly manages to enter a region between cartography and the land itself. "It was as if he had walked under the millimetre of haze just above the inked fibres of a map, that pure zone between land and chart between distances and legend between nature and storyteller."[19]

When a well-drawn map serves as my entry into a place, this kind of geographical alchemy will sometimes take me, through contour lines and the tracings of human enterprise, into the layer of history and myth overlying a landscape. Aerial-photo maps, mechanized and monochrome, should be less evocative, but I find myself all the more captivated by their close detail and relief. Transfixed by the trick of the stereoscope, drawing me across a membrane of paper and suspending me above hills, barns, and trees, I have stared for long stretches of time at photo maps of the upper Qu'Appelle Valley.

From 6,800 feet above the grass, I saw the valley as it was in one moment of 1963. It was November, three years before the flood. I soared over aspen trees that poked their frothy crowns toward me. I glided down updrafts from sandy slopes and out across the surface of beaver ponds. Roads, canals, earth berms creased the valley with sharp intaglio set within a soft and yielding earth. I saw the springs at the summit of the upper Qu'Appelle, sending the Aiktow River to the west and the Calling River, nascent and tentative, to the east.

From this altitude, parts of the valley show distinct wave lines the same as undulations of sand on a riverbed. Only the scale is different. Larger particles moved by more water — in this case, boulders and till arranged by a seventy-five-foot deep torrent of glacial meltwater into these sinuous ridges across a large stretch of valley. This pattern is an uncommon feature on any landscape, and the Aiktow Valley was an especially good example.

Leaving the wave lines, I rested my eyes upon the waters of Middagh Lake, near the divide and the place where Hind shuddered to see the Sandy Hill Cree impounding buffalo. Beyond Middagh, I saw trails. One took me west from the river at the headwaters a mile, and then forked. The northeast fork ran for a quarter-mile and then ended abruptly at a rock. A rock large enough to show up on a photograph taken from 6,800 feet.

## THE ROCK: GENESIS

IN MAPS, journals, memos, newspapers, and photographs, I chased after the history of this rock. And in the end never quite possessed the understanding I believed lay somewhere ahead of me.

Ask a geologist how a giant boulder found its way to the bottom of a prairie valley and the answer will come swiftly, directly: it was an erratic brought south by glaciers and dumped some time during their retreat twelve thousand years ago. Ask a Cree elder the same question and the answer will be a circling and apparently evasive treatise on the significance of stories, the storyteller's responsibilities, and the listener's rites of passage. The geologist, informed by the latest models of geophysical science, offers his opinions freely. The elder, constrained by oral traditions that have bound people, animals, and land together since the first tales were told and songs were sung, speaks carefully, avoiding the actual story and the names of places or characters. "That place, that stone, that boy," he will say, and if a degree of trust and openness has been established through proper gestures of respect, he may say something *about* the story, mentioning bits of the narrative or the messages it contains. But the story itself will remain somewhere else, elusive and beyond an easy knowing.

Such has been my experience when I have spoken about the rock with Wes Fineday, a respected bundle-keeper and ceremonialist of the Sweetgrass nation. I had read texts purporting to be the story of the great rock's origins, but I doubted their authenticity and wanted to hear it properly, from an elder with Wes's credentials. Whenever we spoke about it, though, I could see Wes carefully making tracks around the story itself, as though a border kept him away from the region where it was safe to speak of such things. I felt disappointed and confused at first, only realizing later that he knew better than I what I was ready to hear. And so, although I do not *know* the story, I have heard Wes talk about it, felt its power resonating in his voice, and arrived at my own meagre understanding of its place within the spirit life and wisdom of his people.

The words that tell how the rock came to rest in the Aiktow Valley belong to a core of sacred spirit stories borne in the memories and hearts of a few Plains Cree storytellers. These stories, which can only be told when accompanied by appropriate ceremony and when the snow is upon the ground, carry the primary teachings of the people. They are the sacred narratives, the oral Pentateuch of the Northern Plains.

The genesis story of the rock is sacred because it tells how a place came to be sacred. But it is also one of the restricted stories because it depicts transformation from one form of being into another and because it contains lessons from "the grandfathers" — the spirit buffalo. Cree elders are unequivocal on the grandfathers. They are healing spirits and therefore must not be tampered with.

The stories themselves contain clear boundaries of spiritual knowledge, which are observed by the ones who keep the stories. To earn the right to hear, to bear, and to pass on a sacred spirit story one must first demonstrate to the keeper of the story the required openness, attention, and respect. Later, guided by ceremony and ritual practice, and after attaining a full understanding of the story at all its levels — comprehending it and remembering it with the body, the mind, and the emotions — then and only then may a person be said to know the story and share in its spiritual copyright.

Like many sacred spirit stories, the story of the rock has something to say about the power of spiritual knowledge. It teaches how, in the past, this power flowed freely from people's relationships with animals because the same animals that fed one's body would also feed one's spirit. In the narrative, a lost boy is adopted by the grandfathers and later undergoes certain trials and transformations, changing from human to buffalo and later from buffalo to stone. In the end, the story shows why the rock became, within the Aiktow Valley's rich spirit field, a potent point of contact with the sacred, a place where buffalo and buffalo hunter alike came each summer, crossing rivers and plains to pay homage to the life and wisdom embodied in stone.

## THE PEOPLE: APPROACHING MANITOU

FOR TEN THOUSAND WINTERS and ten thousand summers, the buffalo rock presided over the shifts of the River That Turns, the migrations of the buffalo, the source of the Qu'Appelle, and the hunting life of the plains people.

The ones who followed the herds came to the buffalo rock, but they did not come to barter with the spirits for a favour. To approach the rock was to encounter the holy in their prairie world. The rock was one place where a hunter could join with the mystery and recognize its power in his own life. He would place an offering beside the rock, not as a tithing for good luck in the hunt, but as a sign of his respect for the order of things. And if the man were prepared inwardly, he might come to know the singular flow of Creation, the mingling of his flesh and bone with grass, sky, and granite.

## THE ROCK: WRITTEN RECORD

PALLISER'S JOURNALS mention the rock. He saw Cree people engaged in ceremonies and noted their trance-like state. Hind, in 1858, walked along the Aiktow and upper Qu'Appelle Valleys, speculating on their formation, measuring and identifying rocks. Of the great rock, which he marked on his map of the region, he had this to say: "About fourteen miles from the South Branch is a gigantic erratic of unfossiliferous rock on the south side of the valley. . . . The Indians place on it offerings to Manitou, and at the time of our visit it contained beads, bits of tobacco, fragments of cloth, and other trifles."[20]

The rock was gigantic by prairie standards. According to measurements recorded in the *Blue Jay*, a journal of natural history, the exposed portion of the rock — how much was underground no one knows — measured about 30 feet long, 20 feet wide, and 14 feet high. Hind stretched a tape measure around it at three feet off the ground, and came up with a rough horizontal circumference of 79 feet. With a volume of 4,800 cubic feet, its weight was initially thought to be about 370 tons. Later estimates were much higher. Hind said that it was the largest erratic he had seen on his travels in the North-West. It was certainly one of the largest anywhere on the Northern Great Plains. Facing west, the rock sat in a dish-shaped depression accentuated by the comings and goings of people and buffalo. The surface of the rock's fine-grained, pale-red granite was smooth, particularly where the buffalo rubbed themselves. The granite was composed mainly of plagioclase, potash feldspar, quartz, and pyroxenes. It was pre-Cambrian, among the oldest of rock and part of the mantle that first cooled on the earth's surface four billion years ago.[21]

## THE PEOPLE: PICNICS AND SNAPSHOTS

I HEARD an Indian historian once say that soon after the 1885 uprisings in the North-West, the federal government outlawed any practice of native rites and ceremonies. These restrictions, combined with the hardship of reserve life on tracts of land far from the headwaters of the Qu'Appelle, did much to sever the connection between the Plains Cree and the rock. Like the buffalo, the people came no more to the lands east of the Elbow.

The new people, though, fresh on the land, soon found themselves drawn to the ancient monument, partaking of their own rituals. From 1900 onward, white farmers came to the rock on Sunday afternoons, first by wagon, later by Model T. Setting the week's labour aside, they would sit in the shade of the erratic, eat sandwiches, and talk of hail or the price of sugar while their children climbed the sides of the granite buffalo.

I searched through photographs of these afternoons. The images show for the most part a people who knew that it was just a big rock, who smiled and posed like families on an outing at the zoo, standing in front of the elephant cage. I wanted to find at least one photo that suggested a measure of respect from the settlers, a regard for the rock's life upon the floodplain of the River That Turns. It would show a farmer and his small son or daughter in repose and unaware of the camera. The man leaning against the flank of the rock as he sat in the hollow at its base, the child looking up at the sky or down at the grassy cosmos underfoot. And something in the father's gaze across the valley or in the arch of his shoulders would allow me to imagine respect and humility in the presence of an enduring mystery.

## THE ROCK: ARCHAEOLOGY

THERE IS NO WAY to measure the importance of a holy place. My seventh-grade understanding of science says otherwise, has me concocting a formula: devotion to/interest in a given locality is expressed in total number of visits divided by the number of years for which statistics are available. A simple calculation, the kind used all the time by Banff National Park or Wanuskewin.

But visitation statistics are not available and the people who came to the buffalo rock for ages beyond counting were not tourists. All the same, something in me needed to hear the archaeology.

On the day I headed for the Royal Saskatchewan Museum in Regina to find what record remained of the rock, there seemed hope yet of understanding how history, archaeology, politics, and culture converged in deciding the fate of a sacred prairie shrine.

The curator of Archaeology and Anthropology handed me a fat file about the rock. I thanked her and told her I was looking for evidence of the rock's importance as a holy site. She smiled and said that the question of proof was the centre of a great controversy concerning the rock in the early 1960s. Then she showed me to a table in the museum library, where I sat down, opened the file, and began to read.

By the fall of 1958, the plans to dam the Elbow of the South Saskatchewan were in place. The House of Commons in Ottawa gave its approval of the project in September. The following spring, Prime Minister Diefenbaker presided at the inaugural ceremony before 15,000 people — one of the largest crowds the province had ever seen. In the shade of large elms that would eventually fall to bulldozers, people ate buttered rolls, apple pie, and barbecued beef. Later each guest would take home a horn-handled steak knife as a souvenir of the occasion. Martial music from the Saskatchewan Dragoons Band made its way down to the people from a stage constructed high above the riverbank. Six T-33 jets from the RCAF roared past three times to kick off the official ceremonies. A group of Indian people from a reserve near Dundurn danced on stage. Invited to the ceremony to lend colour to the event, the dancers were from a band of Dakota people whose ancestors had fled north from Minnesota in the late 1860s. They would have known nothing of the stories of the Elbow and the River That Turned — only that the government was damming the river and that they were to perform a dance and make Diefenbaker an honorary chief. This they did, giving Diefenbaker the name Chief Tatonka Moni, as well as a complete eagle-feather headdress and buckskin jacket. The record shows that Mrs. Diefenbaker received a smart beaded buckskin handbag.

Diefenbaker and Saskatchewan's premier, T.C. Douglas, both paid tribute to the forethought of Henry Youle Hind, whose original idea for a dam had been "conceived 100 years ago."[22] They made promises that this would be an "economic turning point in the province's history," and that the dark days of the dust-bowl thirties would never return. The closing of Diefenbaker's address swells with the same hubris that has inflated the rhetoric of every colonizer in our history, from Samuel de Champlain to John A. Macdonald: "It is my honour and privilege to declare the inauguration of the South Saskatchewan Dam Project; to declare it officially underway, a project which in the days ahead will be a symbol of triumph over the struggles of the past, whereby the people of today will lay the foundation for greater opportunity and hope, not only for Saskatchewan but for Canada as a whole. In other words, in building here this great project for the benefit of generations yet unborn, we make our contribution in a spirit of unity among the races [toward] the building of that Canada whose destiny is founded in the heritage of its people. . . . Mr. President, Mr. Premier, my fellow Canadians, I now declare the inauguration of the construction of the South Saskatchewan River Dam!"

With this, Diefenbaker pulled a switch detonating a half-ton of dynamite and sending a mass of river-bottom earth hundreds of feet into the air above the crowd. The farmers and townspeople of the Elbow region let out soft sounds of amazement and then began to cheer. Craning their necks to watch the cloud of alluvium settle, they felt new assurance that such a power would soon bring prosperity to their doorsteps.

That same summer of 1959, archaeologists and anthropologists were dispatched to the upper Qu'Appelle and Aiktow Valleys to assess and recover anything of value that would be under water once the project was complete. In the lands stretching between the summit and the Elbow, they walked, probed, measured, and made notes. The valley felt nothing, did not so much as note their presence. The stones released no shouts. The hills may have shrugged, but that was all. The men in boots and khaki went here and there collecting the evidence of former dwellers. They found much, but nothing that would move the dam-builders to reconsider or reduce the size of the project. A series of prehistoric buffalo pounds, several burial sites, a trading post from historical times, tipi rings at various locations, and a miscellany of artifacts. Most of the takings were placed safely within the vaults of the National Museum in Ottawa.

Zenon Pohorecky, an anthropologist and leader of the expedition, surveyed the fourteen miles from the Elbow to the summit, where the dam was to be stretched across the headwaters of the Qu'Appelle. The document recording all archaeological sites that were in the way of the coming flood was called The South Saskatchewan Archaeological Project 1959. In it, Pohorecky described the rock in detail. He called it the main feature in what he believed to be "a sacred offering and ceremonial centre." At this "Buffalo Shrine," said Pohorecky, the Cree addressed "the spirit of the Manitou."[23]

Digging at the base of the rock, his crew extracted more than one thousand artifacts — offerings left over an undetermined span of time. The inventory included pieces of bone, chert, ochre, spear and arrow points, scrapers, bone and shell beads, bits of leather. Nearer the surface they found items from the fur-trade era — musketballs, crockery, glass beads, copper rings, metal buttons, pendants, and earrings. Piece by piece, Pohorecky accumulated the tribute of countless travellers who had come to pay their respects, and yield something of their tools, adornment, and themselves, to the power indwelling in stone.

Near the rock, Pohorecky found changes in vegetation and soil that outlined large circles where someone had erected structures made of perishable materials. Two of these were twenty feet in diameter; a third was eighty feet in diameter. In subsequent reports, Pohorecky speaks of this larger circle as the remains of a structure made of saplings and used in ceremony, likely a sundance lodge.

The scientists had no instrument or test to detect the filaments running from the rock to the ceremonial lodges to the buffalo pounds to the burial sites to the springs at the headwaters to the animal trails to the gathering of sixty tipis nearby. But the bonds between these points did register in Pohorecky's gut. The day he came to the rock, something jostled him away from the moment's scrutiny and made him shake the dust of science from his feet. He heard the pipit's swirling song, felt the pull of sedges underfoot, and walked into the role of activist.

## The People: Advocates

THE MUSEUM'S FILE left a lot of questions unanswered and didn't say how Pohorecky made his case. Did any of the local people care enough about the rock to speak up? Some farmers believed they would benefit from the irrigation promised by the dam-builders; others, not needing or wanting the water, may have had other thoughts. How many opposed the dam — spoke against it because it would flood a valley of their childhood, of memory, of history, of good pasture, of a rock and ceremonial grounds deserving respect? I wondered what it was that moved a few to speak while most stood by in ignorance or quiet surrender.

Two years after first reading that museum file, I would accompany Zenon Pohorecky on what turned out to be his first trip back to the Elbow region in thirty years and his last field trip anywhere. I would be surprised to see such a short man step out of the van and onto the dirt road. Surprised to see this controversial anthropologist and civil rights activist looking as weary as a pensioned coal-miner: full head of bristly grey hair, a couple of days' growth on his chin, and a mustache above a smile stained by years of smoking. Bearing fifty pounds that he did not have on his original rambles along the valley during the summer of '59, Pohorecky would wheeze as we walked out to the shore of the reservoir.

And he would point across the flat, grey expanse of reservoir and remember his first visit: *We came from the other side, but we saw the springs from here, coming out from this side. We were looking for slopes with the right kind of access to the water — looking for fords in the Aiktow. . . . We figured that the people would have congregated here in late summer. There was a place just southwest of here with about sixty tipi rings. And signs of a trading post nearby. We recorded all kinds of sites, excavated several of them — the oldest were Besant culture, two thousand years old, all along the shore here, the Besant. . . . At the rock, although it had been picked clean by picnickers for many years, we found about 1,200 artifacts. . . . We found vegetation changes indicating a structure the size of a sundance lodge and rocks in particular locations, so we plotted them. . . . Nearby we found evidence of butchering and buffalo bones. . . . It was an important place. I saw it as something good for the people of Saskatchewan, that it could show them that they are surrounded by spirits from the past . . .*

Two months after our meeting at the Elbow, I would receive word that Pohorecky had died quietly at home.

"I'm the son of a man who came over the mountains." That was how Zenon Pohorecky described himself the first time we spoke over the telephone. It was the Carpathian Mountains, he said, and then he told me he was Ukrainian and explained how to pronounce his name: "Rhymes with Gretzky." And he chuckled at this, but I could tell he was proud of his name and origins. We talked several times over a period of months, and I came to know Pohorecky as someone who, despite a career of lost causes, could still laugh at life without bitterness or rancour. This absence of cynicism, together with his commitment to the rights and cultural revival of First Peoples, made him seem innocent, vulnerable. He told me about summer weekends in the sixties and seventies when he would often be invited to attend sacred ceremonies on the reserves. The people accepted him, and he returned the favour by opening his home in the city to visitors from Sweetgrass or Poundmaker who would regularly stay with him for days or weeks at a time.

I never got around to asking Pohorecky why he allowed compassion and imagination to enter his science, why he jeopardized his academic career to defend a rock, but after he died I found among the news clippings he had mailed me a piece from the Saskatoon *Star-Phoenix* that began to answer my curiosity. The story was not about the rock; it was about Pohorecky and his father, the man who came over the mountains.

Michael Pohorecky, the article said, was an intellectual and writer in the Western Ukraine. In the 1920s he escaped from jail where he was being held for publishing articles protesting dispossession of Ukrainian peasant land. Once over the mountains and across the sea in Canada, he sent for his wife and newborn son, Zenon. The family lived first in Edmonton, where Michael joined a Ukrainian newspaper and then quickly founded his own — *The New Pathway*. After moving to Saskatoon, where Zenon spent most of his early childhood, the elder Pohorecky continued promoting the rights of Ukrainians, who in Western Canada were facing new forms of oppression.

Zenon grew up admiring his father as a leader of the Ukrainian people and a champion of human rights and free speech. He discovered early on that he had a talent for art and as a teenager he began to paint murals depicting Ukrainian history and folklore. At his father's side, he learned that it is the story-bearing nation, not the arms-bearing nation, that will triumph over racism and tyranny.

As a university student, Zenon helped form the national Ukrainian students congress. During his undergraduate studies at the University of Manitoba, he shared a locker with another Ukrainian artist and intellectual, William Kurelek. After taking his doctorate at Berkeley in 1964, Zenon, now married and ready to begin his teaching career, returned home to put together a department of Anthropology and Archaeology at the University of Saskatchewan in Saskatoon. That was when he found out that the archaeological sites he had discovered in 1959 and 1960 were on the wrong side of the proposed dam in the Aiktow Valley.

Back in the museum file, the spoor of documents showed that Pohorecky and his group of Saskatoon activists had gained the attention of government. By 1965, departmental memos had begun to fly. Atop each mimeographed letter was the provincial coat of arms — three sheaves of wheat above a lion.

The Museum of Natural History in Regina was convinced that something had to be done; the Department of Natural Resources would have to do something. Women at the museum sent letters dictated by men at the museum to women at the department who opened them for men at the department. Further memos went to the federal organization in charge of the dam project, the PFRA (Prairie Farm Rehabilitation Agency). The memos said the PFRA would have to move the rock. The PFRA said, *Move it yourself.* The provincial government said, *Okay, if someone else will pay for the moving, maybe we can find funds to build a new site on higher ground, as part of our winter works program. Kindest personal regards, Province of Saskatchewan.*

The notion that some noble purpose would be served in shunting the rock out of the way seems alarmingly daft in hindsight. Lucky it was not a mountain. The record has hidden any second thoughts about this. Nowhere did I come across a consideration that the rock's significance might derive not so much from its bulk and form, as from its origin and placement as a sentinel of life at the source of two rivers.

Instead of rethinking the plan that threatened the rock and its landscapes, the main concern was *How do we get this thing out of the way?* No suggestion that the reservoir could be redesigned to terminate farther west, up-valley from the rock and the ceremonial grounds. No discussion that in flooding the Aiktow Valley and the Qu'Appelle headwaters, the dam-builders would destroy an ancient mystery that regulated the bidirectional flow of water between the Elbow and the source of the Qu'Appelle. The rock's holiness came in part from presiding over this mystery, this force that gathered and moved water. To drown the rock and its valley would be desecration enough; the real sacrilege was in acquiescing to the uncivil fallacy of civil engineering: that human controls are superior to the controls in Creation; that dams, reservoirs, canals, and floodgates are an improvement upon the regulations overseen by a rock and inherent within a low prairie divide, a chain of sandhill springs, and a river that turns.

## THE ROCK: EXPERT OPINION

THE ROCK FIRST weighed 380 tons, then 1,600, then only 80, then 1,400. Once it was four tons, but that was a mistake in a newspaper editorial. It would only cost $11,500 to move it. No, it will cost at least $25,000. Then $75,000. *It is too brittle to be moved. We think it could be moved in two pieces on skids. Why not encase it in concrete and then roll it uphill and above the floodline? Or, we could anchor buoys on cables attached to it, and then after the flood, relocate the rock and hoist it to the surface and onto a large raft. Just like the navy does in salvage operations. Wait. What about the folks who moved the ancient monuments to make way for the Aswan Dam construction in Egypt? Let's bring them in as consultants.*

## THE PEOPLE: SAVE THE ROCK

ONCE THE LOWEST CONTRACTOR BID for moving the rock had been chosen, the Save the Rock committee in Saskatoon began fundraising in earnest. University of Saskatchewan students went door to door asking for donations to "save the rock." Even the provincial government said it would throw a couple of thousand dollars into the hat. In the spring of '66, folksinger Buffy Sainte-Marie, born twenty-three years earlier on Piapot reserve in the central Qu'Appelle Valley, headlined a benefit concert along with American comedian and civil rights activist Dick Gregory. Meanwhile, Saskatchewan members of Parliament rose in the House of Commons somewhere east of the rock and said heroic things, demanding the rescue of this "ancient Indian shrine" and pointing out that Canada had recently sent hundreds of thousands of dollars to help move historic monuments threatened by the Aswan Dam project in Egypt. One of these champions was John Diefenbaker, the man who initiated the dam project while he was prime minister, the man whose name now graces the reservoir.

## THE ROCK: VOICES

POHORECKY COULD SEE where this was headed. He wanted the rock to be moved, but resistance to the idea was growing. Skeptics began to question the rock's religious significance. Indian leaders had so far said very little publicly about the rock. Pohorecky began to gather the statements that journalists and other white interviewers had taken from Indian elders. As the debate intensified in 1965, he published some of this testimony in a Saskatchewan Archaeological Society newsletter.

Dan Kennedy (Ochankeegahe) was an Assiniboine elder from the Carry-the-Kettle Nation, west of Wascana Creek and south of the valley. He said that the rock was without doubt a shrine of the plains. He described the ceremonial offerings of strouds (a valuable trade cloth), tobacco, and other cherished items placed at the rock.

Pat Cappo of the Muscowpetung Nation near Pasqua Lake remembered that his grandfather's band of six hundred had overwintered at the rock in 1868, the same year they had taken peace with Sitting Bull and the Lakota. Young girls, he recalled, were never allowed near the rock. This sort of precaution is a traditional gesture of regard for the holy. It is a practice that continues today at important ceremonies, where young women in menses are prohibited. Cappo said that his people stopped coming to the rock after 1901, when missionaries in the Qu'Appelle put a stop to what they saw as heathen idolatry.

Sidney Fineday of the Sweetgrass Cree Nation compared the rock to Christian places of worship. He spoke of religious freedom and suggested that the disrespect shown to the rock would not be tolerated if it were a Christian shrine.

Chief John Skeeboss of the Kawacatoose Nation referred to the time before history, "when Indians flew through the air," made their own tobacco, and healed the sick with plants of the prairie. He remembered the buffalo rock, how members of his own band would sit by its side for long periods without food and water.

The words of the Indians are moving and situate the rock within human memory and stories, but I worry about this sort of testimony. It seems irretrievably compromised by the intrusion of the white interviewer. Journalists and activists sought out these voices, enlisted them to support the cause. This must have been puzzling for the elders, to be asked to address thought and concern to a people who want to know the significance of a place before they proceed with its destruction. Kennedy,

Cappo, Fineday, and Skeeboss knew what would come of this. There is resignation in their voices, little of the defiance I had hoped for.

No indignant speeches, no roadblocks, no tipi vigil in the valley. The descendants of the Cree who welcomed Henry Youle Hind on his journey had long ago learned that to stand in the way of development was merely to delay the inevitable. There is the story of Piapot, the intrepid Cree chief of the late nineteenth century who sat in his lodge astride the CPR right-of-way and halted the railroad construction. For an afternoon. A sergeant of the North-West Mounted Police walked into Piapot's tipi, past the chief, and kicked out the main pole. The tent collapsed, Piapot and his people moved, the CPR went on its inexorable way.

## THE PEOPLE: ASPERSIONS

WHEN POHORECKY STEPPED out of academe to champion the cause of the rock, his colleagues did not follow. He had lapsed from the objectivity of his science and would have to be drawn back into line. Some anthropologists and historians began discrediting Pohorecky and his campaign, accusing him of grandstanding. If it were truly a significant shrine, they said, it would have petroglyphs or markings like other sacred rocks. As for the 1,200 artifacts he claimed to have found at the foot of the rock, such leavings were not unusual on the plains where any prominent feature was an obvious spot for nomadic people to gather.[24]

In the museum file, I came across a government memo, dated January 25, 1966, in which a bureaucrat named Baker sowed doubt regarding Pohorecky's conduct as an anthropologist. He was indignant that the artifacts Pohorecky collected at the rock were not sent to Ottawa along with the rest of the spoils gathered in the initial archaeological expedition. In the memo Baker suggests that in keeping these items, Pohorecky committed an impropriety. He then questions the origin of the artifacts and Pohorecky's honesty: "If the material in Pohoretsky's [sic] possession is not from the erratic, then devious means are being employed to bolster the significance of this particular erratic. . . . I believe that in time, given sufficient rope, this individual will be 'hanged' by members of his own profession. Possibly, the minister may wish to see the contents of this memo."[25]

With Pohorecky now standing at the margins of his profession, the validity of the Indian claims for the rock also came into question. Farmers who had lived for years in the Aiktow area came forward to testify that they had never seen an Indian near the rock. People began wondering why Cree elders who recalled stories of the rock had not been to the rock themselves until Pohorecky publicized its plight.[26] Letters to the editor described the affair as a misguided effort to appease pagan worshippers. One letter writer suggested that pieces of the rock could be sold to help pay for the dam. Taxpayers said they did not want public money spent on moving a worthless piece of granite. The Saskatoon Board of Trade refused to contribute to the Save the Rock Fund. In June 1966, as the waters began to rise in the new reservoir, the National Historic Sites and Monuments Board held a special meeting with the Department of Northern Affairs in Ottawa. Without ever seeing the Aiktow Valley or its rock, they determined that a prairie boulder could not qualify for funding as a historic site.

### THE PEOPLE: RECLAMATION

AS I CAME ACROSS each of these worrisome cracks within the noble cause of saving the rock, I found myself drawn more deeply into the struggle, listening to arguments on each side, searching for whatever it was that made some people want to move a 400-ton monolith that others would just as soon forget.

I sympathized with Pohorecky and his supporters, but in the end had to admit that all actors in the debate were operating from a similar disregard for the order within the prairie rivers. All, that is, except for the Indians, who kept their distance from the squabble, knowing that if they acted in protest, someone would, sooner or later, walk into their lodges and kick out the main poles. I cannot blame them for staying out of a dispute that sidestepped the larger problem of the reservoir design, that did not even discuss the possibility of rethinking a project that would desecrate an entire landscape.

It seems that eventually, as historical and religious meaning became blurred in the minds of all concerned, the rock began to signify the Indians' final hold on lands that had once been so important to the buffalo hunters, a remnant claim that had somehow escaped the general extinguishing of native title. The tide of white civilization had eddied around the rock, leaving it to the spirits of the past. Now those spirits were becoming meddlesome, getting in the way, complicating what should be simple: if you need electricity and water control, you dam rivers and flood valleys. What really had to be extinguished were the nagging concerns about religious significance and Indian claims to sacred places. Establish the rock as a commonplace icon of little sacred or historical value that even the Indians had forgotten, and this last irksome relic of native title can be shunted aside once and for all. The land will then be indisputably alienated from its original dwellers.

Although no one expressed such an intention, or at least not in those terms, the underlying fear of ancient mystery and aboriginal entitlement would have operated upon the minds of the proponents of the dam, inspiring the denial of history required to devalue the rock in clear conscience.

*If the rock was so important, why haven't the Indians been visiting it during recent decades? Why did they show interest only after the controversy began?* These are the questions of people blinkered to the facts of the twentieth century in this region, as though broken treaties, reserve squalor, Indian agents, and residential schools had never happened. Of course the Cree no longer went to the rock and the upper Qu'Appelle Valley. They no longer made trips to the medicine wheels, danced at hilltop ceremonial circles, or visited effigies and countless other sacred sites on private land, many of which had been ploughed under as the primeval grasslands were seeded to hay and wheat. All such places had been left unattended, but not forgotten, for the first half of the twentieth century.

Through the years of cultural annihilation when missionaries and Indian agents discouraged all of the old ways, elders kept the fire of their faith at a low burn. Some holy places and ceremonies would have to wait for a better time. There were too many other issues — such as survival — demanding attention. Keeping the children alive did not leave much time for reclaiming a sense of myth and movement on the land.

The government ban on traditional religious practice was not lifted until the 1950s. Today, a generation later, Cree elders smile at the irony of the same Canadian government sponsoring workshops on "native spirituality" and marketing Indian culture in tourism brochures. The issues of self-government, land claims, housing, and unemployment occupy the concerns of band councillors who now also find themselves discussing whether to allow white people at a sundance or cameras in a sweat lodge.

There are the faithful teachers who, unimpressed by the marketers of dream catchers and sweetgrass, and the deals made in band offices and hotel lobbies, recall a grandmother's respect for the old ways, and who, in returning to the flow of ancestors and Creation, now rise and move like rain along creek beds clogged with the dust of many dry years.

## THE ROCK: SANCTUARY

IT IS A ROCK, only a rock. No one dressed in long robes approaches it solemnly with swinging censer. No bells, no sanctus. It does not rest on a marble floor beneath vaulted ceilings. It has no gold leaf upon its flanks to remind the faithful of its eternal value. The bones that rest within its cracks are not those of the canonized. You can watch it for days and no one will kneel before it or light candles at its side. No one will hide there from the incursions of law and state. It is a rock sitting outside at the mercy of the wind and rain. It is shat upon by birds and surrounded by weeds.

By early 1966, it became clear to the Cree elders that the rock was soon going to be either flooded or moved by the people who possessed the means to execute, but not the wisdom to change, such a plan. Now it was time for a ceremony.

On February 13, a small gathering of Cree elders and dancers offered their last oblations at the buffalo rock. Spectators, mostly white people, arrived out of nowhere, out of the snow and the wind along drifted-in trails bisecting the Aiktow Valley. By the time the ceremony began, one thousand or more people had come to watch. Cars were scattered in a crescent around the amphitheatre a short distance from the Cree celebrants huddled close to the rock. The audience waited in silence, blowing into their mitts, stamping their feet to fend off the chill. Everyone there knew that when the spring run-off came, the valley would slowly begin to flood. If they failed to move it, the rock would disappear under the reservoir. Nonetheless, the bickering and the campaigning were set aside for the day; the voices raised now carried the songs and prayers of the people who could still see life in stone.

Felix Sugar, an elder from Piapot, wearing blue-beaded skins and a black porcupine quill headdress, approached the buffalo rock from the east. He stopped at the edge of a small circle marked by stone cairns, lifted his arms, and bowed, uttering an invocation. A younger man drummed slowly on a round hand-drum and called the Cree dancers to gather. His voice echoed off the Aiktow's hilltops and carried up into the winter sky: "We are Plains Cree! We are a proud people. We bow to no man. We bow here only to our god — Manito — and to his spirit messenger in the great stone!" Then he threw his head back and let out his song, high and mournful, like other songs of the plains, the cry of a hawk or a coyote. To the music of a single drum and voice, the Cree dancers, wearing parkas and blankets over ceremonial garb, began to move slowly around the rock.[27]

## THE PEOPLE: RAISING THE STAKES

THE RESERVOIR, initially dubbed Lake Saskatchewan, began rising in late 1966. Water crept in along the Aiktow Valley over willows and bull-rushes at the bottom of the floodplain. It widened and flowed out over successional zones of drier and drier vegetation until it covered crop-lands and remnants of snowberry, wolf willow, grama grass, needle and thread. It trickled over sandy flats, across bogs, and around the base of boulders. By early December, the water was lapping at the foot of the rock.

The Save the Rock Fund at $28,000 had climbed within $5,000 of the lowest bid for moving the rock. Then PFRA officials announced a new, last-minute estimate. They would need at least $200,000 to move the rock. Otherwise, the rock would be under water in ten days.

## THE ROCK: A SOLUTION

THE TERRIBLE, GRINDING WHINE of rock drills. Men dressed heavily against the cold dawn, standing on the ancient buffalo rock. Drilling fifteen shafts six feet down into the darkness of its volcanic heart. Four sticks in each shaft, packed, tamped down with the fear and despair that urge a people to blast an object of veneration, to tear apart what they could not see as wholeness, as mystery.

Talk had already made new fissures in the rock. Gossip about the claims of archaeology or Indians, about the religious significance of large glacial erratics, had probed its depths, prepared the substrate for the PFRA men to carry out the final act of disintegration with sixty sticks of dynamite.

## THE PEOPLE: SUCCESS AND TRAGEDY

*"Elbow (CP) — A 400-ton rock held sacred by centuries of Plains Indians was blasted to bits Thursday in a successful bid to save part of it from the rising waters of Lake Saskatchewan."*[28]

THOUGH I HAD KNOWN of the blasting and read through the museum file expecting the bizarre climax, when I came across the newspaper clipping, it shook me in the way it must have shaken anyone who had cared about the rock and held out hope for its preservation. The headline, in a perverse attempt to gloss over the sudden barbarity of the act, read "SACRED ROCK PIECES TO FORM MONUMENT."

But it was the set of page-wide photographs accompanying the article atop the *Leader-Post's* front page that hit hardest. The cut-line is "BEFORE AND AFTER." The "before" image shows a ladder against the flank of the rock and two men identified as engineers on top tamping explosives into holes. The "after" image shows ten men in parkas standing in a field of scattered rubble.

In the first, man is the agent of change, crouched over a chunk of his world, using tools and taking action. In the second, man in society reflects upon the consequences of his agency. The ten men — faces shadowed by parka hoods, heads bent low, arms at their sides — stand among ruins in the prairie amphitheatre. They look like a parody of a Greek chorus. You can sense the coming cue. They are poised to step toward the audience, gesture in unison, and elucidate in wise utterance the folly of this grievous action: "Jeez . . . now we have to haul this away and make a monument."

The PFRA executioners spoke to the press later. Custy Harris, the man who detonated the blast, said that the valley was empty and quiet before he slipped the ends of the two wires into the socket of a portable generator. By the time the dust had settled, however, two men on snow-mobiles had arrived. There was a heap of grey and brown fur slung over the back of one of their machines. Harris said that the men had been out participating in a favourite winter sport in those parts — coyote running. When they heard the explosion they came right over to see what else was being destroyed that morning.

## The Rock: As Far as the Indians Are Concerned

DECEMBER 7, 1966. The memo people are busy again:

> *Be advised that PFRA had the rock blown [up] on December 1, 1966. Roughly sixty tons of loose rock has been delivered to the Elbow lookout site. I understand plans call for a suitable monument struc-ture at this location.*
>
> *The remaining rock at the Qu'Appelle arm at one time was going to be used as rip rap on the dam structure. Apparently this idea has now been abandoned and PFRA will merely let the water flood over the remaining portion of the boulder. . . . Because of people wishing to have a souvenir it would be advisable for the monument to be con-structed first thing in spring.*

An interesting change occurs here in the memos. When the rock was a problem, it was referred to as "a rock" or "the erratic." After the blasting, however, as the administrative assistants began consulting on how to give the "shrine" its due posthumous recognition, the memos adopt the Cree name invented by Pohorecky's committee: "Mistaseni," it appears in one memo, or "Mistusinne," as it is spelled in another.

To the culture that floods holy sites and then erects monuments to our residue of guilt, a word like *Mistaseni* is useful. It is a one-word poem, an elegy about past glory, when the noble red-skinned nomads pursued the shaggy monarch of the plains. Pohorecky never felt com-fortable with the word. He knew that it was a crude marketing ploy justified by his cause.

When we met at the Elbow, he laughed at the road signs directing traffic to "Mistussine Subdivision" and he told me how they took the name from Sid Fineday one cold January morning in 1966. Dennis Fisher, a member of Zenon's Save the Rock committee, tracked Sid down in the alley behind the Roxy Theatre on 20th Street in Saskatoon. Sid was busy welding something and the wind blew snow along the alley as Dennis asked his question: "Sid, how do you say 'Big Rock' in Cree?" "Mistah-sini," Sid replied and then returned to his work. Dennis carried the word back into the cold of 20th Street, confident that the public would be moved by its romantic nuances.

*Mistaseni.* This is not the buffalo rock's name; it is a term lifted from the language of the people whose ancestors knew the real names of things. It is a pilfered caption and it rings hollow with contrived nostalgia. We license such words to purify ourselves, to sanctify the ark so that when we have flooded every corner of the land with our colonizing ways, we may cruise with impunity upon the deluge.

> *June 5, 1967. Re: Mistaseni Cairn. Work on the erection of this cairn is progressing rapidly, with the final rock work expected to be completed by the middle of this week. . . . As you may have heard by now, the Mistaseni Rock is made of black granite which does not shear or split like normal field stone. Consequently the cairn has been constructed mainly of field stone with an occasional piece of Mistaseni inserted when possible. This does not seem to have alarmed local people too much, but the biggest concern to the Department is the disposition of the 60 ton of loose rock that is lying on site. I would suggest that this material be loaded on a truck and dumped into Lake Saskatchewan rather than have it lie around for people to chip away at and in general misuse the rock which reputedly has religious significance as far as the Indians are concerned.*[29]

## THE PEOPLE: FRAGMENTS AND HEROES

PEOPLE DID COME to get their piece of the rock. Museums in the region, including one called The Western Development Museum, all got their chunk to display with rueful tale.

The farthest-flung piece went to Ottawa. In the spring of 1967, a fragment of the rock, shaped to requested size, was placed in a crate and shipped to the nation's capital, where it was included in a rock garden in a downtown pedestrian mall. A centennial rock garden, celebrating one hundred years of Canada.

One piece of the buffalo rock rests now at the graveside of one of the Plains Cree nation's most honoured leaders. A month after the blasting, members of the Poundmaker Band Council approached Pohorecky to ask if he would help them bring home the remains of their great chief. Pohorecky knew the story of Chief Poundmaker and how he came to die away from his own reserve.

In 1885, Poundmaker was the chief of a nation of thirty thousand Cree people. The Macdonald government was doing a fine job of implementing Hind's recommendations for the North-West. The buffalo had been gone for a decade and famine had finally brought even the most resistant Indian bands to the treaty table. Poundmaker, tired of watching his people die of disease and malnutrition, agreed to take a reserve in the Battleford area.

Other Plains Cree leaders were considering the merits of taking up arms and perhaps joining the Métis people to reclaim the North-West. Poundmaker would not hear if it. Throughout his tenure as chief he did his best to keep the peace and control the younger, more volatile men of his band. However, after Gabriel Dumont and his forces routed the North-West Mounted Police at Duck Lake in late March, it became harder to suppress the call for war. Within a matter of days, the inevitable happened: a group of young Cree warriors broke rank.

After receiving a message from the Indian agent requesting his presence in Battleford, Poundmaker travelled the twenty-five miles to the post. When he arrived, the town was deserted. The agent had abandoned his office and crossed the North Saskatchewan River to take shelter in the NWMP barracks. The police, afraid that what had happened at Duck Lake could happen there, had gathered the settlers into their barracks. Poundmaker was confused by this turn of events. He had been asked to come to Battleford and did so, fully intending to assure the agent of his commitment to peace. As he waited to see if the agent would return to his post, night fell and a group of his men, now frustrated and hungry, began looting shops for food. The next morning,

Poundmaker regained control of his party and returned to his reserve. Over the next three weeks, however, in what has become known as the Siege of Battleford, the settlement and several farmers' homes in the vicinity were burned and pillaged by groups of Cree men acting in defiance of Poundmaker's orders.

Poundmaker had ample cause and opportunity to throw his support behind those who wanted to regain control of the North-West. As the colonial forces arrived in the territories and began their march north to Batoche, Poundmaker confined his men to their reserve and listened to reports of General Fred Middleton advancing toward the Métis settlements. On May 1, a week after the first skirmish at Fish Creek, a column of 325 Canadian troops under Colonel William Otter was dispatched to the Eagle Hills where Poundmaker was camped with his people. Otter's men were feeling heroic, having liberated Battleford, which is to say that they shooed away the handful of Indians still enjoying the amenities abandoned by the townspeople. No medals were handed out, however, for their performance at Cut Knife Hill the next morning.

At the base of the hill, the lodges of Poundmaker's people were silent, except for babies stirring and the snores of dreaming elders. One old warrior, Piacutch, had risen early for a ride on horseback and heard the squealing wagon wheels of the approaching battalion. He galloped back to the encampment and alerted his people of the coming attack. The women quickly gathered the children, the sick, and the aged and headed for cover on a distant hillside.

Without any attempt to hold conference with Poundmaker, Otter had his men take up their positions along the top of the hill. A Gatling gun borrowed from the American army and two seven-pound cannons were levelled at the lodges below. Poundmaker, though eyewitnesses say he draped himself in a white flag of truce, had little choice but to let his war chief mount a defensive assault. The Cree warriors, armed mostly with muskets, kept the Canadian soldiers on the hilltop where their silhouettes made easy targets. Shortly after midday, Otter counted his casualties and remembered Custer's disaster at Little Big Horn. He quickly called a retreat. A lesser chief might have allowed his warriors to massacre the Canadian soldiers as they gathered up their dead and made their way back to Battleford. Poundmaker, the record shows, restrained his men though they clamoured for vengeance.

After hearing that Middleton had taken Batoche and that Louis Riel had surrendered, Poundmaker sent a message to the general asking for peace terms. Middleton fired back a note saying that he had enough men to destroy Poundmaker and his people and would not make terms of any kind. A few days later, Poundmaker walked into Middleton's camp on a final peace mission. The general immediately arrested Poundmaker and threw him into prison with four of his chiefs.

Poundmaker did everything he could to prevent all-out war in the North-West of 1885, yet in August of that year he was tried and convicted of treason and then shipped off to Stony Mountain Penitentiary. Seven months later, the great chieftain of the sunlit plains was dying in prison. Father Albert Lacombe, a Catholic missionary, persuaded the government to release Poundmaker. His lungs clotted with tuberculosis, his face haggard and his head shorn, Poundmaker walked out of Stony Mountain and made his way back to the Eagle Hills in the spring of 1886. A fortnight later, he told his people that he was leaving to go to the tipi of his Blackfoot foster father, Chief Crowfoot. He then walked 250 miles to the Blackfoot reserve near what is now Gleichen, Alberta. A few weeks after his reunion with Crowfoot, Poundmaker, who had seen his buffalo-hunting tribesmen reduced to beggars in a single generation, died of a white man's disease. He was buried on Blackfoot land in July 1886.

Eighty years later, Pohorecky thought briefly of the provincial laws he would be breaking if he agreed to help Poundmaker's descendants move the body of the great chief back to the Eagle Hills. The decision was not difficult. He had been given an opportunity — small though it was — to do something good by Poundmaker's people, to make one right step on a trail of wrong after wrong after wrong. Once he knew that Poundmaker's relatives and the Blackfoot people at Gleichen had given their consent, Pohorecky offered his department's facilities and his own assistance, asking only that they feed him and give him somewhere to put a sleeping bag at night.

It was a snowy weekend in April when they travelled to Gleichen. Several Cree and Blackfoot elders presided over the ceremonies while younger men slowly removed the earth above Poundmaker. Pohorecky stayed in the background, perhaps whispering suggestions for handling and transporting the remains. Quietly, respectfully, the group returned to the Eagle Hills with the bones of Poundmaker. They buried their chief atop Cut Knife Hill and encircled the new grave with stones gathered from each of the Plains Cree reserves. The headstone is a large piece of the buffalo rock that once watched over the River That Turns.[30]

## THE ROCK: DEDICATION

### MISTUSINNE DEDICATION PROGRAM
### 11A.M., JULY 22, 1967

#### CHAIRMAN:    G. JOEL

| | |
|---|---|
| Welcoming Remarks | – G. Joel |
| Invocation | – Reverend L. Knutson |
| Guest Speaker | – Hon. J.W. Gardiner |
| | Government of Saskatchewan |
| Dedication Address & Prayer | – Reverend L. Knutson |
| Unveiling of Mistusinne Historic Cairn | – Hon. J.W. Gardiner |
| | Centennial Corporation |
| Closing Remarks | – G. Joel |

### FLY-PAST BY ARMED SERVICES BASE, MOOSE JAW[31]

*Chapter Six*

# MONUMENTS
# AND LEGENDS

THE DAY I TRAVELLED to the upper Qu'Appelle Valley to see its renovated land forms, I knew only scraps of the rock's story: that there had been a controversy and a campaign to save it thirty years earlier. I came expecting either to see it resting on higher ground or to learn that it was now beneath the waves of Lake Diefenbaker.

Highway 19 drew me down into the western extremity of the valley where the reservoir's eastern arm ends and the Qu'Appelle is suffered to begin. The first thing that comes into view as you descend the eighty or one hundred feet to the valley floodplain is the straight engineered line of the dam. Stretching for more than a mile across what was once the bed of the Qu'Appelle's origins is the solid, featureless green of an introduced grass on the downstream bank of the structure. It strikes the eye as a kind of landscape topiary. To achieve the same effect in woodland, you simply clip away at the forest until you arrive at a likeness of a bridge or parking lot.

I walked a distance beside the "river," which moved grudgingly along a dyked channel. Brome grass, the calling card of civil engineering and modern agriculture, rested upon the channel's muddy banks like a bad toupee. To the north, at intervals along the valley, irrigation equipment pumped moisture to the crops above. Mallard and wigeon dabbled in twos and fours.

I returned to my car and drove on to the town of Elbow. If the town had a museum — and these towns always have a museum — someone there would be able to tell me what became of the rock.

It was a clean white building on the main street, formerly a town hall or something like a town hall. I have found in every museum a gracious, helpful woman making labels, sorting files, serving coffee and cake to hungry writers, and in a dozen other ways quietly holding the place together. Without her, the collection would fall to ruin in one winter. Such a woman met me at the Elbow Museum, signed me in the guest book, and showed me through the glass cases and aisle ways. Teacups, chairs, combs, harness-work, weaponry, crocks, and gadgets of obscure purpose had been lovingly arranged and tagged for all comers to view.

When I asked about the rock, I was shown to a display of geology and Indian artifacts. Next to other oddities of the earth, I found a fragment of grey stone, or black stone grey with dust. A card beneath, curled and yellow, told the story of Mistaseni, the blasting, and the cairn.

I think I was supposed to feel shock at that moment, but the best I could manage was a weak bout of incredulity. My knees did not buckle, my blood stayed where it belonged. I stood there wondering what to think of all this and then asked if there was a local historian who might talk to me about the rock.

DON BOOK IS A RETIRED FARMER. He drove me in his pickup truck south of the town, past golfers in mint-coloured clothing, to a muddy trail sloping down toward Lake Diefenbaker. The golfers were measuring careful putts within a nine-iron shot of the cemetery where the bones of their homesteading grandparents mingle with soils that have, over time, produced more than durum wheat and divot-resistant bluegrass. The truck seemed to be sliding down the grade, which was wet with the previous night's rain, but Don did not look worried. He too was familiar with the soil.

There it was. A large monument of hewn fieldstone, tipping oddly toward the reservoir. It looked like a victim of seaside erosion, an edifice that slid downhill when its substrate was undercut by rising water. We got out of the truck and Don told me what had happened to the cairn. It was built and dedicated on the headland just above us, he said, where it was intended to remain. Then, twenty years later, golf course developers decided that the site was better suited to a scenic-view fairway. The cairn was in the way. It might have required a special out-of-bounds rule — *Mistaseni is out of bounds. If your ball hits this historic hazard you may take a drop at its base after adding two strokes to your score.* It would have to be moved.

Moving the cairn was not difficult; required very few memos, if any. It was easy to hook logging chains onto the structure and haul it over the embankment where it would no longer block the view. We walked toward the cairn for a closer look. It sat there askew, in high weeds, in the attitude of discarded things. Things that soon gather moisture, grow a shaggy beard, and tilt at the forces that were powerful enough to wash them aside. Don showed me the bare patches where there had been two brass plates telling the story of the rock. These, he said, had been removed and remounted on a new set of small cairns near the harbour.

I asked Don if any of the stone used in the cairn came from the big rock.

"No. That's what they said initially, but I think it was just something to tell people."

"What about the new cairns? Were they made from parts of the rock?"

"I don't think so."

THE CHAMPIONSHIP GOLF COURSE is next to the Lake Diefenbaker Yacht Club, which is not far from the Harbour Inn Condominiums, a new luxury development where "you can drive your golf cart right to your door. . . . Ask about our special golf/condo package."

By following Don's directions to the new set of cairns, I have somehow walked into the midst of West Palm Beach. The fixed-keel boats at the yacht club have names such as *Treasure Lady*, *Heaven Sent*, and *Maranatha*. The adjacent golf clubhouse looks as though it would rather be in southern California. The harbour is actually a flooded coulee of the South Saskatchewan River. What is now a headland overlooking the reservoir's grey expansiveness has become the most recent resting place for the brass plaques commemorating the rock. Two small cairns of fieldstone, one featuring a plaque in English and the other a plaque in Cree syllabics, sit on a grassed boulevard surrounded by paved parking space for the yacht club.

The English plaque says, "This monument was constructed of fragments of the stone removed before the site was flooded and preserved in recognition of its significance to the Indian people." The word *dynamite* does not appear in the text. Only removal and preservation for the sake of the Indians. The story of the rock's arrival in the valley is included, to lend its colour to the drab eulogy. It is prefaced with an "According to one legend" — the official phrase that at once romanticizes and dismisses the mythology of quaintly deluded primitives. People who believe a rock is sacred are tribal, picturesque, and uncivilized. Modern, practical, civilized people — people who believe nothing in nature is sacred — change the course of one river, flood the source of another, and destroy the mythic land between the two.

Looking beyond the new cairns to the distant southwest, I can see the upstream arm of Lake Diefenbaker. To the northwest is a second arm heading to the hydroelectric dam named after James Gardiner, the former premier who unveiled the original cairn in 1967. Looking back to the east, I see what is called the Qu'Appelle or McKenzie arm, forming the waters above the Aiktow and upper Qu'Appelle Valleys. Beyond this, on the eastern horizon, I can just make out the land that was once the undulating crest of low valley slopes. Now, pinched between sky and water, there are eroded cutbanks of prairie and isolated clumps of aspen. Like islands.

*Chapter Seven*

# RIPARIA RIPARIA

I AM FOLLOWING A THIN, charcoal-grey line threading its way along the north shore of the Qu'Appelle arm to try out a piece of local folklore. This is Douglas Provincial Park, a tract of stabilized sand dunes, spear grass/June grass prairie, poplar bluffs, and beaver ponds straddling the eastern end of the arm. People say that this meandering grey line ranging from one to six inches wide is a layer of pulverized buffalo bones — a wrackline trace of the grazers whose annual returnings marked the Aiktow and upper Qu'Appelle valleys' place within the Holocene. As the waves of Lake Diefenbaker rework the sands with each significant rise in water level, the cutbanks erode and release their history onto the beach. Anything that falls to the lapping waves will disappear and reappear according to schedules worked out between sand and water. To my eyes, the grey line looks like sand, perhaps from a darker, ferromagnesium parent material, but sand just the same. Still, people do find buffalo bones along the shore from time to time, and artifacts. One man I spoke with said I could be sure of finding something — a scraper, projectile point, or at least a fragment of flaked chert — if I walked slowly, watchfully along this stretch of beach.

The possibility of coming across an arrowhead dispatches me — with the stoop of any shameless treasure hunter. I have never found anything, partly because I am not sure I really want the responsibility.

I was once out walking with a group of people above a buffalo jump in the valley north of Regina. We were heading away from some tipi rings, when someone found a flawless arrowhead and pocketed it for his collection as blithely as one would pick up a coin from the sidewalk. The magistrate in my brain wasted no time in assuring me that I would be different. I would simply, and with appropriate reverence, leave the piece where it lay.

I am not keen on testing this out with a clean side-notched Avonlea point at my feet. If I did not succumb to the keeping urge and decided to just admire it *in situ*, it might keep me and I might never leave. Something might unravel within me, pluck a strand of atavism wound deep within my chromosomes, sending me into the snowberry to search for a shaft, into the chokecherry for a bow. Not likely. I have held an atlatl and my bones remembered nothing of its arc and cadence. Still, we long to possess something of that wilder time, to recall it safely in our domestic hearts. And so we walk with eyes to the ground in places like this where the fierce world was last seen.

Every damned stone on this beach looks like an arrowhead. Although most of the beach is sand, there is a wavy belt of scattered pebbles running along its midriff, about eight to ten feet wide. It is a Milky Way of even-sized, sharp-edged, and angular stones, the kind my children often pick up and say, "Wow! An arrowhead!" I could spend the week here turning over thousands of pebbles one by one. Some sit atop a little pillar of sand that holds them a short distance above the level of the beach. The surrounding sand has blown and washed away, leaving this miniature landscape of thimble-sized hoodoos.

Among the hoodoos, I find animal tracks. Leaving the trail of ancient hunters for the time being, I rise and follow one that hunted here last night. The unswerving line of coyote tracks draws me eastward along the beach. Other trails of common prairie mammals bisect ours. Animals — mule and white-tailed deer, fox, deer mouse, hare, and beaver — have crossed from the grassland above the beach, which was once the hilltops of the Aiktow Valley, down over the cutbanks to the water's edge for a drink. Turning the tracks into familiar creatures has me cataloguing the place, hanging names on sounds and images.

There is a LeConte's sparrow on the pasture above me. There must be a meadow there of lusher grasses, for this bird will not nest in dry upland prairie. Out over the lake, I see a gull named after the nineteenth-century British explorer whose tragic disregard for local values finally killed him and his entire crew, lost in the Arctic while searching for the Northwest Passage. The Franklin's gull is a small-boned, respectable gull of the prairie, not the sort you see slumming at garbage dumps. Just ahead of the waveline teeters a pair of spotted sandpipers, one of three or four shorebird species that breed along the shores of Lake Diefenbaker. From another pasture the wind carries the song of the Baird's sparrow: three zips and a loose, ragged trill. This bird was, rashly I think, declared threatened in the hit-and-miss effort to draw attention to organisms that are at risk. Recently it has been "de-listed" from the roster of the unfortunate.

Other birds, genuinely in peril, nest here. I have been listening, in vain, for the call of the endangered piping plover. This sparrow-sized shorebird, which nests only on stretches of undisturbed beach, has experienced a cycle of boom and bust here at Lake Diefenbaker. The difficulty has much to do with water-management policy. The reservoir giveth and it taketh away. When Lake Diefenbaker's water level is particularly low in the spring — as it can be for any number of reasons relating to climate and water-management priorities — a lot of prime beach habitat greets the plovers arriving from their wintering grounds in the southern parts of the continent. Drawn in impressive numbers to this outlay of nesting grounds, the birds quickly establish pair bonds, mate, and lay eggs in shoreline nests. Then, in late May and early June, run-off from snowmelt in the Rockies finally makes its way along the south branch to Lake Diefenbaker. If the water mandarins decide to hold back a lot of the water by slowing the outflow at Gardiner Dam, the reservoir level will rise rapidly. It does not take much of a rise to drown a piping plover's nest.

There have been years when the majority of plover nests have disappeared beneath the flood only days before the eggs would have hatched. In rare years, when reservoir levels stay relatively low but more or less constant, Lake Diefenbaker can be one of the best piping plover–nesting grounds in the world. Most years, the water level is higher, and only a small population of plovers can find suitable habitat. However, the overall inland breeding population of piping plovers seems to be stable — the Saskatchewan population, at 1,348, if anything increased slightly during the early 1990s — and so resource managers are now saying that they believe the species as a whole can accommodate itself to life in a here-today, gone-tomorrow environment.

The biologists point out that water levels in prairie sloughs and rivers rise and fall naturally, exposing and flooding plover habitat by turns. The species evolved alongside these ephemeral waterways and has, therefore, adapted to local gain and loss of habitat and to flooding at a natural rate and frequency. This makes sense as far as it goes, but what about unnatural water fluctuations? There is nothing in a piping plover's evolved responses to habitat change that can prepare it for the artificial floods of the timing, rate, and frequency of those it will encounter at Lake Diefenbaker. The government departments in charge of endangered species programs have met with the departments responsible for managing Lake Diefenbaker's water levels to resolve this problem. In the end, nothing substantial came out of the meetings. Only non-decisions, translatable as *Yes, it is too bad about the nests being flooded, but we must be realistic: power generation and recreation are more important than a few sand-coloured birds that no one notices anyway.*

This is June and if there are plovers along this beach, I would have seen them, heard them. The rain begins again, dripping from stratus clouds low and soggy like bedsheets on a clothesline. This has been a wet year, with plenty of local run-off to keep the reservoir level from fluctuating greatly. A survey of piping plovers on the lake in the summer of 1996 turned up only seventy-five birds, a drop of almost three-quarters from 1991, the last survey year and a year of disaster for plovers attempting to nest on Lake Diefenbaker. That year, a winter of heavy snow in the Rockies flushed high levels of meltwater into the reservoir in early June. Gardiner Dam's generators had been running slowly all winter, so the power generation officials decided to trap the flow to boost hydro production. The reservoir rose suddenly and destroyed a hundred plover nests. The records for that year show that only seven young fledged from Lake Diefenbaker nests. The adults, 270 of them, did not move to another place and renest that season. It was too late for that.

In one summer, 270 piping plovers fail to raise young in a province that provides nesting habitat for almost twenty-five per cent of the total endangered world population, which is estimated at 5,532. These numbers should make us concerned about any habitat loss or local nesting failure, unless we are sure of the way plovers react to changes in their environment. Instead, gaps in our knowledge are used to justify the current course of maximizing power generation. We have virtually no data on the status of non-game species endangered or otherwise in this region before the river was dammed. No one will ever know whether, over time, the reservoir has been a benefit or a bane to creatures like the piping plover.

STAYING WITH THE coyote trail, I continue east, east, east, following tracks, tracks, tracks. I hit a rhythm that matches the cadence of naming and step off the shift from what was once here to the assemblage of life I find today. Once: prairie slopes, wooded springs, rocky outcrops, each with their associated plant communities; birds including golden eagles, long-billed curlews, Sprague's pipits, rock wrens, along with a diversity of other creatures from bull snakes to grey hairstreak butterflies. Today: *stipa* grasses atop the cutbanks, a veery singing from a poplar swale, snail shells on the sand, the smell of wolf willow and sage on the moist wind, black terns over the water, a family of gadwall in a bay, and the unseen world of walleye, pike, and perch beneath the waves.

I begin to see exposed fragments of sandstone on the beach. Hind described and illustrated large sandstone outcroppings he found on this side of the valley. There is no way to be certain — the location marked on his map was vague — but these chunks of stone seem to be part of the larger formations he saw downslope, on knolls now under water. As I continue east toward the summit, the pieces of sandstone become larger and more numerous. Some are slabs the size of a small bed. It seems that the pieces of bedrock emerge from the beach as the successive rising and falling of the reservoir erodes the till from the surface of what was the valley crest. Hind found this layer farther downslope, exposed by a flood of glacial meltwater that passed this way ten thousand years ago. Born exactly a century after Hind's visit, I am finding different portions of the same stone exposed by the wave action of a lake that was built when I was a boy.

The sandstone behind me, I pass by the mouth of an inlet leading into a large beaver pond ringed by poplars. I step on the trail, slick and muddy with the passing of furred bellies and wide tails. Sloshing across to the other side and down the beach, I begin finding bones of a large ungulate jutting out of the sand here and there. Rib fragments, a larger bone — perhaps a femur — a couple of teeth, a lower jaw with teeth intact. Though I am not a good enough bone man to tell if any belong to the wilder bovine, each piece I handle draws me further away from the birds and grasses at hand and back toward the landscape we extinguished.

Ahead I spot a cluster of grey sticks protruding from the sand, leaning toward the water like emaciated totem poles. They are dead aspen stumps, about fifty of them in all, piercing the beach in a ragged line that runs from the woods above the cutbank, across the sand, and out into a broad bay of the lake. A few weathered snags thrust at odd angles from the bay itself, where they now shelter walleye instead of weasel or hare. I sit on the beach next to a thick stump that is covered except for its top three or four inches. The sand, damp from the rain of several days, feels somehow like patience. Nature, imperturbable, unaffected by human desire, is the sand that falls from our fingers, receives our footprints, accepts our diggings. Idly, and without hope, I begin scooping handfuls of beach from around that aspen stump. I dig, wondering if there is anything further down to confirm what I already know: I am perched on beach sand halfway up into the canopy of aspen woods that once filled a small coulee reaching back from the valley.

The sand begins sliding back into the small dish I have made. A map in my backpack will show this old coulee, help me calculate how much farther I have to walk before I will be adjacent to the submerged headwaters and summit.

A mile, or slightly less. The rain begins again as I realize that I am sitting directly opposite the amphitheatre from which the great buffalo rock had presided over Aiktow's comings and goings. People once came here to leave offerings and pray for healing.

The bank swallows chittering above my head are heedless. Down the beach, they are nesting in cutbanks created by the reservoir. One colony I passed had fifty nest holes in a bank eight feet high. This is a bird that has thrown its lot in with rivers. When Linnaeus — the great Swedish taxonomist who sat like Adam in his garden and blessed

Creation with names — came to this bird, he looked at its restless life by restless waters and named it at once: *Riparia riparia*.

The river swallow nests here each summer at the submerged headwaters and along the length of the Qu'Appelle and all its major tributaries, wherever habitat allows. *Riparia riparia* looks to what the water gives. It has reconciled itself with the river.

While the swallows riddle the cutbank with their diggings, my hole next to the aspen stump has refilled with sand. I thought of bank swallows yesterday when Don Book took me out to a hilltop in the upper Qu'Appelle Valley downstream from the dam, where the river emerges. He wanted to show me two things he knew I would be interested in: a Red River cart trail crossing from the south side of the valley and a group of tipi rings on a promontory overlooking the confluence of Ridge Creek and the Qu'Appelle.

As we walked across the mixed-grass pasture, the prairie assumed its ancient disk-shape, and the song of Sprague's pipits, upland sandpipers, and Baird's sparrows rose into an overcast sky. A Swainson's hawk ferried low over Ridge Creek Coulee. The stony pasture was bright, lit green from inside with life from recent rains, and ablaze with scarlet mallow, rock cress, and penstemons. We walked, oblivious to a mizzling rain that had not really stopped in two days, and we spoke of many things. Of temperance colonists who made the cart trail in the nineteenth century on their way to Saskatoon, of the forces that removed the buffalo and the Indians, of the forces that create a need for dams and then build them, of trails and circles of stone, of what is gone, of the better past. Don told me that he and his brother found an amulet in a crevice of the big rock when they were boys. Given another chance at life, he said, he would be an archaeologist, not a farmer. Thinking of all we had said and all that required no mention — the distance between today's world and the world he knew when he found that amulet — he told me before we parted ways that he sometimes wondered if he had been born seventy-five years too late.

The tipi rings were as tipi rings always are: hard to find and somewhat disappointing when they finally reveal themselves. One ring had coyote scat in its centre. The Saskatoon Trail was deep rutted where it descended the slope to the valley floor. I looked at these tracings of other ages and felt inured by time, removed from their claim upon history.

The collective regret we have made of our geomancy failed me. I was left utterly without its comfort.

With eyes downcast we stand by tipi rings, follow grey lines on beaches, dig in our dreams for arrowheads, and mark what has been lost with cairns and stories. The trail leading back to the place where we parted company with the holy in this land is not hard to follow; everywhere we see the spoor: ecosystems, plants, and animals in rapid decline; landscapes and treaties broken in the name of the economy; atrocities at Indian residential schools; the events at Batoche and Wounded Knee.

I wonder if grief has taken us as far as it can, if it is time now to move on. As a culture, we have come this distance on a narrative of regret that qualifies our greed, mops up some of the mess we make in choosing grain quotas over buffalo and prairie, industrial agriculture over people, power generation over plovers, and hydro dams over the mythic and the holy. We have been looking to the land for sustenance, comfort, wealth, and pleasure, while dreaming of archaeology and a settler innocence that never really existed. There are signs of change, signs that the mythology of regret may be giving way to a mythology of reconciliation. People are beginning to look to the land for consent, belonging, health, and spirit, while dreaming of mysticism and ecology. Narratives that reconcile us are coming from the science of fostering biodiversity and hope, the natural history of a burrowing owl or a market garden, and the consecrating gestures required to restore a prairie stream or unclog wild tributaries within culture.

NOT FAR FROM THE TEETOTALLERS' trail and the tipi rings is the modest farmhouse of Jim Gallagher, the man who belongs to the pastures we had walked across. Jim's grandfather came to Ridge Creek in 1902. Gallaghers have been tending the land ever since.

When Don and I first stopped to ask permission to see the trail and tipi rings, Jim said little but smiled widely at our interest. The trail is part of the Saskatoon Trail, he said. The tipi rings are over there, and keep your eyes open for a harrow lurking in the grass. Later, as we stopped to thank him on the way out, Jim seemed to want to talk more, so Don shut off the truck and we passed the time covering the usual subjects, weather, crops, politics. Eventually, the conversation turned to irrigation schemes, the dams, and the river. Jim is not the kind to offer judgment casually — he preferred to listen — but it was obvious that he had thoughts on the way the government had used water in the upper Qu'Appelle. I cannot say for certain what his opinions are, but I can say this: he is the steward of what is, in terms of biodiversity, the richest stretch of Ridge Creek, and Ridge Creek is now the primary upstream tributary of the Qu'Appelle River, in effect its westernmost natural headwaters. The length of creek I saw running along the deepening coulee and out its mouth onto the larger valley's floodplain looked to be as fine a piece of riparian landscape as I have seen anywhere in the watershed.

The grass was high and lush, trees and bushes showed no signs of undue grazing pressure, and the stream flowed strong through banks covered with a green profusion of riverside vegetation. No abnormal erosion, no channelizing, no cattle standing in the creek. An obvious diversity of native plants that would take a full day to survey thoroughly. On the stream banks, communities of willow, great bullrush, cattails, mint species, and red-osier dogwood. Above that, species of *stipa* grasses and June grass, beside saskatoons, western snowberry, and chokecherry. Then asters and goldenrod species with yarrow, thorny buffaloberry, rose bushes, and prairie sage.

And above the shining creek, a group of bank swallows drew arcs in the air that knitted the bottom of Ridge Creek coulee to its top.

If this bird, in its adaptiveness and readiness to accept habitats made by people, is a less than ideal indicator of riparian health, it is still my indicator of the possibility of a life aligned with rivers. *Riparia riparia* will return to Ridge Creek next spring, where Jim and his son will be seeding crops, repairing machinery. In late winter, the swallows will leave the lowlands east of the Andes in Paraguay, Argentina, Peru. They will follow the river valleys at the core of the New World, and they will arrive in May to nest at the Calling River and its waterways: Cottonwood Creek, Iskwaohead Creek, Thunder Creek, the Moose Jaw River, the Arm River, Little Cutarm Creek, Scissors Creek, and Bear Creek, and at one hundred other places near ponds, rivers, and streams throughout the watershed. The swallows will come to all these places, and they will come to the shores of Lake Diefenbaker. They will not mourn the passing of the old headwaters. They will get down to the regenerative work of singing, finding mates, digging nest holes, copulating, laying eggs, feeding nestlings, and fending off death. The good work of making more life by the river.

# Part Three

# WEST TO EAST

*I MAY NOT KNOW WHO I AM, but I know where I am from.*

— WALLACE STEGNER, *WOLF WILLOW*

## Chapter Eight

# SUMMIT CREEK,
# AIKTOW CREEK

THE SUN IS SHINING, for a change, as I leave Lake Diefenbaker in early evening to find the outliers of the height of land that once divided water flowing to the Qu'Appelle system from water bound for the South Saskatchewan River. The summit in the Aiktow Valley rests under five fathoms of reservoir, but there are ridges to the southwest that still allot rainfall and run-off between the two basins.

The gravel road ribbons up and down over kame-and-kettle landscape, as I drive over the streams that converge at Ridge Creek's origins, streams moving under the road, barely noticeable, disguised, guttered in steel culverts. My topographic map indicates this stretch of the divide as a slight rise of land running southwest to northeast. Ahead I can see the hill. As I look for somewhere to pull over, I feel a rising in my blood, and I know it is my desire to detect something of the prairie's shift from one river to the other.

I shut off the engine and coast to a stop. On my right is a string of wetlands that feed the upper reaches of Aiktow Creek. This little creek once fed the Aiktow *River*, the stream that would sometimes turn, bringing water from the Saskatchewan River system into the Qu'Appelle by way of the valley of the Great Rock. Aiktow Creek now empties into the reservoir just above the Qu'Appelle Dam. Two miles north of where I stand, another creek that used to drain into the Aiktow River runs from this same summit down to the reservoir. It is called Summit Creek, named for the rise I now stand upon, which on its other side delivers water to Sage Creek, a tributary that runs away to the South Saskatchewan. There is now a broad bay at the mouth of Summit Creek where it enters Lake Diefenbaker. In a deft historical allusion, the latter-day map-makers in charge of describing the new geography that was created by the reservoir decided to call it Hind Bay, after the man who suggested cutting through the summit to join or, in his word, *inosculate*, the rivers permanently.

But here at the head of Aiktow Creek, LeConte's and Baird's sparrows zip-zip their quiet vespers from high growths of cord grass and other plants I cannot recognize from the roadside. There are waterbirds here, too: avocets, ruddy ducks, shovellers, and a marbled godwit. A willet calls once, flying over the meadow, banking in a flourish of black and white wings. I step into the meadow and walk up the rise, feeling for a line that is not there, that exists only on maps and in the minds of riparian ecologists and water managers. Approaching the top, I wait for a falling away, an increase of gravity to overtake me. Perhaps a change in the appearance of the land. At the place that I decide is the summit, I look to the west and see nothing different from the Qu'Appelle landscape at my back. Hummocky moraine, thin brown soil, all cropped in three or four varieties of grain. Nothing to indicate that I am standing at the westernmost limit of the land that belongs to the Calling River. From here, the boundary of a prairie watershed is as mythical as the mariner's edge of the world, as intangible as the International Date Line.

I return to the car unsatisfied, wishing for something to show me the western lip of the watershed. I start the engine and the noise flushes two animals, pronghorn antelope, out of the opposite ditch. They step gracefully, almost blithely, up onto the crown of the road and trot westward ahead of me, unhurried, the white hairs on their rumps erect and haloed by the faltering sun.

The swiftest animal in the Americas, this runner of the high plains used to be common throughout the Qu'Appelle basin. The first Great White Hunter to collect trophies in the region was the Earl of Southesk, member of the Scottish peerage and aristocratic twit-on-tour. The good earl found antelope just west of the Manitoba-Saskatchewan border, not far from the Tantallon area where my mother grew up. In his greatly reworked and contrived journal, Southesk — who spent his idle hours moaning about the lack of genteel company on his tour, reading Shakespeare (he confesses a weakness for *The Two Gentlemen of Verona*), and bathing in an India-rubber tub — says that on June 30, 1859, he went out to hunt "cabrees," the word his mixed-blood guides used for pronghorn antelope. He managed to bag a doe, one of a group of five. Five antelope anywhere near the eastern Qu'Appelle today would be a good record. By the time my grandfather arrived in the region, fifty years after Southesk's shooting expedition, antelope had become scarce. Now they are found only in the western and southern reaches of the watershed, if at all, and, like the two I flushed on the crest of the divide, they are generally headed southwest into the rangeland of the South Saskatchewan Basin.

THAT WAS IT: TWO ANTELOPE, my marker of the tilt in moraine that shifts water away from the Calling River to the larger, swifter South Saskatchewan.

For the rest of the summer, the Calling River would roll on through my days as I traced the edges of the watershed, stood in places where the basin reached its fingers out onto the heights of the plains, then turned down again through pastures and wheat fields in long glacial gouges, down to lowlands, falling, always falling to the east and toward the ultimate drainage into Manitoba and the larger Assiniboine.

After the antelope ushered me across the divide, I stopped the car, got out once more, touched the grass, and turned my back on the western skies. I could hear lark buntings in their song flight somewhere nearby; they were the last I heard that summer. Like the antelope, they are creatures of the drier southwestern reaches of the watershed. Only in the most arid of years will they show up in pastures near the Calling River valley, almost never in the valley proper. Returning to my station wagon, I pulled a U-turn on the summit and began my trip east.

East gained its meaning for me as a six-year-old boy when I started going to East School, a brick box of learning on the eastern boundary of Esterhazy. Our side of town was newer and, we thought, better. There were basements dug each summer on our block and we, the children of potash miners, walked to school in September amid the damp smells of concrete and carpenter's putty, exposed clay, and new lumber. At the eastern edge of the schoolyard, beyond the field that taught me the pain of a soccer ball in the face at ten below zero, loomed a dark, green expanse of bush where the land fell away. On the other side of the bush there might have been tundra, desert, or the enchanted landscapes of Narnia, for all I knew. It was simply The Ravine, a wild and impenetrable fastness whose threshold we never crossed. No one told me that the bush formed the rim of a major tributary of the Qu'Appelle that runs sixty miles from the northwest. Nor did I understand that the more benign slopes where we tobogganed on the golf course in winter were part of the same valley, in fact just around the bend from the schoolyard. Or that a few miles downstream, the creek at the bottom of the ravine passed through my grandfather's land at its confluence with the Qu'Appelle. A hike would have unified the fragments of my early impressions of lowland landscape, threading together my schoolyard, my tobogganing hill, and my mother's birthplace along with all the scraps of creek and valley I saw from the car on Sunday afternoons as we dipped down into the Little Cutarm, back up onto the uplands, and down again on our way to visit family in the eastern Qu'Appelle.

From any one spot along the valley or its tributaries, we have trouble comprehending the sprawl of a 260-mile-long glacial-meltwater channel and the ragged pattern of secondary arteries draining the thousands of square miles of prairie to which it owes its life. How it all fits together — how this or that lowland meanders from the place we go for picnics — escapes our car-window view of the landscape. A woman who lives in the valley north of Regina once told me that she never realized that her parents' cabin at Buffalo Pound Lake is in the same valley. Making my way east across the basin by car, I am subject, more or less, to the same disjointed impressions of the Qu'Appelle country, but I have maps that tie it all together, as well as a desire to make sense of the recurring patterns in prairie landscape.

*Chapter Nine*

## DARMODY FLATS

Aᴀ FTER LEAVING THE ANTELOPE in the west I made my way to a high spot above Thunder Creek on the south side. I passed through some good stretches of native mixed grass along the creek valley's broad margin. Upland sandpipers, Baird's sparrows singing — there must be a ferruginous hawk here somewhere, I thought. West of Williams Lake, a marshy reservoir in the creek, I pulled over to identify a wretched lump of feathers on the roadside: a marbled godwit killed by a car earlier in the day. I picked it up, using my index finger to measure its long, decurved bill snapped in half by the impact. This bill, orange at the base and turned upwards like the nose of Cyrano, is the glory of the godwit, one of the largest shorebirds to breed on the plains. Examining the bird in my hand, I saw that the tertial wing feathers, those nearest the body on the upper surface of the wing, were worn down to their shafts with the abrasion of a year of flight, the long trip from Mexico's Sinaloa or Baja coast to this pasture. I brushed the road dust from its cinnamon-and-charcoal-marbled plumage, walked across the ditch, and placed it through the barbed wire into the kind of grass that brought it here in the first place.

Toward sunset, I passed a great horned owl perched on a hillside boulder waiting for twilight. I decided near Darmody Flats to park and do the same on the highest piece of road I could find. It was, like the

Dirt Hills, a good place for taking in the larger design of highland and lowland in one portion of the watershed. I could see at least forty miles to the west and north, but much less to the south, where the elevation began stepping up toward the uplands of the Missouri Coteau, which form the basin's southwest rim. Everywhere there were puddles shining silver on the kame-and-kettle moraine, silver droplets staining the dark green broadloom of wheat fields now six inches high in this wet year. Down the Thunder Creek valley I could see a series of larger marshes, Ducks Unlimited projects, threaded together by a strand of the same luminous element. From one kettle to the next, flocks of northern shovellers and pintails crossed the darkening horizon. Franklin's gulls surrounded me with their soft cries, and the voices of horned larks rang from above like bells strung on the wind.

MORAINE BORDERING a glacial-meltwater channel — these areas form some of the richest sanctuaries of prairie life anywhere in the region. They are the gifts of the glacier — corridors of semi-wilderness that remain because we cannot plant wheat on such steep slopes, in such stony, light soil. If you pay attention as you drive across thirty or forty miles of the Qu'Appelle watershed, you will notice the shift from cultivated land to native prairie and back again with each drop down into a coulee or valley and each rise to the plains. In this way, the creeks and rivers of the Northern Great Plains form a network of remnant native wildness. Without these glacial and post-glacial waterways — the ice-front channels such as the Arm River, the glacial spillways such as Thunder Creek and the Calling River itself — and without the eroded till plains, hummocky moraine, saline fluvial plains, and kettled till plains associated with these waterways, we would have no native prairie and our countryside would be uninterrupted cropland. Any large pasture of native grass you find here will either form the margins of a creek or river, or cover an expanse of end moraine or outwash plains associated with the water that follows the ancient channels to the Qu'Appelle.

Ancient only to us, of course, the civilization that pays inordinate attention to the top foot and a half of soil, the stuff created by microbes, roots, decay — the organic circularity that will sprout number 1 Hard, field peas, or petunias at our behest. I admire geologists for their radical indifference toward topsoil. To a geologist in the field, the top eighteen inches or so is ephemera, yesterday's news; the real "surface material" begins after you dig past this facade of recent history. By any calendar that applies to rocks, the mile-thick sheath of Wisconsinan ice left for the north sometime this morning. Its tracks, as fresh as a coyote trail in mud, are everywhere: drumlins pointing the way of the glacier's retreat, streams too small to have cut the valley they inhabit, boulder fields and hillocks above potholes where lumps of ice melted away short hours ago.

"The earth's crust on the northern Great Plains is still rebounding from the pressure of glaciers." This was from Lynden Penner, a geological engineer and terrain-analysis expert who let me tag along with his engineering class one day on a field trip to the valley. Glacio-isostatic rebound, he called it. In northern Manitoba, near Churchill, the current rate of rebound has been estimated at about one yard a century. It is a slow bounce, perhaps appreciable to a godwit on her nest above Thunder Creek but certainly beyond the sensitivities of the fifteen aspiring engineers who were up against post-adolescent hormonal rebound on the day I joined Lynden's class.

Soft-spoken, steady, and never in a hurry to pass judgment or draw conclusions, an engineer like Lynden is a dose of reassurance to those of us who worry about the way industry and government use prairie landscapes. It would be easy, I suppose, to dismiss him in a category of scientists and technologists who manipulate nature on our behalf, but I know Lynden too well: as a member of my community, as a good husband and father. I know also that he enjoys the beauty of original landscapes. Like everyone else, I rely on the competence of engineers and scientists everyday. When I'm flying and there is enough turbulence to make me anxious, I try to imagine that there is someone just like Lynden Penner at the helm.

During the drive out to the first site, Lynden gave me a running narrative of the glacial origins of the terrain we were passing over: the floor of Glacial Lake Regina, almost as level as the surface of the lake that formed it; the Davin Moraine; a shallow meltwater channel by the town of McLean; and the Qu'Appelle Moraine just west of Indian Head. We spoke also about three-dimensional aerial-photo interpretation and the techniques of site analysis developed by Jack Mollard, the engineer who founded the consulting firm where Lynden works. Jack's father was born in a sod shack in the Qu'Appelle where his grandfather homesteaded in the 1880s, raising horses for the North-West Mounted Police. Jack left Saskatchewan in the 1950s to take his Ph.D. studying aerial-photo interpretation under the master, Cornell University's Professor Donald Belcher. During World War II, Belcher had been the aerial-photo interpretation expert for the United States military. A technology once used to locate the weak spots on bridges in the Ruhr valley is now used to find gravel pits and outwash plains along the Qu'Appelle and other prairie valleys.

Lynden can look at a splotchy grey photo of farmland taken from several thousand feet in the air and tell you the soil characteristics and parent material — the bedrock underlying the soil — as well as the slope and approximate elevation of any given site. As we skirted around the topic of land use, Lynden said he thought homesteaders would have benefited greatly from aerial photos. Many of the original settlers made decisions on the basis of hearsay and crude geography. It was something of a lottery: one family gets stony, ground moraine and the neighbours get rich, lacustrine soils. "With air photos," said Lynden, "this place might have been settled differently." Differently, perhaps; better or worse is a matter for discussion.

A week or two after my outing with Lynden, I was out walking on the prairie above a large coulee that local people call Snoasis, for a short-lived alpine-skiing enterprise that used the slopes twenty-some years ago. The soil beneath my feet was light and sandy, covered by June grass, spear grasses, and a variety of blooming penstemons and psoralea, including breadroot. It was a remarkably flat area jutting out toward the valley, the kind of land that has escaped cultivation only because the soil is so poor. There is little to be gained from the top eighteen inches of such soil, save for the grass that feeds a few steers grazing their way toward market weight each summer. Just below that topsoil, though, where the roots of blazing star and milk-vetch feel their way into layers of glacial outwash, there is a small profit to be made. As I wandered along the rim of Snoasis coulee across from the old ski lodge now renovated as a country home, a dump truck crawled into view, drawing my attention to a pile of gravel on the horizon and what looked like a gravel crusher. A familiar cramping gripped my chest, a sense of contempt for the ways we violate the Calling River landscapes, combined with guilt and a recognition that the roads I drove upon to get to the valley were built with gravel gouged from equally blessed pieces of prairie. It is all up for grabs; not a pebble is without its price, and no one asks forgiveness or burns sacred smudges over the rocks we disturb from their resting places, or the ones we crush and spread upon our proliferating pathways to take us swiftly from one abused locality to another. Lynden's consulting firm, I knew, would have located this site for the gravel company. That is what the firm's engineers do, and the rest of us benefit from their ability to point out where the glacier dropped a load of gravel for our convenience — an ability that does not falter even when the gravel underlies a landscape just across the valley from home.

Jack Mollard and his brother and business partner, George, remember their father's stories about driving cattle up the length of Snoasis coulee to get to market in Regina. They remember too the location of their grandfather's sod shack in another ravine across the valley and a little upstream. The homesite is now buried under a hundred feet of road-fill where Highway 6 slashes across the Qu'Appelle on a grade that obliterates the coulee's original contours.

I have met the Mollard brothers. They are lanky, garrulous fellows my father's age or older, and they are moral, pragmatic, and reliable, like Lynden, like men you will meet in the country, working in oil, potash, or wheat, helping us carry out the extraction that keeps us in split-levels, minivans, and motorhomes. When their site-analysis data target a familiar pasture or a coulee that recalls their origins, any sentiment these men bear for the land loses out to utility and the overriding pressure for more resource development and better roads — a pressure to which we all lend our weight every time we drive downtown or down to the valley.

ON THE FIELD TRIP with Lynden, one of the engineering students asked, quite sincerely, if anyone had ever found gold associated with Qu'Appelle outwash. We were standing behind the van, and I noticed that someone had scrawled four letters in the fine post-glacial dust coating the rear window: ERTW. I had seen it earlier in the day on a T-shirt: Engineers Rule the World.

Godwits, I can testify, do not. We are a civilization of engineers, bending nature to our will, and we are on the increase, while godwits dwindle, their bright lives snapped off by cars on roads built of stones mined from pastures where godwits used to nest. Yes, engineers rule our world, but that is because we have all become engineers. And, no, there is no gold in these hills, and for that merciful omission, we can thank the glaciers.

## Chapter Ten

# ISKWAO CREEK

BAIRD'S SPARROWS AND SPRAGUE'S PIPITS, the two grassland birds characteristic of the watershed's western reaches, filled the sky with the morning's mandatory psalms. I could smell rose bloom along the sedge-bottoms and even along the mid-slopes where I sat on a chunk of granite, reckoning the span of Iskwao coulee, the first major tributary to enter the Calling River from the north. Here, within four miles of its confluence, I estimated the distance to be a little more than half a mile from rim to rim; perhaps 200 feet of elevation from the creek surface to the plains above. Guessing at span and depth occupied the duller moments of an hour-long vigil. That is the length of time the hawk had been sitting on its own chunk of granite nearly a mile southwest of me along the far slopes of the coulee. But now it was 150 feet lower on the slope, in high grass just above the floodplain. It had pounced on something and appeared, through my binoculars, to be at rest, as though deciding what to do next.

I was watching the hawk for two reasons: to make sure it was in fact a Swainson's hawk and to see if I could tell the size of its prey. Five or six minutes passed with my elbows propped on my knees to steady the binoculars, before the bird launched heavily into the air and teetered over the floodplain, taking an updraft to a third position higher up on the slope. Tapered wings, a dark hood, light underwing coverts and darker flight feathers — it was a Swainson's all right, and it laboured in flight with the weight of its prey: something larger than a vole, perhaps a ground squirrel. Impossible to tell from that distance, but in such habitat, thirteen-lined ground squirrel is more likely than Richardson's. After a pause, the hawk took to the wind again and moved farther down the coulee, this time drawing the attention of a blackbird, which harried it mercilessly. After evading the blackbird, the hawk landed once more on a promontory at a bend in the coulee. Here it leapt into an updraft, bouncing off the face of the slope, this time apparently unburdened by its prey. It soared away and out of my binocular range, leaving me to wonder whether it dropped the ground squirrel at its last perch or during the blackbird's attack. Perhaps it has a nest nearby, I thought. This is late June; it could have chicks to attend.

GOPHERS AND HAWKS; gophers and buffalo: they say that in this land a short while ago you could put your ear to a gopher hole on a calm day and hear the rumbling of the great buffalo herds twenty miles away. When Fort Qu'Appelle was built in the 1860s between Echo and Mission lakes, Hudson Bay trader Peter Hourie saw a gathering of buffalo nearby that he estimated at one million. Such numbers were reported here and there across the Great Plains even in the last twenty years of the buffalo's wild existence. The total population of the plains bison before extermination has been placed at anywhere from forty to seventy million animals, depending on whose figures you accept. The Qu'Appelle basin, 20,000 square miles of the mid-continental grassland, could easily have supported two or three million buffalo in season.

When we remove this many native grazers that evolved along with the grasses and a distinctive ecosystem of creatures ranging from soil microbes to Swainson's hawks, things quickly begin to unravel. One hundred and fifty years may seem a long time in human terms, but it is the flick of a gopher's tail in the long view of the prairie. Already several of the grandest threads within the weave of the northern prairie have thinned and disappeared. There are no large tracts of native grass growing on the fertile, lacustrine soils of the region; no buffalo wolves, no plains grizzlies, no greater prairie chickens, no black-footed ferrets, and no whooping cranes. The antelope, swift foxes, black-tailed prairie dogs, sage grouse, and burrowing owls are almost gone, and much else is in steep decline. The absence of buffalo is not the single cause of all these other losses, but it cleared the stage for the kind of agriculture and settlement that continues to ravage the natural communities of the Great Plains.

The buffalo were the unconscious caretakers of the grasslands. They thundered over vast stretches of landscape, creating diverse plant communities according to the intensity and duration of their grazing in any given area, as well as the number of years since their last visit. For prairie creatures dependent on a narrow niche — say, short grasses with little cover and abundant badger and ground-squirrel holes — the habits of buffalo and the incidence of fire maintained a dynamic ecological patchiness that ensured a fullness of life over the whole of the prairie world. Ranchers will argue that cattle can fulfill this role on native range if we just manage them properly. There was a time when I wanted to believe this hopeful theory, but I have seen too many birds disappearing from large tracts of well-managed cattle range to give it credence any more.

In 1989, I wrote an article for *Canadian Geographic* on the burrowing owl. At the time the numbers in Saskatchewan were down to roughly 1,500 pairs and it was, officially, a threatened species. Researchers believed that Carbofuran, a pesticide used on grasshoppers and flea beetles, was a major cause of the burrowing owl's decline. Recovery programs were just underway and farmers were saving their "ground owl" colonies all over the prairies. Some even agreed to stop spraying pesticides in the vicinity of nests. Things looked bright and I ended the article on a note of optimism.

In 1990, wildlife officials launched an application to have Carbofuran deregistered in Canada. Eight years later, the granular form of the pesticide, used primarily to kill flea beetles on canola fields, has finally been banned. Liquid Carbofuran, the kind used on grasshoppers, remains on the market. The field studies conducted on Saskatchewan and Manitoba canola crops were unequivocal: granular Carbofuran was killing an average of 37.2 songbirds on every quarter section sprayed. Researchers collected hundreds of poisoned carcasses: song sparrows, clay-coloured sparrows, chipping sparrows, longspurs, horned larks, and meadowlarks. The report estimates that in Canada granular Carbofuran has been responsible for the deaths of somewhere between 100,000 and

1 million birds annually. A single grain of the pesticide is enough to kill a songbird. Death is usually swift. With a lethal dose rating three times that of sleeping pills, Carbofuran can kill a sparrow in three minutes.

Meanwhile, during the moist summers of the nineties, grasshopper populations crashed, and farmers in the burrowing owl's range had little reason to spray. Yet, by the mid-nineties, the numbers of burrowing owls in Saskatchewan had dropped again sharply, to fewer than eight hundred pairs, and the overall Canadian population was declining at about sixteen per cent every year. The species' official designation was hiked up a notch to "endangered," the last step before "extirpated." Clearly, Carbofuran was not the only problem. Ornithologists and wildlife officials began referring to "a pathology in the landscape," suggesting that the kind of habitat we have left for the owls is proving to be inadequate.

The local burrowing owl colony near the town of Kronau, once the largest anywhere in the Qu'Appelle basin and now the only colony near Regina, is as good an illustration as any. Less than ten years ago, there were eighteen pairs nesting at Kronau. Last year there was a single pair. It is an unremarkable patch of misused pasture: small, weedy, and overgrazed. Burrowing owls like such places, in part because ground squirrels and badgers also like them. The owls use badger holes, almost exclusively, as nest sites and escape cover, and badgers hunt and dig in places where ground squirrels, their primary prey, are abundant. The sequence appears to be simple: no gophers, no badgers; no badgers, no burrowing owls; however, it is complicated by another factor that closes the loop: badgers also hunt burrowing owls. It all makes for a fine prairie ecosystem as long as there is a sufficient expanse of suitable and contiguous habitat to minimize the impact of any local imbalances or temporary fluctuations in the overall equilibrium.

So why did the Kronau owls disappear? One possible cause, part of the gradual increase of landscape dysfunction, is habitat fragmentation. The Kronau pasture is isolated, far from any other native grass, surrounded by cultivated land, and fifty or more miles from another pair of burrowing owls.

When I go out to Kronau now, I see a severed landscape, a place cut off from the whole and its reservoir of life. After ten minutes of eyestrain through my spotting scope, I might be fortunate to find a single owl. Desolation is seeing such a gregarious bird away from its own kind and peering out of a hole in a disjunct scrap of prairie that short years ago moved to the hover and pounce, hop and flap of two dozen of these creatures. I look behind me to the roads, wheat fields, and summer-fallow running past the horizon, and I wonder how the colony ever lasted as long as it did. Where do you go if you are an owl in such a place, and times get tough? If there are too many poisons accumulating in your prey, if your prey become scarce, if the badgers that make your nest holes become scarce, if your genes become inbred, if the grass grows too high, if the rains flood your burrow, and if researchers will not give you a break from the banding, the blood-testing, the probing, and the transmitter-tagging? We have made recovery plans for the owls, but without places to recover from the stresses of living in a managed, agricultural landscape, the burrowing owl has no hope of recovery.

There is something else amiss at Kronau pasture: gophers. I used to see far more Richardson's ground squirrels in the pasture than I do these days. This creature is the other important grazer of the northern plains and, like the buffalo, it has been the target of widespread exter-mination programs. Both grazers, both key prey species for predators, the buffalo and the gopher are the two "wildlife pests" that farmers have not been willing to share the prairie with.[32] I remember my father reciting an old homesteader's joke that he would have learned from his father, who burned buffalo chips to warm his first prairie shack. It is a jibe at the jodhpurred British naturalist back from the colonies and doing his best to explain the difference between the two extremes of prairie fauna: "It's quite simple, old boy — you see, the buffalo is much laaarga and much fierca than the gopha."

The buffalo may be much fiercer, but the gopher has been harder to exterminate. It adapted well to farmland, riddling cow pastures and eating the farmer's grain. A century of penny-a-tail bounties, drowning expeditions (the "harmless" boyhood pastimes that came to our litera-ture in W.O. Mitchell's *Who Has Seen the Wind*), and campaigns of government-sponsored strychnine-poisoning seem to have made little difference to this our most vilified native rodent — until now, that is. By the destructive logic of extinction, the most abundant of species seem to crash the most precipitously.

The sky-darkening flocks of passenger pigeons recorded in John

James Audubon's time showed it to be the most populous bird species in the Americas; yet fifty years later, they were all but gone.

Prairie naturalists and biologists are just now beginning to wonder if the Richardson's ground squirrel is reaching critically low numbers. Stuart Houston, one of Canada's most celebrated naturalists and bird banders, grew up in Yorkton but remembers passing long summer days on an uncle's farm near Tyvan, where Wascana Creek rises out of the southern reaches of the basin. When I asked him what the gopher numbers were like when he was a boy, back in the 1930s, he said that they had an old Scottish term they would use to describe a place aswarm with Richardson's ground squirrels: "We used to say 'the pasture is *sniving* with gophers.' It's a word. You can look it up in the *Oxford*."

How many pastures once snived with gophers all across the Canadian plains? No one knows. When an animal is abundant — and the Richardson's ground squirrel has been described as one of the most abundant mammals of the New World — no one bothers to count them. Wildlife officials have no baseline data to help them define healthy population densities for the Richardson's ground squirrel.

"All we have to go on is instinct, gut feeling, and anecdote," said Houston, "but I know that on the pastures near Rosetown where I band hawks, ground squirrels are down to one to two per cent of their former numbers. Something is wrong." Hunters, naturalists, farmers — anyone who spends time on the prairie — will tell you the same thing about other places where a decade ago it was impossible to walk five paces in any direction without stepping in a gopher burrow.

These days, articles appear in local natural history publications, highlighting the importance of the gopher as a "keystone" species with important ecological links to the endangered burrowing owl and several declining predators. Persecution from the general public, however, is far from over. Not long ago, an Alberta legislator put forward a bill describing the Richardson's ground squirrel as an agricultural pest and calling for the extermination of the species. His bill was defeated, but the Richardson's ground squirrel remains on the list of animals, along with skunks, rats, crows, and magpies, that one may shoot on sight throughout Canada's Prairie provinces. The absurdity of all our official wildlife listings will reach new heights on the day, not far off now, when the gopher makes the jump to the "threatened species" list without ever resting in that comfortable limbo where the officially innocuous and sufficiently numerous await their turn.

Swainson's hawks long ago stopped wondering about the status of the gopher. In the 1980s and early 1990s, when there was still a colony of owls at Kronau, I used to watch a pair of Swainson's that nested annually in a sprawling old poplar tree just beyond the southern margins of the pasture. They would swoop out over the chewed-down grass where owls, cattle, badgers, and ground squirrels shared a few acres of grass. The female hawk, larger than her mate, would drop like something suddenly too heavy for the air, hitting the ground, where there would be a brief tussle before she took to the wing with a limp gopher in her talons.

When Swainson's hawks nest, one of the main items on their daily menu is Richardson's ground squirrel. Houston has been studying this hawk for more than thirty years and has banded more of them than anyone else in Canada. The decline in Swainson's hawks began, according to his records, in the mid-1980s — which aligns it exactly with the decline in the burrowing owl, or at least our recognition of its decline. In the past, he would often find three or more gophers in the nests he visited. In 1995, however, he did not see a single Richardson's ground squirrel in a Swainson's nest.

While the gopher is becoming less common in the countryside, it often thrives in good numbers on the margins of prairie cities and towns: in schoolyards, railway easements, boulevards, airports, and exhibition grounds. When the burrowing owl began disappearing rapidly from rural sites in the early nineties, colonies in Moose Jaw and on the edges of a few dying towns became the last ones of size anywhere on the Regina-Moose Jaw plains. Even so, over the years these sites have lost owls, and some colonies have disappeared entirely. In the final stages of local extinction, the last representatives of the northernmost burrowing owls in the world gather in degraded, pathetic habitats: on trashy boulevards, among rusting machinery, baseball backstops, and railyard detritus. These are not places to recover; these are hospices for a doomed animal.

The burrowing owl may be beyond saving here in the northern extremities of its vast range. We are standing by, watching a rapid range retraction that we are powerless to slacken, much less reverse. There is still time to help the Swainson's, I believe, but I get worried when I see these great prairie hawks retreating to the same despairing strips of land left to the only dense populations of gophers they can find. In the 1998 Regina spring bird census, for the first time since I began taking part in the mid-1980s, I did not see a single Swainson's hawk in my count sector. The next morning I was out walking in our neighbourhood and heard the piercing alarm call of a gopher coming from across the traffic heading downtown on Saskatchewan Drive. I looked over to see if I could catch a glimpse of any on the grassy boulevard and saw instead a small Swainson's hawk flying low over the lawn on the lookout for a vulnerable gopher.

Another time when I was driving along a street in the city's industrial district — "rad and brake" shops, weedy vacant lots, equipment yards, all separated by chain link fences — on the periphery of my vision I spotted a large bird launching from a utility pole ahead of me. It dropped low over the street, struggling for altitude in the heavy July air. It was a Swainson's and it flew directly over my car, carrying a ragged, bloody ground squirrel. I stopped the car, jumped out and turned to follow it as it laboured in ponderous flaps south, just clearing the tops of cars on Victoria Avenue, one of the city's busiest streets. It headed on farther south where a nest of young hawks waited God knows where. It was in the middle of the city. Facing north again to open the car door, I saw a smaller hawk, the male, lift from another pole and follow the path of its mate.

In 1996, the same year I watched the Swainson's take a ground squirrel in the Iskwao Creek coulee, news reports announced that life had suddenly become more perilous than ever for the bird that a few years ago was our common grassland hawk. Swainson's hawks overwintering on the Argentine Pampas were dying in droves from pesticide poisoning. Biologists described corpses littering fields in the states of Córdoba, Buenos Aires, and Las Pampa. They were mostly adult Swainson's and mostly from the Canadian plains: nine leg bands were from hawks banded at nests in Saskatchewan and Alberta. In all, 3,909 carcasses were found. Given the high rate of scavenging and the size of the area, the researchers estimated a total kill of well over 20,000 Swainson's hawks. The Canadian population of this species is thought to be somewhere between 40,000 and 100,000. No one has ever done a thorough census.

You hear reports of this kind of devastation and wonder if there is any hope for wildness. The pesticide in question was monocrotrophos, an organophosphate that Hitler's scientists developed to use in chemical warfare. It is banned in North America, but farmers in the Third World still use it on grasshoppers. Chemical warfare — what are the Argentine farmers thinking? *Are* they thinking?

Reading a report in the newspaper, I learned that it was actually a farmer who noticed the hawks dying and called Swainson's hawk researchers in the United States. The global context behind the massacre is that the Argentine government wanted to increase its cash crop exports to Europe. To bring more land under production, they introduced irrigation to a grassland area that had never been cultivated before. They provided landowners with incentives to plough the pampas and start growing alfalfa, sunflowers, and other crops. Grasshoppers that were adapted to reach a population equilibrium amid the full diversity of range vegetation began eating the crops. The farmers, with new tractors and irrigation equipment to pay for, were quick to react with the strongest poison they could buy. Monocrotrophos was sprayed from crop-dusting planes and by air-blasters pulled by tractors.

I have watched Swainson's hawks following tractors near Regina to feed on the insects and rodents that the machinery will turn up in the furrow. They would have done the same in Argentina to catch grasshoppers disturbed by the crop-sprayers. Some would have died immediately from direct contamination. The majority would have been killed by lethal doses of the poison received when they ate the grasshoppers. Some would certainly die in the weeks and months following the contamination. Those that received lower dosages and survived the spraying would almost certainly be impaired in the long term. Many would not have been healthy enough to migrate the 7,000 miles to their nesting areas, let alone mate and rear young successfully. Others might migrate and then not be able to produce viable eggs. There is no escaping these thoughts now whenever I see a Swainson's, whether it is one patrolling the CPR line in the city or a more fortunate individual with its own gopher patch along a grazed-down strip of valley rim.

Like gophers and buffalo, this hawk was once an abundant prairie animal. Only ten years ago, seeing a Swainson's hawk was a simple matter of looking skyward on a sunny day. There was almost always one in sight. My field notes for the summer of 1989 record a count of 212 Swainson's I saw along the Trans-Canada Highway as I drove from Regina to Calgary. The number did not seem remarkable to me at the time, but I look back at such field notes now with a longing for the days when Swainson's hawks were part of the background of a summer afternoon, like the skunky fragrance of wolf willow in June or the hurdy-gurdy of grasshoppers in August. Prairie people, at least those who pay some attention to wild creatures, are beginning to notice the absence of hawks.

On the day I left the headwaters of the Qu'Appelle to head east through the watershed, I stopped for gasoline at a place that was part garage, part confectionery store, part fishing-tackle shop. Coaxing the last few cents of gasoline up to a round figure, the proprietor, a man his mid-forties, started talking to me — about birds. He had noticed a book piled on top of my backpack and camping gear in the back of the car.

"I see you've got *Birds of the Elbow* too," he said.

We talked for several minutes about the book — it was the first one he had ever bought — and about hawks and eagles, the birds he noticed most. He said he thought the book was remarkably current because it even had the story of the Swainson's hawks killed in Argentina. He knew some of the details of the tragedy, enough to affect his regard for the bird.

"We used to see Swainson's hawks all over the place . . . but this summer there's been hardly a one." He shook his head and thought for a moment.

"I found a dead one once. Got it mounted and it's in my living room now. . . . If they keep this up in Argentina, my bird might become a collector's item."

He smiled awkwardly, hearing his own words dissipate into the light rain we stood beneath, and then he added, "I hope not."

If hope and goodwill were enough, we would have burrowing owls on pastures all over the Qu'Appelle region. We still have a chance with the Swainson's hawk, but this time we will have to do more than focus on the species at risk. We might start by creating and protecting gopher sanctuaries so that the last native grazing mammal we have in numbers can once again proliferate and help restore our afflicted and fragmented landscapes.

## Chapter Eleven

# EYEBROW MARSH
# TO BUFFALO POUND

FROM ISKWAO CREEK I DOUBLED back west to see the valley's first major wetland, Eyebrow Marsh, a set of dykes and channels engineered for duck production on the floodplain. Miraculously, two immature whooping cranes had spent the previous summer there — the first in half a century — so I was eager to have a look at the place. As I neared the valley rim from the north, I saw a truck and an all-terrain vehicle at the side of the road and two men talking. I stopped to see if they knew anything about the marsh project.

"Interested in *our* ducks, are ya?" asked the man in the truck. Considering the ATV, I thought they might be with Ducks Unlimited, but I asked what he meant by "our" ducks.

"We feed 'em, so they must be ours." He smiled. I was from the city and I might be a government pencil-pusher of some kind, so he was letting me know that, as a farmer, he was not pleased about welfare ducks eating his crops.

Qu'Appelle Basin Water Control Issue Number 34: waterfowl crop damage.

THE NEXT DAY, another water issue came my way as I rested at the side of a road that bisects the valley north of the town of Keeler. The terrain falls in shallow, broad steps to the floodplain in that portion of the Qu'Appelle, and each step forms a broad, grassy saddle running parallel to the main valley. I was parked on one of these subvalleys, a yawning trough surrounded by low hills to the north and a slightly higher set of hills to the south. The side-hills, long, reclining, and voluptuous, were covered then in a thick green pelt of short grass. Trees were somewhere to the east, an adornment of wetter landscapes farther downstream.

A clean white pickup truck approached from the valley bottom and stopped opposite me, the driver's arm dangling from the open window: "Nice day, eh? Have you seen a motorboat come down the river this morning?" As I replied I caught a glimpse of the lettering on the side of his door: "SaskWater."

His name was Reg and he was gathering hydrology data for the provincial Crown corporation in charge of fixing all the mistakes and oversights of Creation in this part of the world. Reg was looking for the rest of his survey crew, a couple of engineers in an aluminum boat putt-putting their way downstream and measuring the river's channel capacity. He had left them at Eyebrow Marsh three hours earlier, and they were to rendezvous with him here at the bridge. They were an hour late. Reg returned to the bridge to keep watch, and I asked if he would mind my joining him.

Some local farmers were requesting that the river's channel capacity be increased between Eyebrow Marsh and Buffalo Pound Lake.

"I think this is the sixth time they've asked. We measure, tell them it won't work. Couple years later they ask again, and we go out and do the measuring again." Reg told me that he was responsible for the "dry geometry," the measurements above the surface of the river and up onto the floodplain.

"I can't see it ever working here," he said. "Just look at this place. It's a broad, flat floodplain with hardly any slope. To increase channel capacity here enough to allow landowners to irrigate would take a lot of improvements."

We talked about improvements. Channelization, dyking, dredging, straightening, rip-rapping, and other erosion-control measures. As I began to ask him what he thought, personally, of such manipulation of a river, another truck pulled over and into the ditch adjacent to the bridge. Two farmers stepped out of the battered, pasture-worn Dodge, which appeared to be held together by a patina of dried mud and rust. Perhaps they had come to retrieve the five Hereford steers loitering on the road. We walked down to ask if they had seen any boatloads of wayward engineers that morning.

In this part of Saskatchewan, it is not uncommon to find two farmer-bachelors, usually brothers, living the peasant life, and surviving on a few acres of cropland and pasture — holdings that would never be enough to support a family or anyone with loftier ambitions of modern comfort. These two men, both somewhere in their sixties, or nineties, had every sign of having lived a long time without benefit of female attention. Reg and I introduced ourselves. One of the men said his name was Stan; the other said something that might have been a name or a curse. They had a week's stubble on their purple-red cheeks, and the whites of their eyes were glazed pink from years of living in the prairie sun. Stan had apparently left his dentures at home for the day. We asked about the Herefords. No, he said, for once the escaped cattle belonged to their neighbour. They had come to repair the riverside fence that had lost its footing in the recent flood. They hauled their gear out of the back of the pickup, working in the silence of men who know one another's movements and habits nearly as well as they know their own. I could see they had done this job countless times, whenever the river rose enough to take a bite out of the silty bank, swallowing with it a span of their fence.

Reg and I helped them hoist the fence back into place and took turns with a twenty-pound maul, whacking the replacement posts — lengths of half-rotten ash and poplar — into the ground. When we were done and the barbed-wire fence was up and looking slightly less rickety than before, I asked Stan and his partner what they thought of the irrigation idea. There was a pause while they considered why I might be asking such a question, and then Stan said, "Can't say it's much use to us at our age — what are we gonna do with irrigation when we can't afford the equipment?"

They agreed that it might be nice to have a few acres of irrigated land to grow their winter supply of hay each year, but they had come this far without irrigation and they could take it or leave it from here on.

If an irrigation project were ever approved for this stretch of the Qu'Appelle, SaskWater would then triple or quadruple the flow they currently allow into the system from Lake Diefenbaker at the Elbow. Such increased capacity would then make it easier to justify more irrigation and channelizing farther downstream to Buffalo Pound and beyond.

I have a map of the watershed drawn in the late fifties for the Hydrology Division of the PFRA. It indexes topographic plans for more than twenty irrigation projects that would turn the entire length of the Qu'Appelle river into an irrigation channel. Through a merciful blend of economic and geographic circumstances, this grand scheme was never fully implemented. Only two or three of these projects ever came to be, and most of the river has never been channelized or used for irrigation. As long as the PFRA and SaskWater are afoot in the watershed, however, the threat remains.

Reg and I parted ways and walked back to our respective vehicles. Something moving at the edge of my vision yanked me out of my thoughts of irrigation and river damage — two small birds chasing a larger one that was tilting and flapping erratically a few feet above the valley's northern slopes. Two blackbirds on a crow. No. I looked again and they changed to larger birds: two red-tailed hawks chasing a golden eagle. The eagle had white on the base of its tail and in its flight feathers; it was an immature, like the one I had seen in April above the ceremonial circle in the Dirt Hills. I stood watching the trio fly in and out of view behind hilltops: a golden eagle, the monarch of the prairie skies, chased away by a breeding pair of red-tailed hawks, a forest-edge species that has proliferated with farm shelterbelts and now appears to be replacing grassland raptors.

"An eagle!" I shouted to Reg who was just opening the door to his truck. I pointed. "It's a golden eagle!"

The water manager turned, nodded politely, and then stepped into the driver's seat and drove away.

*Chapter Twelve*

# Buffalo Pound and Arm River

AFTER A HALF DAY OF TRAMPING through the coulees and over the high grasslands of Buffalo Pound Provincial Park, where Hind was hosted by the Cree in 1858, I stopped at a town to make some inquiries. I was looking for the name of a leaseholder who held a parcel of land east of the park that is said to be a good example of the valley floodplain as it was a century ago. Uncultivated land on the Qu'Appelle bottomlands is as rare as an afternoon without wind on its uplands. I had heard also of an "ancient burial site" in the vicinity, and I thought I might at least determine if it was more than legend enlivening a farmer's pile of fieldstones.

The town museum was closed, but a sign on the door said that keys were available. I drove down main street looking for anyone who might know the keeper of the keys. I found an elderly lady wearing a muumuu, thongs, and a hairnet as she sprinkled her geraniums. Mrs. Dirmel, she said, two doors north, had the keys.

I knocked on the door; a boy answered. Mrs. Dirmel was not home, but Mr. was. Two shouts of "Grandpa!" from the boy filled the doorway with a large man who had the sunburn and hat-creased hair of a grain farmer just in from the fields. An affable sort, he was amused by my strange inquiries and invited me into his kitchen where we could spread out my topo maps and his rural municipality map. Finding the leaseholder names on the RM map was easy, and he knew the family that leased the land where the old burial ground was said to be found. He remembered hearing something about the place and would call the man up to ask permission on my behalf.

As the phone call passed through NHL playoffs and weather talk on to the question at hand, the half of the conversation I could hear made it clear that there had been a burial ground but that it had been destroyed in a gravel-digging operation.

"No . . . just a fella here from the city is interested in it is all . . . oh yeah, Babcock Construction was it? . . . all dug up then . . . well, I guess that's it then. Alright."

After the phone call Mr. Dirmel's manner changed. He seemed a little nervous and avoided my eyes as he explained the tragedy to me. "But, grandpa," said the boy, a thirteen-year-old who could read an RM map, section, township, and range, with all the skill of a small-town lawyer, "I know there's still something up there because Gary took a group of kids up on that hill last year to look at it."

No answer from Grandpa.

Something is not right here, I thought, and I was beginning to feel less welcome. I said I'd be on my way if he could just give me the phone number of the other leaseholder, the one who grazed the native grass bottomland I had come to see. As I gave my thanks and prepared to leave, Mr. Dirmel seemed to want to make amends as though he had been inhospitable. He began talking about a Red River cart trail nearby and some tipi rings on his own pasture land in the Arm River Valley. If I was interested, he'd show me them sometime when the cattle were out of the pasture. I thanked him for the offer, said goodbye, and walked toward the car, puzzled by Dirmel's change in demeanour and disgusted by the rapacity of gravel contractors.

I went straight to a phone booth and rang up the farmer who leased the bottomland. The voice on the other end of the line was guarded and curt. I explained my interest in the land and assured him I would be on foot and would not open any gates. He was worried about his cattle being disturbed. Without exactly saying "no," he grumbled on as though I had asked permission to take his youngest daughter for a weekend in Vegas. Finally, he said that I might not like his bull, but I could try my luck, just don't complain to him if I'm trampled.

Then, before I said goodbye, I thought I would mention the burial ground that used to be on his neighbour's land above the valley rim. Had he heard about its destruction? There was a long pause and then a derisive chuckle, "Well, I'm not saying whether it's there or it's not there. Let's just leave it at that."

I hung up, knowing I would have to find other places to walk the following morning. I had long ago used up my quota of mercy when it came to out-running range bulls. What's more, I knew that the rural instinct to guard the landscape from intrusion was intact. Three men were doing all they could to protect a burial site, a place of great local value, from the likes of me — someone who, for all they knew, had a car full of picks and shovels and every intention to pillage their historic treasure. Anyway, I had my answer. There is something of archaeological interest on the valley rim in that stretch of the Qu'Appelle — something worth a couple of white lies.

THE SUN DID NOT fully set until almost ten o'clock that night. As I watched from my camp abreast of the Arm River, the sky performed its usual twilight trick spilling streaks of peach and fuchsia into darkening violet. A gibbous moon drew up over the narrow banks of the river, and downstream, where I would wander the next morning without any leaseholder's permission, blessings, or misinformation, came the trill of a toad, two hoots of an owl, and the confiding, querulous cries of other riverside creatures that I would leave undisturbed in the shroud of their darkening world.

Morning saturated the little valley with a yellow light diffused through low cloud cover. The Arm River shone like a platinum serpent poured into jade. It was the most green of days in a green year. The run-off from a winter of deep snows flowed into rain-filled days in May and June, changing every rivulet in the basin into a creek. Before subsiding into ribbons of reflected sky, streams such as the Arm River had over-flowed their banks in spring, recharging marshes and fens long dry, broadening the margin of water-borne life on the prairie, and calling avocets, snipe, yellow rails, and willets to their sedge-meadow sides. The flanks of coulees and the moister places at the toe of every slope were an exuberant green gemmed with points of lilac, pink, and yellow. Making my way along the north side of the shallow valley, I waded through patches of geum and antennaria the size of a city lot.

My immediate excuse for the walk down the Arm River valley was a bison kill site downstream somewhere amid the folded hills. Kill sites don't reveal themselves on the landscape like burial sites or even tipi rings; and with neither the precise mapped location nor the tourist's desire to gaze upon the archaeological facts of the place, I made a poor explorer, a less-than-methodical bone hunter, as I traipsed from sedge meadow to cactus bloom down the valley bottom.

The flight song of a Sprague's pipit blowing on the wind above me was all the evidence I required that this was once a great buffalo ground. This once abundant prairie bird, sometimes called the Missouri skylark, has a breeding range that almost exactly covers the historical range of the northern herds of plains bison. From the Red River in the east to the foothills of the Rockies and north to the forest edges, wherever there were buffalo on the northern plains, there was the swirling flight song of the Sprague's pipit.

The bird itself is something of a ghost. Although it is common on pasture land, most modern farmers and ranchers live in its precincts without ever actually seeing the bird, without knowing it exists. Yet the song is always overhead on summer days; it is the ambient pastorale of the northern plains, a thin spiralling series of notes falling from the blue, with no bird in sight, as though the sun had added music to its repertoire. The pipit is there, however, four or five hundred feet up into the air, a mere fleck against the sky. You can find it if you know how to look for it and account for the wind's ventriloquism.

On my Arm River walk, I had to strain my eyes and neck for several minutes before finding a pipit fluttering far overhead. Through my binoculars I could see it flapping into the wind to hold position. Every few seconds it would set its wings and coast — and then it would release its song. After a count of two or three, the notes would reach my ears, while the bird in my binoculars had already resumed its flutter. And the song, meanwhile, would fade away into the valley's soft parabola four hundred feet below.

On most summer days, for the twelve or fourteen thousand years of post-glacial life in this region, pipits looked down from their wind-perches and saw a prairie pocked with dark brown forms that assembled and flowed in distinct patterns across the valley, patterns shaped by orientation to water and wind, by the threat of predators, and by a complex of other considerations in the herd-mind of the buffalo.

Those patterns have been absent from the Arm River Valley for 125 years or more. The grass, the river, and the pipits remain, representing just enough for the imagination to conjure up its own kill site. Lying back on the woolly-stemmed forbs and grasses to look up at pipit specks, I felt I could retrieve Earth's grand reminiscences of recent days: the thunder of forty thousand hooves, the cries of the hunt, the bawling clamour of death.

I saw several places that day that looked like good candidates for kill sites, not knowing or caring if they were the actual locality recognized by science and museums. There is satisfaction in such uncertainty, in the failure to locate with exactitude a place that hides among other places that look equally possible. It is something like seeing a pipit on the wing. You never really get a good look at one; no identifying field marks or *National Geographic* views. It is always a remote dot in the sky that you must take on faith as a pipit. It is this way for many of the prairie's most characteristic forms. You live in ignorance of them, unaware of their role in forming what you have come to know as grassland ambience. Later you learn of their existence or history and their belonging to certain places. Beyond that, you may be granted a brief and distant glimpse, which will only confirm what you already knew: this is the fierce and mysterious life dwelling here, made multiplex by the radiating, spiralling creation of a region that just yesterday shrugged off its mantle of ice.

Sprague's pipits and the killing grounds where great shaggy beasts spilled their blood for the people of the plains are best pondered at such a distance. Sequestered away in the hills, the old buffalo haunts, now guarded by range cattle and ornery landowners, have gone dormant beneath the airborne dreams and songs of a prairie bird that will sing on the wind, I was once told, for up to three hours at a time. This extravagant defence of territory, covering the whole of the native grassland that receives the pipit's benediction, proclaims for all to hear that *Creation still holds title to the prairie.*

*Chapter Thirteen*

# LANIGAN CREEK

"**P**LEASE JOIN THE CHOIR in singing the responsorial psalm."

*You care for the earth, give it water*
*You fill it with riches;*
*Your river in heaven brims over*
*To provide its grain.*

*And thus you provide for the earth:*
*You drench its furrows,*
*You level it, soften it with showers,*
*You bless its growth.*

*You crown the year with your goodness,*
*Abundance flows in your steps,*
*In the pastures of the wilderness it flows.*

*The hills are girded with joy,*
*The meadows covered with flocks;*
*The valleys are decked with wheat,*
*They shout for joy, yes they sing.*

It was early summer in the land of Judah, in a year of plentiful rain. Psalm 65 was written for just such a season, and we sang it from the pews of St. Mary's Roman Catholic Church in the town of Lanigan. In the far northern reaches of the watershed, Lanigan is at the head of the creeks that bundle into Last Mountain Lake, the basin's largest body of water, a seventy-mile serpent that bites into the Qu'Appelle Valley at the town of Craven.

I was standing behind rows of stout, well-fed farmers and farmers' sons, who were leaning back in their pews at the rear of the church. A sombre, football-fan priest (a Roughrider season-ticket holder) waded into the gospel reading and sermon. It was the parable of the sower: "The seed that falls on good ground will yield a fruitful harvest. . . ." The farmers knew their ground was good — not quite the rich, heavy clay of the Indian Head or Regina's glacial lake beds, but good enough to yield a four-bedroom house, satellite TV, and, for some, a motorhome or a cabin at Stony Beach.

The man who originally delivered this parable to a crowd of people overlooking the fertile Jordan River valley was referring to yield and harvest metaphorically, of course, as a way of illustrating the expansive power of the Word. Two thousand years later, however, the pews of St. Mary's were filled with people who heard the "yielding a hundredfold" and thought of their fields of sprouting wheat bound for abundance, notwithstanding early frost, hail, or the vexations of wheat midge or Bertha army worm.

Later in the mass we prayed together in antiphon. The lector read: "For the care of God's good earth, for the care of seeds and plants, and trees . . . we pray to the Lord."

We answered: "Lord, hear our prayer."

"For a good harvest . . . we pray to the Lord."

"Lord, hear our prayer."

The closing hymn was "God Whose Farm Is All Creation."

God has not always been a farmer and we didn't always sing and pray this way. God seems to have given up the hunter-gatherer life some-where between twelve and eight thousand years ago. That was when the songs and prayers about planting and harvesting began. Stories too — in fact, the Judeo-Christian Genesis myth could be described as a story that explains how we changed Creation from a wild garden into a farm. *The world was once a garden where we ran naked and gathered what we needed, and God provided as long as we followed his rules, but we got bored with this, broke the rules, and so God sent us off to look for places where we could grow our own food.* The rest is history: we wiped out the hunting peoples and then the herding peoples whenever we needed their valleys to replace the ones we had farmed into wasteland.

"We are the people of the next valley." Rob Wright, ecologist and fireside sage, tossed this declaration into the embers once as we sat by a fire in the lee of jack pines, beneath a boreal sky. We were with our families far north of the Qu'Appelle country, on a week-long trip in which we failed day after day to demonstrate to our offspring our innate ability to divine walleye and pike from cold water. After the children bedded at dark each night, we would stay up and talk for hours beside our shared hearth. Tin cups and bellies warm with tea and Cointreau, we told family stories and solved a great many of the difficulties facing modern civilization. Our campfire synod agreed that most of our problems began when we hammered our hunting spears into ploughshares. From that point on, it has been one valley after another — Euphrates, Nile, Ganges, Rhine, Seine, St. Lawrence, Mississippi, Hudson — evicting the local hunter-gatherers and pastoralists, replacing them with farmers who soon multiply, filling the valley with a civilization that venerates the tiller's short-term residency, calling this "settlement," while dismissing the hunter's long-term residency, several thousand years of seasonal migration and ecological congruency as mere "nomadism."

Most of the children and grandchildren of those who first farmed the Qu'Appelle have moved on to other valleys now — the Peace, the Bow, the Okanagan, the Fraser — or to Western cities, where the progeny of the hunting peoples they displaced are also congregating. The Qu'Appelle's rural communities, like its soils, are growing thinner each year.

When we started farming the soils in this region eighty to one hundred years ago, the "A" horizon in the topsoil averaged from four to eight per cent organic matter. Today it is half that and dropping. Most of the nitrogen that the prairie had secured over thousands of years disappeared soon after the sod was first broken. In a native grassland, the bulk of the nitrogen is in the root zone, bound up in humic acids and carbon compounds so complex that they remain a mystery to soil science. Whenever we cultivate a piece of prairie, we oxygenate the soil and increase its temperature, leaving the nitrogen exposed to bacteria that specialize in consuming nitrates. As soon as we plant our cereal crops in this kind of soil, the nitrogen store drops again sharply. By selling our organic matter and nitrogen on the international market, we are, in effect, exporting the life of the soil that fed the buffalo and prairie peoples in a sustainable cycle over thousands of years.

It is the story of dryland grain-farming wherever it is tried, from the plains of Ethiopia to the pampas of Argentina. Break the native sod, create an economy based on short-term gains, deplete the soil of its nitrogen after a century or so, and then move on to the next unploughed pasture on God's farm. Today, however, we have been able to delay the inevitable by using external supplements from the world of petrochemicals — artificial fertilizers produced here in Saskatchewan by our own SaskFerco. The nitrogen brewed up by SaskFerco in the form of granular urea and anhydrous ammonia has allowed Saskatchewan's farmers — even those on the most marginal of soils with as little as two per cent organic matter — to outstrip nature's limitations. While we once stored the prairie's fertility in the first few inches of topsoil, we now keep it in a SaskFerco warehouse that their promotional material assures us is "the size of three football fields."

Government and university agrologists have devised a new method of dryland farming to complement the regular doses of artificial nitrogen. They call it no-till farming, referring to its cardinal rule: avoid cultivating cropland. Traditionally, prairie farmers have tilled their land at regular intervals to discourage annual weeds. Of course, more topsoil and nitrogen disappear with each cultivation, so by avoiding this kind of yearly tillage, the farmer can reduce the depletion of nitrogen significantly. The alternative weed control recommended by the no-till experts is herbicides, lots of herbicides. This makes the method extremely expensive for small farmers and extremely lucrative for the agribusiness corporations that produce the chemicals and spraying equipment, and support the research and government programs promoting no-till. Rising fertilizer and herbicide prices, meanwhile, have pushed many farmers into debt and below the poverty line, contributing to rural depopulation across the plains.[33]

How long the land can continue to produce on this input/output equation is anyone's guess. No one has ever tried this before as a basis of dryland farming. Some soil ecologists believe that before long, however, the soil structure itself will disappear. The capillaries within the soil, so important to the uptake of moisture and nutrients, will simply collapse. Then the most fertile lands on the continent will look like the cracked mud at the bottom of a dry lake bed. For that is all that will remain: clay bereft of tilth and nutrients, unsuitable for growing anything.

Organic farming is beginning to gain favour as an alternative; however, its methods require a lot of tillage for weed control. This too can be disastrous, if the level of organic matter and nitrogen added — in the form of animal wastes and "green" manure crops — does not match the rate of nutrient extraction through cultivation and cropping. The debate between advocates of organic farming and advocates of conventional farming skirts around the more basic and challenging questions facing agriculture around the world. The real problems relate to scale and boundaries. We have too few farmers using too much machinery to feed too many people too cheaply too far away. While our mechanized, cash-crop agriculture depletes the fertility and organic matter of our soils here on the prairie, global trade in farm produce contributes directly to overpopulation, famine, and desertification on other continents. By shipping grain to countries that once fed themselves, we fuel population explosion in parts of the Third World. We call it aid and disaster relief when we send food to a famine, but if we relieve anything it is our sense of guilt in seeing the victims of the global marketplace starve to death on our television newscasts. Add enough food to any region where there are more people than the land can support, and you will see the population increase further, ensuring even more profound ecological crisis and starvation.

Soon after we started exporting grain, we began calling our prairie landscapes the Breadbasket of the World. Along with the national anthem, phonics, and multiplication tables, our schoolchildren have been taking in the notion that Saskatchewan farmers feed the world. In the farm crisis of the 1980s, psychologists suggested that this shibboleth and the pressure it bears was contributing to the sense of guilt and failure behind the high suicide rate among prairie farmers. Yet if you ask grain farmers today what motivates them, keeps them going in tough times, they will tell you that it is this vocational duty to "feed the world." The ad agencies promoting designer herbicides or genetically engineered seed have not missed this bit of agricultural mythology. SaskFerco, for instance, closes its ads with the phrase, "Helping Saskatchewan Farmers Feed the World!"

So it goes — suicidal farmers here, starving peasants there, ecological destruction everywhere. Sooner or later the mathematics of population growth will overwhelm our manic attempt to feed the world, and the land will have no more life left for us to export.

From the outset, this destructive scale of production and trade has been made possible by our willingness to adopt more and larger machinery as it becomes available. To accommodate this fetish for machinery, we have had to redefine certain words, three in particular: wealth, economy, and efficiency. A fourth value, independence, has refracted our understanding of these first three. *Efficiency* now means that you can manage a task with fewer people and "with greater independence." *Economy* now refers to an aggregation of independent and competing producers and consumers. *Wealth* is now simply a measurement of the stockpile of resources gathered by any independent and competing economic unit: nation, producer, consumer.

The original definitions have not disappeared entirely, of course. Just as I still know in my gut that the best fertilizer for any land is the farmer's footsteps, I recognize at some level that wealth, economy, and efficiency become meaningful only within a context of *inter*dependence. The truth of these values resides in community, and the original model for community is the Creation itself in all its complex interrelationship.

EFFICIENCY, ECONOMY, WEALTH, and interdependence all amount to the same thing in the natural community you will find on a prairie hilltop. Here and there on the wooded hillsides that make up much of the valley's north-facing slopes, there are small grassy openings — ridges and knolls where the drainage will not support tree growth. I passed part of one afternoon in the middle of such a clearing, on a knoll high on the slopes of a stretch of the valley downstream of Lake Katepwe.

The patch of prairie was no more than eighty feet in diameter, the crown of a hill oriented to the west. The grass had not been grazed for a number of years so it was high and thick yet neither thatched nor lodging over. I sat on the summit, surrounded by hundreds of silverleaf psoralea in blossom, electric blue flowers set among silver green leaves. A dense growth of porcupine grass supported the blooms, waving out-stretched awns, five inches long, catching the sunlight as they danced away from the wind, each with its spiralled bands of dark purple-brown alternating with straw yellow, like needle-thin candy canes. Sprays of Western wheat grass showed blue-green here and there through the other grasses, but the species that dominated the circle of prairie was blue grama grass. Atop each stem of grama grass was a mauve flag, an inch-long inflorescence, perpendicular to the stem. Strips of grama grass, taking the sunnier xeric spots on the hill, looked like parades of miniature standard-bearers pausing to catch their breath on a climb. At the margins of the clearing, where the poplars provided some relief from the sun, I could just make out small stands of big bluestem coming into flower.

Beyond that fringe of big bluestem, the world shifted into the ecolo-gies of aspen woodland, but in the centre of the clearing where I sat, everything but the birdsong and a few decaying poplar leaves said "prairie." I concentrated my attention on a smaller circle of the place, a piece barely larger than my outstretched hand and immediately to the right of my folded right knee. It was a relatively barren sample of prairie, the surface strewn with flakes of limestone among tufts of pas-ture sage, some young blades of Western wheat grass, one eight-inch seedling of snowberry, a mat of moss phlox well past bloom, and one plant of blue grama dangling its yellow stamens into the little breezes that passed just above ground level. There was evidence of other lives that had come and gone: two curled maple leaves from last fall; a frag-ment of almost fully composted animal dung, likely deer; four wing cases of ladybird beetles; and two from some larger beetle. In the half-hour of my vigil, several other animals came and went, showing their interest in my hilltop sample. A blue darner damselfly flew in briefly to prod the grama grass stems. Small red and black ants crossed the circle at a rate of one every ten or twenty seconds. A prairie butterfly, the common wood nymph, hovered once above the tips of the grass blades. All in a circle smaller than a dinner plate.

The sandy soil; the larger animal that left the dung; the regimen of moisture, sunlight, and evaporation; the plants with their specialized niches and give-and-take with soil micro-organisms and insects — all dwell within an ecology that despite change and local cataclysm (fire or a burrowing animal) stays whole and true by way of Creation's authentic efficiencies: interdependence, symbiosis, community succession, and the cycling of energy and materials through trophic levels. The circle I drew around the little patch of prairie of course existed only in my mind. I could have drawn wider circles concentrically, taking in the community of organisms that use the clearing and then beyond its apron of saskatoon bushes to the surrounding woodland world. Even from my seat, I could hear and see spotted towhees, orange-crowned warblers, black-capped chickadees, red-eyed vireos, clay-coloured sparrows, eastern kingbirds, western wood pewees, and, above the hillside, a red-tailed hawk on the wing. When I stood to walk around the clearing, I found a wood frog and several more hilltop butterflies: two species of fritillary, common sulfurs, a pearl crescent, two kinds of hairstreaks, and more common wood nymphs. Two animals seemed to dominate the clearing, at least while I was there. If I strayed to look at bluestem or another plant near the edge, a pair of eastern kingbirds, protecting their nest somewhere in the shrubbery, chased me back to my place in the middle. The other dominant species was the ant, which usually abbreviates a prairie sit. I was a local cataclysm and perhaps an opportunity to the ants. In my boots and up my pant legs taking microscopic mouthfuls of me, they were doing their best to return this large reservoir of nutrients and energy to the soil. And the mouthfuls will ultimately make their way down to the Qu'Appelle, cycled through countless other lives, metabolized and reconstituted in the ephemeral moments of the ecological neighbourhood reaching out to the river as skunk, black currant, ruffed grouse, red-osier dogwood, snowshoe hare, aspen, great horned owl, coyote, bullrush, muskrat, caddis fly, minnow, leech, walleye, and so on.

Everything eventually comes to the river on such tributaries. A sound human culture, like an ecosystem, thrives according to the rate and quality of what it takes and what it relinquishes. It is the relinquishing, the sacrifices, that interest me when I compare the efficiency of a piece of prairie with the efficiency of a modern farm. After the countless reincarnations that carry the energy and nutrients of the hilltop downslope to the Calling River, the molecules that once formed life up on a grama-grass knoll will return again to the land for local cycling before they are finally borne away to distant deltas and seas. Throughout, the river holds fertility and loss, life and death together, forming the final measure of efficiency.

That, I tell myself, is what prairie rivers once were and what they could be again: the living communal measure of true wealth and efficiency, recognized and upheld in our bond with neighbours — town and country, native and immigrant, human and non-human; the lifeblood of a renewed public ethic that would evaluate each technological opportunity that turns our heads, asking always, What are we giving up, what are we losing, and what are we doing to our water and our people when we take up this new tool? Would this labour-saving device or this new marketing system satisfy the river?

*Chapter Fourteen*

# SOUTH FROM
# LAST MOUNTAIN LAKE

THE CAR RADIO ANNOUNCED the names of five people recently inducted into the Saskatchewan Agricultural Hall of Fame. Three of them were scientists; the other two, I assumed, were farmers, although I know of journalists and policy-makers who would qualify for this dubious honour.

I was on my way to an acreage south of Last Mountain Lake, where I would spend the day with two field researchers whose chances of becoming hall of famers were no greater than mine. Their science does not insert genetic material from a trout into barley; their data do not demonstrate that one man and a computer can raise and feed 80,000 chickens. The two researchers I was to spend the day with were out looking at rivers, creeks, and stream beds, assessing the health of our riparian landscapes after a century of intensive agriculture.

When I arrived at Tom Harrison's place on the sandy plains south of Last Mountain Lake, he was finishing his business with a gas-line surveyor. This was one of the details of outfitting his bit of prairie heaven: a modest trailer hidden by an aspen bluff and anchored to the flank of enough native grass to satisfy him, his twenty-five cattle, and a border collie.

Tom is a range specialist for the Saskatchewan Wetland Corporation. "Glorified technician," he scoffed, cowboy modesty as ready as rope at branding time. "I spend most of my time designing grazing systems."

Tom walks convincingly in cowboy boots. Long, lean frame; polite, deferential manner; tanned face with lines-around-the-mouth smile; and a crescent-shaped scar next to each eye ("I had an accident-prone childhood") — he is the young man every ranch-mother wants her daughter to wed and wishes she had done so herself thirty years before. The quality of our pastures might improve significantly in this region if more of the landowners Tom dealt with were female.

I had come out to Tom's acreage to learn something about his riparian-areas research project. We would spend the day in the field with one of his summer research assistants, a young woman from Regina named Les Hall, who was taking inventory on a few sites on the Qu'Appelle and its tributaries immediately upstream of Lumsden, just a short drive south of Tom's.

Les works for Tom because she loves native grass, perhaps even more than Tom does. He grew up on a Saskatchewan farm. Les has the zeal of the convert; she is the city girl who, after leaving home, discovered how she felt about prairie landscapes. Away at an environmental studies course in Victoria, Les became fascinated by the possibilities of prairie restoration. She had heard and read about a large restoration project in Wisconsin, and it caught her imagination.

"Before long it was all I could think about. I realized I had been living on the prairie without really knowing what it was. I didn't know if I had ever seen real prairie, even though I had been living in a Prairie province. That was three years ago. I moved back to Regina and started my master's degree in geography, focusing on prairie restoration."

At one point in our day, Les told me that she wants to do something right by the land, to somehow make amends with the prairie. There was no mistaking her reverence. She seemed to be watching where she placed each step, and she was slow and gentle with the plants, admonishing Tom, only half jokingly, when he yanked a Solomon's seal up for a better look. The teasing between Tom and Les carried on through the day, forming the surface of an affectionate regard for one another. Once, with Tom out of earshot, Les admitted she envied his ability to read a landscape. "It's one thing to grow up with it as Tom has," she said.

"He's a rural person. It's another to have to learn it as an adult. He's just more at home in the landscape. Sees more than I do right away."

Tom has taught himself the taxonomy of riparian plants, but his first love showed itself when we backed away from the river's edge to visit the upland prairie of a "riparian" hillside. Gracefully and easily, he pointed to the "increasers" and "decreasers" on the pasture — the grasses and forbs that either multiply or diminish under the selective nibbling of cattle. I mentioned that I had trouble separating fescue from bluegrasses. A moment later, Tom had located some of each, showing me the distinguishing floral characteristics. When I said that the pasture seemed to have no native wheat grasses, he immediately found a stand of Western wheat grass, helping me to learn the look of its ragged, blue-tinged blades and gnarled, trashy rootstalks.

The day passed pleasantly, as days will when you crouch over flowers and grasses next to a river. We complained about heedless farmers and channelization, keyed strange flowers, discussed prairie restoration, and swapped stories about the state of our prairie waterways and the ignorance of the water mandarins. Tom said he knew of farmers who bulldozed strips of riparian aspen woods as a method of controlling beavers. At a recent meeting of water and conservation managers at which Tom delivered his presentation on riparian-areas research, an official from SaskWater approached him afterwards, saying, "Those riparian areas are having an impact on agricultural Saskatchewan."

"I didn't know how to answer the guy," Tom said. "Here was a SaskWater representative saying basically that flowing water is a threat to agriculture unless it is controlled."

As we came to each inventory site along the river, Tom and Les made their measurements and estimations, sitting on the bank and filling out forms with values and check marks representing channel movement, confinement, and entrenchment; stream regulation; stream-bank soil texture; stream dimensions; channel sinuosity, gradient, and orientation; upland vegetation; and erosion classes and causes. They would speculate on the causes of anything unusual we found at a site: a large maple tree tossed into the river channel from its original position on the bank fifteen feet above; a ridge of raised soil covered by tame grasses separating a farmer's field from the riverbank; a wide strand of unvegetated silt along the stream channel; a shortage of hydrophytic (water-loving) plants such as willows for long stretches of channel; destabilized and slumping banks everywhere; a two-foot thick deposition of silt from the spring flood that almost buried the brome grass understorey in a maple woods; badly overgrazed river banks; carcasses of calves, their ankles bound with the orange twine that was used to drag them into the maples; more trees down in the river, one with a trunk as stout as a beer keg, its branches in flower though it was already dead.

Punctuating their commentary was a continuous dialogue:

"Any border between the crop and the woods?"

"Nope."

"Stream width?"

"Ten, maybe twelve metres."

"Bank width?"

"Twenty, no thirty metres."

"What's the stream edge like?"

"No emergent vegetation and lots of bare soil."

This went on as Les and Tom rated and recorded the indicators of riparian health in this portion of the watershed. After the measurements and estimations at each site, they would toss a square of metal tubing called a quadrat into the riverside vegetation. By taking this random sample of plant life, estimating the percentage of the quadrat covered by leaf litter, bare ground, and each plant identified, they can determine species richness and composition. Finally, before moving downstream to the next survey plot, Les would photograph the site.

Throughout the day, Tom spoke about the way agriculture affects the river: "One of the primary causes of unnatural levels of erosion like we are seeing here is channelization and dyking. Erosion and deposition are supposed to be in a sort of equilibrium along a river as it moves across its floodplain. . . .

"If you want to improve these areas, you start by adjusting the stocking rates [cattle per acre] and the timing of grazing. . . . We're seeing spots where all the understorey has been grazed and all that's left are the large trees. . . . What happens when the mature trees die in an overgrazed riparian area? There are no young trees coming up to replace them — the understorey is grazed away as high as the cattle can reach, and there's nothing on the ground but an inch of Kentucky blue-grass. If you've seen bluegrass roots you'll know they don't go down very far — they can't stabilize the banks. The natural equilibrium main-tained by hydrophytic plants like willows and rushes is gone. There is nothing left to hold the streambank. . . .

"The sediment load in this river is far too high. It was never a clear river, but before we started cultivating the prairie it would have been much less cloudy. . . .

"Brome grass will show you how cultivation affects a riparian area. Away from the fields on a native hillside there's no brome invading, but as soon as you get near the interface with agriculture — whack! You've got brome grass up the wazoo."

When we returned to Tom's place at the end of the day, I asked where his own cattle were. He said he was pasturing them on a rented quarter section not far away, to give his own 160 acres a rest. Before I left, he took me out to a vulnerable spot on his pasture that he is rehabilitating. It was not a riparian area, but the kind of place cattle soon destroy: a blowout in sandy soil next to a moist area. Tom pointed to plants growing in what had been bare sand the year before. Looking up from the new grass, he smiled a satisfied, proprietary smile, pleased to see the rush of native growth stabilizing soil that had been blowing for years. From somewhere on the flats of Tom's prairie, a Baird's sparrow and then a pipit sang out their ancient and abiding songs.

## Chapter Fifteen

# PELICAN POINT

THE SUNDAY I ATTENDED St. Mary's in Lanigan, I went out to see the Wolverine Community Pasture, a large piece of native upland grass managed by the federal government a few miles north and west of town. Sixteen thousand acres of grass in two parcels of light alkali soil, the land is drained by creeks that send their water to Last Mountain Lake, the longest natural lake in southern Saskatchewan. "Natural" has been compromised to the degree that the lake is now managed and supplemented with inflow from the Qu'Appelle River near the town of Craven. But at Wolverine Pasture, where Delwood Creek winds through the mixed-grass prairie, it was easy to forget the incursions of modern water-control schemes. The rudbeckia was in its yellow and black-dotted splendour, gaillardia spangled the grass with its bright flakes of orange, and grassland birds were everywhere casting songs into the breeze. Two Swainson's hawks gripped the wind above their prairie world, teetering toward the grass and its promise of voles and gophers.

Later, a few miles away, on Wolverine Lake, I watched white pelicans fishing in flotillas, and a dozen yellowlegs and semi-palmated sandpipers. The shorebirds were the first back from the north, an unfailing sign of the summer's turn toward cooler days when the skies would ripple and clamour with the thronging waterbirds of autumn. In the nineteenth century, another naturalist in another July looked at similar landscape north of Last Mountain Lake and thought he saw Judah in a wet year, the promised land, or at least land that promised to complete Ottawa's colonizing destiny:

> *The following notes from my journal will illustrate the flora in the vicinity of Long Lake [Last Mountain Lake] as seen in the first week in July, 1879. Flowers are a most conspicuous feature of the prairie. Hedysarum and various Astragali vieing* [sic] *with the lily and the vetch in lovliness* [sic] *and luxuriance. Often whole acres would be red and purple with beautiful flowers, and the air laden with the perfume of roses. Sometimes lilies* (Lilium Philadelphicum) *are so abundant that they covered an acre of ground bright red.*[34]

This testimony came from John Macoun, the head botanist on the Canadian Geological Survey, the last official expedition sent to the North-West to settle once and for all the question whether the prairies could be farmed and settled. The financiers and politicians who owned the land companies and railways wanted a positive report, but these gushing descriptions of a region that was soon being referred to in Ottawa as the "Fertile Garden of the Northwest" exceeded all expectations. Palliser's report had been pessimistic; Hind was somewhat encouraging, for he did recommend settlement on the plains, but he was too prosaic. What was needed was an explorer-visionary with a gift for turns of phrase that would catch a peasant's eye when printed on leaflets promoting immigration. Macoun, who saw crops where others saw deserts, was the man for the job. His book, published in 1882, is like a farmer's almanac full of nothing but sunny weather forecasts: "The soil is unsurpassed for richness. . . . an excellent farming country is entered upon. . . . eminently suited for grazing purposes. . . . these hills are flanked by marshes and hence protected from fire. . . . good poplar for building purposes will be found on the hills. . . . as there is abundance of timber in that section and good water, a large settlement will spring up in a year or two."[35]

Macoun knew something of birds and was moved by the abundant avifauna he found near his camp north of Last Mountain Lake:

> *Multitudes of pelican, geese, ducks, avocets, phalaropes, water hens,*
> *and grebe, besides innumerable snipe and plover everywhere, in the*
> *marshes at the head of the lake or along its shores, or on small islands*
> *lying to the south of the camp. This was early in July and experience*
> *tells me that not one tenth was then seen of the bird life assembled in*
> *September and October.*[36]

According to Macoun and the Canadian Geological Survey the plains were fertile and verdant, its natives few and docile, and the land reserved by God for farm settlement. By 1883, the Canadian Pacific Railway had bisected the region and the flood of settlers was underway. Two years later saw the events at Batoche, Fish Creek, and Cut Knife Hill, culminating in the hanging of Louis Riel in Regina and the incarceration of Big Bear and Poundmaker. Unaccountably, in 1887, the dust having barely settled from this police action, the lieutenant governor of the new North-West Territories, Edgar Dewdney, wrote a letter to the minister of the interior advising him that what the territory really needed, now that peace had been restored to the land, was a nice little bird sanctuary. Sir John A. Macdonald was delighted by the idea. In June of that year, Macdonald and thirteen members-in-council passed an order to preserve much of the marsh and nesting islands at the head of Last Mountain Lake. This one letter from Dewdney, unlike the several he had written earlier petitioning Macdonald to grant the people of Riel and Dumont their own land, got immediate results. The North-West, it seemed, was a place where native peoples and native birds were relegated to reserves, but half-breeds need not apply. Macdonald was a political realist; he knew his constituents. Grant a few miles of shoreline to wild birds, and local settlers may whine about losing some hayland; do the same for a community of half-caste Frenchmen, and all of English Canada will call for your resignation.

So it was that Canada's first migratory bird sanctuary came to be. It was 1920 before the Canadian government designated another sanctuary anywhere in its domain. The Last Mountain Lake National Wildlife Area, as it is called today, has expanded to cover 14,300 hectares of lake, island, wetland, and prairie. In addition to its status as a national wildlife area, the reserve has been designated a Ramsar site and a Western Hemisphere Shorebird Reserve.[37] When Canada's Globally

Important Bird Areas are established in the next few years, Last Mountain Lake will almost certainly be on the list.

The sanctuary is recognized internationally as an important staging area for shorebirds, as a resting and feeding area for the world's remaining population of whooping cranes on their fall migration, as critical habitat for more than ninety species of prairie waterbirds, including the American white pelican and the endangered piping plover, and as a reserve and research area containing thousands of acres of mixed-grass prairie. It gives the Qu'Appelle basin a foothold of ecological well-being, an anchor to the original order of life in the region. Walking its trails past buffalo rubbing stones and cattail marshes, down a peninsula to the water's edge, you can lose sight of fencelines and farms, and rest, finally, on damp beach sand where it is possible to allow your dreams to sweep southward over the long lake and its history, until the prairie world comes near to completing itself within the circle of your imagining.

South along the lake's narrowing slash into the belly of the watershed, before the CPR and Dewdney's advice, there was Isaac Cowie in his Hudson's Bay fort, Last Mountain House, at the foot of the lake, trading with the Assiniboine and Cree for pemmican to fuel the northern fur industry, cursing the camp of Indians across the lake from him at Little Arm Bay — Young Dogs, he called them, a band that would sooner raid than trade, which made them in Cowie's eyes a shiftless and unproductive lot; and before Cowie, there was Daniel Harmon, the young North West Company trader who dealt briefly in 1804 with Indian people on the east side of Last Mountain Lake and who was unable to sleep on much of his trade journey to the Qu'Appelle Valley and the great lake, so convinced was he that at any moment he would be "torn to pieces by wild beasts"; and after Cowie and the Hudson's Bay Company selling Rupert's Land to Canada, after Macoun and the survey, there was the on-rush of settlement, and Last Mountain Lake became for a short time the preferred avenue of north-south transport between the new settlement at Davidson and a hill known as Last Mountain, a small western outlier of the Touchwood Hills; and this region from Davidson to Last Mountain had been bought up by an English land speculator, William Pearson, who in the early 1900s commissioned freight barges and steamers to carry landseekers, lumber, livestock, and other goods to the new settlements along the lake, with their fresh bloom of lumberyards, grain elevators, and shipping docks, until a branch rail line was completed in 1911 and the steamboats were docked, the last an elegant two-hundred-passenger steamer with a fully upholstered and wood-panelled cabin, the *Lady of the Lake*, she was called, officially the *Qu'Appelle*, and it made its last runs hauling picnickers up and down the lake before it too was hauled up onto the shores in 1913;[38] and after the branch line connected the lake to Regina, people began coming out from town and nearby farms in the summer heat, to be next to an expanse of water, blue relief from the dust-grey streets and overworked fields, and they built cottages on the shores, rows of clapboard and tar-paper shacks queuing up the slopes from the water's edge to the valley rim, at places they named Lumsden Beach, Buena Vista, Regina Beach, Kedleston Beach, and Pelican Point.

PELICAN POINT IS A SPIT of sand at the inside of the lake's dog-leg bend eastward, across from the inlet of the Arm River where the Young Dogs once camped. Pelicans used to rear young there on the point. Bob Symons saw them in the 1920s or 1930s, before the water managers placed a dam at the outlet of the lake, raising the water level and flooding much of the spit and its ground-nesting birds. Now the only nesting colony for pelicans in the entire Qu'Appelle basin is an island in the bird sanctuary on the north end of the lake.

Robert David Symons, one of the prairie's finest naturalists, artists, and writers, grew up in Sussex, England. Like Ernest Thompson Seton before him, he came to Canada as a young man, dreaming of wild places and noble savages on the frontier. He lived the remainder of his life on the plains, valleys, and forests of the Canadian West, making his way as a horse-wrangler, a wildlife officer, and a homesteader, before returning in his retirement to southern Saskatchewan, where he had first learned the songs of prairie birds and the landscapes of coulee, coteau, and butte. His health failing, he and his wife, Hope, spent their last years in a small house in Silton, a village just above the east arm of Last Mountain Lake. They summered at Pelican Point in a tiny shack surrounded by scrub maples and caragana, which Symons, with the Englishman's love of naming homes, christened Meadowlark Cottage.

I went looking for Meadowlark Cottage after reading every book Symons published. If someone were to ask me to name a hero, I would without a pause say Bob Symons, though I never had a chance to meet him. He died long before I reached adulthood and learned that the prairie world was good for something more than pot-shooting. Those who knew him say he was an irascible so-and-so much of the time, given to sullen moods and self-righteous diatribes against materialism and "mechanized mankind," but they remember too the irrepressible dinner guest and raconteur and the man who knew the Northern Great Plains better than any white man of his day. They say that he could look at almost any landscape photograph taken in the region and identify the location, and often the precise place, where the photographer had stood to take the picture.

His books, published in the sixties and early seventies (two were Doubleday Book-of-the-Month selections) were exciting to read for they spoke to me about my home landscapes and history. Symons was our first home-grown voice of protest against the excesses of agriculture and the diminishment of native peoples and wild places on the prairie. His artwork, like his prose, was not always polished, but it arose from a natural authenticity and identifiable style that I find compelling, as much for its honest interpretation of nature as for the character it reveals in Symons himself. As a naturalist who writes about and some-times paints prairie landscapes, I was immediately drawn to Symons, the story of his life, and the persona he created in his books.

One midsummer afternoon a few years ago, I walked up the hill from Pelican Point to find Symons's tiny cottage at the end of the road. It was still there, entangled by bushes and trees gone weedy, a dark little hovel on a hilltop now given to grander structures. Virtually all of his writing was done from his desk inside the cottage, where he could look out upon the landscapes of Last Mountain Lake and spin his tales in terse, lively prose. Here he wrote books with such names as *Many Trails, Silton Seasons, Where the Wagon Led, North by North-West, Still the Wind Blows, Hours and the Birds,* and *The Broken Snare*.

I spoke to a man watering his patch of grass down the road from the cottage. He said he remembered Symons as a "peculiar" man — *he was a writer, you know, kept to himself a lot, not that friendly*. In *Silton Seasons*, Symons expressed some disdain for the weekend visitors to Pelican

Point, their petunia and bluegrass landscaping, and their ignorance of the wild gardens that survived in pastures just beyond their cabins. One of my favourite passages from *Silton Seasons*, which contains his reflections on village and country life near Last Mountain Lake, describes a small amphitheatre of native pasture a short way from his cottage. I walked there on my visit and found the tipi rings he loved to sit amid, imagining former dwellers. I sat there too, on a large boulder imagining his imagining and listening for the tenor of his words again:

> But over the first steep hill, on the upland, is a little hollow or amphitheatre, green with prairie grass and bright in spring with nodding clumps of wild onions. This is a farmer's pasture, because these undulating slopes of downland have not been thought worthy of the ploughshare's consideration. Few people come here, for this is the bald, rocky prairie which no cars can traverse, no motorboats navigate, and where no golf can be played. Within three hundred yards of the cottage, it is as remote as Tibet and as full of mystery. . . .

> I sit sometimes on a marbled and gilded limestone rock and look towards this old camping ground, with my thoughts out of time and date, and I think I can hear the thumping of hobbled horses — lean, fleet Indian mustangs. They crop the young grass, and pause and look intently now this way, now that, blowing softly, then they crop again — but their ears are not still, and flick back and forth, for they were foaled on these plains and know its hazards. Steadily they tear the squeaking grass, and their jaw muscles work back and forth over the bony structures below their liquid eyes.[39]

If I could be a ghost like Symons, perched above Last Mountain Lake, evoking older phantoms that belong to its hills and shorelines, I would call forth buffalo hunters and pemmican traders, men who fished here to live, couples who danced on the floorboards of *The Qu'Appelle* as it chugged from Valeport to Glen Harbour, farmers who watered their Clydesdales in a bay, wives who washed their children's breeches in the shallows, and summer people who raised the first summer shanties on the hillsides above Pelican Point, high enough to avoid the rising waters of springtime, when the point itself would half disappear before the waters receded and the great white pelicans arrived to claim their own summer sites along the jetty.

Pelicans still come now and then to the southern end of the lake. When we visit Regina or Lumsden Beach on summer weekends, we see small squadrons flapping white and black wings over the point and riding the thermals on their way to the marshes at Valeport. Many of these are non-breeding adults and subadults, but some are nesting birds from the colony at the head of the lake. Fifty miles is nothing to a hungry pelican.

A HUNDRED MILES IS nothing to an excited birder. When the call goes out that something rare has shown up on Last Mountain Lake, the bird-listers from Regina and Saskatoon converge on the beaches of Little Arm or Pelican Point to scope the waves for the living, feathered marvel, the scrap of dislocated biodiversity that was, until now, represented by a blank space on their checklists.

The waters from Little Arm Bay to Pelican Point and east beyond Regina and Lumsden Beaches and Valeport have proven to be the region's best waterbird hotspot in late fall. The birds seem to use Last Mountain Lake as a north-south migration corridor, and so the keenest of Saskatchewan birders go out in October and November looking for their annual serving of rarities: red-throated and Pacific loons; Clark's grebes; surf, black, and white-winged scoters; Barrow's goldeneyes; Thayer's and glaucous gull; gyrfalcon; and jaegers. Oh, such names! To a birder these words are titillating and suggestive of an ardour satisfied. Birding, at least as I have known it, is the polar opposite of the Zen ideal of *hatori*, to live above desire. Birders wear desire on their sleeves. We are lit by a desire to have the lake show us something new or unexpected: a huge raft of mergansers, a diving osprey, a late warbler. It is unmitigated desire and, like aging lovers, we complain about the poor prospects and extol the good old days when alcids and eiders threw themselves at our feet.

Still, on a good day, we will sometimes come upon a bird that has seldom or never before been recorded in the province — a slaty-backed gull from the Pacific Rim, a black-legged kittiwake or king eider from the Arctic. Walking the old rail bed that fifty years ago bore train coaches that bristled with beach umbrellas, picnic baskets, and day-trippers from Regina, we peer through German and Japanese optics at specks on the water, muttering that the "hooded mergs" (mergansers) are scarce this year, and where the hell are the loons today; remember that yellow-billed loon two Novembers ago, just before freeze-up? And we lament the subdivisions that consume more of the natural hillside along the lake each year, and curse the people who build monster-homes with attached dwellings for their sport-utility vehicles, folks who love "nature" as long as it doesn't chew on their Lombardy poplars.[40]

The first time I went bird-watching at the south end of the lake, I knew nothing. Nothing about birds, about the lake itself, its history, or its engineered interflow with the Qu'Appelle. It was easy to embrace its scalloped landscapes, the recurving bay at the inlet of the Arm river, the bouldered beaches along Kinookimaw, the vast marshes at Valeport, the poplar bluff atop Little Arm. Innocent of its history or its tenure, I walked the land and let it come into my senses.

It was fall and our tour leader identified a low, thumping sound as a ruffed grouse. Although I had shot them as a boy — we called them bush partridge — I had never seen a ruffed grouse on its drumming log, so I left the group eating lunch and wandered toward the poplar woods that reverberated with soft thumps. I crawled on my belly through the thicket-laced understorey toward the sound, eventually finding the bird rooster-posed on its log, beginning each solo with a few creaky flaps of its wings, rapidly accelerating to a low-pitched, air-thrumming whirr. On my way back out of the woods, a patch of aspen two or three acres at most, I noticed cleared areas and roadways arranged in a pattern that said "campground." Someone had built and then abandoned a public campground on the site not long ago. Rejoining the group, I asked if anyone knew what had happened to the campground. The answer surprised me, made me a little uneasy about our presence there. The old campground, it turned out, belongs to an Indian band, along with all the land from Kinookimaw to Little Arm. No one had mentioned that we were guests or trespassers on reserve land. There were no houses other than the cottages at Kinookimaw, and those were full of white folks like any cottages on the lake. As far as I knew, the nearest reserve was forty miles east at Piapot. Like most Saskatchewan people, I had driven through reserves before, on highways where you receive the white man's car-window summary: run-down bungalows, rusting Fords, barefoot children on the roadside, happy dogs everywhere. The standard approach is drive on through, watch for pedestrians, and, whatever you do, don't stop until you pass the "YOU ARE NOW LEAVING RESERVE LAND" sign.

It felt strange to be walking on Indian land that first time at Little Arm, partly because we were trespassers and partly because the land did not fit any of the categories I knew. It was not public land, but it was not private either, for it belonged to a group of people — and a group to which I did not and could never belong. It looked much like any farm or pasture land I had seen before, except that there were no fences or livestock, and no signs of grazing or cultivation.

Later I learned that the reserve is called Last Mountain Lake. It belongs to a group of Indian bands from the Touchwood and Qu'Appelle reserves. They share profits from the cottage subdivision but do not use any of the land to house their own people. It has become a popular area for Regina Beach people to fish for perch or walk their dogs, and for a long time the timbers of the abandoned railway bridge spanning Little Arm Bay made for a pleasant, if somewhat treacherous, stroll to the hillsides farther north and west up the lakeshore.

I still return each fall, sometimes in the company of birder friends, to look for rare birds on Little Arm and Kinookimaw Beach. When the birds are thin, my thoughts turn to the land's recent ironies. Here was once a camp of Indians who would not trade with the HBC; today their descendants manage a small piece of it as resort property; the rest is left alone. Where are the people, the descendants of those who had to put up with the early traders on this lake, Cowie and Harmon? How do they use and regard the land that the treaties allowed them? Do they regret their great-grandfathers' hospitality when they hear the new-comers claiming that the treaties removed the Creator's title over the prairie and placed it into the hands of governors, land developers, and settlers? Do they wonder if there is a way to rescind hospitality, to with-draw the trust offered by forefathers who never dreamed that this fraudulent transfer of title would be used to evict them, the prairie's long-dwellers, from their ancient precincts, confining them to reserves, small scraps of land from which untold generations would wander like displaced birds drifting over a jetty on outstretched wings, over the old grounds, now cultivated, dammed, and built upon — not recognizing that here their ancestors summered and raised young; here they gathered before moving for winter?

## Chapter Sixteen

# PIAPOT

DOWNSTREAM OF THE OUTFLOW of Last Mountain Lake where it joins the Qu'Appelle Valley at Craven in a series of channels and control structures, where the dykes were recently raised because the annual country music festival did not want its campers to get soggy; downstream of the Grande Fourche, as the *hivernant* called it during the last century, past a smattering of acreages occupied by retired people and commuters, the valley turns from northeast orientation to east, the woods on the southern slopes thicken, and bog orchids begin to appear at floating fens where small tributaries run into the bottomlands.

Here the great Cree statesman, Chief Piapot, loath to confine his people anywhere, but having no choice, finally agreed to take a reserve. The treaty-makers had wanted him to take land elsewhere, but he held out for a reserve in the Qu'Appelle, where his band would have opportunities in towns developing nearby as well as land suitable for both farming and ranching.

This I learned from Florence Carrier, an elder I visited on the Piapot reserve one afternoon in the summer of 1996. Florence told me that Piapot was a fierce defender of his people's right to religious practice. As an old man he was thrown in jail for three months for defying a prohibition against Cree ceremonies. I had met Florence the year before in an introductory Cree language class she was teaching in the city.

I phoned her and told her I would like permission to walk around her reserve, looking at plants, birds, and landscapes. I asked her about protocol and yammered away, trying to assure her that I would not do anything disrespectful or inappropriate: I was not looking for traditional stories, I said, or cultural property, only an opportunity to get a better look at the way reserves in the valley strike a bargain between wild space and domestic space.

There was a long pause and then, "You'd better come see me and we can talk."

ON THE DAY I WAS to go to Piapot, I stopped by the drugstore to get supplies. Florence is an elder of a Plains band, which means she must be given tobacco in such circumstances. "What kind of tobacco?" I asked an archaeologist at the museum.

"Player's Light is good. And don't be giving them pipe tobacco or anything like that. If you ask a simple question or courtesy, offer four cigarettes. Four is a sacred number."

Another friend said it was appropriate to also bring a small gift, so I picked up a box of chocolates with the cigarettes. Sometime after I had left the city, the bizarre symbolism of this came to me: these vestiges of New World plunder — processed tobacco and Pot of Gold chocolates — are all I have to bear me across the gap between my race and Florence's. I was nervous.

Just north of Regina I drove past a fenced enclosure where the city's largest manufacturer keeps a "wild animal park" with deer, elk, geese, and a few beleaguered buffalo. The park is intended as a friendly buffer zone between the company's steel-pipe foundry and the community. From the highway, all that I could see on my drive out to Piapot was a trio of ersatz tipis made of steel and lined up one, two, three like cigar-store Indians.

The entrance to Piapot reserve has a large sign proclaiming "Ahaw Tawaw Nehiyaw Patinak" — Home of the Plains Cree. When I arrived at Florence's place, she was outside, packing her tent, campstove, and lawn chair in preparation for a weekend trip to a gathering at Neekaneet reserve in the Cypress Hills. I helped her tote some of the gear over to her brother-in-law's house, a short walk away. He was planning to go early and would save Florence a campsite.

The gathering, Florence said, was a celebration, a ceremony of prayer and thankfulness for having passed through another winter into the season of regeneration and life.

"First prayer, then joy. First sacrifice, then joyfulness," she said chuckling softly as she placed her chair into the truck. "It is always this way with us."

I could see she was excited about going to Neekaneet. As she spoke, a smile would flicker now and then across her round face, or she would chuckle "heh, heh," amused by something — such as when she told me, "The government in the old days outlawed our ceremonies but now they are encouraging us to do it! Heh, heh!"

It is hard not to envy this life that praises seasons, honours the God indwelling in Creation, and holds religious ceremonies in valleys and on hilltops. Non-aboriginal people are fascinated these days by the rituals, stories, and philosophies of the first prairie dwellers. Corporations hold workshops on cross-cultural themes, inviting elders in to smudge the attendees with sage. Cree teenagers peddle dream catchers door to door in Regina. People seeking new therapies or a new faith go to medicine men and make four-day vision quests in the woods. Some of this arises from a legitimate and respectful sharing of cultural gifts, but some is bound to be touristic, shoddy, and exploitive, a glib commodification of the sacred.

The year of my visit to Piapot, two white people were married on the reserve in a ceremony presided over by an elder who is open to sharing traditions with non-Indians. The groom was an airline executive from Switzerland, in his fifties, and the bride was a Canadian woman in her forties. I watched a special television news report about the wedding. The usual effect of the TV camera in such circumstances is to drain the dignity, power, and meaning from even the most public of rituals. I was expecting a sham ceremony cooked up by a shrewd elder who saw an opportunity to take advantage of two white people with a lot of money and enthusiasm for "Indian culture." In the end, however, I saw little that seemed cheap or disrespectful. The two betrothed spoke softly and with great understanding and respect for the traditions of the Cree. They referred to their own experience and made no grand summaries about indigenous religion. They seemed thoughtful and unhurried, and had nothing of the tourist in their demeanour.

The camera showed the man as he prepared for the event and entered a sweat lodge with his closest male friends. The woman did the same in a separate group with her friends. The journalist, an aboriginal woman herself, did not allow the camera or her interviewing to intrude upon the proceedings. We watched the men and women emerging from their respective sweat lodges. They appeared peaceful, if somewhat dazed and drained, and as they blinked into the glare of daylight and stretched their spines, their faces shone. There was opportunity to say something flippant or ponderous, but no one did.

The wedding ceremony itself was moved into a round tent when the afternoon rain began. The light, diffused through cloud cover and the white tent walls, saturated the scene with rich colour. The couple wore ribbon shirts, a modern garment that people from various Indian nations have adopted for use on ceremonial occasions. The elder burned sweetgrass and sage and spoke both in Plains Cree and English to the gathering of friends and Piapot residents filling the tent. Afterwards people murmured quietly and smiled at the newlyweds.

As they would for any wedding ceremony, the couple paid for these services. The elder has been known to stage cultural shows for small groups of tourists, particularly Europeans, many of whom seem to have an unlimited enthusiasm for things Indian. The lines between culture and entertainment, education and sideshow, respect and exploitation are narrow enough here for some controversy. Some elders say that this is wrong, that the Cree ways of being and believing are not to be passed around so openly, before cameras and crowds of non-Indians. The white man has stolen everything else, they say, and now they will steal our culture. Others have said that the Creator gave the First People these traditions and this wisdom about how to live on the land not so that they could hoard it and protect it, but so that it might be shared among those who need it most and will regard it with respect. White people too come from the Creator, and if they are ever to live here well, they must learn some of the original ways.

Watching the televised wedding, I soon forgot about these issues. The colour and songs of the land itself took over and redeemed what

could have been a tawdry depiction of Cree ceremony. In the background, behind each of the speakers interviewed, behind the
canvas-covered sweat lodges and the Indian dancers, were the shimmering side-hills of coulees bound for the valley. As the bride spoke,
answering questions about why she wanted to have an "Indian wedding," a meadowlark sang out its clear and liquid notes. Later I heard a
vesper sparrow. The green setting and the birdsong somehow sanctified
the event, carrying it above human longing and argument.

Florence laughed again when I handed her the cigarettes and chocolates. I thought it was my awkwardness, but later she told me that if I
bring gifts to other elders, I should try to bring something more appropriate — perhaps a blanket rather than Pot of Gold. We got into my
station wagon and went for a tour of Piapot, Florence showing me the
place where she grew up across the valley, the settled areas, the farmland. As we coasted down the road that took us through the village past
the gas station, band office, and school, Florence gestured at the far
valley walls and told me her grandfather's story of how the Qu'Appelle
was formed by a great torrent of water cutting through the land. Her
grandfather, she said, was a hard-working farmer who had no patience
for laziness and drunkenness.

   As a child, Florence was away from the guidance and teachings of
her family for ten months of the year. Along with every other school-
aged child from the Qu'Appelle reserves, she was taken to the
residential school at Lebret, where she was forbidden to speak her language and taught that Indian ways were wrong.

   In the early years of the century, the federal government began to
restrict the movement of Indian people in Canada, more or less confining them to their reserves. When Treaty Four had been signed in
1874, the Indian leaders understood that reserve land would be merely
a home from which their people would be free to travel to meet their
economic and social needs. There was no mention of confinement. After
the turn of the century, however, white settlers began complaining to
their governments that Indian farmers from local reserves were coming
into town to sell their vegetables, poultry, and eggs at prices the white
farmers could not match. It was unfair, the farmers said, because the
Indians owned their property in common and had the advantage of free

agricultural equipment and assistance. Soon after, legislation was passed to restrict off-reserve movement — part of what is now known as the Indian Act, one of the darkest pieces of jurisprudence enacted in a Canadian legislature. This measure to undercut the early agricultural efforts of First Nations seems especially sinister, when you bear in mind that for the first generation after the reserve system was established, settlers were complaining that Indian people were inept and lazy farmers, unwilling to lift a finger to help themselves. The law restricting people to their reserves was finally lifted during the 1960s, but it had already done its damage. In the preceding decades, the cliché of the helpless, shiftless Indian on social assistance took its place at the end of the long and degrading line of Indian forms we have constructed: innocent child of nature, bloodthirsty savage, conquered warrior, vanishing people, wise orator, powwow princess, flop-house drunk.

Now, most members of Piapot and the other Qu'Appelle bands live off-reserve in towns and cities where the economic base can support their growing population. You will still hear farmers and city people remark that there should be a penalty for living off the reserves, that if status Indians live in cities they should lose some of their treaty entitlement. Repealing the Indian Act has not removed all that confines Indian people.

All the more remarkable are the few farmers with land adjacent to reserves who learn to live gracefully with the contrast between their values and manners and those of their indigenous neighbours. Jack Semple grew up on a farm that bordered on Piapot. His house was a stone's throw from the boundary, and his nearest playmates were Cree boys. He remembers Saturday nights on the farm when their living room was full of men and boys from the reserve, all crowding around the television to watch the drama of Mahovlich, Bauer, and Delvecchio. Whenever it was *Hockey Night in Canada*, fans from Piapot would, as if drawn by some silent summons, show up on the Semple doorstep. On other nights it might be to borrow five dollars or to ask if the Semples had any chores they needed help with, or to use the telephone. TVs, electricity, and telephones had not yet come to Piapot homes; in fact electricity and telephone service has come late to most of Saskatchewan's reserves. Some Qu'Appelle reserves are just now receiving full telephone service.

Piapot men and boys hunted year round on the Semple fields for rabbits, grouse, and deer. Jack's father and older brothers hired men from the reserve regularly to do farm work: repair a fence, cut the hay, build a pen. One of these hired hands, Clayton, became a family friend. If there were no chores that needed tending when Clayton came by, they would put him to work building something, a bench perhaps or a set of flower boxes. Jack remembers Clayton as a man who could do a little of everything. He was a carpenter, a mechanic, an artist, even a barber. Every month or so, when there was no hay to mow, Mr. Semple would have Clayton give all the boys a trim.

These days, Jack is widely known as Canada's finest rhythm and blues guitarist. He is the quintessential born musician — someone who experiences life and memory by ear. Jack takes in the day's melodies and rhythms in a reflex as automatic as the one that lets him breathe. In the spring, he will sometimes ask me to identify a birdsong he has been hearing in the neighbourhood, recreating it for my ears in perfect pitch. The music of the Piapot Cree remains in his sonic archives too. He recalls as a boy in summer sitting on the valley rim and listening to the chanting voices rise up from the bottomlands, lifted by a low, throbbing drumbeat: Piapot's people, hockey fans and hunters, remembering to give thanks and celebrate.

From time to time when Jack's band is playing a Regina gig, he will feel a hand on his shoulder during a set break, turn and see Clayton's aging face: "Hey, boy, looks like you could use a haircut!"

WHEN WE RETURNED to Florence's driveway, I could hear the buzz of clay-coloured sparrows out the car window. A catbird and a yellow warbler dove back into the chokecherry bushes like bits of ribbon yanked on unseen strings. In Florence's neighbourhood — a scattered grouping of homes — the yards are separated by natural contours and vegetation. The lay of the land is hummocky moraine with small grassy hillocks and poplar-filled swales. The neighbour's place is always "just over the bush" or "past that hill." Gravel roads arc around the aspen and chokecherry bluffs, binding each household to its neighbours. Any mowed or culti-vated area is small compared to the expanses of vegetation left to wild grasses and bush. Always the buffer of nature; no two yards join in hedges or mowed grasses. There are no hedges. Only wolf willow and wild roses blooming within smelling range of most doorsteps. I could live in such a place, I thought to myself. But I am not Cree, my great-great-grandparents did not live in portable lodges that allowed them to take in the entire bioregion as home — a word that hovers uneasily above the government-issue bungalows of Piapot.

A people who have always regarded tens of thousands of square miles of the earth's surface as their dwelling place, will, when placed in houses on circumscribed tracts of land, make different choices in the way they strike their bargain with the immediate landscape. The interface between culture and nature on a prairie farm is cut neatly by a geometry of fences, lawns, and flower borders. At Piapot and the other Qu'Appelle reserves, however, the margin is usually a small and ill-defined area of rough grass cropped short around each house, enough room for the vehicles, a small deck or patio, a barbecue, perhaps a shed. Some houses have gardens and flower beds. Planted shelterbelts are almost non-existent; most houses are as exposed to the elements as a tipi on a hilltop.

At the same time, the margin for agriculture on a reserve is much narrower than it is on privately owned farmland. The fields veer around large aspen bluffs, sloughs, and yard sites; pasture land is often lightly grazed and left to native grasses. Economics and quota systems have encouraged farmers to plough, drain, and clear so they can maximize their seeded acreage, while Indian bands, despite their poverty and their large areas of land that agronomists would say is "reclaimable," have been less inclined to strip their land of its native vegetation.[41] You can see it clearly on an aerial-photo map or even as you drive past the boundaries of a reserve onto the surrounding farmland: a patchy collage of bush, meadows, pastures, and sloughs on one side of the line; miles of unvaried grain crops on the other.

Patchiness is important. The diversity of vegetative communities that I found at Piapot and many other reserves impressed me. Ecologists talk about patchiness as a precondition of biodiversity in some ecosystems. On reserves, it comes from letting nature get out of control from time to time. The Cree, Saulteaux, and Assiniboine people have never been averse to wildfire. "I like to see the green-up afterwards," they will say, referring to the flush of native grass after a pasture burn. And they will laugh and shake their heads when they remember how near the flames came to their own front doors. Again, the buffer is narrow; acceptance is wide.

At Piapot I could not see evidence of recent burns, but the aspen bluffs on the uplands and the ash-poplar-maple-elm woods in the lowlands had a complexity and a vertical structure that implied a history of fire. Within one section of woods, I was finding patches of even-aged young aspen regenerating thickly amid the skeletons of an old burn, next to a stand of middle-aged trees with a closed canopy and, not far away, a clutch of large mature trees that were dying back, breaking off as snags, and leaving holes in the canopy. This kind of variance makes for changes in the degree of light reaching the understorey and the forest floor, which in turn allows for a diversity of shrubs, grasses, and flowers.

In grassland, the effects of fire are similar, but even more dramatic. Encroaching shrubs die back, the thatch of previous years' growth disappears, the soil recovers some of its nutrient investment in the form of ash, and suddenly species that have been absent or scarce begin to flourish. Our mixed-grass prairie, unlike tallgrass, can go for long periods without fire, but it too will benefit from a burn every ten years or so, particularly if natural grazers are absent.

WALKING FROM THE CAR to Florence's back porch, I tried to assimilate the variety of natural landscapes I had seen on our tour of Piapot and the neighbouring reserve, Muscowpetung: subvalleys behind hills that at one time or another calved off the valley slopes; small coulees with intermittent streams; sharp hogsback ridges; a good mix of native grasses on a variety of slope regimes and none of it grazed heavily, much of it unfenced; a larger coulee with a healthy stream that had not been fouled by livestock; and on the valley floodplain, a vast network of sedge meadows and marshland through which the river winds, emerging and disappearing from behind bullrushes and sandbar willows. It was the valley bottom in Piapot and Muscow, wet from wall to wall and in some places entirely flooded, that left the strongest impression on me. It had the look of a great wetland, first-rate habitat for aquatic invertebrates, waterbirds, and marsh sparrows. Later I was to read a newspaper report that made it clear that this flood had been caused long ago by the same agency that dynamited the buffalo rock at Aiktow.

Dams built in the 1940s by the PFRA have kept thousands of acres of Qu'Appelle reserve bottomland under water for the past six decades. Bottomland is among the richest, most valuable agricultural land in the region. Losing their share of floodplain cropland — in Muscow's case it was one-fifth of its total acreage — has made it difficult for these Indian bands to support themselves. On most of the Qu'Appelle reserves there are some families that like to farm, although much of the arable land is rented out to non-indigenous neighbours. Either way, by flooding fertile lands on reserves, the Canadian government has diminished the land base required for the economic autonomy that Indian peoples desire and our policy-makers promise.

Indian bands and band councils talk a great deal about land these days. Every acre counts when you are feeding and housing more people year after year. I was surprised at the number of houses on Florence's reserve, yet there are not enough. She worries about her band's growing population. Feeding, educating, and housing more people on a limited land base has been partly responsible for the exodus off-reserve to Regina and other cities where it is easy for young people to become lost in the maelstrom of white culture.

As we approached the doorstep, Florence continued to talk about young people losing touch with their traditions, taking on white people's ways, and becoming destructive and disrespectful. From the porch I noticed several Richardson's ground squirrels and their diggings around the yard. When we moved into her kitchen for coffee I could hear the occasional whistle of gophers just outside the window. Our conversation settled into the room. There were cupboards lined with teapots and china, and a large calendar on the wall featuring a Charlie Russell rodeo painting. I thought of the rural kitchens of my childhood where I listened to aunts and uncles talk. Florence spoke slowly, returning again and again to the same simple theme: respect is everything.

Elders often talk about the importance of respect: respect for tradition, for the old ones, for all Creation. You hear it on news reports: "At the road-block, the elders said they are praying that the company will begin treating the forest with respect." It begins to sound like rhetoric, the jargon of the disenfranchised. We become impatient, wishing for some deeper pronouncement or detailed advice, and in the end we are as deaf as Hind in the lodges of Mistickoos. In Florence's kitchen though, whether it was her gentle, unassuming way or the lazy afternoon music of clay-coloured sparrows and gophers drifting in through the window, the idea of respect came into my thoughts as if for the first time. Later that day as I drove back to Regina, I remembered reading in Wilfred Thesiger's *Arabian Sands* how the Bedu, the indigenous dwellers of Arabia's Empty Quarter, would chastise Thesiger for tossing a single date stone into the campfire. This surprised him until he realized that their reaction was more than superstition; it was a social injunction that served their long-term interests as dwellers of the sands. Dates were a staple for the Bedu in their land of scarcity and barrenness, and they considered the date tree to be a great gift from God. To be careless with a date stone, rather than planting it where it had a chance of feeding others some day, was to be disrespectful of one's home, one's people, and one's god.

Nothing less than respect will do for even the least in Creation, even for the dirt and the stones beneath our feet. Florence told me she believed we should not be removing stones so carelessly. They have their place, and it is dangerous to toss them around and break them apart as if they have no purpose, as if we own them. A people who will at least pause in respect before they plough their gardens, gather field stones, or take a hillside's store of gravel are capable of gratitude and of recognizing limits, the community of ownership, and the need to conserve. Respect — a gesture, a prayer, an invocation, a recollection — intervenes as the pause between desire and use, between appetite and acquisition. Respect alone may not reunite us with the prairie, but it seems a fair place to start.

*Chapter Seventeen*

# CARRY-THE-KETTLE

AFTER PIAPOT, I TRAVELLED through most of the reserves in the watershed,[42] spending an afternoon or a morning touring the wilder places, patches of upland prairie or aspen woods. Occasionally, I would meet with an elder before heading off on my own, but most often I simply paid my respects to the chief or band administrator. For a gift I used a blanket instead of chocolate plunder.

Every day had its discoveries: that stands of wild lilies can grow in patches as big as a baseball diamond; that ninety per cent of female inmates in Saskatchewan prisons are aboriginal; that white-throated sparrows breed in the Touchwood Hills on the old burns of the Gordon Reserve; that the Gordon residential school, which was being demolished during my visit, had been run for sixteen years by a man who extorted sexual favours from students; that ring-necked ducks and ravens summer in Muskowekwan; that the gas station in the nearby town of Punnichy has posted a blacklist, next to the "NO CREDIT — DON'T EVEN ASK" sign, displaying the names of sixty people who cannot rent videos anymore, names such as Dustyhorn, Sunshine, Poorman; that there are sizable stands of ungrazed big bluestem prairie at Ochapowace; that dogs on Indian reserves don't chase cars; that little boys carrying bows and arrows or BB rifles on the roadside will invariably wave; that in 1907 the Canadian government swindled 33,000 acres of prime agricultural land from the starving people of Kahkewistahaw; that it is possible to become lost within the cobweb of trails in the back-country of Carry-the-Kettle.

Finding my way back to the road at Carry-the-Kettle, I came upon the reserve's powwow and rodeo grounds, a clearing of native grass where the Assiniboine people have made ceremonial circles within the jurisdictional squares of their land entitlement. Ringed by aspen bluffs, the Carry-the-Kettle powwow grounds are as lovely and wild as any I have seen. Standing by the shade structures, the wind swirling through dead poplar staves, I had trouble filling the emptiness with the carnival atmosphere of powwows I had attended: pickup trucks, campers, and tents stippling the landscape in ragged concentric circles around the dancing grounds, the innermost ring of tables and vans where people hawk fried bannock-burgers, "Indian Tacos," turquoise jewellery, dream catchers, and "Mother Earth" Nevada tickets that promise $1,000 to the one who tears away the paper window to find three images of Turtle Island in a row.

The nearest summer powwow to our cabin in the valley is at Standing Buffalo reserve. Standing Buffalo, a reserve of Dakota (Sioux) people at the joining of Pasqua and Echo Lakes, holds a powwow each August in the open air, beneath a great, girdered steel canopy on the valley bottom.

One time at the Standing Buffalo powwow, I passed a piece of the afternoon talking to an elderly Cree man from Kawacatoose reserve in the Touchwood Hills. He was alone at the picnic table where I had sat down to feed bannock-burgers and fries to my three children. Once the children were settled into their meals, I looked across the table at the man, who was relaxing after his supper. The patch on the shoulder of his jacket read "Mike," and his hat advertised the Moose Jaw Wild Animal Park. We made eye contact and Mike began to speak. It was as though he had been waiting for someone to sit down and pass the time. The main event, the Grand Entry of all the dancers, was almost an hour away, so our conversation took on the easy pace of people who have nothing to do, nowhere to go. Mike remarked on the children, smiled at them, and said he wished he still had three little ones like that. His girl — she's nineteen today — she's in the traditional dance competition. Good dancer too. Adopted her when she was ten months old, just a little thing. Started dancing when she was only five. She's a good girl — never drinks or tries drugs — smokes a little, but . . . Now he spends all summer driving her from powwow to powwow. It's getting harder each year with his glaucoma. Not supposed to drive at night. Forgot the drops today. His own parents were ninety-six when they died and they could still see forever. Like eagles.

Mike's eyes were glazed with a blue film and he squinted through wire-rimmed bifocals. I noticed bank swallows bisecting the air above the powwow stadium as he told me about his reserve, Kawacatoose, about the bush fire that almost burnt down his house that spring, and about returning to Kawacatoose from Northern Alberta where he worked in construction while his wife packed chickens in a poultry plant.

Before we parted, Mike again looked at the three small faces beside me on the picnic-table bench. He smiled, shaking his head, as though they were remarkable and rare creatures: *"These are your children!"* he said. I was not sure whether it was a statement or a question. Then he looked me squarely in the eye without saying anything, and I saw myself in him, an old man whose little ones are grown, and I wondered whether I was enjoying them as I ought to and whether I should give in to Karen's desire for another baby. Later that night, as I built a fire in the wood stove at the cabin, I thought again of Mike, and somewhere within me, the possibility of a fourth child began to glimmer, warm and right.

A few minutes before the Grand Entry, Mike rose slowly from the picnic table. "I gotta go watch my girl," he said.

I thanked him for the conversation and said we might see him in the stands.

"I'll be there," he said, "you watch for me."

Toward the head of the Grand Entry procession, after the World War II and Vietnam war vets, were a pair of RCMP constables in red serge. As they queued up at the entrance to the stadium, waiting for the introduction, the male constable, fair-skinned and blond, began attempting what he thought to be powwow footwork, thinking he might be funny or that he might prove he was not uncomfortable to be a white man among Indians. His partner, a tall and striking Indian woman, a single braid emerging from her hat, shook her head and turned away in embarrassment at his decision to cut-up as they awaited the most solemn moment of the powwow. Once the dancing procession began, the constable and the treaty commissioner, the only two white men among the parade of hundreds of powwow people and dignitaries, both shuffled along awkwardly, thinking of each footstep. They looked like miscreant bridegrooms doing a rendition of the foot-sliding wedding march down a dusty church aisle.

The dancers themselves, from four-year-old girls to men in their eighties, were attired in an astonishing array of every material that has graced the human form — as well as several that were making their sartorial debut. The traditional dancers shook and turned in buckskin, porcupine quills, pewter, silver, turquoise, fur, feathers, teeth, bones, claws, and beads. Some young men used bird carcasses or limbs to decorate themselves. I recognized wings and tails from sharp-tailed grouse and red-tailed hawks, an entire sharp-shinned hawk skin, and a golden eagle head. Eagle primary feathers adorned most costumes. I worry about the collecting of these birds, especially the hawks and eagles. Officially, a dancer must earn each feather with acts of personal honour and community service, and body parts are to come only from existing costumes or from birds found dead. But headdresses and feathers are bought and sold for powwow regalia. Unfortunately, wherever money and honour mix, there is wide opportunity for abuse. I suspect that more than a few wild hawks and eagles are sacrificed to pride parading as honour, or honour too easily gained.

Road-killed porcupine, on the other hand, is never hard to find in this region. Porcupine quills and fur crown many heads at a powwow. One five-year-old boy I watched at Standing Buffalo preened his porcupine-fur headdress as he waited for his turn to compete. Staring into the crowd absent-mindedly, he licked the palm of his hand like a cat and then ran his fingers carefully through the guard hairs so that they would stand erect in a fan of black and gold across his crown.

Even more stunning than the hide, fur, and feathers at a powwow, however, is the way some costumes incorporate modern synthetics, applying them to the basic forms of the circle, the fringe, the feather, the eagle, and the bear. Anything that glitters, gathers light, and celebrates colour can be found on a fancy-dancer's body. Nylon, satin, spandex, acrylic, and mylar appear in swatches, strips, and ribbons of phosphorescent green, pink, yellow, red, and orange. Pieces of metal or glass are added for extra effect. Shards of glass or mirror are glued onto sleeves. There are entire "jingle dresses" made out of hundreds of lids of condensed milk and chewing tobacco cans, each lid curled into a small cone. Some costumes feature sequins sewn into a mosaic of a feather or an eagle in flight.

Plains Indian cosmology, while recognizing that the Creation dwells most powerfully in original materials, does not make a sharp aesthetic distinction between the natural and the artificial. The entire material world available to our senses — the manufactured as well as the natural — is good until we make it otherwise by our use. Used appropriately and with respect, then, almost anything can serve to adorn a fancy dancer. One teenaged boy at the Standing Buffalo powwow, arrayed in vibrant splashes of Day-Glo green and yellow, had attached to each shoulder a compact disk, forming the centre of an orange mandala. Each time one of these CDs connected with the sunlight, his shoulder would flash with borrowed fire. The sight of such a symbol of contemporary culture on the boy's costume startled me. It was likely nothing more than a way of adding flash to the outfit, but it struck me as such a sophisticated reference, a bit of irony tossed in the face of anyone who would prefer to think of Indians in simple categories. Terms used by tourists become troublesome here. You hear stories of European visitors upset because the Indians at a powwow are not "authentic" enough, meaning they do not appear to be living in the nineteenth century, a time when all Indians apparently had an unquestionable innocence.

My children, who have not yet acquired the cultural prejudice favouring natural materials and people, thought that the CD shoulder patches were the coolest decorations in the whole powwow. To them, the blend of new and traditional wares does not matter. What matters is the effect, the movement, the colour and light. Questions of purity or authenticity and preconceptions about how Indians should look or behave come from a perspective that is bound to miss the truth being celebrated when the descendants of Piapot, Standing Buffalo, Poundmaker, Big Bear, and Kawacatoose gather to dance on a summer's day. A powwow is a finally a forum for celebrating the hybridity of modern plains culture. Full of ambivalence and transition between old values and new ways, a powwow is a heterogeneous blend of the life that Indian people inherited from their forebears and the modern life that they have adopted.

The survival borne of this blending is what makes faces shine and eyes glisten as the Grand Entry reaches its whirling, stamping, pitched glory, the throb of drums echoing in the hundreds of hearts encircling the dancers. The Grand Entry announcer said something, during his patter of hoots and warrior cries, that to me sounded like a declaration of indigenous vitality and survival. He had a beat-up cowboy hat pulled down to his ears, and his upper body was wrapped around the microphone stand. His lips pressed against the microphone cover with every exhortation to the crowd: "Put your hands together for the Ladies Fancyyyyyyyy Daaaancerrrrrrrrs!" I eventually tuned him out, but once, when he dropped his voice to a lower pitch, I started listening again, just in time to hear him say, stressing each word loudly, deliberately, and slowly, ". . . because we are here to celebrate that we are Indian people, alive, true, beautiful, and strong — here, here today! Heeeeaaaayaaaaoooooyahhhh!"

There it is, I thought. Despite every persecution and disadvantage from massacres, disease, the buffalo extermination, the land swindling, the abuse and repression in residential schools, the duplicity of Indian agents, the constraints of the Indian Act, the prejudice, poverty, and anguish in our cities, and despite the consequent loss of respect for self and Creation, the hunters who shoot too many animals and leave carcasses to rot, the false shamans who sell "native spirituality" to confused white people, the dream-catcher car ornaments, and the Nevada tickets that gamble with Mother Earth and the Spirit Buffalo — despite all, the people of the plains are here today. They are not back in some nobler past time, and their cultures remain viable because even as they shift to incorporate the tools and trappings of modernity, they remain distinctively Indian in many ways: in the way they regard time, the way they handle tragedy, the way they mourn their dead, the way they use humour to disarm or approve, the way their stories assume an inter-communication between all the elements of the Creation, and the way they remain hospitable, still welcoming into their homes — as Mistickoos welcomed Hind — the very people who have always taken away more with one hand than they have given with the other.

## Chapter Eighteen

# STANDING BUFFALO

"WE USE THIS ONE FOR COLDS." Velma Bear, an elder at Standing Buffalo, stroked the top of a bergamot flower as we walked beneath a ridge on her reserve, enumerating the lives and medicines offered by the valley. She and her partner, Andy Goodfeather, were giving me a tour of Standing Buffalo despite drizzle threatening to become rain.

"Wild onions. You have to leave some or they won't come back, eh? There's a wild turnip, but too small to take yet. A lady sells them on the reserve. . . . Fish come up the creek to lay eggs in the spring and you can snare them and dry them. . . . That's mint there — Grandma used to pick it and boil it and put it on our eyes. It felt so cool and good."

When I arrived and presented Velma with the tobacco, she excused herself and walked over to the edge of her yard to bury two cigarettes at the base of a small poplar. As we drove from site to site in Andy's truck, we spoke of the long trek made by Chief Standing Buffalo and his people fleeing persecution in Minnesota. An outbreak by one group of Dakota people in 1862 brought reprisals from the white settlers and American army. Many bands, even those such as Standing Buffalo that had not participated in the uprising, were left with little choice but to abandon their reservations. After crossing into Canada's North-West, Chief Standing Buffalo camped with his people in the Weyburn area until he died in 1869. The band dispersed and one group came to settle here at

Sioux Crossing, where Jumping Deer Coulee enters the Qu'Appelle. They were granted a reserve in 1878 as non-status Indians.

We talked too of more recent history. Velma pointed down to the lakeshore where the Roman Catholic Church took some of the band's lakefront property — land that could earn them some revenue. But our conversation always returned to the other beings with whom they share their small reserve. When we stopped to get out and walk, Andy and Velma would list animals and plants in a duet of naming:

"Oh, there's all the berries: the gooseberries, the blackcurrants, the pincherries, hawthorn berries — they're good after the first frost."

"Just like the rose-hips."

"Then there's the ducks, the geese, the swans . . . blue herons, the turtles."

"My son found a big turtle the other day. And there's the green grass snake."

"That one will fight you."

"There's a snake den down in the coulee."

"Salamanders."

"Lots of deer, and now and then a moose or elk, but somebody usually gets it, just like that!"

They went through all the mammals, squirrels to woodchucks to coyotes. Even the bugs got a mention. They wanted to show me the richness and abundance of their world, and I felt privileged to receive it.

Later, Velma would show me fifty or sixty dried wild-turnip (*Psoralea esculenta*) bulbs braided together like onions in a root cellar. White and hard as cue balls, they clacked against one another when she passed the bunch to me. I was surprised at their uniformity and at how hard and clean they were. "You have to soak them overnight before you cook them," Velma said.

After the inventory of Creation, we went up to one of the hilltops overlooking Pasqua and Echo Lakes where the bones of the second Chief Standing Buffalo rest alongside those of his wives and relatives. He was killed, Velma said, in a skirmish with the Blackfoot in the Rocky Mountain foothills. The people bore him up to his grave on a blanket tied between four horses.

Distant thunder rumbled overhead as we searched for the hollows that marked the place where Standing Buffalo and his kin were buried.

The rain fell on the June grass, on the scarlet mallow, and on the thread-leaved sedge; it fell on bottle caps and empty cans of Pilsner; and it fell on our shoulders and our hair. I stared through the grey air to the valley and the lakes with their fringe of cottages.

"Up here!" Velma called. I ran to where she stood looking down at eight shallow depressions in the native grass. "My daughter used to say that when it rains it is Mother Earth washing everybody." Velma smiled, remembering something else. She told me then about a Fort Qu'Appelle man they once caught digging up graves, scavenging for artifacts. And she asked me to not tell others where to find these graves.

We spent the rest of our time together at a ceremonial grounds, where Velma described the rites of their annual sundance, the meaning of each element and role, the preparation, and the rules of respect. To recount here any of these details would be to diminish and confine the most reverential seasonal event in the lives of Plains Indian people, the midsummer ceremony that attends to the health and wholeness of this land and its dwellers. As Velma spoke, her language filling the space between us and around us in the truck cab with the images of a Dakota ceremony, I began to consider the possibility that such ritual might have actual consequences, that there may be a real, ecological function to ritual and prayer, particularly when enacted in community. All that we learn and experience as children of modernity blinds us to this possibility. We know that, beyond providing ethnic colour, the religious practice of an animistic people might at best exert a psychological and social effect, influencing personal and communal ethics. We know this in our very bones, and try as we may to see any real communication between a praying people and their land, we see only superstition and crude devotion to the material world, which has always been more easily moved by a plough than by prayer.

Something in Velma's reverence, though, allowed me to imagine — if only for the short time we sat talking and watching the rain run down the windshield — the original antiphony that once echoed between the people and these hills and coulees. I came as close as I will ever come to grasping a sense of what it would be like to know differently, to know the truth that the land is sentient, that it listens and responds to the rites of those who were formed in its embrace. The moment evaporated, but it has left me wondering about the ones who live on the reserves strung along the valley; about the resurgence of the pipe, the sundance, the medicine bundle, the sweat lodge, and ceremonies of fasting and prayer; about the elders and keepers of the stories gathering medicines, offering tobacco, and burning sage and sweetgrass.

From Henry Youle Hind we have some idea of how common it was in this valley to come upon the visible signs of someone's ritual attentions to the land. The Qu'Appelle that Hind saw in 1858 was festooned with the blessings and propitiations of its dwellers:

> *In the valley of the Qu'Appelle River, we frequently found offerings to Manitou or Faeries suspended on branches of trees; they consisted of fragments of cloth, strings of beads, shreds of painted buffalo hide, bears' teeth and claws, and other trifles. Our half-breeds always regarded them with respect and never molested or liked to see us molest these offerings to Manitou.[43]*

This land still needs gifts from the people who heard the river's call, who dug breadroot and told stories of a lost child becoming a bird, whose prayers, songs, language, and very breath reciprocated with the wild otherness here like water swirling in and out of an eddy at streamside. An American ecologist-philosopher named David Abram has made some important observations about the intimate interchange between the people of an oral culture and their land.[44] Our intelligence, our imagination, and our senses, Abram suggests, took their present form in relation to other sentient bodies. Our species evolved in the presence of hillside, savannah, and forest shadow, knowing the feel of fur, bark, and shell; the savour of salt and honey; the music of crickets and grass sparrows; the aroma of wood smoke; and the sweetness of fruit blossom. At the same time, these "animate others" in what Abram refers to as "the more-than-human world," received *our* imprint, felt *our* presences, and evolved accordingly. This intimacy implies a cosmos in which thoughts, words, and acts of respect or disrespect carry real power.

If Abram's persuasive philosophical and historical arguments are correct, then how can we not do ourselves and our country good by returning to communication and engagement with our co-inhabitants? Now more than ever our human communities need intermediaries, shamans, and ecologists who will travel on our behalf across the gulf that we have created between ourselves and the rest of the Creation, learning what we must do to regain the favour of this land.

I keep a list of examples of surprising ecological resilience and recovery in the watershed, of unaccounted-for restraint and forbearance in the face of economic opportunity. This record includes a note on the quality of water in the Qu'Appelle system. A limnologist who studies the history of water quality in the Qu'Appelle lakes once told me that, given the nutrient load our sewage and agricultural run-off injects into the river, the lakes should be even more turbid and eutrophic than they are. He showed me his data for the twentieth century. The figures indicate extremely high phosphorous and nitrogen levels in the lakes, and yet the algae blooms are not as serious as one finds in other lakes with similar nutrient burdens. There is no scientific explanation, he said, for the relative resilience and clarity of the Qu'Appelle lakes.

My afternoon at Standing Buffalo had me asking myself, "What if?" What if the unscientific explanation is ritual attention to the sacred? What if propitiation keeps the river and lakes from further ecological degradation, keeps the PFRA and SaskWater from enacting more irrigation and channelization projects? What if prayer and ceremony are responsible for the reappearance of native grasses on disturbed soil, the recovery of the beaver, the return of the bear and the elk in the east valley, the sudden interest in native grassland, and the summer visit of two young whooping cranes at Eyebrow marsh? For these and other anomalous blessings I am willing to give the benefit of the doubt to shamanic intercession and propitiation.

## Chapter Nineteen

# CALLIN'S TERRAIN

VELMA HAD CALLED THE MOVEMENT of Standing Buffalo's people from Minnesota to Sioux Crossing a migration. Another migration to Sioux Crossing made ornithological history seventy years ago. In 1929, a Fort Qu'Appelle bird bander caught a bank swallow at Sioux Crossing and slipped a coded, metal bracelet around its leg. Six years later, in June 1935, it was found dead in a river valley several thousand miles to the south. It had spent the winter along the banks of the Rio de Dios, which flows east of the Andean plateaus where the Tiahuanaco people once built their stone temples.

This remarkable record would have been lost to popular natural history, tucked away in the files of the United States Fish and Wildlife Service's Bird Banding Laboratory in Maryland, were it not for the passion and pastime of E. Manley Callin, the Qu'Appelle Valley's great chronicler of bird life.

Callin lived in or near the valley for almost all of his seventy-four years, from 1911 to 1985. He scarcely left the valley in search of birds and made almost all his bird observations in the eastern half of the Qu'Appelle. His book, *Birds of the Qu'Appelle, 1857–1979*, is recognized as one of the finest records of regional bird life written for any part of North America. The book's 122-year span of bird accounting gains much of its authority from Callin's own field observations, which cover the latter half of that period. For sixty years, beginning at the age of fifteen, Callin kept meticulous records of the comings and goings of birds in the valley. His pocket notebooks show the date he saw each species arrive in spring and depart in fall, and document unusual numbers of birds, rare species, and breeding records. These notebooks, as well as the records of other observers, fill a file cabinet that holds 297 folders — one for each of the Qu'Appelle's bird species, from common loon to snow bunting.

Poring over Callin's book the first time, learning of the places where ravens nested in 1875 or where passenger pigeons were last seen, was like rummaging through an ancestor's attic. Each species account drew me further along Callin's pathway amid the intimate and abundant lives of the valley. Fifteen years later, I still check with Callin every time I see an early warbler or a wayward gull. The August night a saw-whet owl woke me from my sleep, I wandered out into the dark to listen, and when I returned to the cabin I lit a candle to see what Callin had said about saw-whet owls singing in summer:

*Saw-whet owl* **Aegolius acadicus**
*Permanent resident, seen and heard irregularly. . . . The monotonous and long-continued but pleasant notes are heard occasionally at night in late winter and early spring; except for 1 date of April 26, all "songs" were heard within the period February 9 to April 5.*[45]

AS I TRAVELLED EAST from Standing Buffalo, stopping now and then to watch a kestrel, a flock of pelicans, or a lark sparrow, *Birds of the Qu'Appelle* accompanied me, informing my experience of the transition from arid mixed-grass prairie to the moist aspen-oak parkland of the east. Less than two hours by car, three or four days by canoe, the trip bears the traveller across broad ecological boundaries along a moisture gradient that at specific locations marks Canada's western limits for big bluestem grass, side oats, grama grass, bur oak, and nannyberry. Less distinct, but just as revealing of the west-to-east shift are those animals that share a zone of intergrade and hybridization with a genetically approximate counterpart whose continental range overlaps with their own along a few miles of the valley. The smooth green snake, for instance, has been classified into western and eastern subspecies according to the number of scales on its belly. But the ones in the Qu'Appelle, including those my children find on our hillsides east of Katepwe Lake, always show an intermediate number of scales, blurring the official demarcation between eastern and western forms. Birds in Callin's stretch of the valley are an even greater conundrum for the taxonomist.

### Eastern Wood Pewee  Contopus virens
*Probably a regular but uncommon summer resident in the extreme eastern portion of the valley. We have no summer records west of Echo Lake.*

### Western Wood Pewee  Contopus sordidulus
*Probably a regular but uncommon resident as far east as Round Lake, where it is replaced by the Eastern Wood Pewee.*[46]

The ranges of the two wood pewees overlap in the valley, according to Callin, from Echo Lake to Round Lake. Since the publication of the book, the overlap zone has been extended. In the past four years, I have heard western wood pewees singing twenty-five miles east of Round Lake at Scissors Creek and eastern wood pewees singing forty miles west of Echo Lake, near Craven.

The two birds that animate the east-west shift most vividly, however, are the eastern and spotted towhees. These two are among the valley's most characteristic birds, for although they are almost never seen on the plains above, in summer virtually every hillside rings with the notes of one or the other — or both. When Callin wrote his book, ornithology still regarded the two towhees as subspecies of a single species: the rufous-sided towhee. In the eighties and early nineties, however, field studies and DNA work determined that they were genetically separate enough to be considered two species. The year the American Ornithological Union announced the split, I found a female towhee floating belly-up heading east on the current of Katepwe Lake. I was up to my knees in the lake casting for northern pike when the dark lump appeared on the waves, trailed by a tress of tail feathers. She was a pathetic, bedraggled little Ophelia, passing beneath overhanging maples and willows whose leaves fingered the wavelets as she passed. It was late June, the height of breeding season, and her brood patch was bared to the sky. I picked her up. The fierce glow of her red eye stared up at me. Her feathers were all slicked down against her coral skin and the scapulars on her back showed no spotting. It was an eastern towhee, the only female of the species I had ever seen near enough to identify. What mishap, I thought, would send a mother towhee into the lake in a week of clement weather?

Since that encounter, I have begun taking greater notice of the towhees around Katepwe Lake. Most are spotted, some are eastern, and a few are damned confusing. I have watched "eastern" towhees, with all the right field marks, singing the song of spotted towhees. And there are several spotted towhees in our stretch of valley that sing a blend of the two species' songs.

Nature will not always yield to our categories. In Callin's half of the valley, taxonomy falters in the face of the flow of genes and life wherever east encounters west. The towhees are a prominent example, but there are several other east-west couplings among bird species whose ranges overlap in the valley. The wood pewees form one; indigo bunting (eastern) and lazuli bunting (western) form another; and eastern bluebird and mountain bluebird a third. All these examples almost certainly produce intergrade or hybrid offspring in the valley, though proving it, particularly in the case of the wood pewees, would require DNA testing.

### Whip-poor-will **Caprimulgus vociferus**
*Undoubtedly this species did occur many years ago as a rare transient and possibly as a very rare summer visitant; now apparently absent.*[47]

IN THE 1860s, an early missionary from Ontario, John McDougall, camped along the Qu'Appelle River just downstream of the Big Cutarm Creek.[48] He was on his way home after spending several years in the North-West. That night he heard a birdsong that transported him to the eastern forest of his youth:

*In the evening shade, as we were sitting beside our camp-fire,*
*suddenly I heard a cry which thrilled through my whole being: "Whip-*
*poor-will!" "Whip-poor-will!" came echoing through the woods and*
*up the valley, and in a moment I was among the scenes of my child-*
*hood, paddling a birch canoe along the shores of the great lakes, rioting*
*among the beech and maple woods of old Ontario. For years I had not*
*heard a whip-poor-will and now the once familiar sounds brought with*
*them a feeling of homesickness.*[49]

If a mixed-blood pemmican trader raised upon the plains had been travelling from the east and crossed paths with McDougall that night, he might have heard from the same spot or not far away the first songs of some prairie birds familiar to his ears: chestnut-collared longspur, Sprague's pipit, and Baird's sparrow. In Callin's terrain, fingers of the eastern and northern forest ecologies interdigitate with fingers of prairie so closely that a naturalist can easily find places where the songs of woodland birds hidden in the coulees mingle with the songs of prairie sparrows claiming the grassy hilltops. Some of the woodland birds breed in biogeographic islands or corridors in which there are plants and animals whose nearest conspecifics outside the valley may be more than a hundred miles north or east. The plants include alder-leaved buckthorn, speckled alder, and several orchids and ferns, while the list of isolated birds runs from Swainson's thrush to Canada warbler to white-throated sparrow. The Assiniboine system into which the Qu'Appelle River drains is a corridor connecting the valley to the north and east, a natural pathway along which elk, black bear, and moose enter the eastern Qu'Appelle. The Assiniboine's biogeographic reach extends 150 miles upstream into the northern mixed-wood forest and 200 miles east downstream into the Manitoba lowlands. Along this wildlife channel, northern flying squirrels have entered the Qu'Appelle and advanced as far as Round Lake. From the east, the Assiniboine influence brings northern red-bellied snakes and snapping turtles to the valley. Now and then one of the fishermen of Tantallon will hook onto a channel catfish that has swum all the way from the Red River, up the Assiniboine, and into the Qu'Appelle. Respect for range map boundaries is not in a river's job description.

*Chapter Twenty*

# ELLISBORO TO ROUND LAKE

B Y THE TIME I HAD REACHED the village of Ellisboro, one of the oldest and smallest of the valley's settlements, there were clear signs that I was entering a wetter landscape. The grass in the ditches was getting higher and yellow splashes of black-eyed Susan began to appear, indicating greater rainfall. The valley itself had begun to change in profile. The hills seemed slightly higher and broader, whereas the floodplain was narrowing. Instead of the abrupt, angular shift from valley wall to valley bottom that characterizes the western Qu'Appelle, there was now a gentler sloping away from a wide range of hills down to the floodplain. The entire southern valley wall was heavily wooded, hilltops as well as coulees, and the white trunks of birch trees were becoming more frequent. The north side of the valley was showing a gradual increase in woody growth as well. Near the inflow of Summerberry Creek, the river disappeared into a meandering forest of large Manitoba maples and American elms. As I drew nearer Crooked Lake, the valley became deeper again, and the floodplain changed from fields of cropland to marshy hayland meadows. There were hang-gliders dangling on updrafts above the grassy northern slopes of the valley.

Crooked Lake follows a picturesque S-curve in the valley's meander, and this shape at one point thrusts the south hills, dark green with poplar and birch, sharply into the lake, forming a steep and dramatic headland. The effect seems out of place in a prairie landscape and draws the memory to hilly land farther east on the continent, to the wooded lakes of the Adirondacks or Gatineau.

At Round Lake the bur oak redefines the face of the valley again. Although there are oaks as far west as Crooked Lake, this tough, fire-resistant tree does not really dominate the landscape until just downstream of Round Lake. There is a place where I watch for the change along the north rim of the valley. Rather suddenly, the grassy hilltop sprouts a row of stunted dark-green trees, forming a ragged, toothed fringe on the horizon. These first oaks have always looked like scruffy soldiers to me, a local militia standing on the ramparts guarding the entrance to the valley that enlivened my earliest years. Here the valley deepens again, the floodplain narrows to a strip along the river, and the hills on either side expand to become a range of rolling woodland, thick with oak, birch, poplar, and maple, save for the odd, south-facing ridge where the sun recollects the prairie in tallgrasses.

### Bank Swallow  Riparia riparia
*Regular and common summer resident, especially in the valley, where the cut banks along the sides of the valley, the lakes, and the river provide suitable habitat and nearly unlimited nesting sites.*[50]

The river downstream of Round Lake travels a sinuous course through a mosaic of marsh, hayland, cropland, meadows, and woods. Later in the summer, during my stay in the eastern Qu'Appelle, I would join two local naturalists from the town of Whitewood on a morning paddle down the river east of Round Lake. From the canoe, we would record fifty species of birds: in the skies there would be gulls, kingfishers, red-tailed hawks, and turkey vultures; on the river, common mergansers and eleven kinds of shorebirds foraging on their journey south. As always, there would be bank swallows, forty of them in two colonies.

Much of the bank swallow's appeal, apart from its impressive migration between far-flung valleys of the New World, is its gregarious nature. This bird is social in all turns of its life. Bank swallows hunt together, roost together, migrate together, and breed together. They nest in tight gatherings we like to refer to as "colonies." Their nesting, in fact, is synchronized so that all young within a given colony will be exactly the same age.

Like our own species, this bird likes to dig. After arriving here from their wintering grounds east of the Andes, the bank swallows set to work either redigging available nest holes in old colonies or digging new holes in whatever banks the river or human digging offers. Using their bills to remove pea-sized mouthfuls of dirt, they excavate their burrows two or three feet deep into the side of a sandy bank, usually near the top.

Ornithologists studying social nesters such as the bank swallow have asked why they bother to nest together. The answer appears to be predators. Their best defence against any attacker is to use numbers to fight it off. The bank swallow is extremely effective at what biologists refer to as "mobbing behaviour." Any threat too near their colony will be dive-bombed by dozens of swallows. Search far enough for the roots of human community and you will arrive at the same principle. Paleoanthropologists now believe that the rudiments of our own social behaviour evolved as a means of protection against the beasties. We may have first begun living in tribes or clans as a way of fending off predators that specialized in cave-dwelling hominids. A sabre-toothed tiger is far less formidable at the mouth of your cave when four or five of your kin are standing next to you brandishing pointed sticks.

Such points of consonance between the evolution of a wild culture and that of our own arise from a common ground that is so easy to forget; but remembering can be as simple as holding a live wood warbler, quivering and vivid, in your hand. Like small birds, our individual lives are vulnerable and evanescent, and preservation — cultural or ecological — still comes down to kindness between neighbours.

*BRING BOOTS AND A LAWN CHAIR, something to eat and drink. Watch for the red and white truck on the side of the road. Honk your horn when you get there.* I followed the instructions and, shortly after I honked at the thick woods not far downstream of Round Lake, John Pollack came walking out to greet me. Carrying my lawn chair, I followed him into the dew-drenched forest along a deer trail widened by his biweekly visits. Every two weeks for five summers, John has been coming to this twelve-acre plot in the east Qu'Appelle to band songbirds. He is halfway through a ten-year monitoring project — part of a continental effort called MAPS (Monitoring Avian Productivity and Survivorship) — and makes eight visits during each breeding season. He has banded hundreds of song-birds of more than thirty species, gathering brood productivity and survivorship data while learning what he can about the way species composition relates to habitat.

John is a circumspect and attentive man, not given to rash or unfounded assumptions, but he told me that he believes surprises are still to be found in the distribution of plants and animals in the eastern Qu'Appelle. It remains a relatively unexplored region, he said, and needs more field survey work to determine population densities, even for vertebrate animals, and to pinpoint the location of rare plants, lichens, and mosses. He spoke with some pride of the day he spent with Vernon Harms, one of the prairie's foremost field botanists and Saskatchewan's expert on rare-plant distribution. Harms located several provincially rare plants on John's survey site and in the immediate area. The site contains a marl bog (that is, one with calcareous water) in which Harms identified several bog orchids, sedges, and mosses as well as the locally rare *Impatiens biflora* (spotted touch-me-not). Other rare plants they found nearby included Virginia grape fern and enchanter's night-shade.

The profusion of greenery at my feet as we walked into the site could have harboured any number of uncommon plants. The forest floor was riotous with grasses and flowers, mosses and lichens. Around every bend, there was a shift in vegetative community, creating a diversity of habitat within the woods. John's MAPS site is in a large coulee watered by a creek that is supplemented by springs and checked here and there by beaver dams. The woods surrounding the creek are mostly large balsam poplar, Manitoba maple, and green ash. Changes in micro-topography, tree density, and canopy characteristics provide the conditions for a mix of habitat ideal for bird study. John uses eight banding nets, mist nets made of a mesh so fine that they all but disappear in the light-dappled gloom of the poplar forest. In full sunlight, however, they look like badminton nets woven from spider silk. Held aloft by aluminum poles, they have long horizontal folds or pockets where the trapped birds rest between fits of whirring entanglement. Some species struggle more than others. "Chickadees and vireos don't go down without a battle," said John. "They'll fight you all the way."

After a tour of the nets to collect birds, stuffing each into its own cotton drawstring sack, we scurried down another one of John's paths — a narrow meandering rabbit-run of a trail — until we arrived at a lawn chair in the middle of the woods, resting on a small sheet of polyethylene and looking like a hastily abandoned picnic. This was the banding station: a chair; a plastic sheet to catch any bird that falls during the banding process; pliers and a box of banding rings; and a binder containing five years of data. To the right of the chair and just above it, jutting out from a green ash, was a broken stub on which we hung the quivering sacks of birds to be banded.

Among the first bunch of birds were two adult red-eyed vireos, a hatch-year least flycatcher, an adult female northern waterthrush, an adult female chestnut-sided warbler whose brood patch proved her as a local breeder, a hatch-year common yellowthroat, and three raucous young downy woodpeckers. Throughout the morning we banded twelve species of songbirds, many of which were migrants that winter in the tropical rainforests of Central and Southern America.

As John banded each bird, cradling it in the palm of his hand, the head gripped between two of his fingers, he would give me details of moult sequence and of aging or sexing the species. He passed a female Tennessee warbler into my hand so that he could spread its underwing and point out the fourth primary feather from the wing-tip. The tiny quill was fresh and perfect, fully grown, while the third from the tip was just emerging as a pin-feather. In your hand, the wing of such a bird is an insubstantial, translucent thing — a bit of light gathered into the most delicate of interlocking forms: vanes, shafts, barbs. The whole structure is at once improbable and sublime. We take it on faith that such a marvel is merely a blossom at the growing point of a long evolutionary tendril, but that is finally an inadequate explanation. Examined closely, a bird's wing still leaves you wondering at the Maker or the making.

Opening my hand, I watched the warbler take to the air in one whirring, consummate, fluid stroke: first leaping away, twisting its head, and then righting itself in mid-air, it unfolded its wings and, flicking them effortlessly, regained its element. I could release birds one a minute for an entire morning, I think, and I would to the last feel the quickening of life, the sudden miracle that bears a bird across the forest canopy. It takes a leap of faith, though, for me to accept that the same pinions will bear a bird across the Gulf of Mexico. Preposterous as it may seem, this Tennessee warbler, like many of the birds in the Qu'Appelle Valley and in John's banding plot, flies twice each year between breeding grounds in North America and wintering grounds in Central and South America. Ornithologists now use radar to count the migrants whirling down out of the spring sky and coming ashore along the Texas coast. Arriving here on its breeding grounds in late May, a Tennessee warbler will, before departing again in early August, glean several thousand caterpillars from the trees within the acre of forest it requires to raise a brood. Accurate figures on warbler prey are hard to come by. Science still knows little about the ecology that binds together wood warblers, their prey, and the forest vegetation they require at both ends of their migration.

Ornithologists and birdwatchers, however, have gathered ample data to demonstrate that something is awry in these relationships. Long-term banding and surveying projects such as MAPS and the North American Breeding Bird Survey, as well as recent radar efforts, have shown that many songbird species are declining in numbers, especially the neotropical migrants. The likely causes are legion and easier to list than to remedy: forestry practices, biocides and other environmental contaminants, tropical deforestation, urban sprawl, and a variety of other perils from our overconstructed world, including illuminated office towers, window-glass, and house cats.

One cause of songbird decline interests me because it brings to mind again the buffalo and the ecological dominoes we sent tumbling across the continent when we removed its primary grazer. Several species of songbirds, particularly in the eastern half of North America, are raising fewer young from their nests because they do not know how to deal with a new threat — the brown-headed cowbird. The cowbird was originally known as the buffalo-bird for its habit of following the herds as they ranged across the Great Plains. Whenever the buffalo moved, the buffalo-birds came with them. (These birds are still roamers. Callin refers to a male cowbird banded in the Qu'Appelle in early summer,

June 13, 1929, that was found only two weeks later in San Juan, New Mexico.) This mobile way of life made it difficult to stay in any one place long enough to raise a brood, so the buffalo-bird came upon a strategy for getting more sedentary birds to raise its young. Science calls it brood parasitism: one bird laying its eggs in another bird's nest. The songbirds of the Great Plains, having evolved alongside the buffalo-bird, have developed adaptations that protect them from any long-term nest-productivity problems that brood parasitism might present. Some species simply toss out the alien egg, while others build a new nest on top of the old one. Those that accept the egg and adopt it as their own have apparently adjusted their own productivity to accommodate the frequent fostering of an extra nestling.

Now, remove the buffalo and the buffalo predators. Bring in sedentary grazers, horses and cattle, on farms. Clear woodlands on the northern and eastern flanks of the Great Plains. The same bird, the buffalo-bird, suddenly becomes an enemy of songbirds. We gave it a new name to reflect its new dependencies. It is now the cowbird and our cattle have brought it into the clearings in our fragmented forests, where it has found new and receptive host species, many of which have not had time to adapt and therefore are raising young cowbirds instead of young vireos, warblers, and thrushes. A single cowbird hen can lay forty eggs in one summer. Once a cowbird chick is a few days old, it fills the nest, taking most of the food brought by its foster parents and starving out its nest-mates.

No one has studied the effects of cowbirds in the eastern Qu'Appelle forests, but John sees his share in and around his MAPS site. In other places, particularly the forest fragments of eastern North America, biologists have found that anywhere from thirty to seventy per cent of monitored songbird nests receive at least one cowbird egg.

Toward the end of my morning with John, he banded two female red-eyed vireos — a species that has been hit hard by the cowbird expansion. Once, in the coulee east of our cabin, I found an adult red-eyed vireo feeding a cowbird fledgling perched on a poplar branch. Some encounters with wildness are not beautiful: fish, pale and putrid, wedged overhead in the branches of maple trees where the creek tore through at high flood a week earlier; a bloated deer carcass with raw holes where coyotes have chewed out the genitals and rectum. It is the same with a cowbird begging for food from a vireo half its size. Fascination and revulsion keep you there, staring at the spectacle. The cowbird quivers grotesquely, shrieking for its meal; the vireo, thin from the expenditure of calories required to satisfy such a demanding hunger, cowers to avoid being knocked from the branch by its monstrous child. When the time and angles are right, the parent rushes headlong toward the cowbird's red gape, jamming a beak-full of grubs into its maw like a reluctant zookeeper in the lion's cage.

# Chapter Twenty-one

# OCHAPOWACE

ON ONE OF OUR ROUNDS to check the mist-nets, John noticed an animal track, a long slash on a muddy piece of trail sloping up from a spring.

"Bear. That wasn't here on our last round," he said. Bear tracks are unmistakable in mud. A bear had clearly walked down that piece of trail some time during the previous fifteen minutes.

Black bears have been a minor nuisance on John's MAPS site, but he is more than happy to put up with their knocking down his nets if it means this native predator is returning to the eastern Qu'Appelle in numbers. The resurgence of bears is one of a few positive signs that some of the east valley's wildness remains and is recovering. John and other local naturalists are seeing ravens these days. Once a common bird along the valley, the raven likes seclusion when it nests and so it retreated, along with the wolf, to the northern and eastern forests. But now the great black birds are seen regularly enough in summer that many birdwatchers believe that they may be breeding in the Qu'Appelle's heavier woods.

There have been reports lately too of golden and bald eagles spending the summer in the eastern Qu'Appelle. Elk are again bugling in the larger coulees downstream of Round Lake, and even the odd moose wanders into view now and then. Bears, however, are as good an indicator as any of the eastern Qu'Appelle's status as a half-wild land-scape. During the remainder of the summer of '96, I was to hear several stories about bears in gardens, on roads, woofing at farmers and berry pickers. In a semi-wild country where there are still farm people on the land, a large and sometimes dangerous animal such as the black bear will enter the local lore in tales of a big brown one hiding in the out-house, of a boy chased to his doorstep when he was waiting for the schoolbus to arrive, of a large bear shaking an oak tree to knock the acorns down. Some individual bears, identifiable by their pelage, become familiar to local farmers: "We had a cinnamon-backed bear a few years back" or "There was that white one in the seventies, remember? Some hunter got it eventually." I was not to see any bears myself — only their spoor now and then — but they were always on my mind when I was in the oak woods or following a creek.

THE BEAR, in the original fireside narratives of this continent, has always been an intermediary between humans and the land. People change into bears, bears change into people, people mate with bears, hibernate with bears, go to live among bears. Cree lore shows this animal — like humans, versatile, omnivorous, and able to walk upright — to be a crea-ture that helps us to couple with or enter the wildness that surrounds us.

Mindful of the animal's power as an interlocutor between them-selves and their home landscape, the plains peoples have sometimes borrowed the bear's energy and characteristics by making its name their own. It was Velma Bear who showed me around Standing Buffalo reserve, and when I stopped in at the band office for the Qu'Appelle's easternmost reserve, Ochapowace, I requested permission to hike from a young band administrator named Darlene Bear.

Ochapowace has some of the wildest and most inaccessible woodlands in the Qu'Appelle basin. A large creek, Iskwaohead, on the east side of Ochap, slices toward the valley from the south, creating several square miles of intractable forest. The reserve's northern limits cover the entire south shore of Round Lake, where the shaded slopes of valley are com-pletely wooded. There are no houses or development on this part of the reserve; the land is left, at least so far, for berry picking and hunting, even though it could easily and profitably be leased out to cottagers, who have covered the other side of the lake with shoreline cabins, decks, boat launches, and docks.

Round Lake is not only the line where the valley takes on its distinctive eastern character; it also forms a boundary, as sharp as the contrast between wooded slopes and bare, between indigenous and non-indigenous people in the region. There are six reserves in the area, side by side, running from Crooked Lake to Round Lake. The next reserve due north of these is more than one hundred miles away on the edge of the boreal forest, where the nearest ravens and bears are to be found as well.

After walking through Ochap's prairie above the valley and the woods on its flanks, I went down to the beach where a sand jetty, the tip of an alluvial fan, curls out into Round Lake. Despite a jet-trail overhead and evidence of shoreline parties, a quiet stretch of beach like this allows me to countenance the original allure of the Qu'Appelle Lakes.

I had the shore and likely the entire south side of the lake to myself, except for the odd spotted sandpiper teetering among rocks. There were several massive cottonwood trees at my back. I wondered if they were of the eastern variety. I was calculating the effort required to get up and count the teeth on a leaf to see which species it was, when a splashing behind me and away from the beach took my attention. Thinking it might be something large, perhaps a bear come down to the water, I turned and found a family of cedar waxwings bathing in a rain puddle.

Two song sparrows, one on either side of me, sang from shoreline willows and testified to a specific harmony of moisture, space, and leaf where land and water meet. It was a dead calm day. Only one fishing boat on the water and as it passed down the lake, the surface rose and fell in long, slow swells, like a large animal breathing. Out in front of me, a couple of paces into the water, three barely submerged boulders poked their noses out and back in again as the wake came to shore. They looked much like spy-hopping sea lions I have seen on the Pacific. Long moments of stillness held the lake before giving way to the sudden hurl and plash of a walleye off the point. I became sleepy and my gaze fell to the wrack-line in front of me: poplar branches clipped by beaver, water weeds, dead crayfish, snails, mussel shells, and drying algae — the detritus of a windier day. I picked up a small orange leaf for a closer look, exposing a tiger beetle, alive but playing possum. After I replaced the leaf a few inches away, he still held his ground. When I looked for him a minute later he was gone. I checked the leaf and there he was. I shifted the leaf again and tried to catch the beetle moving, but something else took my attention and again he managed to slip under the leaf while I was looking away.

The afternoon, like the beetle, disappeared without my notice. It was time to leave Ochapowace and go to the other side of Round Lake where my cousin Gary lives with his wife, Sharon, in a lakefront cabin I could just make out from the sand jetty. There would be supper, talk of bird houses and purple martins — Gary has two thriving colonies — and Gary would tease me about risking my life at Ochap.

Round Lake folks stay clear of the reserves. The trench between whites and Indians at Round Lake deepened a couple of years back when a seventy-three-year-old cottager named William Dove was slain by two men and a teenager from a local reserve. The men appeared at Dove's door asking for assistance with a flat tire. They had been drinking heavily. Nonetheless and perhaps out of fear, Dove went with them out to the highway where their truck had broken down. After Dove tried to repair the tire for them, the men decided they would take his car and they began beating him. He died later of the injuries.

AFTER SUPPER AT GARY and Sharon's, we went outside to sit by the fire pit and look out over the lake. The sun well down and the moon not yet risen, an all-embracing darkness fell upon the valley as I walked out to the end of Gary's dock. I tried to glimpse the sand jetty where I had spent the afternoon at Ochapowace. The south wall of the valley was formless, inky black against the paler sky. Not a single light or any other sign, for that matter, of the inroads we have made upon the Qu'Appelle's grandeur.

On summer nights such as this, warm and still, the cottagers of Round Lake will sometimes send floating candles off into the darkness of the far shore. Later in the evening, a lantern sailed into view from the west as we sat by the fire listening to Gary explain that his birds are never bothered by neighbourhood cats, a phenomenon that he attributes to the local rate of feline heart failure, or .22 calibre coronary, as he calls it. Out past the dock, the lantern, a tea candle on the bottom half of a milk jug, was taken by a current and pulled southward to the middle of the lake. We watched it in silence, a single light rocking and shimmering as it glided imperceptibly across the water. As its glow faded, dwindling to a mere spark against the great black ramparts of Ochap's wooded hills, a second spark appeared just east of it, definite but dim enough for me to doubt my eyesight. As the near light faded, the far one grew brighter, as though they were passing one another on separate currents. The possibility that there may be someone on the other side of the lake — sitting in the dark and launching candles from the beach where tiger beetles were now emerging from their leaf-blinds — had me imagining how different the floating candles must appear from that far shore.

From our side, in the cottage subdivision, standing amid every accoutrement of our electrified civilization, the people of Round Lake look out and see their frail candles float off into the apparently uninhabited darkness of an unknown shore. Candlelight, flickering against a black emptiness, is perhaps reassurance that light prevails over dark, civilization over savagery.

But from the side where there are no boats, no barbecues, no yard lanterns, and only the articulate shadows of night and the ways of oak, bear, and hawk, anyone on the beach looking north would see the dazzle and sparkle of the new civilization, the incandescence of a culture that sheds light so gratuitously. And separating that spray of artificial light from the enfolding darkness behind and above would be the gradient of light running from the harsh glare of a thousand cabin lights to the soft glow of stars overhead.

On that peaceful night, anyone on the far shore would have seen the first small candle on its translucent boat crossing that same gradient of light mirrored in calm waters. Rocking tentatively on wavelets kicked up by vagrant breezes, it would have drawn nearer: a strange offering adrift on the lake, a light on a calm night from the people who have flooded this landscape with the glare of an alien culture. Then the second candle, like a reply released from the invaded shadows, issued toward the domain of glowing tungsten and mercury vapour; the two candles pass in an exchange between the side of the Qu'Appelle country that is domestic and ablaze with destructive enlightenment and the darker, wilder side where there are still bears, and Bears.

A candle floating across a lake is not propitiation or reconciliation, but on that night I wished and almost believed it could be. Returning to the landscapes of the eastern Qu'Appelle where my grandfather made a start ninety years ago, I knew I had some of my own propitiating and reconciling to do in the days to come. For intermediaries, I had at least the dreams and stories of forebears if not bears. Their pathways, I hoped, would show me how we came to abuse the river and the prairie, how we began to unravel the warp and weft binding Swainson's hawk to Richardson's ground squirrel to badger to burrowing owl to buffalo to buffalo-bird.

As I left Round Lake the next morning, a desire to start all over again at the water's edge, to float offerings of light against the dark, lingered in my thoughts, bearing me eastward into the country drained by the Little Cutarm.

# Part Four

# LAIRD OF THE LITTLE CUTARM

*THE STORIES PEOPLE TELL have a way of taking care of them.*

— BARRY LOPEZ

## Chapter Twenty-two

# BY THE RIVER

ALL WATER RUNS TO THE VALLEY. I am driving in a steady rain that has been falling since eight o'clock last night. The radio says it is sunny this morning in Regina and "throughout most of the Grain Belt," but here, in the eastern Qu'Appelle, the rain has been falling for fourteen hours and there is no line of blue on the horizon.

I have come here to look for big bluestem grass, Eastern wood pewees, chestnut-sided warblers, old pathways, and family stories. The grasses and birds will remind me that it has been too long since my last visit; the pathways and stories will remind me why I am a visitor, why I live in a city two hundred miles from what was once my grandfather's valley.

Next to me on the passenger seat, my Uncle Babes talks about the road conditions; runs his faded blue eyes over crops he has been watching for sixty summers. Babes, a retired farmer and a bachelor, has come along for the ride to see what his nephew from the city is up to; to help me open up the farmhouse where I will live for several weeks, amid the landscapes where my ancestors and the prairie came together in one generation and parted ways in the next.

I slept last night at my Aunt Evelyn's in Esterhazy, a town fourteen miles north and west along the Little Cutarm creek from the McRae homesite where she, my mother, and six more brothers and sisters lived as children seventy years ago. For the McRaes, as for thousands of other settler families, theirs was the slice of prairie history pressed between the heroic era of ox-and-plough pioneering and the postwar era of mechanized, gasoline-powered agribusiness. Their father, Jock McRae, was able to support a family at the mouth of the valley of the Little Cutarm Creek because of water. The hills of oak, spear grass, and bluestem surrounding the McRae farm sent water past its fields and yard site in one set of springs, one creek, and a long oxbow curve of the Calling River itself.

For the McRaes, these waters meant fish in the nets in May, mink in the traps in December, and the makings of good strong tea or stronger Scotch brews year round. Though none of my relatives had the gift of the water witch, I grew up hearing stories about people who felt the pull of waters, who lived their lives within the confluence of the Little Cutarm and the Qu'Appelle: Jock adrift on a floe of river ice at spring flood; the boys wading across the river to visit the Finn girls on the south side of the valley; my aunts and grandmother washing clothes in summer at a bend in the river; drinking from the Little Cutarm after eating far too many saskatoon berries; scooping carp by the basketful from the creek; burying the still in a sandbar to hide it from the RCMP.

This was their water, flowing and available, quenching thirst and hunger, and flooding their alluviated fields with rich sediment from the plains above.

The McRaes, as I said, were no diviners. The eastern Qu'Appelle, however, is a landscape scoured and filled by currents above and below, and has raised its share of men in whose hands a willow fork will twist toward hidden springs. Jock would have known the local dowsers well enough, but apparently never saw the need for their craft on his land at the mouth of the Little Cutarm. There never was a well on the home place. The McRaes have always believed that there was no groundwater available. It would take a good dowser and a test drilling-rig to prove this wrong, but the lay of the land, its abundant surface water, and obvious capacity to channel water to the main valley have left me looking for other ways to explain the lack of a well.

From what I know of my grandfather, it seems possible that he preferred water that moved in the light of day. Where he could watch its trickle, drink from its gathering pools, set his traps along its shores, hunt and walk its bottomlands.

Discovering good water on your property is still regarded in this region as a smile from God, ranking with other graces, like fertile land or beautiful daughters. And men who can find underground streams with a willow fork or two copper rods are still respected and granted special status here. By the shores of Round Lake, up-valley from the homesite, I have listened to my cousin Gary talk of local water witches. Of the time he watched the copper rods bend in the grip of a dowser for whom the gift was strong. Of people in the valley who, after hauling their water from town for years, hired a water witch to locate a well. The witch walked the property, the willow bent, the farmer dug, one spadeful, two, and water bubbled out onto the grass — to run thereafter as an artesian well, sixty feet from the back door.

Several of Gary's stories were of a water witch whose sorcery is legendary in the eastern Qu'Appelle — a diviner remarkably named Wizener. More than once, Gary has watched the willow fork twist so violently for Wizener that the bark has torn in his grip. One time, Gary tried holding the fork himself over the same ground. Nothing. Then Wizener grabbed hold of his wrists and immediately Gary felt the surge of a strange energy moving through his hands.

When talk turns to water witches, Gary will eventually dig out a set of copper rods and offer to run a test to see if his visitors have any hydrological inclinations. Without disclosing the location of the spring that runs beneath his back lawn, he sends the candidate, rods in hand, out across his property. I walked with ponderous and slow steps over his lawn gripping the coppers and proved I was as incompetent a finder of wells as any McRae. Not so much as a shimmy. My wife, Karen, on the other hand, had the coppers crossing and uncrossing in all the right places. She found the first spring immediately. Then, thinking it was beginner's luck, we tried her out on another subterranean flow that Gary knew of down the lane. Again she located the water. I should not have been surprised by this; Karen has always been something of an underemployed clairvoyant, inclined to the witching arts. She now tells people that she is the second dowser to be discovered by Gary. One of these days, I'll have to see if she can find water on the home place.

But I have come back to the eastern Qu'Appelle to perform a divining rite of another kind. Grappling with stories and memory instead of copper rods or a willow fork, I want to locate the currents, running beneath the surface of family mythos, that drew us away from the valley and the Little Cutarm where a young Jock McRae once mucked a spring out of the shale at creekside.

THE WATER THAT MY WINDSHIELD wipers throw onto the road will make its way, above ground or below, to the floodplain of the Little Cutarm Valley. We are now less than a mile from where I am to live for the next several weeks. The house, built by my grandfather for his eldest son, rests on the verge of a promontory 350 feet above the valley bottom where the Little Cutarm spills into the Qu'Appelle.

From the house, once my Uncle Henry's farmstead, it is a one-mile walk downhill and across the creek to the cellar depression that marks the original McRae farm. Henry was a larger-than-life character I knew only from family stories. Everyone called him "Sonny," just as everyone called Uncle Everett "Snooks," and still calls Uncle Laurence "Babes." I think I was in university before I learned that my uncles had real names. Sonny died a young man in 1949, leaving a wife, three small sons, a farm, and a memory that has taken on the mantle of tragedy in the McRae family myth. He was thirty-nine years old when he died; I'll be thirty-nine in October.

Sonny's widow, Aunt Bertha, or Bea, carried on farming with the help and hindrance of Jock, her father-in-law. Aunt Bea, intelligent, tough, able-handed, is of that disappearing breed of rural women who once elevated farm life above a crude wrestling with nature for sustenance. She lived in the house for almost sixty years — alone for the last twenty — finally giving in to the concerns of her sons and, reluctantly, selling the farmsite and taking a suite in Esterhazy.

For much of the last ten years of my grandfather's life, he made himself at home in Aunt Bea's house, as though in losing his eldest son he had some claim upon it. His own daughters had not married farmers, and lived in cities or towns. He tried living with Evelyn in the nearby village of Tantallon, but away from his fields, the cattle, and pigs, his spirit soon withered. By the 1960s, even before my grandmother had died, Jock was more or less living on the farm with Aunt Bea. Almost all my memories of my grandfather occur in Aunt Bea's house, where he lived out his last years on the valley rim above the home farm at the mouth of the Little Cutarm.

Passing by familiar fields and my cousin Jerry's abandoned house, I am feeling uneasy about inhabiting Aunt Bea's place when she is no longer there. Although the land and buildings now belong to a young farmer who lives in Stockholm thirty miles away, and although I called Aunt Bea and asked for her permission, I can't help feeling like another interloper, another McRae making himself at home in a place where he has no claim.

As I turn onto the long approach that heads to Aunt Bea's and the valley, the rain picks up its pace. Rivulets trickle along the ditches and fill up the holes in the road's gravel surface. I begin to notice a remarkable thing. For the past mile and a half I have been seeing frogs crossing the road in front of the car. Dozens of frogs. More frogs than I have seen in the last ten years altogether. They stretch themselves out in wet, elastic hops that carry them quickly over the road. Now that I am halfway along the approach and passing fields that my grandfather once cultivated, the frogs are becoming even more numerous. Wood frogs, chorus frogs, large green leopard frogs, even the odd tiger salamander. The frogs leap out of the knee-high wheat, onto the gravel track, take three sticky hops and dive back into the grain on the other side. I have not seen the likes of this before, and may never see it again. These amphibians must not have heard that North American populations of their species are in steep decline, that the thinning ozone layer, background levels of toxic chemicals, or some other ecological abomination is killing them off.

It dawns on me that the frogs are all moving in the same direction — following the rivulets and ditch-rivers down to the valley. It is an extraordinarily wet year and as I get out of the car, slosh toward Aunt Bea's house, and find a wood frog greeting me on the doorstep, I allow myself to wonder whether rivers have edges we cannot see, whether this small cottage is nearer the banks of the Calling River than it appears to be.

*Chapter Twenty-three*

# TANTALLON

I UNLOAD THE CAR, place my things in Aunt Bea's kitchen and walk through rooms to see what my memory has done to the walls and fixtures. A faint tincture of fuel oil coming from the little brown stove in the living room returns me to Christmases and Eastertimes: the same small room wall to wall with cousins, aunts, and uncles around a great table with legs like lathe-turned tree trunks varnished black; Aunt Bea and the other women serving food; the men laughing loudly; Jock in his chair wearing braces and smoking roll-your-owns.

The local repairman for the electrical company will be here in half an hour to turn on the power. I have just enough time to locate the well in the yard and see if there is any chance of getting it to pump water into the house. I walk out through Aunt Bea's gate and across the driveway where the corrals used to be. In rubber boots I wade knee-deep into the soggy brome grass, searching for signs of a well lid, as Babes shouts directions from the driveway. This is a familiar feeling — bent over at the waist, high-stepping in boots through a wet emerald-green place, looking for something hidden in grass. I half expect to hear the chatter of a marsh wren, to see a muskrat splash in front of me. I part the growth, and right where there might be a mallard nest, I find a plywood lid covering the well.

Something too small to be a muskrat scurries down into the well as

I remove the cover. A deer mouse. The clouds toss a spate of harder rain into the drizzle, and I think about following the mouse downward to have a look at the pump. I know almost nothing about wells, even less about pumps.

When I reach the bottom of the ladder, the deer mouse is there waiting for me next to the pump. It eyes my boot, no doubt weighing the pros and cons of risking a human-assisted run to daylight. The pump comes with levers and gauges, but no instruction manual. Having determined that, yes, the well appears sound; yes, I will need help to get it operating; and no, I cannot catch a deer mouse in my hands at the bottom of a well, I return to the wet world above. Babes, who is not surprised by any of this, recommends we go into the village later and see if my cousin Jerry can help.

The village is Tantallon, once a commercial and cultural centre for the district, now a dwindling assemblage of potash miners, retired farmers, and a few children waiting to grow up and move away. One of the only towns located on the bottomlands of the Qu'Appelle Valley, and the easternmost of these, Tantallon has spread its cluster of households across the floodplain from the north hills to the south. The river is pinched tight against the southern wall of the valley, where it curls through the edge of town beneath a bower of arching Manitoba maples.

A *bower*. I can't think of the south side of Tantallon without lapsing into an idyll that is part wish, part memory. I wish I could say I grew up in Tantallon, but in fact I lived there only one year as a small child. All of my earliest memories of life and landscape come from the turn of seasons we spent by the riverside in the three-storey house that we called the Mansion. My grandfather bought the Mansion, which had originally been built by W.C. Paynter, a town father and one of the founders of Saskatchewan's co-operative movement. My grandmother lived with us, and from time to time Jock would come down from Aunt Bea's to stay for a day or two. I remember standing beside the old man in his upstairs bedroom, watching him sit and slurp strong tea from a saucer.

If there is a single configuration of landform and vegetation that has shaped my landscape sensibilities, it is the world I saw from the Mansion's verandah. To the south, maples along the riverbank, the Qu'Appelle slipping past secretly, and beyond, the southern wall of the valley rising almost four hundred feet with rank upon rank of poplar, oak, and birch. To the east, a rough lawn in the yard, shaded by giant elms and maples, and then, at the edge of the property, the town bridge with its two broad arches of concrete spanning the river. When my father was hired at the potash mine, we moved to Esterhazy, north of the valley. It was only a fifteen-minute drive to Aunt Bea's and Tantallon, so we visited often, but we were distanced further by the industry and suburban aspirations of our squared and modern subdivision of miner families — people recruited from the failed economies of Ontario and the Maritimes.

And the valley was no longer the setting of daily life. River, bridge, maples — the view from the Mansion — was supplanted by new images of the valley and Tantallon, the roadside impressions of a visitor.

Driving to Tantallon on weekends, we would descend into the valley from the north on a winding road that showed the valley sweeping in a great curve from the west horizon through the village and away to the southeast. The village itself — a rink, a clutch of shops and hotel facing onto Main Street, elevators along the CPR line, and houses poking through foliage increasing with proximity to the river — looked in this aerial view like an elaborate model-railway set.

I still feel the tug of memory and anticipation when I come over the lip of the valley from the north, watching for this first glimpse of Tantallon's rooftops. I remember a small oil painting of Tantallon hanging on a wall in our Esterhazy house. An artistic aunt on my father's side painted it when she came to the village for my parents' wedding in the late 1950s. She sat on the north hills and brushed in the village with small dabs of colour against the yellow and green of the valley slopes. Tantallon summarized, simplified, and suspended in one June afternoon forty years ago. As a boy, I stared at this painting and the rows of Tantallon houses looked to me like gemstones or bright sea shells strung together and laid on golden cloth. This small painting conspired with the roadside panorama of Tantallon to post me, in sentiment and desire, high upon the verge of the valley, far enough to see the beauty and quiet of village life, too far away to see its decay and delinquency. Learning the lie of the distant view has not completely removed me from the hilltop. A part of me remains there, looking down at a village coloured by time and unfettered nostalgia: 1962, a mansion shaded by elms and the river running by the south side of town.

THE ELECTRICIAN IS HERE NOW. As he checks the breaker box, we make conversation. Our words, idle and cursory, tumble into the emptiness of Aunt Bea's back porch, against rain-spattered window panes, until we settle on a subject of interest.

"So, how do you know the McRaes?" he asks.

"I'm a relative. Bertha is my aunt — married my mother's brother."

"You related to Kevin McRae?"

"He's my cousin Eddie's son. He still lives on a farm a couple of miles from here, doesn't he?"

"Yep. He works at the mine. My son's been dating Kevin's daughter."

There it is again. The electrician's son dates my second cousin's daughter. I haven't lived here for thirty-five years, but the interconnections of blood, marriage, and courtship form a web that is impossible to avoid. Yesterday, Aunt Ev told me that even the new landowner, the young agribusinessman who bought Aunt Bea's place, is married to one of my relatives. This was disappointing news, for I had been creating a caricature in my mind of a thoughtless, absentee mega-farmer who had no filial relation to the soil he overtook. Now it turns out that he has wed Becky Sutherland, daughter of my second cousin who lives on the land a few miles north of here, where my great-grandfather Donald Sutherland homesteaded exactly one hundred years ago.

When the electrician is finished, Babes tests out the stove by making a pot of Red Rose. Emboldened by strong, sticky tea, we head for Tantallon to find a McRae who can help with the well. The rain has let up and a gap in the overcast appears in the west. Rounding the curve before the steep grade down into the valley, I feel myself wincing inwardly, afraid to look at the village from the north-hill view, afraid to see what is missing or ruined since my last visit. One more curve and the Tantallon of 1996 appears above my steering wheel. Golden light from the hole in the sky lights up the gables of town, the back of the hotel, the curving face of the rink, the too-straight strip of grass where the rails of the CPR once bisected the valley in a sweep from Bear Creek to the Little Cutarm.

The road hauls my station wagon to the valley floor and into town past the rink and what appears to be an oversized statue of Bambi's father: a beacon to trophy hunters who come from far and wide to bag the large white-tailed deer found in this end of the valley. Main Street, with more empty lots than full ones, appears to be utterly desolate, save for the litter of trucks latched onto "the store" like piglets on a sow. What surprises me, as we cross the abandoned CPR line and turn off Main Street, is the vitality of the neighbourhood on the east side of town. The homes appear to be occupied for the most part, and are well-tended, with gardens, swing sets, and driveways lined with clipped hedges. I'm not sure what exactly I expected to find, but it was not these marigolds adorning the walkways and eight-year-old boys riding bicycles.

Babes directs me to Jerry's house. The last time I saw my cousin, he was still living a mile east of Aunt Bea's in a big old farmhouse. According to Babes, Jerry and his wife, Iona, quit farming a couple of years ago and moved into this two-storey home behind the United Church. The house is a graceful old building with a verandah and trees all around; probably built in the 1920s and still in fine condition.

We park out front. I follow Babes up the front steps. He walks through the verandah, the entrance, and into the kitchen and hollers something incomprehensible — "wharthellarya" — as I stand in the doorway admiring the woodwork on the stairway to the second floor.

"Nice place," I say to Babes.

"No one's home."

Without Jerry's help, there is little hope of my getting Aunt Bea's well to run, so on the way out of Tantallon, I stop to draw water at the town pump. As I fill up my jugs, a small leopard frog bathes in the puddle beneath the tap.

We head back to Aunt Bea's to cook up a supper of new potatoes and carrots from Babes's garden and bread and a casserole from Evelyn's kitchen. After supper, I take Babes back into Esterhazy. Stopping to talk with Evelyn for a moment before returning to the farm, I mention something about liking the feel of Jerry's house.

"Well, you should," she says, "Daddy built that for Frank Baker in the twenties."

Evelyn then tells me that the floor plan is identical to the McRae house at the mouth of the Little Cutarm and that if Jock had ever finished his own house, it would have looked exactly like this one he built for Baker.

DRIVING SLOWLY BACK to the farm alone, I compare my memory of the McRae farmhouse — it was an abandoned ruin even when I was a child — with the grand edifice I had admired earlier in the day in Tantallon. And I think about why my grandfather never completed his own house; why the McRaes grew up in a building that had only one interior wall, ladders instead of staircases, an ash pile instead of an outhouse, no fixtures, and no glass in the top-floor windows. The official family story blames a bank failure that occurred just after the house was framed, but the disrepair of the McRae household was ultimately, I believe, an expression of Jock's personal regard for the necessities of life and how he should engage himself in attaining them. In his mind, the house was a manor fit for the gentry compared to the low-roofed shed of his own childhood in Scotland. And as for its shortcomings, the staircases and windows would come as soon as he could take time away from the farm, the carpentry jobs, trapping, hunting, and other gainful enterprises. This distance between my grandfather's view of the house and its reality — a place where the boys sleeping upstairs would wake on winter mornings with their hair frozen to the wall — is somehow reconciled in my mind by the one decorative flourish that graced the old house.

On the west side, receiving the afternoon sun, was a small piano window with panes of cut glass leaded together in a simple gothic pattern. A piano window, but never a piano. In my recollection of the house in its abandonment, the window's bevelled glass shines clean, hard, and smooth within the weathered grey of siding and sill. When the old house was eventually torn down and hauled away, the only piece anyone saved was this small, anomalous reference to gentility.

Rounding the curve toward Aunt Bea's, I watch storm clouds rising above the Little Cutarm Valley where the village of Hazelcliffe, population eight, rests upon its floodplain a few miles upstream of the homesite. By the time I reach the yard, the downpour has begun. In the kitchen, rain is skinting through the screen of an open window, and a puddle is already forming on the table.

I clean up the kitchen and slide into my sleeping bag, listening to the storm and thinking of Tantallon. Tantallon, somehow still alive despite the depredations of modern culture and economy.

Darkness from the edge of the valley has wrapped itself around the little house like swaddling. The rain falls into sudden pools of blue light with each flash from the sky. I begin to read through a book of Tantallon history that Aunt Evelyn loaned me. *Tales of Tantallon*, one of those chronicles "dedicated to the memory of our pioneers" that every prairie town publishes sooner or later. I turn the pages looking for parallels and connections between people: the links of blood, marriage, and ethnic origin that bind together a local settlement on the plains. A thought comes of another parallel, as recent as the rain pounding against the window: Jock McRae had ten grandsons. Jerry is the second eldest; I am the second youngest. Tonight we both are dry under rooftops raised by the hands of our carpenter grandfather.

## Chapter Twenty-four

# THE CROFTER'S TRAIL

I GREW UP LISTENING to stories of Tantallon and the McRaes and their neighbours in the districts locally known as West Valley and Valley View. West Valley is a seven- or eight-square-mile string of valley that includes the bottomland and hillsides immediately west of Tantallon. It ends, as near as I can tell, two miles west of the confluence of the Little Cutarm and the Qu'Appelle. Valley View is a larger district, roughly fourteen square miles, bordered on the west by the rim of the Little Cutarm Valley and on the south by the rim of the Qu'Appelle. The northern limits seem to be the correction line between townships 18 and 19, and the eastern boundary is the road that leads north from Tantallon to the town of Gerald.

The people from these districts are familiar to me as characters in stories I have been hearing all my life. The same stories, told again and again, reworked, supplemented, argued over. The hot summer day that Snooks fried an egg on the flat boulder in the yard. Mrs. Hugh Irvine and her infamous henshit tea. The woman up the valley who chained her sickly brother-in-law inside a granary, keeping him barely alive on gruel and water. Jock feeding his pigs on mash leftover from his home brew and then delivering them drunk to a happy end at the slaughter-house. The Hudasiks, the Irvines, the Tinnishes, Doc Morrison, and the Kallios. Ghosts that haunt roads, sleighs that tip over, fish that jump into the frying pan. Peddlers, gypsies, Indians, Christmas pageants, house dances, and threshing crews.

Reading *The Tales of Tantallon* that first storm-lashed night at Aunt Bea's, I began to get a feel for the tilth of the West Valley culture, the ground in which the McRae stories grew.

The earliest white residents of the Valley View and West Valley districts were three men: Thomas, James, and John William Brown. These three Englishmen were brothers, I believe, though it is not clear from the book, and they appear to stem from a family that emigrated from Northumberland to Canada in the 1850s. They came to the Qu'Appelle Valley area in 1884 by way of Minnedosa, Manitoba. After clearing and breaking a few acres, the Browns retreated to Minnedosa for the winter. In spring they returned to their new homesteads on the north rim of the valley and seeded their land. Then they departed once again to settle matters in Minnedosa and retrieve their respective wives and children. James Brown's sixteen-year-old son, David, stayed behind to tend the homestead by himself for the spring and summer.

By the time I got out the topo map to locate the Brown homesteads, the rain had slackened to a steady hiss against Aunt Bea's house — the sound of water that has been falling forever, drowning out all memory of drier nights. According to the legal description for the homestead, David Brown spent that first summer exactly one mile east of Aunt Bea's house, where I lay reading his story.

The year was 1885. The young Brown would likely have been living in a log shanty, perhaps a tent. His nearest white neighbour was a Scotsman some miles away in the next district to the east. He would have heard his father and uncles talking of Indians and the possibility of trouble. The Cree and Métis in the North-West Territories were on the verge of taking some kind of action to protect their lands and way of life. And so David Brown, the first white person to stay for a spring and summer anywhere near the Little Cutarm Valley, was not altogether surprised when he saw a large band of Cree warriors ride by one morning. He was down along the banks of the Qu'Appelle, cutting brush, when he heard the sound of drums approaching from downstream. He hunkered down in the willows to wait as the long procession drew near, eventually passing by him in single file, Cree men on horseback, wearing paint and full battle regalia. Months later he learned of the events at Batoche and Duck Lake and realized what he had witnessed on that spring morning.

Much that stands between me and the significance of early events in this landscape collapses when I read such stories. The young Brown, crouched in the brush, wide-eyed in terror and fascination, draws me from the origins of the eastern Qu'Appelle culture to the larger dramas of the Northern Great Plains, the violence and injustice we have euphemistically titled the "Opening up of the West." Whether it was a desire to place myself at that moment of intersection between the origins of West Valley and the turned-aside dreams of Riel and his people or simply a fascination with the connecting threads of history that trail behind our lives, I kept reading the Brown family story until I managed to draw a remote connection between the battles of 1885 and my grandmother's family, the Sutherlands.

One of the three original Browns who settled in Valley View served with the colonial forces at Batoche. John William Brown, who seems to have been an uncle of David's, enlisted from Minnedosa when he heard about Louis Riel's rebellious stand along the banks of the South Saskatchewan. Thomas Brown, J.W.'s eldest son, was the first male child born to settlers in Valley View. Although I never met the man — he died seven years before I was born — he married my grandmother's little sister and was, therefore, my great-uncle. Though her name was Janet, I knew my great-aunt always as Aunt Jo, the kind spirit who inhabited the other half of our riverside mansion. In my memory, Aunt Jo is always laughing, serving tea in a room with a china cabinet full of elaborate figurines and fine cups and saucers. Beside her is my Uncle Will, the man she wed in a second marriage the year I was born.

Uncle Will, a soft-hearted man of great dignity and patience, brings me round again to my grandfather. Will Miller and Jock were childhood friends in the county Caithness of northern Scotland, where they had grown up in rural poverty and the same wretched social conditions that had persisted since their ancestors had been evicted from their Highland homes a century before. In 1906, the two of them set out for a place in the New World where any man could live like a laird, graze cattle in waist-high grass on hillsides, and hunt along streams in wooded valleys brimming with deer and grouse. The same place

Scottish emigrants had been singing about on ships and trains for thirty
years:

> *We're sailing west, we're sailing west,*
> *to prairie lands sun-kissed and blest —*
> *the crofter's trail to happiness.*[51]

Land-settlement agencies and the Canadian government might have
exaggerated the abundance of the prairies in general, but the eastern
Qu'Appelle almost lived up to the billing. To Will and Jock, Valley View,
West Valley, and Tantallon were as yet only names in letters from friends
and relatives who had been immigrating to the region for the previous
fifteen years. Encouraging letters from Caithness settlers, who described
an abundant land of open and rolling plains much like the glaciated
lowlands around the Caithness towns of Banniskirk and Halkirk. The
letters would surely have mentioned as well a great, wooded valley and
a river, with tributary streams coming in from smaller valleys. Word of
such land would have caught the attention of a young man who liked to
hunt, who had no doubt walked south from Halkirk far enough to see
the distant hills looming upstream above the River Thurso, and who
had heard his elders speak of the lost McRae homelands high in the
mountains of Kintail and Glensheil.

By 1906, the ethnic landscape surrounding Tantallon had already
been established. The Scots, mostly Caithness families, had claimed
Valley View and much of West Valley to the west and north of the village. The first Caithness people to come were Bill and Hugh Henderson
in 1891, settling on the next section east of the original Brown homestead where sixteen-year-old David spent that first summer. Local
people still call a prominent ridge on that section Henderson's Hill — a
long gentle slope jutting into the valley at the mouth of a small tributary
ravine coming in from the north. After the Hendersons came the Foxes
and then a flood of other Caithness families: Williamsons, Sutherlands,
Hamiltons, Millers, Shearers, Lamons, Bruces, Campbells, Coghills,
Moodys, Gunns, Malcolms, Sinclairs, and McRaes. At least sixteen families in the districts surrounding Tantallon came from Caithness county.
Most settled in Valley View.

Immediately east of Valley View and north of the valley is a district that was settled predominantly by Icelandic people, with the odd Scotsman or Englishman here and there. The early Icelandic families named their new home Holar, Icelandic for "hills." Below the Holar district, where the valley east of Tantallon takes a sharp turn south, is a region that was homesteaded by Englishmen and a few Caithness families at the turn of the century. If you drive the road that runs along the valley bottom south of Tantallon today, you will pass several farm-gate signs showing the surname Kingdon, one of the early English families in the district.

While Scottish newcomers were settling into Valley View and West Valley districts, on the other side of the valley people with surnames such as Kautonen, Luhtala, Kivela, and Polvi were homesteading. On this stony, heavily wooded land, these families established what came to be known as New Finland, for most of them had emigrated by steamship from the port of Hangoniemi, Finland. The first homesteader in the district, however, was a Russian Jew, Harry Jacobsen, who arrived in 1889. Jacobsen belonged more properly to the district immediately south of New Finland, to which fifty families of orthodox, Yiddish-speaking Jews came between 1886 and 1907, fleeing religious pogroms in Russia. Among these people, who formed the first successful Jewish farm settlement anywhere in Canada, was the founder of the now famous Bronfman family, Ezekiel Bronfman.

Both the Finns and the Russian Jews made large homes and barns out of poplar logs, the Finns typically squaring the face of each pole. Over the hewn logs, joined neatly at corners with a distinctive saddle and notch jointing, the Finns always installed diagonal willow lathing. Over this they added plaster and whitewash made from lime burned in local hillside lime kilns. The result was a white finished surface covering the logs, keeping out dust and cold.

One afternoon when I was walking through the provincial wildlife lands on the south side of the valley opposite the mouth of the Little Cutarm, I came across several of these Finnish buildings with white mud and plaster over lathing and squared logs. The homes have been long vacant — no one has lived in this part of the valley for years — but they have weathered remarkably well. Even in their decay, these structures continue to evoke a proud beauty, a gracefulness that other homesteads lack. It is something in the textured whiteness of the remaining plaster, and the mindful work that such an exterior implies.

As I poked around these old farms, I thought about the Finnish family that I knew from family stories. Charlie and Sanna Kallio raised ten children just across the river from the McRaes in the unofficial borderland between West Valley and New Finland. On moonless nights, the McRaes looked out over the valley and saw the lamplight of the Kallio household surrounded by the dark bottomlands. I have found places like this farther west in the Qu'Appelle, where in winter the southern constellations overarch a valley darker than the night sky, a black trough that surrounds the electric glow of a farmhouse on the floodplain, shining like a stud fallen from Orion's great belt.

And I thought of the visits that my mother and her sisters once enjoyed at the Kallios, drinking strong Finnish coffee and laughing as they ran from the house to the steam-bath shack. Steam bathing was a small luxury the people of New Finland brought with them from the old country. As a Northern people's tradition, it transferred well to the climate and wooded slopes of the eastern Qu'Appelle. On cold Saturday evenings, the McRaes would pile into the sleigh and head for the Kallio farm, where they would enjoy one another's company in the moist heat of the steam bath, visiting as they brushed their backs and legs with rushes gathered from the riverbank. The snow, dry and crisp in mounds at the base of maple trees, waited just outside the shack's envelope of heat and steam. When the warmth had penetrated every pore and found its way to their bones, the Kallios would fling open the door, step through its passageway, and jump into the white drifts, rolling wildly in the fallen crystals, and laughing all the more at the sight of the McRaes who were wreathed in steam and staring, incredulous, from the inside of the shack.

The Kallios, however, were locally famous for more than their steam baths. Charlie and Sanna had raised a surplus of enchanting daughters, nine in all, who knew their way around kitchen, barn, and garden. Between the McRae farm at the mouth of the Little Cutarm and the Kallio farm, a path was worn into the grass by the feet of McRae men crossing the bottomlands and wading the river to call on the prettiest girls in the district. And so, the two families eventually joined in marriage what the river divided in property: Snooks married a Kallio girl named Viola, and Sonny married her older sister, Bertha.

*Chapter Twenty-five*

# NARRATIVES OF
# ENDURANCE AND JOY

Wʜᴇɴ I ᴛʜɪɴᴋ ᴏꜰ Aᴜɴᴛ Bᴇᴀ it is always with an awareness of her place among all the McRae daughters and daughters-in-law as the one who lived her life out on the land within sight of the home farm; and with an awareness of the dignity this granted her, the dignity of a woman who shaped her spirit and flesh against the weight of the uncountable tasks of growing things, feeding people, keeping house and farm together. Tasks made somewhat lighter by the small pleasures that stitch work into life's fabric — the warm, yielding life of bread dough against her palms, the cultivated extravagance of delphiniums in the garden, the comforting whiff of tobacco on a cool April morning's walk to the henhouse. And yet, for all this, I know that life was hard for her, as it had been for my grandmother Millie. Both women had the usual labour and worries that fall to the farmwife — animals, children, and gardens to keep alive. Both had few luxuries, until late in life. Both gave time, attention, and patience to the same ornery Scotsman who had all but declared himself Laird of the Little Cutarm.

The world that circumscribed the lives of the McRaes in poverty or plenty, anguish or serenity — the world of Valley View, West Valley, the Little Cutarm, and Tantallon that I have known from family stories — has gone from the life of the eastern Qu'Appelle like the summer mists that leave the bottomlands at daybreak. Where once there were twenty households in a district, now there are three or four. Young Finns no longer cross the river on Sunday afternoons to play softball at the McRaes' three-corner field.

On that first night at Aunt Bea's I thought about the loss of this nascent rural culture and about all that connects a family mythology to the actual, cold, unembellished experience of living off what your back and spirit will bear. It has, I believe, something to do with what Wendell Berry has called the "customs of necessity."[52]

In a rural peasant culture, says Berry, the dull, callus-forming tasks of daily survival become rituals lending significance to what would otherwise remain meaningless drudgery. He refers to "minute strategies of endurance and joy," arguing that "the sense of familiarity finally crests in ritual . . . which tends not only to protect the individual's sense of himself in relation to the place, but the place as well."[53]

Berry uses the word *ritual* carefully, I think, because the quality of one's relationship with the land in how one comes to feed one's self is, ultimately, a matter of "religion" — and here again I mean not church doctrine or private piety, but the ligaments that bind us to one another and to the land. With this in mind, when I consider who left and who stayed among the McRaes — who felt the tie most strongly — I find at least part of the answer to my question about the link between family myths and the tasks of daily subsistence.

As one would expect, the McRaes who grew up and stayed to live a rural life near the home farm were also the ones who as children were charged with the chores of sowing crops, feeding animals, harvesting and processing the yield. The two boys who did most of the farm work stayed nearest home: Sonny on the adjacent quarter, and Babes on the McRae land itself. Of the four girls, only the eldest, Evelyn, had regular chores on the farm, in the kitchen, and in the garden. She also spent many a winter night helping her father skin and stretch muskrat, mink, and coyote pelts. Her sisters, before the age of eighteen, all moved away to cities where they met young men who had also left home and farm for industrial jobs. Evelyn, however, fell in love with the neighbour's boy, Lewis Tinnish. She married him and stayed close to home, living first on the Tinnish farm and later in Tantallon, taking prizes at the town fair every year of the last sixty for her garden produce, flowers, baking, and canning. Her three urban sisters gave up most of these homely skills in favour of the supermarket long ago.

This correlation is unremarkable until it is seen in light of another relationship involving the family stories themselves. Most of the narratives, naturally, tell of events that occurred as moments of relief or contrast within the recurring patterns of work and rest. Something that happened while picking berries, while bringing in the cattle, at the weekly house dance, on the daily sleigh ride to school. It was a life lived in place and remembered as counterpoints along a baseline of diurnal and seasonal repetition. A life that entailed at least the possibility of a religious relationship with the land that fed and was in turn fed by similar rhythms. The stories would not be remembered, told, and listened to without that life, without the customs of necessity and repetitions of labour between land and mouth.

Of this signifying ritual, all that remains sixty years later are the stories, now themselves rituals in the telling and retelling. They are the ragged, leftover bits of an almost-culture, the remnants that kept some people tied to the place of their birth, while others were drawn or forced away to localities where the boundaries of culture and economy have expanded out of sight, where the customs of necessity have been traded for dubious varieties of leisure, and where local mythology has no ground in which to grow.

Such a bond between narrative and locale has also meant that the McRaes who stayed nearest the farm have the best memory for the stories and feel most obligated to preserve them, like heirlooms they take down from the shelf and polish from time to time. While Babes, the introvert bachelor, has always kept his memories somewhere behind the washed blue of his eyes, Evelyn and Johnny in later years vied with one another to see who would become the primary repository of the McRae histories. Before Johnny's death a couple of years ago, I used to enjoy listening to him and his sister argue over dates and details of circumstance, each convinced that the other was improvising from a fictional theme. Meanwhile, my mother and her other two sisters, who as children were more or less spared the menial tasks of farm life, can remember only scraps of some of the stories and have come increasingly to rely upon Evelyn for details.

Some details are left out, of course. The McRaes and their neighbours lived through much — poverty and pain, envy and greed — that does not surface in family mythology. Stories handed down from our forebears are much like the china cabinets and chiffoniers left to us. They all come with a protective coating of varnish.

Given this gloss and the knowledge that to a significant extent the people of the West Valley and Little Cutarm — like rural people throughout the plains — participated in the undoing of their own culture, the McRae stories would seem a dubious oracle. Yet, at some level, I have always regarded these stories, as well as those from my father's family, as a source of elder wisdom; perhaps my only source. Now, as an adult who presumes to evaluate land use in this region, I return to these accounts of the way my grandparents lived, just as a man will return sooner or later to the flawed faith he was born to. The model is incomplete, shot through with human failing, but it is the only model that has a claim upon my blood. The stories of the West Valley and the Little Cutarm, with their pathos, hyperbole, heroism, and drama, have come down to me as relics from a recent distant age, signifying the possibility of living with dignity and respect in this landscape. From such narrative I take my bearings and find my way in a world where ritual is gone from our relationships with the land, where religion is relegated to a moribund orthodoxy, where mass culture has replaced the experience of local culture, and where a malignant consumerism destroys thrift and responsible economy.

No more than a shadow of that long-ago world in the valley west of Tantallon, the stories, nonetheless, are worthy of my attention. Holding them in my memory, guessing at the truths they leave out or hide, has shaped my thinking on landscape, culture, and nature more than any other influence in my life. When I walk the grown-in trails through the tallgrass at the foot of Bruce's Point, it is to touch the world worn bare by the feet of my mother's family, to trace the pathways and the tales that tell me what was good in their contact with the land, what least effort they made to resist the pull of the industrializing, homogenizing economy beyond, and what attention they paid to the customs of necessity that bring together a family and a landscape.

*Chapter Twenty-six*

# HAMONA

T*HE* BRIDGE WAS JUST *a culvert across the [Big] Cutarm. We were warned to walk in the centre of the bridge. I remember how we clung to each other and carefully walked in the middle. The road was deeply rutted by wagons and, in the morning, the dewy grass lay thick over the road and felt so good on our bare feet.*

*The flowers along the way were red columbine, blue fringe gentian, yellow water lilies, all in the creek. The wild rhubarb stalks we used as sun shades. Wild morning glories and hop vines covered the shrubs by the side of the road. There were birds singing and wild fruit in abundance. Noon hour and recess were never long enough. We played pom-pom pull away, prisoner's base, ante-I-over, cricket, and hopscotch.*

*We walked to the creek at noon for drinking water. We tried to dip it where there were no minnows. I still remember the warm musky taste of the water.*

— A CHILD OF HAMONA COLONISTS REMEMBERS SCHOOL NEAR
THE BANKS OF THE BIG CUTARM IN *THE SPY HILL STORY*.

KICHEKISKAPETTONANO SEPESIS AND KISKIPITTONAWE SEPESIS, Big Cutarm Creek and Little Cutarm Creek, the McRaes and the Paynters, personal utopias and social utopias — the parallel outflow of tributaries and narrative swirled around and within me as I swam upstream in the waters of the Big Cutarm on a late-July afternoon. It was hot for a change. Only the black-eyed Susans would see me, so I had slipped out of my clothes and into the water-lilied, sun-dappled world of the Qu'Appelle's last tributary. Rounding a bend where I could see a meadow of bergamot and harebell, I hauled myself out onto a flat rock. I lay there letting the sun and wind pull the creekwater droplets from my skin. An eastern wood pewee sent its distinctive *peee-ah-wee* song from the woods nearby as I drifted into a waterside reverie. A brief one. There is always something pushing you back into the water — mosquitoes, horseflies, wind. This time it was fish. A school of creek chubb had discovered my feet dangling in the water. Chubb are curious and will nibble on anything you drop into the water — bread, sausage, toes, anything.

And so I dove back into the Big Cutarm, touched its stony bottom, and pulled my way along the stream bed through braided currents of warm and cold water. Downstream of me, at the creek's opening upon the main valley, I had spent the afternoon at the source of my muddled daydream, a no-place that people once called Hamona.

Before my lungs gave out, I opened my eyes to the clear yellow glow of sunlight coming through the undersides of lily pads. The reverie had shifted and now looked like vain desire: *swim far enough upstream in this water and I will come to a mingling of tributaries where the Cutarm Creeks, Big and Little, share a culture, a history; swim farther and I will arrive at the no-place born in the country of my grandfather's mind.*

I rose to the surface, kicked once, and continued upstream. Ahead I was assured of nothing but more bends in the creek, more meadows of bergamot, more wood pewees. More of Kichekiskapettonano Sepesis.

THIRTEEN DAYS OUT OF SCOTLAND, nine by Atlantic steamer, four by CPR locomotive, my grandfather Jock McRae and his compatriot Will Miller arrived in Tantallon on June 29, 1906. Coming to the eastern Qu'Appelle was Will's idea; he had an older brother, Dave, and a cousin, Angus Hamilton, who had already settled near Tantallon. Jock had no close relatives in the region — other McRaes had emigrated to the United States — but he would have known several of the families from Caithness, his home county in Scotland's northern lowlands.

And the names of the Caithness families would have come to mind as he stepped off the train and reached for his tobacco.

*The Hendersons, the Bruces, the Coghills, the Sutherlands. And the Williamsons too. All scattered out here somewhere in this glen or not far beyond. That letter from Mrs. Hamilton to mother said there's work among the Icelandic home-steaders east of town. Told me to make sure they intend to pay with more than a bed and meals. So. This "Tantallon" is not much. Just a scruffy row of stick houses and shops with mud in between. And the "hills" they wrote to us about are just the flanks of a great trench, not really hills at all. . . . Strange, from down here they look like hills, for all that. Dark green there on the wooded parts, must be oak. There's sure to be deer in there. Grouse too. And me without a rifle. It'll take a month's wages to remedy that. Will's brother Dave will get us some work, he said. Enough to fill our bellies anyhow. Fine for now, but I want more from this country than a full belly. To live well enough on my own, to walk down this road as I am today — free of the chains of debt and duty that weigh a man down in Banniskirk.*

Tantallon was barely three years old in 1906. The local history seems to suggest that the village sprang up spontaneously a few minutes after the first train hurtled down the new CPR line that came north into the Qu'Appelle Valley from Scissors Creek across the mouth of Bear Creek "Canyon." Bear Creek, the only place in the watershed that I have heard people call a canyon, is a steep-walled tributary that enters the Qu'Appelle southeast of Tantallon. The CPR line, until it was pulled up a few years ago, ran across Bear Creek and Scissors Creek on high wooden trestles that hoisted the train aloft on its descent from the plains into the main valley. Once on the bottomlands, the rails turned sharply west at the village to follow the valley three miles before heading far-ther north up the Little Cutarm Valley in an easement that bisected what eventually became my grandparents' farm.

For two young Scottish immigrants, the name Tantallon would have had a familiar, though aristocratic, ring. The village received its title from an early Scottish settler, Senator James Douglas. Douglas was a local aristocrat of sorts, one of the first four Saskatchewan senators and a Presbyterian minister who had once served as a chaplain with Her Majesty's forces in India.

Local lore has it that when Douglas first visited the region in 1883, the year after returning from service in India, he saw mists running through the valley at the foot of the hills. The scene reminded him of the Highland glens of his childhood, and so he decided then and there to file for a homestead. The reminiscence must have outlasted that one misty day for he later named his new farm on the valley rim after the Douglas castle on the North Sea — Tantallon. From Tantallon Farm in the 1890s, the Douglases managed the region's post office. When the new CPR line began to attract buildings to the valley bottom in 1903, the post office moved and the name went with it.

The house built by Senator Douglas stands yet, a local landmark in the Holar district. Though no Douglas has lived in its shelter for many years, the building is well-kept by the two women who live there now, farming what were once the senator's fields. An impressive brick structure that has not lost its air of patrician grandeur, it overlooks Tantallon from the east, glowing like the beacon of civilization and rectitude it once was to settler folk: a light into the murky heart of an unredeemed land. Generations of east Qu'Appelle people, including the McRaes, have looked upon the Douglas home as a monument of rural aristocracy, attesting to the possibility of a more cultured, elegant existence on the plains.

Once I took my mother and her sister, my aunt Doris, out to the land at the mouth of the Little Cutarm where they grew up. After we had walked around the site, picking up old bedsprings and stove parts, I noticed my aunt staring off toward the eastern horizon. I asked what she was looking at. "The old Douglas place," she said. "We always looked for it from the yard. The sun made the windows shine and we were convinced they were made of gold . . . Funny, can't see it at all right now." We strained our eyes that afternoon, and though it was clear and the light was at our backs, we could not find the Douglas family's New World citadel. Trees, the oaks that fringe the valley rim, had grown up in the intervening years, blocking the view to Tantallon Farm.

Walking north along main-street Tantallon on that June afternoon of 1906, Jock and Will would have passed several buildings that had been erected by two brothers who more or less created Tantallon out of their own peculiar brand of social reformist ideals and commercial enterprise. Edward and William Paynter had by this time put together the makings of a prairie town main street: a grocery store, a furniture store, a creamery, and a hotel. The hotel was named Ruskin House, after the British art critic and social reformer, John Ruskin. The two-storey building, with its name painted in large lettering across the facade, fell somewhere short of the architectural ideals outlined in Ruskin's *Seven Lamps of Architecture*, but it was a major edifice for those times and the first of its kind to be built in the eastern reaches of the valley. "Architecture," said Ruskin, "is the art which so disposes and adorns the edifices raised by man, for whatsoever uses, that the sight of them may contribute to his mental health, power, and pleasure."[54]

These days, Ruskin's artistic and social vision does not often arise in Tantallon's café conversation, but the name Paynter is still associated here with three generations of store merchants who stocked shelves floor to ceiling with whatever it took to keep the people of the valley fed, shod, and clothed from the turn of the twentieth century to the 1970s. "If you can't get what you want anywhere else, you can get it at Paynter's."

I remember as a child coming to Paynter's on our visits from Esterhazy and thinking that this must be the oldest retail enterprise in the New World. The archetypal store of my memory was a great, cavernous place with long, wooden counters and air smelling sweet from the general store aroma of chewing gum, bath soaps, and a half century of inventory. The tin ceiling seemed impossibly high; it might well have been a cathedral's vaulted nave. Was it oak that trimmed the glass cases? On the main counter, there was green wrapping paper on great rolls and a dizzying display of candy.

The thin-lipped, balding man with round spectacles behind the counter, in pressed shirt and apron, had an air about him that the clerks I knew from Esterhazy stores seemed to lack. I suppose it was part pride of ownership and tradition, part Presbyterian rectitude, and part watchfulness for short candy-thieves, but I have imagined too that if I looked hard enough into my recollection of this store-clerk son of W.C. Paynter, I could see a trace of his origins within what was a remarkable attempt at communal settlement and co-operative living on the Northern Great Plains.

For five years, from 1895 to 1900, the original Paynter brothers and their wives and children lived with several other families in a collective that would today be known as a commune or "intentional community." They called it Hamona, after the prophesies of Ezekiel (39:16): "And also the name of the city shall be Ha-mo-nah. Thus shall they cleanse the land." The land of the Paynters' Hamona was in the valley, not far downstream from where Tantallon was to spring forth a few years later.

It was the last decade of the nineteenth century. The customary optimism of settlers in the North-West had been beaten down by several years of depression and drought. Across the prairies, lone homesteaders were failing and abandoning their claims within a year or two of "proving up." Heroic frontier individualism had tripped in the furrow.

In the minds of Christian idealists such as the Paynters, the solution lay within the precepts of a social reform movement that ran from Robert Owen through John Ruskin to the utopian writings of William Morris and Edward Bellamy. Responding to the havoc caused by laissez-faire capitalism and industrialization, these British and American reformers advocated close-knit, co-operative communities to be formed in an alliance between rural peasants and industrial workers. In the early nineteenth century, Robert Owen tried out his ideas with "villages of cooperation," including one short-lived effort in Indiana, called New Harmony.

Later writers, including Ruskin, Morris, and Bellamy, adapted these "Owenite" ideals to fit within liberal Christian thinking. The Paynters, and perhaps some of the others who joined them at Hamona, had read much of this literature. One book, I believe, was fresh in their minds.

During the last decade of the nineteenth century, a utopian novel by American journalist Edward Bellamy had captured the imaginations of liberal-thinking readers throughout North America.[55] In *Looking Backward*, the narrator is a young Bostonian who, on the eve of December 26, 2000, casts his thoughts back over the previous hundred years. Employing this device, Bellamy attacks the excess and injustice of nineteenth-century capitalism, and proposes a future of social harmony, a new economic order characterized by co-operation, common ownership of property, and full employment. This book, and to a lesser extent, the anarchist utopia set out in Morris's *News from Nowhere*, provided the basis for the charter and constitution drawn up by the Paynters in 1895 to establish the "Harmony Cooperative Industrial Association" at its inaugural meeting in their home town of Beulah, twenty miles into Manitoba. Remarkably enough, *Beulah*, a Hebrew word meaning "the wedded," also comes from Old Testament prophecy. Toward the end of *Isaiah*, the prophet promises the Israelites a better place where they will one day be wedded to the land:

> *Thou shalt no more be termed Forsaken; neither shall thy land any more be termed Desolate: but thou shalt be called Heph-zi-bah [My delight], and thy land Beu-lah: for the Lord delighteth in thee, and thy land shall be married. (Isaiah 62:4. King James version)*

In Article 1 of the charter that ultimately wedded ten Beulah families to a piece of the Qu'Appelle Valley, the socialist utopian vision of Bellamy mixes with Protestant notions of fallen man and Providence. Here the tenets of Hamona's foundation are disappointing. The same hubris that tainted most settler endeavours — the European article of faith that the Creation is man's servant to possess and exploit — was laid down in black and white when the Paynters and their confederates signed the charter:

> *Feeling that the present competitive social system is one of injustice and fraud and directly opposed to the precept laid down by our Saviour for the guidance of mankind in subduing all the forces of nature and the evils springing from the selfishness in the human heart, we do write under the name of Harmony Industrial Association for the purpose of acquiring land to build upon for its members to produce from nature sufficient to insure its members against want and the fear of want.*[56]

The constitution then goes on to mention plans for stores and factories and "to provide educational and recreative facilities of the highest order and to maintain harmonious relationship on the basis of co-operation for the benefit of its members and all mankind in general."

In forming the association, the Hamona colonists also followed the famous Rochdale Principles, a set of guidelines originally drafted by what is widely recognized as the first modern co-op, a grocery store organized by weavers in Rochdale, England, in 1844. The language of the prospectus that the Paynters handed out to recruit members for their co-operative looked back to the foundations laid by Rochdale and forward, somewhat ambitiously, to the provisions we have since come to take for granted, and lately to disparage, in the modern welfare state.

Section 4 declared that the "Department of Agriculture" would look after "farming and stock raising operations of the association, care for forestry, lawns, gardens, boulevards, and parks."

Section 6 anticipates socialized medicine. A "Department of Sanitation" was to oversee "the general healthful condition of the homes of the members, factories, and other buildings belonging to the association, to give instruction in the laws of hygiene and furnish medical treatment and medicine to members and their families without personal charge."

According to Section 8, the "Department of Cuisine" was to maintain "general charge and supervision of all hotels, restaurants, co-operative kitchens, etc."

At the first meeting, at which this grand scheme was adopted, the association elected one of its elder members to be president. Samuel Sanderson was a Quaker of the full-fledged thee-and-thou variety, whose family had granted shelter to escaped slaves during the American Civil War. The Sandersons were a part of the Hamona experience from beginning to end. In 1896, less than a year after the founding meeting, there was a wedding at Hamona between Ed Paynter and Jemima Sanderson, one of Samuel's nine daughters.

In 1895, Sanderson and the two Paynter brothers harnessed a team to a wagon and set out from Beulah to find Hamona. They headed west into the Qu'Appelle where Will had already taken a homestead the year before, just beyond the mouth of the Big Cutarm Creek.

I have daydreamed about the Hamona scouts driving the last few miles to their promised land, arriving at the small log shack William had built to fulfill his homestead requirements. Hot, covered in a film of dust, sunburnt from their brows to their shirt collars, the three of them step off of the wagon, stretch the kinks out of their spines and stand on the first level of hills up from the valley bottom. The needle grass and a scattering of wild vetch blossoms surround their boots. From there, with the prospectus in their hands, ideals and enthusiasm in their hearts, they look out over a wild, uncultivated bottomland, envisioning a model community that seems every bit as distant as Bellamy's utopian Boston one hundred years hence. Yes, this place will be Hamona. It has fertile land for crops, timber near at hand for fuel and construction, and a strong creek nearby for water supply.

More important than any of these requirements, however, was a map of the proposed Great North West Central Railway, which showed a line that would soon be built past their doorstep, connecting them to commercial centres in Manitoba. Rail transport was essential, because, despite their rejection of mercantile capitalism, the Hamona colonists had no intentions of becoming self-sufficient and would be nearly as dependent upon trade as any other settler community. This reliance on trade and rail transportation weakened Hamona and contributed to its eventual demise. Utopians like the Paynters, despite their radical politics, were still economically and philosophically European men and, as such, blind to the new land's sufficiency and invitation to live within its graces, not upon its resources.

During 1896 and 1897, the founding families gradually moved from Beulah to the new colony along forty miles of muddy, axle-breaking trails. By 1898, Hamona was a community of fifty people who, instead of building the boulevards, lawns, and hotels of the prospectus, were learning locally appropriate skills and trades from their Métis neighbours.

Felix Hayden, a Hudson's Bay freighter originally from a Métis settlement on the Red River, had established one of the region's earliest homesteads just across the Big Cutarm from Hamona. The historical record mentions that Hayden taught the colonists how to make lime powder by burning limestone in hillside lime kilns. The Hamona people used lime to cement their foundations and plaster their walls, but with Hayden's assistance they also established a small lime-producing industry that became the colony's mainstay during its first two years. By 1898, Hayden and the colonists were hauling hundreds of bushels of lime along the thirty-mile trail to the town of Moosomin, where they could trade it for groceries and supplies.

I have found enough references to Felix Hayden in accounts written by people recollecting their childhoods at Hamona to suggest that he was a resource without which their experiment might not have lasted the first winter. He was an expert axe-man, and it is easy to imagine him showing the colonists some pointers on how to build with the local poplar. An account given by Basile Hayden, one of Felix's sons, provides a detailed picture of their own home, constructed several years before the Paynters arrived with the original colonists. Built entirely of local logs, the Hayden house had a sod roof, a floor of white clay dug out of the hills, a limestone fireplace, and windows made of fleshed deerskins. Reading the words of Basile, I was reminded again of the Métis ethic of local subsistence and its contrast with the white settlers' dependence upon distant economies. The Haydens were not wishing for a train to pass by their property. They were remarkably self-sufficient, interdependent only with their neighbours and within their neighbourhood. They made candles from animal fat, wagon wheels from elm trees, nails from ash wood, and yeast from wild hops. They hunted for their meat, gathered seneca root, grew a few vegetables and some grain, and ground their own flour between stones.[57]

The details of such an unmediated life in the valley always interest me. But there was more here than an example of local subsistence. There was the Haydens' hospitality. Half their blood made them a rejected people, the nation put down at Batoche, and yet they welcomed a colony of white people into their stretch of the valley. I began looking for some form of contact with the Métis man who, for saving the colonists from their own ineptitude, deserved more credit than history had granted him. Out driving one afternoon, I caught sight of a neatly stacked woodpile next to a small house along the road above the Big Cutarm. It occurred to me that there might be Haydens still in the area. Several phone calls later I tracked down a granddaughter of Felix Hayden's. I would find her in Rocanville, I was told, a town a few miles south of the valley, near the source of Scissors Creek.

Her name is Jean Larose, and she lives in a seniors' housing complex with her husband, Greg. The afternoon I went to visit them, I brought along my uncle Babes who had known Greg since the 1930s when they were chums at Tantallon School.

The apartment had that afghan-on-the-couch, ceramics-on-the-coffee-table comfort I have come to expect in the homes of older prairie people. The walls of their kitchen and living room were covered with pictures and icons, several colour photos of recent generations, one or two black-and-whites of older generations. As I sat down at their kitchen table, I caught a glimpse of hummingbirds scooting back and forth at a feeder just outside the apartment window. While Babes and Greg reminisced, Jean, in her soft, deferential voice, began talking about her childhood — first on the plains south of the valley at a French and Métis settlement called St. Marthe and later in the valley where the Haydens and other families moved to be near St. Joseph's, a new church built by the east Qu'Appelle Métis in the 1920s. Just the day before, I had been looking in the valley for signs of St. Joseph's and had found only a small cemetery where the settlement had once been. A patch of big bluestem and sunflower prairie completely encircled by oak woods, the hillside cemetery, with its stones and crosses glinting in the sun, reminded me of other prairie mandalas I have seen: medicine wheels, ceremonial circles, tipi rings.

Jean showed me a photograph of herself and Greg standing in the snow at St. Joseph's on their wedding day. It is late winter and you can see bare trees on the valley hills in the background. The image of the newlyweds, young and happy, carried us back to an era and a life that the citizens of Hamona would have understood.

The men chuckled at each others' stories while Jean whispered hers to me across the kitchen table.

*My father, Basile Hayden, went to school with Mr. Paynter, Roy, son of Ed Paynter. And with Mrs. Paynter, who used to be a Parker. They were both from Hamona. Dad and Mom moved out onto the plains here. At St. Marthe. That's where I was born, east of St. Marthe. Some people were Métis; some were French. Discrimination? Oh yes, very much, when I went to school at St. Marthe. The feeling is still with me. The French treated us very badly. Very badly. It made you feel like you weren't good enough for them, you know?* Here Jean remembered the names, listed them one after the other, the names of the St. Marthe people who made her and her family feel unwelcome.

*In winters, we would move nearer the river for water for the horses and cattle. We had a little log house there and a barn by the river. It was land in the valley that nobody owned. Not so far from that bridge going toward the DeCorbys' now. Just a little shack for the winter, eh? Other families would live year round in shacks in the valley. They would have a garden and just live there. In those days they'd just live wherever they could make a little house, eh? Didn't bother with taxes or anything.*

*We spoke French all the time at home. Learned English only after we moved* to the valley to live year round. That was when they built the church at St. Joseph's. Dad got a job on the railroad. Old Edouard Pritchard had a store in the valley there. A priest, Father Passaplan, wanted to build a church there. In the name of St. Joseph. So Dad and Edouard Pritchard and all the Pritchard boys, they all got together and they built that church. I remember seeing it come up. How they cut the logs from the bush and squared them. How they plastered it with mud.

When we all moved to the new settlement, there were always house dances. Didn't have a hall or anything. They would go to the neighbours and gather there and they would lunch and have a dance. Dad played the fiddle and my brother Bill would be the caller. Arthur Pritchard would play the accordion or guitar. We made our own fun.

We lived off whatever the land would give. We had chickens, milked cows, picked berries. We would dry vegetables, the beans and the corn. Even dried saskatoons. Later we would soak them overnight and then cook them. In summer we would dig seneca root. You know what seneca root is? We would dig that, wash it clean, sell it in town in Rocanville here. It was shipped away. They said it was used as medicine.

Dad would trap in the winter. The men would go hunting for venison. They didn't always hunt in season. It was against the law, but they had to. They killed partridges and prairie chicken. Sometimes there were a lot of bush rabbits and that was delicious meat.

And they made lime in the hills. They'd dig a deep, deep pit. And they'd have to have this certain kind of stone. A white stone. And they'd have to line that thing and they'd have to cut cord wood. And they'd make a fire right underneath the thing and that fire would have to go for many days and nights. Later, Dad would take a piece of the lime and put it in water and it would foam up and then he knew that the lime was ready to use.

They would mix that with dirt to plaster their log houses. And they would take that white lime and whitewash the building. The rain would come and wash it off. It never stayed. They'd have to do it every year. . . . They were tough people.

Now a French family owns the land where St. Joseph's was. Last year they bulldozed the buildings that were left. So it's all gone.

The native and adaptive ingenuity of Jean's grandparents must have been a great help to the Hamona colonists, who soon discovered that their own skills — which they had initially thought ample because their

ranks included a millwright, a teacher, a candy-maker, and a printer —
would need broadening. Nonetheless, with Felix Hayden's help and the
strength of their ideals, the people of Hamona raised a village with several log homes, a store and creamery building made of fieldstone, a log
stable, an ice house, carpentry and blacksmith shops, and a school, also
made of stone. The school and store served the surrounding homesteader community as well as the Hamona colonists.

In addition to the lime-kiln products — plaster, cement, fertilizer,
quicklime, and whitewash — the co-operative began to produce its own
brand of butter, packaged and sold as "Hamona Butter" in a store in
Moosomin. To handle all transactions of goods and labour within the
colony, the association issued scrip to members in one- and five-dollar
denominations. Using this Hamona money, they paid all labour —
skilled and unskilled — equally, following their motto "A man's endow-
ments fix the measure of his duty."

The co-operative also conducted a small local trade in cattle, pigs,
and poultry. Further afield, the Paynters secured an exchange with the
Ruskin Colony, a sister co-operative in the interior of British Columbia.
For a load of flour ground from wheat that they grew on some rented
land at Beulah, the colony received a rail shipment of lumber, Fraser
River salmon, and fresh fruit from Ruskin.

And so Hamona apparently survived despite the depression and the
difficulties of establishing any kind of co-operation within a colonial
political economy that remained suspicious of collective endeavour.
Whit Huston, thinking back on life at Hamona, said in 1941 that "the
association always paid its accounts and was well regarded by
the people with whom it did business. The members had a higher standard of living than have many farm people these days." There were
births, weddings, sports days, picnics, toboggan parties, concerts, sing-
a-longs, dances, Bible studies, and Sunday afternoon political debates,
all on the slopes of the Qu'Appelle, where the wind now presses the
grass down against the foundation stones that mark Hamona's day in
the sun. According to a local historian named Gilbert Johnson, who
interviewed many of the Hamona colonists in their old age, "people
who were members have since testified that the years spent at the
colony were among the happiest . . . of their lives."[58]

THE AFTERNOON THAT I SPENT at the "provincial recreation site" that now surrounds the ruins of Hamona, I found no evidence of the contingencies that brought this experiment in co-operative living to an end after five years. Nothing mouldering in the shade of the caragana hedges or in the bottom of the cellar depressions could explain why Hamona suddenly dissolved in 1900.

Nor was there much evidence of recent recreation at the site. An empty garbage container and a couple of rusted pop cans that looked to be circa 1975. The roadside cairn marking the site is missing its plaque and has become so overgrown with caragana and brome grass as to be all but invisible to passing vehicles. During my visit, passing vehicles amounted to one pickup truck and one tractor with hay bailer in tow.

Brome grass and sweet clover have grown up around the interpretive panels erected by the government some time ago to explain the Hamona story to anyone who might stray far enough to arrive at such a remote place in the eastern valley. Words from the prospectus, an image of the butter label, a diagram of the lime kilns, and photos of the Paynters — all pocked with bullet holes and streaked with barn-swallow poop.

When I see this kind of inattention and decay so common at Saskatchewan's historic sites, my first reaction is annoyance at the disrespect shown to such places. But then I recall my visits to well-funded and maintained interpretive sites, complete with staff in period costume, turnstiles, souvenir shops, boardwalks, multimedia presentations, and hands-on archaeology. And in the comparing, I realize that I prefer my experience of history to be mediated more by time than by the developers of tourism and recreation opportunities. I enjoy being alone, crawling on my hands and knees, looking for foundations in places like Hamona, where the land is set aside for public use but the history is allowed to return to the earth by the grace of benign neglect.

Using maps that I had obtained over coffee and cookies at the Spy Hill Museum, I located the remaining evidence of Will Paynter's home at Hamona. Through a curtain of maple saplings, I stepped down into the cellar depression, a dish in the earth as evocative as any prairie concavity — a buffalo wallow, a pothole, a curlew nest. There I sat in the blue-green shade, recounting the reasons given for Hamona's demise.

First and foremost of all the causes, given Hamona's reliance on trade, was the failure of the Great North West Central Railway, which had promised to build a line directly across the Hamona property. The second cause, more difficult to weigh after the passage of a century, was religious and philosophical dissension. Although most of the founding members of Hamona were Christian, they came from a variety of denominations — Presbyterian, Catholic, Quaker. Initially, their religious differences were superseded by the ideals of social justice, co-operation, and harmony within the community. A letter written by Ed Paynter in 1939, however, mentions a later philosophical division caused by a handful of new radical members:

> *During the last two years of operation, a number of members were admitted who professed or advocated socialistic, or what would now be called communistic doctrines. They wished to abolish family life, and individual homes, and all live in one large apartment building with a public dining room. . . . Some of the extreme left wing even advocated free love as part of their plans, and all of these parties were staunch advocates of Atheism.*[59]

And so, Ed Paynter, the Presbyterian who had founded Hamona on Christian principles and who had led the colony in hymn-singing sessions, returned in the spring of 1900 from a recuperative stay in British Columbia to find the membership voting to disband rather than devolve into an outpost for free-thinking libertines.

A third factor was not insurmountable but may have compounded the growing disharmony in the village. This was the challenge that every co-operative community faces sooner or later: how to deal with slackers in an economy that does not reward individual effort. Some Hamona members were upset by what they saw as laziness in their brethren. As I reclined on a carpet of creeping charley in the Paynter cellar, I wondered if any of these less industrious members were also the advocates of free love and communal dwelling. It occurred to me that a certain degree of overlap in this regard could easily have divided the colony along lines too sharp for reconciliation.

For Hamona, as for all failed settler utopias, there are a number of "what ifs" that compromise our assessment of its demise, its forgone possibilities, and its legacy. What if, instead of "subduing all the forces of nature," the Hamona colonists had formed a moral and religious bond between themselves and the land? If their mores, values, and world view had accommodated the spirit of the place or adapted to the example of the local Métis? If they had planned for local subsistence instead of long-distance trade? Given the right outcome for all these second-guesses, is it possible that small, locally responsible, economically and ecologically sound villages along river valleys might have become a valid model for prairie settlement? The unequivocal No that answers this inquiry is voiced from the decades of history before Hamona: the buffalo extermination; the treaty signings; the Métis subjugation; clearing the plains and making them safe for the legislated rush to survey and fill the "empty" lands by applying a Homestead Act and a system of land entitlement that separated settlers from one another, distributing them evenly over a surveyed grid, inhibiting human community, damaging ecological community, and satisfying only John A. Macdonald and the directors of the CPR.

I CLIMBED UP out of the cellar depression to the maples growing from between the foundation stones of Will Paynter's home. The mourning dove that had not stopped calling since my arrival broke cover from a low limb in a flurry of rose-blush wings. Caraganas, brome grass, cellars — the usual signs of failure and abandonment on the prairie were all there, but as I crouched and crawled from foundation to foundation and touched the weathered cornerstones of Hamona houses, I sensed nothing of the desolation that has overtaken me in similar places, at ghost towns or homestead sites where the taint of hardship and misfortune hangs in the air, undiminished by decades of wind and rain.

Walking west from the recreational site, I came to a flat area on the valley slope, a quarter-acre patch of alien grasses lusher and greener than the surrounding growth. Sitting down in a hollow where the brome was highest, I could just see through the tops of the blades to the far wooded hills on the other side of the valley. A flat site, luxuriant growth, just west of the main grouping of foundations — before I opened the map, I knew I was in the middle of the colony's original stables. And as this took my attention, I realized why I could not sense failure in the remains of Hamona. Scraps of testimony I had encountered the day before in the files of the Spy Hill Museum made sense of Hamona, its legacy in shaping Tantallon, the private utopias of immigrant settlers, and the collectivist dreams of this region. Archived thought and utterance flowed into the voice of an old man, Ed Paynter, looking back on the Hamona days and the genesis of Tantallon.

*Yes, that five years at Hamona colony was as beneficial to the adult members as five years at University.[60] In the history of this province, Hamona stands as a landmark, not of endings or despair, but of beginnings and hope. It was a proving ground for ideals of social justice, agrarian reform, and commonwealth that over the next forty years made their way onto the platforms of municipalities, farmer organizations, and political parties throughout southeastern Saskatchewan. I call your attention to the graduates of Hamona and the work they went on to accomplish. The United Grain Growers, the Comrades of Equity, the Co-operative Elevator Company, Saskatchewan Municipal Hail Insurance, the Co-op Creamery, several local distribution co-ops, and later the Wheat Pool and the Co-operative Commonwealth Federation — all remarkable organizations in their time that were either formed or advanced by the efforts of people who had experienced co-operation and community first at Hamona.*

*My brother Will and I became active in several of these organizations, as we moved from Hamona to help build the village of Tantallon eight miles upstream in the valley, where the new CPR line crossed the river. It was 1903, and I was elected to be the first village overseer, a combination mayor and utility man. On Main Street the next year, Will and I established the territory's first co-operative creamery, one of the first producer co-ops anywhere on the Canadian Plains. Will ran the Paynter Bros. store with help from our brother Reynolds, while I opened the Ruskin House hotel across the street.*

*Tantallon was a going concern in those days. In some ways, more cosmopolitan than the streets of Regina are today. In Will's store or at the railway station, it was routine to hear three or four languages spoken all at the same time. Hungarian, Finnish, Gaelic, Yiddish, Icelandic, French — on Saturday mornings it seemed that Europe had arrived on Main Street.*

*I was also working as a grain buyer at the Colonial Elevator, where I had ample opportunity to talk to local farmers about politics and reforming the grain marketing system. I would tell them that the only solution to the matter was for the farmers themselves to organize a co-op elevator company. Later, when Mr. Partridge of Sintaluta began to organize a farmer-run marketing co-operative — the Grain Growers — I got involved. He used to visit Tantallon, and we would talk long into the night, making plans and exchanging ideas on how to tackle the CPR and the Winnipeg cartel of grain companies.*

*By 1907, Will and I and a few other local men had formed a political organ-ization — the Comrades of Equity, we called it — to represent farmers' interests. I was the provincial secretary and then the members selected me as a candidate to run in the upcoming Dominion election. The Tories and Grits could not have cared less about the plight of prairie farmers and their abuse at the hands of the grain cartel, so I had no trouble gathering support in what was then called the Saltcoats riding. The comrades unanimously approved what was for those days a very radical platform. Plank number one called for govern-ment ownership and operation of grain elevators. Plank number two called for public ownership and operation of railways, telegraphs, and telephones throughout Canada. Plank number three demanded equal rights for all and absolutely no special privileges to any individual, municipal body, province, or dominion. Although it was not formally a part of the platform, most of us also campaigned in favour of the vote for women, as I did later as a member of the Grain Growers.*

*The Dominion election came and went in the fall of 1908, and I did not gain a seat in Parliament, but I polled the largest independent vote in all of Canada and in the eastern end of the riding, I gathered more votes than both the Tory and the Grit candidates. More important, we got our ideas out to hundreds of Saskatchewan farmers who began to spread the gospel of equity, fairness, and co-operation throughout our young province.*

*Now it is 1951, a half century after Hamona, and I see a Saskatchewan that has co-op stores in every town, producer co-operatives and marketing boards that ensure that farmers are not cheated out of the fruits of their labour, and Crown corporations that provide universal access to telephone service, personal insurance, bus transportation, and electrical power. Some of our Hamona ideals — things like socialized medicine — have yet to be adopted, but give these prairie people another fifty years, and who knows?*

*Someday . . .*

SITTING UP TO MY EYEBROWS in the grass of what was once Hamona's barnyard, I looked out across the Qu'Appelle bottomlands and felt something of Paynter's optimism. I saw for that moment how such landscape gives rise to optimism, big dreams. Throughout this continent, places like the eastern Qu'Appelle remind us why the Great North American conceit of man's perfectibility in the New World has outlasted five hundred years of failure, why it continues to serve as our sustaining myth.

We still believe we can do something new here. And that belief pushes small improvements in from the margins of our social contract. Small experiments, utter failures, five-year attempts at utopia quietly germinate in the thin topsoil of our time upon this difficult land and then emerge later as minor triumphs — co-operatives, agrarian reform, a politics of social justice, medicare.

The day my grandfather walked down Tantallon's Main Street in 1906, past Ruskin House, the Paynters' stores, and the new co-op creamery, the only utopia on his mind was the common immigrant's dream of freedom and a better life in a new land. The possibility of owning property was utopia enough to a crofter's son who had seen his father and uncles struggle to feed families on what could be coaxed from a few acres rented from the local laird.

On the day you said goodbye to Caithness, Johnnie McRae, what did your imagined Qu'Appelle country look like from your mother's doorstep? Was it a place where a man could have a field of oats, a few pigs and cows, and fair hunting without having to answer to kirk and county, earl and baron, bailey and magistrate? And in the living out, the years at the mouth of the Little Cutarm, did your private utopia measure up?

I can testify only that it did not last, for the trail up to Aunt Bea's has fallen out of use, the mink and beaver have not been trapped since cousin Gary hung up his gear for good, and no one has made whisky from Little Cutarm water since God knows when.

Still, I believe and dream in ways that deny the facts of what has happened here in a century's passing. And I find myself wondering whether something of our immigrant ancestors' willingness to turn away from the old and take a chance on the new has survived the failed utopias and lost rural cultures. When I go to the eastern Qu'Appelle now, I bear with me my own utopias and imagine ways of reinhabiting the countryside, reclaiming rural culture. Blending the Paynters' social ideals and my grandfather's aspirations of self-sufficiency, in my daydreams I gather like-minded souls with a prospectus for Hamona II. We take another five-year lease out on utopia, build our community in the valley, and see where it leads.

## Chapter Twenty-seven

# ENTERING THE GARDEN

THE NIGHT I ARRIVED on my Aunt Evelyn's doorstep in Esterhazy, having driven in heavy rain from Round Lake, I felt distracted by a mild sense that I had come to the wrong place. That I would knock on the door and someone else's aunt would open it. Aunt Evelyn lived in Tantallon, always had. The Tantallon that I knew had taken its shape around a centre that was my dear and generous aunt.

I knocked on the door. Rain dripped from the eaves overhead, ran down the sidewalk. A moment later, Evelyn was standing in the doorway — my mother's big sister, the eldest of the McRae girls, bare of foot, sharp of tongue, and substantial of flesh, looking as plump and sleek as bread dough in a bowl. While we hugged and she fussed over the two bags of saskatoon berries I had brought, I tried to shake the feeling of dislocation in finding my aunt in another town.

Our memories and recognitions rely upon context, live within places. Walking along open prairie, I will sometimes hear a birdsong that is familiar, that I know I have heard countless times before but still cannot recognize in that moment, in that place. The song continues unnamed until I come to a rise where I can see a wooded coulee ahead. Trees. A redstart. Of course.

There she was — seventy-six years old, living alone in a seniors' housing development on the west side of the "Potash Capital of the

World," four hundred feet higher than and a dozen miles north of the valley where she had spent her life. Like most of her neighbours, Aunt Evelyn had recently and reluctantly moved in from the countryside. Children and grandchildren begin to worry. It isn't safe living alone on the farm or in a dying village, they say. You should move to town; most of your friends have. Besides, it'll be easier to do your shopping there, and the doctor will always be near at hand.

As we stood outside in the warm rain, Evelyn pointed up and down and across the street, naming Tantallon and valley people living in the duplex units identical to her own. "That's Babes's two doors down. Dolly's there across the street. Your Aunt Bea is in the second one that way. And that one next door is Aleck Mercer's."

"It's a little Tantallon," I said, as Evelyn took me out back to see the gardens. The "gardens" were in fact one long garden that ran behind the houses, knitting together the lots with rows of corn, peas, potatoes, tomatoes, and beets. The boundaries were visible only to each gardener: "Babes's patch starts over there with that row of tall corn. He works his own lot and his neighbour's."

As Evelyn described each gardener's strengths and weaknesses, I realized that what looked to the outsider like unassuming peonies and petunias out front and carrots and cabbages out back, was in fact a sort of Grand Prix of seniors' competitive gardening. Evelyn pointed out the garden that appeared to have the lead, as of mid-July: "You'd never know it from the garden, but he's ninety-one years old. The man *lives* in his garden."

As far as I could see north and south along the rows of vegetables, there were no delinquent gardeners. I compared it to my experience of community gardening in the city, where by midsummer heads of thistle and pigweed would burst forth exuberantly in a few plots, identifying the less virtuous among our collective of growers.

Here, in the gardens of Little Tantallon, neat piles of thinned carrots and cabbage leaves lay at the end of every row. The pathways were clean and wide, and each plant was surrounded by an apron of loamy black soil. Between each housing unit and the accompanying garden was a small metal garden shed and a patio. On the patios, in tidy rows, there were usually several buckets and plastic containers of various sizes, each brimming with rainwater. Every eavestrough up and down the block terminated in a rain barrel or a bucket. Even in this rain-filled summer, the gardeners of Little Tantallon were not about to let heaven-sent moisture go to waste. Besides, the Esterhazy tap water, as Evelyn reminded me, is hard dreck — enough to scare the petals off a pansy.

During a pause in the rain, I walked along the border of the gardens, thinking about the other gardens these people had left behind in the country. Gardens that had filled pantries and root cellars for forty or sixty winters until one year the gardener stopped coming. Other immigrants will now till the earth — the European weeds brought here from the east by our forebears who carried seeds of sow thistle, mallow, fox-tail, and fifty other species in sacks of barley or oats, on the soles of their boots, and in the manes of their work horses. Quack grass, pigweed, lamb's quarters, and other colonizers of open ground will reign for a time, the middle kingdom in a succession from ancient and diverse prairie to a climax homogeneity of brome grass.

Evelyn asked me to pinch a couple of new potatoes from Babes's patch. "He won't mind," she said, "and get a few carrots and an onion while you're there." That night we dined on Babes's produce slathered in butter, sour cream, and fresh dill. When Babes showed up later for a visit, his brow was set in full scowl above a nose that looked like one of the tubers on my plate. He aimed his chin and belly toward Evelyn and accused her of raiding his garden. They exchanged a few cursory brick-bats — "Keep your hands off" and "Stingy old so-and-so" — picking up where they had left off in the most recent skirmish of a mostly benign mock battle that has been going on for years.

Sitting and talking with Babes and Evelyn that evening I could feel myself arriving at a familiar place. Something in their speech, not only the diction, but the way they pronounced words, placed them together in declarations and descriptions, always drew me nearer the world of West Valley and Tantallon. It returned me to other after-supper times, the voices of my grandfather, aunts, uncles, and cousins. Listening and taking pleasure in the cadence of their descriptives, rising and falling in talk of last night's storm, this fall's deer hunt, or the prospects for a wedding. An oozing sore was "mattery," *calm* was pronounced *cam*, the Palmers were the *Pammers*, and deer were always "jumpers." Sentences were sprinkled with certain cuss words: *buggers*, *bloodys*, and *bloody-wells*, the latter pressed into service during discussions of someone else's debt or responsibilities, as in "that young bugger is the father and he bloody-well better make her a bride before too long." Not quite a local dialect, but as it fell from the tongues of my relatives it became for me the recognizable vernacular of Tantallon, a cultural relic that, like the hewn log-and-plaster homesteads, is part of what is distinctive and vanishing from the eastern Qu'Appelle.

Evelyn talked, and I followed the well-worn trail of my grandfather's arrival in the valley with Will Miller ("They got off the train in Tantallon and walked straight up the hill to Angus Hamilton's"), the Sutherland family coming west in 1896 ("Dan Bruce brought them to the valley all the way from Wapella in a sleigh box"), and Jock and Millie's early life together on the Ormiston farm ("Mrs. Ormiston was an educated bride from Ontario but didn't know how to boil water until Mother showed her").

And so it went on into the night. Outside, rain trickled between the rows of carrots in the gardens of Little Tantallon. Inside, I waded into a flow of stories that ran in long alluvial tributaries to the great valley twelve miles and ninety years away.

# Chapter Twenty-eight

# CARPENTERS AND MASONS

THE DAY AFTER JOCK made his way up main-street Tantallon and up the hill to the Hamiltons', he began picking up carpentry work in the valley. His first job was to build a home for a local settler named Cranston, in the Holar district east of town.

The current owner is an old bachelor whose family bought the place from the Cranstons in the twenties. There was no answer at the door when I went to have a look at the house, so I had to settle for what I could see from the outside. Two storeys with dormers, paint long gone, exposing boards weathered to wasp-nest grey. No sagging or leaning, it stands four-square and well-trimmed on its moorings, perched on the hillside like a Cape Islander hauled up from fished-out waters. I am easily impressed by carpentry — the McRae builder trait has yet to surface in my portion of the gene pool — and so I paused for a few moments to admire the workmanship in a simple frame house that has withstood ninety winters since my grandfather first hammered it together.

Jock, I have been told, took jobs on farms from time to time as well, though I suspect it was not his favourite means of livelihood. In the early years, he would hire on with threshing outfits, sometimes travelling far from the valley. Evelyn gave me a picture of her father with six other young men from one of these threshing crews. It is a posed photograph taken in a studio in the town of Strasbourg, in the north arm of the watershed, near Last Mountain Lake. My guess is that it was taken somewhere between 1910 and 1912.

Shining faces, some Anglo-Saxon, some Slavic, some perhaps Scandinavian — all youthful and tanned, freshly scrubbed free of the dirt they had been breathing, eating, and cursing for days. During a break in their labour — a Saturday or a rainy day in September — they took a wagon into town wearing the only clothes they had brought from home. A sign outside the photography studio welcomed threshing crews. They walked in, shuffled chairs, joked with one another until the camera was ready, until it was time to stand and stare down a lens into the long and unbidden future.

I had not seen this early image of my grandfather until Aunt Evelyn showed it to me on that rainy evening at her place in Esterhazy. I must have stared at the photo for some time. "It's the only copy but you can keep it, if you want," she said. She flipped the photograph over and wrote on the cardboard backing, "This goes to Trevor Herriot for his project." All the furniture and photographs in Evelyn's charge have similar phrases written on their undersides: "This goes to Barbara" or "This goes to my dear Nicky."

And so now my "project" is under the supervision of this gathering of seven stook-hoisters fresh from the fields of Last Mountain Lake, in the fall of 1910 or 1911. My grandfather, front row on the right, looks out with piercing eyes that suggest blue even in the monotint; one side of his brow is slightly raised, his mouth set in the faint curve I have seen upon the faces of my cousins. His forelock falls onto his forehead from beneath a woollen cap. Cheeks clean-shaven as always; ears like jug handles.

Sometimes I look at his image and see the proud swagger of a young man who has found that charm and good looks have their uses. Other times, his eyes flicker with the uncertainty of the novice poacher he was in those days, and I see a hunger and expectation, a trace of desire. Once, by the lamplight of my desk, as I counted quarter sections on a map of the eastern Qu'Appelle, the face of my young grandfather caught my eyes, and the pride, hunger, and desire had turned. Innocence had fled; in its place, there was affliction, anger, grief. Many harvest times ahead, life would eventually be wrung dry of all that it promised.

The tall man standing behind Jock, a bit to the left and looking somewhat less rakish in the same turtleneck sweater and tweed jacket, is
Uncle Jack Sutherland. By the time the photo was taken, Jock had married Jack's sister, Millie. The two men got along well and so they shared
farming duties on some land in the valley bottom four miles upstream
from Tantallon where the Little Cutarm entered from the north. In 1914,
Jack went overseas to fight the Kaiser. When the war ended, he resumed
farming with his sister and brother-in-law. A few years later, Jack
packed up and moved northwest to homestead anew in the Peace River
Country. He remained a bachelor all his days.

I saw Jack Sutherland but once. It was the early 1970s and he had
retired to live in a small house in Winfield, British Columbia, which was
at that time a sunburnt village in Okanagan orchard country. I remember
it as a hot day. We — my parents, two sisters, my brother, and myself all
packed into our Dodge Coronet, tent-camper in tow — wheeled into the
strange quiet of Winfield. We were probably fresh from mini-golf, a trip
to see the Flintstones theme park, or some other roadside banality. We
stopped outside a building that resides in my memory as a weather-
beaten shanty surrounded by fruit trees. Out of the dark and cool
solitude of the shack, came a red-nosed, white-haired man who was to
me a living relic from my grandfather's time. Jock had been dead for a
few years, but here was his friend and brother-in-law, living in a place
where peaches grew on trees and cartoon characters beckoned from the
boulevard. Though Jack was in his nineties then, he was healthy and
straight-postured. He gave us peaches to eat from his own trees. The
juice flowed over my knuckles and onto my wrist. Nothing that sweet
ever grew in the Qu'Appelle.

Or in Caithness. On his boyhood wanderings along Caithness county's
nearest thing to wilderness — the valley of the River Thurso — my
grandfather might not have stopped to pick a berry, but I can well
imagine him walking with the stoop of the artifact hunter, looking for
the "stone fruit" of former dwellers. Trails leading upriver from the village and through his home parish would have brought him to some of
the ancient grounds of the Sutherland clan marked by stone walls and
hilltop ruins. A passage from *A History of Caithness* describes this picturesque stretch of the River Thurso: "Here the banks on each side are

steep and richly clothed with brushwood; and on the summit of a pre-
cipitous rock, said at one time to have been surrounded by the river,
and accessible only by a drawbridge, may be seen the ruins of a castle,
which about the end of the fifteenth century, was inhabited by a chief of
the name of Sutherland."[61]

Jock's parents would have known the local Sutherlands, a family
name a notch or two higher than the McRaes on the register of Caithness
peasantry. No castles anymore, but a croft with a bigger garden, a byre,
and animals to fill it. Whereas the ancestral McRaes, known in clan lore
as "the Scattered Children of Kintail," had merely taken refuge in the
Caithness lowlands after the lairds denuded Kintail and Glensheil of
their kind, the Sutherlands had longer, nobler roots in the county predating the Clearances. Nevertheless, the desire to find a better life in
Canada overtook Sutherlands and McRaes alike. In 1883, Donald
Sutherland boarded a steamer leaving Scotland on the floodtide of
Highland emigrants. His wife, Margaret, and their infant daughter
came several months later to join Donald in Whitby, Ontario.

Farming prospects were poor in Southern Ontario and so twelve
years and five children later, Donald headed west to search for land in
the newly opened Qu'Appelle country in the District of Assiniboia,
North-West Territories. His bachelor brother, Alexander, had already
homesteaded in the eastern Qu'Appelle, and Donald would stay there
for the summer to scout for land before sending for Margaret and the
children. Any spare time they had, Alex and Donald hired themselves
out as stonemasons, raising stone buildings and foundations for settlers
in the region.

The stonework of my Sutherland ancestors have become New World
ruins in less than a century. We seem to have accelerated the ruin-making
process. Walking among the stone remains — though they are hardly
ancient grounds — is no less stirring an experience of antiquity, for the
differences between my world and Donald Sutherland's are at least as
great as those between Jock and the fifteenth-century Sutherlands who
built the castle along the River Thurso. Sometimes more stirring. While
staying at Aunt Bea's I set out to find a barn foundation that Donald
and Alex had made for Walter Brown in the early years of the century.
The barn had blown down in the great cyclone of 1916, and so I knew
the remains would be hard to find, particularly since the records

showed that they had not used cement between the stones, only sand mixed with lime burned in a kiln from limestone they dug out of Common's ravine.

I went in the evening, remembering that half-buried stones of other prairie artifacts — tipi rings, foundations — are easier to find when the setting sun throws shadows onto the grass. There was a herd of forty or so large horses, Percherons or Clydesdales, grazing in the north reaches of the pasture. It looked like somebody's pregnant mare–urine operation. The tenant living next to the pasture gave me his permission and said he didn't think the horses would pay any attention to me — mind you, they weren't his horses and horses can be funny.

With this ambivalent licence, I stepped over the barbed wire and into the pasture. I was wearing shorts and knee-high rubber boots. Fine gear for wading through sedges and cattails, not so fine for leading a steeplechase ahead of forty stampeding brood mares.

When I heard the stallion snort, I was crouching to examine stones that were organized enough to be the remains of the barn. Then there was an impressive rumbling sound, the sort that will come from the percussion of 160 horse hooves headed one's way. I stood up, saw that the stallion was in full gallop at the apex of a triangular mass of horse-flesh that would soon intersect my torso, and I decided it was best to run. Abandoning family archaeology, I bolted for the fence in a forty-yard dash. Both boots tried to stay behind, coming half off, and lending my departure all the grace of a B-circuit rodeo clown in swim fins. In three strides I was face down in horse manure and grass, my knee gashed open on a piece of Sutherland masonry. With the horses bearing down on me, I regained my feet, hobbled the last few paces to the fence, and hurled myself over the top wire. The stallion and his harem wheeled at the fence, slowed to a trot, and returned to their fly-swishing and alfalfa-chewing duties. As I left the scene, heart pounding, blood trickling down my left leg and into my boot, I laughed at the spectacle I had created, and wondered at the heavy symbolism there might be in horses chasing me from remnants of my great-grandfather's stonework.

IN THE COLD EARLY WINTER of 1896, Margaret Hamilton Sutherland brought the children out west, including my grandmother Millie and her brother Jack. The train dropped them off in the town of Wapella twenty miles south of the valley. Donald was not there to meet his family. Instead it was a Caithness friend, Dan Bruce, who would take them by sleigh to his farm on the edge of the Qu'Appelle — above a place my aunts and uncles still call Bruce's Point, the steep hill at the eastern verge of the Little Cutarm's entry upon the Qu'Appelle, near Aunt Bea's house, which itself is on land that once belonged to Bruces.

On the sleigh ride north Margaret's cheek would have felt a wind that cut more sharply than any she had known in Ontario. It was drier, but not unlike the on-shore gales she remembered from visiting the North Sea as a girl. And the lamps shining from distant Jewish homesteads across flat, treeless prairie — like beacons for men at sea. It would have been four hours over the plains before Dan steered the team onto a trail that switchbacked down into the valley. If there was a moon, Margaret would have seen, over the horses' heads, the long curves of the Qu'Appelle and the inky-black shadows of wooded hills that twenty-five years earlier had sheltered the Métis and the Cree. In 1896, though, only a few brave Finns and a Scottish bachelor or two lived in the West Valley. Tantallon was yet to be and the Paynter brothers had just begun their colony at Hamona.

The following spring, the Sutherlands homesteaded on a piece of prairie in Valley View three and a half miles north of the valley and two and a half east of the Little Cutarm. Log cabin, sod roof, a passel of children — the customary homesteader arrangement. Life rolled on from there into the future that branched out toward the union of Amelia Sutherland and John McRae, another house, and another set of life histories. The gravestone at Valley View Cemetery says that Donald died in 1910. He was forty-nine, but had a bad stomach, perhaps bleeding ulcers, perhaps cancer. His widow, Margaret, became a local healer-midwife, birthing babies and mending bodies throughout the district. Farm work fell to the eldest son, Jack, the man I saw sixty years later in the Okanagan shanty, the man in the threshing-crew photograph, standing behind my grandfather.

The fellow to Jack's right in the photograph is Allen Vance, Jock's hunting and trapping partner. He is wearing a scarf around his neck and a wide-brimmed hat, tilted back onto his crown in an awkward attempt to appear self-assured. Instead, vulnerability mingles with fear in his eyes. He is poised to say something. Something tentative, worrying. His image shows nothing of the man eulogized in the local history of Spy Hill: "Allen Vance was a great hunter and trapper all his life, and a very good shot. He always went north of Russell [Manitoba] to hunt moose or elk, and loved his jumper meat."

Jock would have met Vance while he and Millie were living in Spy Hill in their first two years of marriage. Jock was working as a carpenter for a man named Robert Greer, who along with his wife, Hannah Sanderson (of the Samuel Sanderson family of Quakers), had been a founding member of the Hamona colony. The Greer and Vance families had bonds that extended back to Ontario. Although Allen farmed his father's land, he did some stonemasonry as well and may have worked in Greer's employ from time to time.

Splitting stones, trimming joists in the molten air of July afternoons, the stonemason began telling the carpenter of crystalline November days in spruce forests. The bull elk, the lynx pelt, an abundance of mink. Every summer, Jock heard more of Vance's stories from the trapline. And the invitation to join Vance next winter remained open. In late autumn, when the snows came, there was always something to keep Jock close to home. The first winter, 1910, Millie gave birth to a child. The night of her labour, after fetching his mother-in-law out of the cold, long darkness of December, Jock felt a strangling pressure take hold above his sternum and a stab running through his left shoulder and arm. This event, true though it may be, is a favourite piece of melodrama that the McRaes love to recount at family reunions: Jock falls to the floor in pain, his heart failing him at the same moment that Millie pushes her baby out into her mother's hands. Trembling in the corner of the room, he faces his first son and his first angina attack at the age of twenty-five.

Family mythology notwithstanding, it strikes me that a man of my grandfather's mercurial nature might simply have been so shocked by the crucible of his own responsibility and passage into fatherhood that his heart simply gave out beneath the strain. It was years before he had another bout of angina.

More winters and more sons. There is a photograph, taken in the summer of 1918, of the family in a new Model T with the top down. Jock sits in the driver's seat, glaring at the camera, slouching in the seat, left arm draped over the wheel of the contraption he would have scarcely known how to control, the other slung around the back of the seat and around his two eldest sons — Sonny and Snooks. Millie has been stowed in the back seat with a toddler and an infant, Babes and Johnnie respectively. She looks weary, and, given the date for the photo, she was very likely pregnant with the fifth child: another son, Donald, born the following April.

By this time, Jock had accepted Vance's invitation and had begun leaving Millie and the boys each fall to hunt and trap for several weeks in the north near the town of Hudson's Bay, Saskatchewan. In the stories, which are vague, he just slips north into the secrecy of the Big Woods, returning in time for Christmas, arms laden with glistening beaver and muskrat pelts. Whatever else may have happened on these trips, I can only imagine.

Where did he and Vance live up there? Did they do their own cooking and housekeeping? And who taught them where to place a mink trap, how to erase their trail at a set, how to skin and stretch a beaver pelt? These are hard-learned skills, some of which Vance may have acquired as a boy in Ontario, but certainly not available to a Caithness lad. From David Thompson to the trappers on snowmobiles today, white men who go to the North-West for furs have always relied upon a Métis, Cree, or Dene woman to fill their needs. Long before the likes of Jock McRae came to the bush, Scottish trappers and traders from the Highlands, the Orkneys, or the Hebrides had been taking, and leaving, "country wives" in the North-West. It is easy for me to imagine my grandfather, not known for his capacity to go long without the attentions and labour of a woman, heartily embracing the creature comforts of this tradition.

One family story tells of what happened at home one winter while Jock was away in the north. In November of 1919, Jock and Millie's youngest son, Donald, contracted pneumonia and died in a matter of days. No more details than that; not an account of my grandmother's grief and panic as her baby's breathing became more laboured each hour, nor even a mention of how Jock handled the news when he returned in December. But once when we were walking through Valley View Cemetery, my mother looked down at the tiny headstone above the grave of the brother she never met, and told me, in the weak, breaking voice she reserves for matters solemn or pathetic, "Mother always said that there was something not right with Donald. She said he was blind. She'd light a match in front of his eyes and they'd not move at all . . . and he never cried."

In the fall of 1921, the trips to the north came to an end. Allen Vance, perhaps daydreaming of trails through rime-covered muskegs and forests of shaggy black spruce, rolled his threshing machine into a ravine on the edge of the valley. In the words of *The Spy Hill Story*, "he was killed instantly." That is who I see in the threshing-crew photo: not the man who "loved his jumper meat," but the man killed instantly, tragically, by an inelegant machine and his own trust in its providence. And, remembering an uncle and a cousin, I see the faces of McRae men whose encounters with later generations of machines put to rest my grandfather's dreams of patrilineal dominion over a piece of the New World.

After Vance died, Jock never went north again. He took to hunting alone in what became his home range within the Little Cutarm and Qu'Appelle, and for the next twenty-five winters ran a trapline along a nine-mile stretch of the valley bottomlands.

*Chapter Twenty-nine*

# BANK DEPOSITS

ON THE AFTERNOON I TOOK my mother and Aunt Doris out to walk over the old yard site at the mouth of the Little Cutarm, I thought of the derelict house I saw there as a child: siding stripped grey by the years, doors open, windows gone, the smell of damp flooring and mouse urine, and the holes in the walls where the McRae girls, craving calcium or some other mineral, would tear off chunks of plaster to gnaw upon. The building was salvaged for lumber twenty-some years ago, and it has probably been at least that long since these two urban McRae sisters walked the place together and allowed its ghosts to recall their origins.

As we walked, one memory arose, settled and faded into the next, spanning the years of their life in the house my grandfather built in 1921: the house they were born in seventy years ago; the house they left as teenagers some fifty years ago; the house that was empty soon after and that became in my time a wind-worn monument to the floor-sweeping, pail-slopping existence that was once here, until it vanished leaving nothing but stories behind. Stories that weather the memory as peak moments capped and hardened by humour, grief, or drama — odd figures crystallized within the soft, eroding drift of days and left standing like hoodoos in the heart's terrain.

There is the story I call The Soul's Awakening. This was the title of an illustration that hung on the living-room wall of the McRae home, where the girls admired it every day of their childhood. It was one of those inspirational religious paintings still found in the church basements of this region: a radiant young woman, eyes turned upward to a glow from beyond the picture — is it heaven or a vision of the Lord? — her hair and face as dazzling as any Hollywood star's of the 1920s, but different, for her countenance is flooded with innocence and wonder at the cause of her awakening. And Margaret looked just like her when she came home for visits from the city — Margaret Tinnics, Lewis's big sister, the neighbour's girl who had moved to Regina to work for Government Telephones and who came home sometimes on Saturdays with gifts for everyone, hats and coats for her parents and siblings, and a huge steamer trunk full of clothes she had grown tired of and donated to the girls back in West Valley; and who had fancy combs and brushes and fashion jewellery; and who told of the modern conveniences that made life richer, easier, and more exciting in the city; and who had changed her name to Marguerite Tinnish because it looked and sounded better and you could do that in the city; and who was glamorous and sophisticated and generous and rich. When the McRae girls knew Margaret was coming for a weekend they would sit and wait for her high on one of the hills so they could see a long way down the valley and watch the road for any sign of her, and as they waited they imagined themselves one day taking the same road to a life where instead of jumper stew and baring your arse to the breeze, there would be market food and porcelain toilets, a life worth coming home from, like Margaret, bearing trinkets and the glow of a soul's awakening.

I walked over to the edge of the foundation while my mother eased her way into the bottom of the cellar depression. Aunt Doris picked up something oval-shaped and nickel-plated.

"It's from the front of the old stove." She paused, looking up from the artifact to her sister rummaging in the cellar.

"Remember how the oven door was broken and mother had a stick of oak jammed between it and the floor to keep it closed, and we'd always run through the kitchen and trip on it?"

We looked for places, patches of ground they remembered: for the flat rock on which Snooks swears he fried an egg one scorching day in July and for the maples growing rank like weeds in the rich soil of the squatting place the McRaes called, with a nod to gentility, "the ash pile," and for the place where Jock would stand in the yard to direct his voice up toward Bruce's Point, where his daughter-in-law Bea would be standing a half-mile away on the edge of the hill to take his order — and here Aunt Doris faced the point, pressed her chin down to lower her voice, and offered her best rendition, with r's rolling and t's slurred, of the old man shouting "Bring me some buttermilk!"

Something brought the Lebanese peddlers to mind: Sam and Leo Joseph, swarthy exotic-smelling fellows, coming down the valley road with two dray horses pulling a van full of brushes, linen, spices, and an assortment of products — everything from egg-beaters to gopher poison — for easing the housewife's burden. Millie would always feed them and then invite them to stay the night before they passed on up the Qu'Appelle along their circuit. And then there were the railcar hobos, jumping off the train as the CPR made the turn from the valley into the Little Cutarm at the edge of their fields. Like the itinerant peddlers, they knew the yard, had it marked: "kind lady, bread." One tramp used to come regularly for a slab of bread dipped in bacon grease — a treat he could rely on from the farm where the line turned north at the first creek west of Tantallon.

My mother wanted to walk down to a certain bend in the river where they would go to wash clothes in the summertime. The washing place, she said, was just west of the confluence of the creek and the river, where a stretch of sand formed the instep of a bend. We made our way down to the river, following a trail across a cultivated field that had been colonized by bluegrass, crested wheat grass, and alfalfa. I was surprised to find a good-sized patch of big bluestem, the eastern Qu'Appelle's showy native tallgrass, that appears to have reclaimed a corner of the field. The trail petered out into a maze of game pathways entering the willows alongside oxbow ponds. These stagnant ponds found everywhere along the length of the valley are the scars of the Calling River's recent history — crescent-shaped chunks of river that were cut off from the active channel when it formed a shortcut between the nearest points of a meander.

A bend in a prairie river like the Qu'Appelle can wander a long way in fifty years. As we crashed in and out of the bush, it occurred to me that the old washing place is more than likely a silted-in oxbow pond by now. There was no point in explaining meander mechanics to my mother, so I searched through the riverside willows until I found what is now the first bend west of the confluence. And then she told me again, as she had dozens of times before, how the McRaes washed their clothes.

"In the summertime, on a warm day, Mother would hitch up a horse to the stone boat and take us girls down here to the river for the afternoon. On the stone boat the horse pulled two barrels: one empty and the other loaded with dirty clothes. We'd play in the shallows at the riverside while Mother piled up stones and built a fire under a barrel of water. The water'd get hot, and she'd start scrubbing the clothes on her washboard. We helped her hang the clean things on the willows to dry. By then we'd all be hot, so Mother, red in the face from the heat and the work, would come into the river with us and we'd all swim and splash around. Later, when it was time to head back to the house, we'd put the clean clothes in one barrel and fill the other one with river water to use in the kitchen. Every two weeks or so we'd do that."

In 1858, James Austin Dickinson, the surveyor-naturalist on the Hind expedition through the Qu'Appelle country, came across a group of Saulteaux women downstream from Crooked Lake as he paddled his way along the eastern half of the river. The women were washing and playing in the river. The life of these women, who scurried, laughing, to retrieve their clothes on shore, was alien and inscrutable to Dickinson, good servant of God and Queen. It is Dickinson I think of when I consider all that separates me from the riverside lives of the women in my mother's washday reminiscence.

My family's laundry is handled by Karen and a box that comes from Sears — an electrified, engineered box that churns soap packaged in Toronto with water filtered, chlorinated, and piped forty-five miles from Buffalo Pound Lake to our urban basement. Convenient, little scrubbing required, but no nickering horse, no soughing willows, no sandy shallows in which to splash with the children.

Wascana Creek, old Pile o' Bones, runs through Regina a half-mile south of our house, but washing clothes there would be futile — an exchange of one kind of filth for another and possibly a violation of civic bylaws. Doing laundry once every two weeks at the river, though it was undoubtedly less pleasant than it appears beneath the gloss of memory, was one of the lighter tasks within the unending cycle of chores that passed through the hands of my grandmother and other women of her class and time. Indoor plumbing has eased many of these tasks, and we have to a great degree formed our culture by changing the way our mothers, wives, and daughters feed and clothe the members of their households. The costs, in terms of community and ecology, however, have been high.

When we stepped away from the riverside and began piping water into our homes, out of taps and down sewers, we lost touch with what may be the only sound way of living on the prairie — in respectful proximity with the gathering of scarce water. I will sometimes sit on the rim of the valley above the Big Cutarm, or the south end of Lake Katepwe, or other places where the Métis settled in the Qu'Appelle and I will try to envision the land sectioned in long lots running back from the river, up the round hills to the prairie above. Given a different history, a different outcome at Batoche and Duck Lake, the Métis system of land allotment might have kept us nearer the waterways and valleys that have sustained prairie people for thousands of years. Living out of sight of the river has put it out of mind, allowing us to forget that beyond the artificial and tenuous support of petrochemicals and an economy dependent on distant trade, water — its quantity and quality — is still the great arbiter of life in a semi-arid climate, the genius that shapes the character of our households, our communities, and our poetry as a grassland people.

As we walked back from the washing place it occurred to me that we might all be better off if we spent more time at river banks and less at the other kind. What if we gave our riverbanks credit for all that we borrow from them? What if we made careful withdrawals and deposits worthy of the river? What if we made up for our debts there? If we calculated the interest charged by a river, the price of our endless borrowing, the possibility of foreclosure? And if recovering from "bank failure" involved building a fence to keep the cattle out of the willows?

THE FIELDS ON EITHER SIDE of the McRaes' washing place, now in the hands of strangers, were part of the land Jock first cultivated with his brother-in-law, Jack Sutherland, before the Great War. Jock and Millie lived with Jack until he went overseas. After returning a decorated soldier in 1918, Jack bought the portion of the farm south of the river, leaving Jock and Millie the north half section, which included the land at the mouth of the Little Cutarm and amounted to a total of roughly 135 acres of arable fields. In the spring of '22, the McRaes, with five children now, moved into a pair of granaries by the creek while Jock began building what would become their home for the next thirty years. In the fall they moved into the house, an unfinished shell, for the winter. Walking into the front entrance, they would have had to take care not to step into a large hole in the floor that led down into the dirt cellar. Above their heads was a hole in the ceiling with a ladder that took the boys up to the second floor, where they slept. This area of holes and ladders, meant eventually to become a stairwell, was separated from the rest of the main floor by a wall — the only interior wall in the building. Other walls and the stairs would come later, as money allowed. Likewise for the upstairs windows, which had cardboard instead of glass.

Jock never got around to making these improvements. The following year, the Tantallon Home Bank failed, taking with it all Jock's savings and those of many of his neighbours. He took some relief work building a local highway during the Depression. There were times when Millie would ask for money to buy some necessity — thread for mending or some sugar for canning — and Jock would launch into an uncontrollable rage. My mother and aunts always stop short of using words such as *hit* or *struck* or *battered*, but I do not doubt that my grandfather was violent at such times.

After the bank failure and throughout the Depression, the McRaes, like many people in and around the valley, often lived on credit from the village grocer. Jock was on good terms with Frank Baker, who along with his brother Harry, owned the Red and White Store in Tantallon. In the twenties and early thirties, Frank was both a supplier and a market for Jock's home-brew enterprise, giving him spoiled fruit to make his mash and then stocking the underside of his counter with quart sealers full of the final product. On occasion, Jock would do carpentry for the Bakers and in fact built a house for Frank, the house in which my cousin Jerry now lives, the house that showed me what the McRae home might have been had Jock acquired the money or inclination to finish it with staircases, walls, and windows.

On Jock's Saturday trips into town, Frank would always send him home with a load of groceries for the family and a dime bag of candy for the little girls. This went on for several years — the McRaes provisioned by a long and unpaid account at the Red and White. (Not a trace of shame from Aunt Evelyn as she talks of this. If anything, she seems proud of her father's cavalier attitude toward financial matters, and she tells the story's resolution with particular relish.)

By 1934, the burden of charity to destitute customers pushed the Baker brothers out of business. They both moved out to the coast, although in 1940 Frank and his wife returned to live once again in Tantallon. That same year, Jock, now in his fifties, secured a well-paying job supervising carpentry at the construction of the Yorkton airport. Returning home with cash in his pockets, he went straight to Frank Baker's to square things up on a line of credit that had run for almost twenty years. Frank took the roll of money, put it back into my grandfather's hands and said, "Forget it, Jock. I don't own a store anymore."

Even in the hardest of times, then, the McRaes never went hungry or barefoot, unlike many prairie farm children who made it through the teeth of the thirties. There were always the fish and grouse their father brought to the table and some income from moonshining and trapping. "Daddy always seemed to have some money" is the phrase I have heard my mother and her sisters repeat. "We used to sneak nickels from Daddy's pants when he left them on the chair." Then they mention Christmases ("We always had something on Christmas morning") and the Kallio girls admiring their clothes — hand-me-downs in parcels that arrived regularly from the relatives in Scotland.

If Jock always seemed to have a few dollars on hand it was at least in part because whatever he earned he kept at home. After the collapse of the Home Bank in '23, he never trusted a financial institution with his money again. His cash and grain cheques went into a brown tin box alongside letters from home. The box now sits on my bookshelf between a piece of the McRaes' brick chimney and a stone axe that I found above Bruce's Point. Evelyn gave me the box last year along with some old photographs and letters. Such a container encloses more than one man's distrust of banks. There is also his desire and ultimately his failure to hold something back from the world at the end of the rails that turned up the Little Cutarm Valley — the world in Winnipeg, Regina, and Ottawa, where those stingy buggers who signed the grain cheques sat at desks devising new ways to squeeze every last penny out of a man. But he had no box that would keep his children, his holdings, or his community back. Few could resist the pull of industry, affluence, and modernity from beyond the valley. Such is the allure of our civilization: liberated from the supposed ignominy and drudgery of growing our own food, the descendants of Jock McRae and his kind live in households where energy arrives in shrink-wrapped, microwavable portions and departs — no ash pile here — with a clean, porcelain *swoosh*.

# Chapter Thirty

# FAITH

IN BOXES WERE NOT ENOUGH to protect the culture and economy of places like West Valley. For the farmers of my grandfather's generation, there was no strongbox that could resist the powers that have homogenized and industrialized prairie farms and landscapes. If there ever was such a container, it was the long-abandoned ark of our covenant with the land. A religious bond is needed, always has been, whether the people are hunter-gatherers or potato farmers, Shinto or Christian: a bond maintained by exact ethical guidelines telling how the Creation is to be used and honoured, which tools and practices sustain land and community, and when to restrict our reach and interdependencies.

Nevertheless, prairie people have not entirely lost their ancestral predispositions toward the preservation of the tribe — the urge to help a neighbour, the desire to draw a circle around community and local culture. There is a natural conservatism in the ethics of anyone who has known hunger and who has learned to feed a family by hunting or growing things. While remote, anonymous forces of history and economics assailed their communities, our grandmothers saved pieces of string, made the best of scarcity, wasted nothing. The men, following their own primitive longings, blustered and tilted at these invisible dragons terrorizing the land, never realizing that with each shift from human and animal power to fossil fuels and machinery, they were feeding the same monsters.

Somewhere along the way, our tribal and moral instincts gave in to the prospects of wealth. Christian doctrine, as it appeared in the hymnals in Tantallon's church and in churches across the plains, was, if anything, a barrier to encountering the sacred in the land, an ethic that could justify any measures taken to convert the land's communal gifts into private prosperity. By the time the people of my grandparents' generation had reached old age, the communities they had cultivated in the New World's fertile soils had already begun to wither on the vine. Religion saved no one. Church-goers and back-sliders alike presided over the dispersal of their families, the loss of their neighbours, the demise of their neighbourhoods.

NO ONE WOULD HAVE MADE the mistake of calling Jock McRae a pious man. He had enough sense to see through the local gathering of self-anointed, jewels-in-my-crown pew-sitters and to withhold his faith, like his money, from all dishonest, unreliable institutions. To his kind, religion was a civilizing bulwark from the Old World, a useful source of small talk when confronted with an unctuous member of the Ladies Aid, and perhaps even a bet hedged against damnation — though I doubt he subscribed to that piece of fiction either. Being a Christian had little to do with the material world at hand and played no role in determining how his farm was to be worked or how a new machine might change his relationships with the land and his neighbours.

Evelyn claims that she heard her father refer to the deity once and only once — apart from cussing, that is. It was the July afternoon my mother was born in 1927, when a hailstorm swept in from up the valley. The hailstones were large and falling fast, striking the single pane of glass at the window above the bed where Millie slept with her newborn at the breast. Jock, my great-aunt Jo, and several of the older children held pillows up against the window to absorb the impact of the stones and in that way managed to keep the glass from crashing down upon mother and child. When the storm subsided, they removed the pillows and looked out the window. In that unearthly green light that follows a prairie hailstorm on a hot day, Jock surveyed what remained of his prize oat crop east of the creek and across the road, then raised his eyes skyward and asked, "If there is a God in heaven, why would He take my oat crop on the same day He has given me another mouth to feed?"

Inside the tin box, among a pile of curled and yellowing photographs and some letters from Caithness relatives, is a letter my grandfather wrote to his mother on the death of his father in 1931. Signing it "fondest love to all, Johnnie," and doing his level best to sound as if he just put down the Bible from his daily scripture reading, he wrote, "It must be great consolation to you now Mother to know how good and how near as possible Father always tried to live up to the teachings of Christ and the Bible. I have often remarked to many people here, where I am sorry to say, the majority don't give much thought to the hereafter, how sincere my Mother and Father were in the teachings relating to the World hereafter."

I laughed when I first read this, trying to imagine my grandfather a devout elder of the Presbytery. Then I thought of his regard for the valley and the times I have stood upon its rim, aware that his faith in the possibility of renewal in this land is part of an inheritance that resides in me yet, inextricably bound up with my own affections for these hills and waterways. But that faith did not come from a church or the religious dogma he could recite when necessary. It came from the river and the oak trees, the warm rank smell of a gutted deer and the confiding lilt of meltwater in April — or from his apprehension of these things. The grandfather of my memory, of family legend, and of my own imagining was too interested in the feel and flavour of the world at hand, the here and now revelations underfoot and overhead, to be infected by a theology that turned its adherents away from the sacred and the redemptive in this everyday Creation, toward false piety and the vague "World hereafter" such piety might purchase.

There were, of course, other faiths that distracted the immigrant homesteaders of the Qu'Appelle. Reading the letter home brought one of them to mind: the orthodoxy that says a farm worked by machines and the energy in fossilized animals is an improvement over one worked by people and the energy in living animals. Dreams of subsistence and dreams of utopia in the New World are the ghosts you meet in the empty barns and farmhouses. They have not been long dead. Most expired or moved away in the short piece of one century that took farmers out from behind draft horses and seated them atop four-wheel drive, air-conditioned, hydraulically enhanced, computer-on-board traction units, ushering in an agriculture that allows one man to cultivate, seed, weed, and harvest thousands of acres without need of neighbours and without ever setting foot on the soil.

I wish I could say that my grandfather resisted the flow of modernity and preferred horses to tractors, but it would be a lie. Instead of spurning the very progress and mechanization that destroyed his world at the mouth of the Little Cutarm, Jock embraced each labour-saving "advance" enthusiastically, as bedazzled by the modern implements as any farmer of his time. Few people saw then where the line of agricultural advancement would lead, and though I cannot blame my ancestors for following blindly, I believe that before my grandfather died he had glimpsed the fullness of what this faith in progress had cost his family and his community.

*Chapter Thirty-one*

# THE LAIRD
# DOESN'T PLOUGH

A HALF-TON TRUCK DROVE UP and parked by Aunt Bea's picket fence on the morning of the third day of my stay. Two men, large fellows in their early thirties, got out and walked up the sidewalk.

I met them at the door. The one in front, holding the other side of the door and staring at me, looked like a matinee idol — six foot three, clean-shaven, cropped bob of wavy hair, square jaw, tanned skin. In $200-hiking boots, a clean shirt, and designer jeans, he was indistinguishable from the legions of young men in the city out for drinks on a Friday night after a week of arranging stock portfolios or peddling multimedia "solutions."

"Who are you?" I said. The words surprised me. I hadn't talked to anyone but ghosts for forty-eight hours and my subtlety in conversation had fled.

"Who am *I*?" he said, "Who are *you*?"

How was I to know that the farmer who had bought Bea's place didn't look like a farmer? I had never actually spoken to the man to get permission. Gary had made all the arrangements with the landowner. But there I was, unshaven, in a torn sweatshirt and bare feet, looking like some kind of squatter, permission or not.

I invited them in, apologizing sheepishly, and introduced myself with a long, rambling explanation of how this used to be my aunt's place and we used to come here a lot and I needed a place to stay while I poked around the Tantallon area and so I called my cousin Gary and he said that you said . . .

The other man, who appeared to be the landlord's assistant and who was providing the background chortling, looked around the porch as we spoke. The landlord, whose name was Monty, shifted conversation to the well and the cattle. I asked him about his crop north of the house. There didn't seem much point in mentioning that, as second cousins, his wife and I shared the same great-grandfather, Donald Sutherland. I was a writer from the city and that was enough to define me as a stranger — and a nervy one at that.

Though he lives almost thirty miles away to the northwest at the town of Stockholm, Monty farms a lot of land in this area. A lot of land. Land that not long ago supported ten or fifteen farm families who lived next to their fields.

According to Aunt Evelyn, who only exaggerates when the truth is inadequate to the task, three of these industrial-scale farmers work virtually all the land in the township — 23,040 acres. I had spoken to Babes and Evelyn about the changes wrought by modern farming methods.

"Monty's got a machine," said Ev. "He pulls it behind that bloody big tractor of his and he can do Bertha's field in two sweeps! Two sweeps!" Babes nodded in agreement. They are fascinated and appalled by turns at the way farmers work today. It saddens them to see the landscape empty of the families that were once their neighbours. In all the abandoned houses that punctuate the landscape of Valley View, all the rickety monuments to their time and its passing, they know the way the staircases turn, the way the hallways run, the places where the children used to carve their names in the woodwork.

In the next moment though, they will praise one of these younger land-swallowing farmers: "He's a good farmer, mind you. That field was producing nothing but weeds and stones and now he's got it into shape." This, referring to one of the fields that until recently was worked by Aunt Bea's son, Jerry. Jerry is the kind of farmer this land can ill afford to lose: intelligent, humble, neighbourly, and kind-hearted. He did his best on the family farm, but never acquired the obdurate wilfulness that lets a farmer subdue the land in the modern way with high-powered machinery, heavy dosages of nitrogen and herbicide, and an infinite line of credit at the bank.

There is no denying that Monty's crops are lush. I look at the fields around Bea's house and down the road by Jerry's now empty house and I can see that they are thick and even with the dark green of wheat in a wet summer. Not a weed or a thin patch in sight, perfectly uniform, and, to the aesthetic of homogeneity, quite lovely.

But I am unable to regard these immaculate, broadloomed land-scapes without thinking of the costs to community, both human and ecological. The dominant model of agriculture, supported by government programs and university research, has made farmers ever more dependent on petrochemicals and banks. From the synthetic fertilizers, pedigreed seed, and toxic cocktails of crop-spray to the outsized, fuel-guzzling, computer-enhanced implements and the trucks hauling the yield to the inland terminal, our farmers are pumping gas and money into the land at a frightful rate. How long we can sustain this kind of agriculture is a question we studiously avoid in our regard for the future and our definition of economy.

I spoke to a farmer in the Holar district northeast of Tantallon about the rising costs of farming. I had stopped at the roadside to admire a single bur oak he had left standing in his wheat field in a small concession to nature. He saw me and wondered if I needed help, so pulled over to check. Talk turned to his truck and the trip he had just made into Esterhazy. He had been at the bank to get a little more credit. Had to buy something for the fall harvest. A new tractor or grain truck? No, he was just replacing a drive belt for his combine. It was going to cost $2,600. Without it, the combine, worth $215,000, would not run. After I drove on, it struck me that a large-scale, high-input farmer might well burn more gas on trips to the bank than any one of the ten farmers he has superseded would have used in a year of cultivating, seeding, and harvesting a farm of more reasonable proportions.

But the small farmers — people like Jerry who now lives in Tantallon and sells insurance — were proven to be "inefficient" by the terms of our deviant economy. Babes tells me that the only small hold-ings that remain in the district belong to people who work full-time at one of the potash mines. To come to male adulthood in Valley View or West Valley these days is to face a simple choice: either mine the land —

potash and fertile topsoil are the primary extractables — or turn your back on your father's land and head for the city.

Complicating all of this is the role of the individual farmer and his relationship with the public. It would be easy to describe mega-farmers as the villains in this scenario. But the cold truth is that we — the ones who let others produce our food, who sup at the far end of a table provisioned by a thousand sins against human and wild community — are equally guilty as long as we draw life from the supermarket. A man like Monty is only picking up the task that we have allowed history and happenstance to place at his feet. He is no more or less greedy than the rest of us. In the short term, the system "works" for farmers and consumers alike, enabling us all to buy our food cheaply and without the supposed indignity of having to grow more of it ourselves. The land continues to turn its tricks, for now; the river receives whatever runs downslope from the fields and the cities; and no one, or everyone, is to blame.

ON AN AUGUST AFTERNOON two weeks into my stay at Aunt Bea's, Fair Day, I sat down to watch the light-horse judging with a group of Tantallon bachelors and widowers on the bleachers behind the town rink. Old men wearing comfortable pants and shoes: no woman anymore, no farm anymore, no hurry anymore. Among them was John Polvi, son of one of the first men to be born in the New Finland district south and across the valley from the McRaes. By the time Jock set up his family on the Little Cutarm, the Polvis had been residents for twenty-five years.

In the late thirties and early forties, John worked locally as a hired hand while continuing to help out on his parents' farm. As he spoke to me, his eyes narrowed down to see if I was really listening, and his lower lip, pursed and jutting, let out words in rapid phrases formed within the mould of the language he learned first.

"You know what I remember about old Jock McRae? I remember once I was ploughing a field in the valley. I was just fourteen but I was driving a team across this field there. I made a turn and was just starting to come along the row when I looked up and saw this tall man on the hillside. Just standing there, watching me, holding his rifle.

Scared the hell out of me. Jock always had this *look*. I was scared of him, I was, for a long time."

My grandfather's favourite farm implement was the lever-action .300 Savage he carried everywhere in the crook of his arm. With his angina furnishing an honourable discharge from farm duties, he had elevated himself to the role of laird and overseer. Until Sonny and Babes were old enough to handle a team, there were always hired men on the McRae farm harrowing, binding, and threshing in the three-corner field and on the flood-enriched acres along the river.

"Daddy was a crude farmer," Evelyn will say, "but a good manager. He always made sure the hired men were out in the field at the appointed time." The scowl and the Savage on his arm served him well as farm-management techniques. So well that, outside of trapping season, he seldom bothered to rise from bed before 11 AM. At nine he would holler for Evelyn to bring him his first cigarette of the day. He'd smoke in bed, then turn over and sleep through the morning until eleven, at which time he expected his porridge to be waiting for him, hot from the stove. After breakfast he would make his rounds to see that the work was getting done. After a mid-afternoon nap, there might be some light duty before supper. Evenings, spring, summer, and fall, were for hunting. He never worked the fields himself.

Neither Evelyn nor any of her sisters can recall seeing the old man so much as sit upon the seat of a binder. But they remember him walking the fields behind Babes to make sure the harrowing was done to his standards. The only farm machine he liked to operate was the threshing machine, which had obvious appeal as the most complex and modern device on the farm, the gizmo that not only saved labour but produced immediate, impressive results: the summer's yield in golden heaps of grain for market.

In later years, after World War II when the tractor and the combine came to redefine farm work, Jock found that he liked driving gas-powered machinery over the fields. By then he was sixty years old, somewhat less volatile, and content to sit high in a tractor seat and survey his domain. Hired hands became unnecessary and expensive, so he and Babes ran the farm more or less alone. The .300 Savage only came out during jumper season, but he still lorded over the land at the outflow of the Little Cutarm as though his rule had been handed down in direct succession from the House of Stuart. During these years he became known locally as "the Gov'ner," an irreverent nickname coined by his eldest grandson, Eddie, who was a chip off the old block and then some.

Jock may have been a laird in his own mind, but to his neighbours, who kept their fences mended, their barns tidy, and their houses painted, he was a rough and neglectful farmer — just barely a class above the local Métis farmers downriver past Hamona, men who had the same pernicious habit of hunting or trapping when they should have been tending their livestock or fields.

Jock didn't bother with fences. Didn't believe in them. Good fences did *not* make good neighbours, just a lot of unnecessary obstruction for the hunter and unnecessary work for the farmer. Besides, everyone else had nice fences, so he didn't need any.

This line of thinking irked one neighbour in particular, Alexander Irvine, the next self-appointed laird up the valley. Irvine, who seems to have been the prototype for the dour Scotsman, lived a mile and a half west of the McRaes just upstream from the Little Cutarm. The right mix of similarities and differences between the head of the McRaes and the head of the Irvines set the two West Valley lairds at odds in most of their dealings as neighbours. Both had emigrated from Scotland after the turn of the century, dreaming of new land where they could establish their own family holdings. Both married good Scottish lasses and set up households in West Valley. Both prospered in the early years and then lost their savings when the Home Bank collapsed. Both adopted the latest farm implements early and eagerly (Irvine was the first in the region to use a threshing machine).

Unlike Jock, however, Alex was a fastidious and ambitious farmer. A few chickens, a few pigs, a small herd of cattle, and 135 acres of arable land were all Jock had and aspired to. Irvine, meanwhile, had one of the larger farms in the district — 800 acres of fertile bottomland — and yet somehow found time to travel the province buying and selling horses and cattle. He owned land in Tantallon and a business: a garage and farm machinery dealership. An upstanding and prosperous landholder, Alex Irvine was the sort of man who is said to be "active in community affairs." He was a school trustee, a town councillor, and a member of the Agricultural Society. When the RCMP patrol passed through the valley on their way to Wapella on winter nights, the constables would stay at the Irvine home. Jock, on the other hand, steered clear of community organizations and preferred to spend his winter days along his trapline and the nights stretching skins. He looked upon the RCMP as a nuisance, not as potential house-guests, for when they paid a visit to the McRae farm it was to look for illicit furs or the still they knew McRae had stowed away somewhere. Once it was to look for stolen grain.

Alex accused Jock of the theft, after following a sleigh trail in the snow one late winter night from his grain bins to the McRae driveway. When the police arrived to arrest Jock, he led them out to his own bins, let them see that he had no extra grain, and then tracked the cutter trail over the Little Cutarm and farther down the valley. This was mischief McRae could not take credit for. The constables followed the trail another mile or so east to its termination in the yard of one of the poorest households in the district, that belonging to Alex Irvine's improvident brother, Hugh. Through the winter, to keep his wife and their passel of children from starving, Hugh had sold every last bushel of grain from his bins, leaving no seed grain to use in planting his spring crop. He knew that Alex would have plenty to spare, but wasn't about to beg favours from a brother who had never given him anything but scorn. Instead, on a moonless night in March he hitched up the team to his sleigh, drove up the valley to Alex's bins, and shovelled a few bushels of grain onto the sleigh box. McRae, whose yard lay halfway back to Hugh's own empty bins and who was already a suspected poacher and moonshiner, could take the heat.

Hugh was arrested for stealing his brother's grain, and Jock had another reason to dislike Alex Irvine. Even an old skunk from Aberdeenshire like Irvine might have had the common decency to forgive a brother in a time of need. Lord knows he didn't have the common sense to recognize a prize steer if it sat down to tea with him. But that was another point of contention: cattle, black Aberdeen Angus, to be specific.

Each of the West Valley lairds believed his own herd of Angus to be the finest in the valley. Although the woods and steep slopes of the Little Cutarm provided a natural barrier, Jock's footloose cattle were notorious for wandering into the neighbour's pasture or escaping down the valley road to fraternize with their bovine colleagues. Irvine, with his large livestock enterprise, would regularly herd a hundred or more of his stock along the five miles of valley road into Tantallon, where the heifers and calves could be shipped by railcar to market in Winnipeg. The McRaes always knew when Irvine was coming down the road with his cattle — they could hear his low Scots cattle-drover shouts rolling in from the west as the herd approached. This was the alarm for the McRae boys to tend to their father's herd of twenty-five Angus, which, being cattle, liked to join any passing parade. One time, however, something went awry, and Irvine's market herd enticed six of Jock's finest away from the creekside without Babes's or Sonny's notice. By late afternoon, when Jock made his count and realized what had happened, Irvine — whose figuring skills were as sharp as any prosperous Scotsman's — was halfway to Winnipeg on the morning train with his cattle and six stowaways besides. Jock headed to town and got Frank Baker at the Red and White to send a telegram to the Winnipeg stockyards: "SEIZE IRVINE. STOLEN CATTLE. COMING ON NEXT TRAIN. J. MCRAE." Then he hopped aboard the afternoon train to Winnipeg. There must have been a remarkable exchange of choice English and Gaelic descriptives upon the stockyard loading platform when he arrived. One way or another, the two Tantallon cattle barons sorted the matter out, for Jock rode back home in a boxcar the next morning with his half-dozen confused though well-travelled cattle.

There is one story, though, of Alex and Jock working together on a project of unmitigated civic and spiritual service: the moving of the new Tantallon United Church. In 1925, church union among the Presbyterian, Methodist, and Congregational denominations across Canada made official the Protestant consolidation that had been happening for decades in prairie communities such as Tantallon. The ladies of the Tantallon congregation decided it was time the village had a real church. Until then, services had been held in various places in the village — Paynter's hardware store, the Odd Fellows Hall, the school. The project began when Mrs. Parker, "Granny Parker" to most, stood up at a meeting of the Ladies Aid, waved a five-dollar bill, and announced that she would donate it to buy the material for a quilt.

"With your co-operation, we will make blocks for the quilt. Each of us must endeavour to have these blocks covered with autographs at ten cents each. This will be the nucleus of our church building fund."

This old lady knew a thing or two about collective effort. Thirty years earlier, she and her husband had helped to build the co-operative community at Hamona. Two of her sons married girls from the Sanderson family and her daughter married W.C. Paynter's son, Roy — the bespectacled storekeeper of my earliest memories in Paynter's store.

The five-dollar plan worked. The quilt and other projects raised $1,000 — enough to buy the school building and cover the costs of forming a new foundation for it on a corner lot along Main Street. There were even funds left over to outfit it with pews and choir loft. But first the building would have to be moved down Main Street.

How my grandfather became involved at this point is not exactly clear. He was not the sort to volunteer for church projects and had little time for the socially and spiritually ambitious members of the Ladies Aid. This was the 1920s, when respectable Protestant ladies busied themselves reading temperance tracts and listening to their ministers deliver rousing orations on the most pressing social concern of their day — insobriety. Yet Jock McRae, known sinner and enemy of temperance, had stepped forward in the congregation's hour of need and volunteered to move Tantallon's new house of worship. Main Street, the ladies all said, would be Jock's road to Damascus. There were doubters. Even some peevish enough to suggest that this was no act of contrition, but simply a favour for Frank Baker, that pillar of Tantallon's Christian community who donated the lot for the new church in the same spirit of generosity that persuaded him from time to time to offer his thirsty brethren, the husbands of the Ladies Aid, a draft of Little Cutarm springwater. Temperance is fine for ladies, but what of Fellowship and Good Cheer — without these to inspire how could a man stomach the other cardinal virtues?

Given this overlap of spiritual and convivial values and the commonplace ironies that characterize life in a prairie village, it somehow made perfect sense that Tantallon's first church would be hauled into place by the local moonshiner and ne'er-do-well. And that he should have to complete the task in partnership with his neighbour and nemesis, Alex Irvine.

I would guess that getting Irvine to team up with Jock would have been a simple matter of appealing to his pride, which by most reports was substantial. He was not about to let that heathen McRae take all the credit for bringing the new church to its foundation. Besides, he had a team of horses that would put McRae's old nags to shame.

With the whole of Tantallon out to watch the great event, the chiefs of the two West Valley clans — the McRae and the Irvine — stood shoulder to shoulder behind sixteen horses, hands gripping the reins, brows furrowed in resolute and, some said, heroic expression, neither man glancing sideways, each basking in the approbation of the townfolk gathered on the street, each wishing the other would fall off the skids. The old schoolhouse creaked and groaned its way down Main Street and onto fresh footings without mishap. New pews were built by local men. And the good Reverend Winchester donated a pulpit, at which in due time he stood and delivered the inaugural sermon, commending his flock for rallying behind this most worthy of causes, while confining himself to only one or two volleys in the direction of those who, fearing the circumspection of the Lord or led astray by the insobriety of a Saturday night, could not find it in their hearts to attend service on this glorious day.

Over the years Alex Irvine and my grandfather saw many friends eulogized and children married in that church. Alex died in 1957. His son, Douglas, moved back onto the home place and took up farming that same year. Jock lost a noble adversary but lived to see one of his oldest grandsons, Jerry McRae, marry Irvine's eldest granddaughter. The two families were joined again when one of Jock's great-granddaughters, Thelma McRae, married one of Irvine's grandsons, Rodney. Thelma and Rodney live on the original Irvine farm and keep some cattle in the valley bottom on the pastures that once fattened Alex's prize-winning Aberdeen Angus.

The church, seventy years after its trip down Main Street, continues to serve Tantallon's dwindling flock. On most Sunday mornings, Aunt Evelyn makes the drive from Esterhazy to attend service. Afterwards, she stops by the town pump to get her week's supply of Tantallon water. Water and church are the two Tantallon amenities she has been most reluctant to do without.

My parents were married in the church in 1956. One of the photographs from the wedding shows a mass of people flooding out of the church onto the steps around the bride and groom. Everyone is smiling and making the gestures people make when they are released from the quiet shelter of a church into the expansive light of a midsummer afternoon. At the back of the crowd, on the top step and off to one side, is my grandfather, looking smart in his double-breasted suit, standing as straight as a poplar in good soil. He has just lit a cigarette and is squinting away from the church, away from the congregation on the steps and lawn, to something, or nothing, in the distance.

## Chapter Thirty-two

# SWINE

*I* LIKE PIGS. *Dogs look up to us. Cats look down to us. Pigs treat us as equals.*

— WINSTON CHURCHILL

IT IS ENTIRELY POSSIBLE, given my grandfather's range of interests in this stage of his life, that he was — as he stood there on the church steps after seeing his last daughter married off — thinking of pigs. *Do they have enough chop? In this heat, they'll be looking to the mud for relief. Better get Babes to check on them now before we have to go. God knows he won't think of it himself.*

Jock had a soft spot for his pigs. His cattle were valuable and fine animals, but the pigs he could confide in. Pigs bring a sense of collegiality to the barnyard. They will look for you and greet your arrival at the pen, tossing their heads with fond grunts of recognition. Not that they are to be entirely trusted. Full-grown swine will take gustatory advantage of whatever falls into their domain, even the farmer himself should he slip in the mud. In that regard, they are like a good many of their attendants: apparently honourable and high-principled until faced with a question of immediate economic gain. No fuss about tomorrow, no qualms about biting the hand that feeds them, as long as that hand will make a tasty meal today.

Come fall, Jock would throw open the gates of the pig pen and let his sow and her brood out to run for the day. The acorns had fallen from the oaks by then and the blue jays and squirrels were getting the best of them, but in Jock's mind, acorns were a treat for his rooting shoats. The pigs for their part were happy to oblige, to hearken back for a day to their wild Eurasian ancestry, their dim racial memories tweaked by the glorious truffle taste of earthworms, mycelium, and acorns. First, though, the sow would usher her charges into Millie's turnips and beets. The garden sown in May, weeded daily from June to August, would have been at peak production and ready for harvest. Jock may have simply been thoughtless in letting his pigs annually destroy the garden just as it came to maturity; he may have thought, foolishly, that Millie and the kids should be able to shoo the pigs from the garden, but I suspect that he in fact harboured some contempt for the soil-grubbing work of gardening and much of its produce. All that greenery was food fit for a rabbit, not a man. Only his precious taties mattered and they were off in a separate patch, safe from the intrusions of swine.

Having mulched the winter's vegetables under their forty cloven hooves and ten snouts, the pigs would disappear into the woods, later to be retrieved a mile west where they had made themselves unwelcome at the Tinnishes' farm. Always lingering at the margins of this story is the image of my grandmother, her drawn grey features a mute protest of hurt and disbelief. She was ever the productive though much-abused partner, the provident, stable one who created home and family despite adversity — and impetuosity and rage. She suffered greatly at the hands of a fool who, always eager to grab a mouthful of the moment's bounty, could not see what today's appetite and disregard would do to his own best dreams. Women of Millie's kind are like the land in this respect: abiding, long-suffering, and, as Walt Whitman would have it, "accepting such leavings from man." Plough and seed, the farmer's desire overtakes the land. And whether that desire be sound or selfish, the land yields, sacrifices humus and health to the wilfulness of uneconomic man.

But the victim drama is never that simple. From another angle, the image shifts, and in my grandmother's inability to save her garden I see the dangerous distance between farmer and consumer. In this gap, the consequences of our public impotence multiply — the impotence that we, the ones who eat supermarket bacon and turnips, so readily accept as we allow the land to be gouged, fouled, and exhausted by the remote and heedless forces that keep the messiness of growing food well beyond our dooryards, out of hand, out of sight, out of mind. The consequences multiply because today thoughtless men with too much power are able to do more than release a passel of pigs into gardens tended by their wives and neighbours. They can unleash intensive "hog operations" consisting of 10,000 pigs that create the sewage equivalent of a large town's, which they pump into lagoons and spread over fields, putrefying the air and land and threatening the local watershed and groundwater. If the investors experience any "community resistance," they simply roll out their public relations plan assuring citizens that every precaution of science and agri-food engineering has been taken to ensure that public health standards are met. The Saskatchewan Wheat Pool, now thriving some distance from its origins in collectivist rural justice, recently created a special hog-production division to take advantage of low grain prices and a bullish global market for ham. They call it Heartland and have begun building massive pig factories all over the province, twenty in all. Crowded in metal pens where they will be fed, watered, and medicated by machine, the pigs in this Heartland will never see the sun. And no one will give much thought as to whether they might enjoy a run through the oak woods.

After Millie died in 1963, Evelyn persuaded her father to move into town for the winter. He spent most of his time reading, but Evelyn says that by springtime she realized that town life was killing him. He couldn't recognize her anymore; his memory began to go. So Evelyn asked Aunt Bea if she would let him stay with her for a while up at the farm. He was fine after that. "His mind cleared as soon as he saw the pigs."

This story about Jock makes me wonder if a farmer who finds such solace in pigs might be trying to understand or justify his own appetites. Pigs are hot-blooded, impetuous, headlong creatures, as my grandfather surely was, and the hog pen, with its daily round of gluttony, lust, and violence, circumscribed and reflected this passion in a way that made its expression at once horrifying and exhilarating, bestial and safe. Indulging himself, sleeping in late, expecting his porridge hot when he finally rose from bed, eating foods — canned soup, fresh fruit, the frozen cream off the top of the milk — that the rest of the family rarely tasted, he likewise indulged his pigs. Once, on the day eight of his shoats were to go to market, he had the boys dump into the pig trough the mash left over from a recent batch of brew. After the pigs had gorged themselves, Sonny loaded them onto the wagon and hauled them to the stockyards in Tantallon, where they waited for the train in a holding pen and began to stagger and squeal, kicking at one another and dancing in circles, as the tale goes, capering for a crowd that soon gathered, so that by nightfall half of Tantallon had come to the stockyards to watch eight pigs drunk as lords on McRae's home brew.

As for indulging his emotions, Jock gave his anger as much free rein as his pigs on their annual trek for turnips and oak mast. His temper was dry and brittle, as ready to light as the hillsides he was known to set afire from time to time, dropping a match just to see the flames roll and jump, and the green-up of prairie afterward; to see the power of something wild and out of control, something that even as late as the sixties once ran up the hill past Bruce's Point to the edge of Bertha's yard where it scorched several power poles, which he blamed on the CPR — damned sparks on the track . . . they should pay. And they did. His temper was at low burn most of the time and his eyes would flash at the least provocation, from a blue lambent glow to the full conflagration of his wrath. Millie, Snooks, Johnnie, and Babes in particular were the usual tinder in these holocausts. Too often, the rifle was handy, a prop to drive the point home when Babes needed discipline for not doing his chores, and Millie or Sonny would have to wrestle it from his grip to save Babes's hide. And there was the time a man from the rural municipality came to seize the south half of the field west of the creek. Jock had not paid his taxes during most of the thirties, had little patience in general for civic affairs, less for tax collectors. So when the man who drew the short straw finally made it out to the mouth of the Little Cutarm, he was greeted by an armed and angry Scotsman cursing him roundly and assuring him he would be dead before he set foot upon the bridge. The rifle was empty. Sonny, as he had done many other times and would again, had gotten to the gun first and removed the cartridges. The rural municipality eventually took the field; sold it to the neighbours.

The old man's roughshod anger, running headlong from its open

pen, most often trampled Babes, the quiet, diffident son, who took each cussing and threat to heart, shaping his character against it, fearing his father enough to do whatever he was told (and once it was "go and drown yourself in the river" and he tried but the goddamn river was too shallow), fearing ridicule if anyone found out that he was visiting Agnes Kallio, and walking backward to the riverbank so no one would suspect his interest in a girl.

Sixty years have now passed and Babes, the long-lived bachelor, is approaching eighty-three, the age at which his father died. He — the resilient and childless one who outlived his brothers and the events that broke the father-to-son lineage on the land at the Little Cutarm — likes to go for long drives these days to look at the countryside and stop in at the café in Tantallon. Heading east from Aunt Bea's along the old road into Tantallon, we stopped one evening to watch horses in a pasture, got out to feed the stallion, a great black Percheron — "look at the balls on that bugger!" — with sixteen brood mares and twelve colts, and then we drove down the road past the Valley View Cemetery where Babes's brothers, sister, and parents are now, then made our way down the winding and venerable hill trail overarched by ash, birch, and oak, stopping to pick a mouthful or two of pin cherries, translucent red, before coasting out onto the valley floor and directly down Main Street, where we waved at one of the Howie girls, sixteen or seventeen, newborn in arms, one of many town girls who smile at Babes and tease him whenever we stop to say hello — she will be a good mother but he wishes that young bugger Arnason would marry her — and out of town again to check a patch of high-bush cranberries south of Bear Creek that he is keeping an eye on, and there flushing a jumper, a young buck, at trailside, and talking all the while about his last herd of cattle, how he misses them, how he cried like a fool when he had to give them up thirteen years ago, how he still thinks of one Hereford cow and her two daughters, all good mothers, good at nursing their calves, protecting their young, and when we turned onto Aunt Bea's driveway there was a doe with two fawns on the trail.

THE NEXT DAY came up bright and windless, the light crossing the Qu'Appelle and into Aunt Bea's garden. In the pasture, just beyond the yard, a group of cattle were gathered round a blue cube that wasn't there the day before. Babes had been up earlier, taken a fifty-pound salt block from the porch, hauled it to the fence, and lobbed it ten paces into the pasture.

It was then I remembered that Jock's dying words were addressed to Babes: "Ye'll look after me pigs, b'y, won't ye?"

*Chapter Thirty-three*

# HUNTING AND GATHERING

*THAT CROFTER'S BOY FROM BANNISKIRK is out along the upper reaches of the River Thurso again. The best trout fishery in all of Caithness, but the rightful property of the members of the Strathmore Angling Association. And so the boy stands wet to his thighs in the shadows of pre-dawn, one eye out for the trout keeper, his line hidden in the water's black, intimate depths. The river has made its way from the heights of Cnogman Gall and Cnoc Gromuillt, past Dallawillay Lodge, through Loch More, along the doorsteps of Strathmore Lodge at the foot of Beinn Chaiteag, turning sharply north to water the towns of Tormsdale, Freechurch, and Westerdale. The boy has made his way walking south all night, by moonlight, through the streets of Halkirk, across Sutherland and the Caithness Railway, down to the floodplain along trails worn first by Pictish men on the hunt. Boy and river meet at a pool, where the riffle is right, where trout have begun to rise and kiss the surface, making it shimmer with bands of silver. Before the sun has lit the head of Achlachan Moss, he has stowed his line and started back for Banniskirk, two speckled trout in his coat pocket, the scent of the river in his nostrils.* [62]

AS A BOY I USED TO WONDER what my grandfather was thinking as he sat and smoked in his favourite chair next to the window in Aunt Bea's house. Now, the better part of thirty years gone by, I stand in the place where the chair used to be, still guessing at those thoughts, watching the old man, the blue can of Player's at his elbow, the crinkled roll-your-own between two flattened, yellowed fingers, the glistening blue eyes, great lugs for ears, sun-cured skin the colour of tobacco. I was fascinated by the moles on his bare forehead and by the angular beauty of his long fingers working shreds of tobacco into a troughed paper rectangle. He would sometimes hold the scrolled cigarette out to me, pinched between thumbs and forefingers, to let me lick the paper's gummed edge. The drag of my tongue on dry paper, the taste of glue, the spicy smell of the tobacco are all curiously entangled in my last memories of my grandfather.

Looking out the window to the fringe of trees that marks the place where Aunt Bea's yard gives way to wooded hillsides, I could see through an abrupt opening in the oaks to the far side of the Qu'Appelle floodplain. It is the only view of the valley from the house, and when the sun shines low in the west, the river itself shows up as a bright wisp in the distance curling across the bottomlands. On the evening that I stood where my grandfather used to sit on many other evenings, the sun did its part. There was no missing the shimmer of water, quicksilver against deep green, cobalt blue. Someone, I knew then, had made that opening in the oaks to gain a view of the river.

Whatever virtues Jock McRae had, whatever small sum of patience, care, contentment, and tolerance he managed to acquire he owed to the hours he walked along the river and the bottomland, where he fished, hunted, and trapped from the Christie Bridge downstream to an oxbow bend two miles west of Tantallon.

Gun in hand, he always went alone, no one else to blame or turn his rage upon, except for the times Ivor Luhtala or John Hudasik would get into his trapline, hanging his mink traps on trees to say "MY LAND. KEEP OFF." When he found them, the willows would fairly curl with the swearing. Once he caught Hudasik in the act, and after Hudasik had picked himself up off the snow and run home to call the RCMP Jock was called into court and fined for assault. But he told the judge, "I'll punch the bugger and be back here again if he ever touches another one of my traps." Most days, though, he was alone on the river with his dream of subsistence, walking the bottomlands, satisfied that he was feeding his own in the most direct way the land allowed — with jumper meat or grouse or duck or the goods he could buy with money from furs or whisky made from water that sloshed out of a spring in shale at the side of the Little Cutarm on its way to the Qu'Appelle.

Some winter mornings, from November until the ice came off the river, he would leave the house at seven. Evelyn watched him go: an old beaver hat tied down over his ears, puttees from his knees to his bootlaces, a biscuit in each hip pocket, and always the rifle slung over his shoulder. Several hours after sundown, at nine or ten, he would return with a deer or some mink or a beaver, done in after trudging the eighteen miles through snow, checking sets, prising frozen carcasses from sprung steel, and resetting traps and drowning-rigs. More than once, he came home wet and frozen to the thermals, having confided too closely with the river and fallen through rotten ice; or, having gambled with the Qu'Appelle at spring break-up, when swollen with meltwater from the plains, it would sometimes run heedless as a prairie fire, thrusting ahead of itself floes of ice large enough and fast enough to carry away bridges and small buildings. In such as this, he, calculating his chances and leaping from one bobbing floe to the next, would try for the northern bank, and if the next leap was too far he would stand his ground on a chunk of ice, feet braced, swirling around each turn in the channel, trapped there waiting for a better floe to come by, sometimes riding the river all the way to the bend by the Little Cutarm, where he could jump for the willows and haul himself, clambering like a muskrat on mud, onto the bank and home again. And this in the dark, and Millie waiting with a lamp at the window and hot tea on the stove, sick with fear that this time he would not make it back.

There were times toward his final trapping years that he did not make it back. After several hours of darkness, Sonny would take a team and the sleigh box out along the river, looking for the old man by lamplight. Sometimes Sonny found him stumbling back home slowly, after resting in the snow to recover from an angina attack. Other nights, he would be still down in the snow, his breath short and quick, waiting for a better heartbeat and life to return.

And it always did by the river. Life came from the bottomlands year round, and every season was hunting season. There were no hunting laws, or at least none that concerned Jock. Jumper meat, frozen and kept in barrels, salted and canned in sealers, disappeared when the RCMP stopped by. And the constable eyed the seven guns on the rack by the door but forgot to check the oat bin — or did they forget, or even care that a man fed his eight children with deer meat fresh in June? And would they have cared if they had found the smoked fish or the nets used to catch them in spring?

Once the ice had gone off the river and the current had settled to the same unhurried meander that has spread twelve thousand summers worth of fertility across the floodplain, Jock would send one of the older boys out to string a net from bank to bank, fastening each end on a tree. The next morning, the little girls would watch as their brothers hauled in a load of fish — walleye, northern pike, goldeye, and suckers — churning, finning, and flashing in the sunlight. There was always too much for one family and plenty to share with the neighbours, the Finns in particular, who relished fish of any kind, even the suckers. Some years, certain species came out of the Calling River and up the Little Cutarm to spawn, and the McRae kids would stand in the creek and catch them by hand. Evelyn remembers in 1936, the spring Sonny and Bertha were wed, she and Bea bagged suckers in gunny sacks in the Little Cutarm, tied the sacks up in the current, and sold them to the Finns for a dollar a bag.

Jock kept the best fish, some to eat fresh, some to can, and some to smoke. He accomplished the smoking by suspending fillets over smoul-dering oak chips in a barrel dug into the hillside behind the henhouse.

The authorities may not have known or cared about the fish and deer salted away, but the RCMP stopped by regularly to check the McRae house for illicit muskrat pelts. When word came that the police were heading west from town to check houses, Jock would boost Evelyn up into an alcove he had built into the ceiling and pass up to her dozens, sometimes a hundred or more, of muskrat pelts that she, skinner's assistant and holder of weasel feet, had on many nights helped skin and turn inside out to cure on the stretchers before they could be stacked in a corner of the room: the ruddy brown late-winter pelts soon to be bartered and sold to the local fur buyers, Barney and Eli Kaplun, father and son from the local Jewish colony south of the valley, who would come to negotiate with Jock and end up staying for the better part of a day, haggling for hours over pennies a pelt until Jock would bluff, "That's it then. I'll ship the lot m'self — including the twenty-eight coyote pelts and fifty beaver — to Robinson in Winnipeg. He'll give me a fair price." And the Kapluns would turn and walk as far as the CPR tracks, bluffing too, before they stopped, came back and agreed to the seller's price.

The RCMP never caught Jock with any ill-gotten furs, even during the Prohibition years when house searches were frequent. They knew Jock McRae had a still somewhere — everyone knew that — but as often as they tried, they couldn't find the damned thing.

The liquor-making process was not complicated. It started out as a mash of prunes, figs, dates, and whatever other fruit the Baker brothers had invested in the Little Cutarm distillery. When enough days had passed and it came time to run off the liquid, Jock would wait until dark and cover the windows with grey woollen blankets so no one could see that McRae was up all night running his brew from a copper boiler through a curled copper pipe and into a five-gallon glass carboy. At the first word that the RCMP were making their rounds, the carboy went into the woodpile and the mash went to the pigs. The boiler and pipe, most incriminating of all, got special treatment. These Sonny and Snooks took down to the river and buried in a sandbar. The Calling River, bearing this insult, insignificant among the varied and countless delinquencies it has suffered at the hands of men, kept Jock's still well and long, until the day came, months later, to dig it up and draw off another batch of Little Cutarm brew.

ON A HEADLAND ABOVE A SHALE outcrop that drops sixty feet straight down from the valley rim, I sat for most of one afternoon and evening watching the river. The outcrop, or "slide" as locals refer to these scarps, is not far downstream of Tantallon. Through my binoculars I was able to turn from watching great blue herons standing on the floodplain's stagnant oxbow ponds to look a couple of miles upriver where a building mover was jacking up yet another house to be extracted from Main Street.

As the day wore on, the herons struck dramatic hunting poses in silhouette, each with attenuated body and sinuous neck ending in a thickening at the head and then elongated to the dagger bill. Backlit by the sun in this way, they looked less like birds and more like exotic musical instruments emerging from the muck. When I was a child, there were still a number of large heron rookeries spread along the length of the Calling River, particularly from Buffalo Pound east. They have disappeared one by one during my lifetime, and now the river hosts only a few small colonies with two or three nests. Pesticides, human disturbance, the raccoon invasion from the east, and other factors have helped to empty the tree nest rookeries that once enlivened the Calling River with the wild, primordial squawking and flapping of young herons.

The wetlands and grasslands so important to certain colonial-nesting birds — herons, grebes, pelicans, burrowing owls — on the Northern Great Plains are becoming quieter places year after year, despite our best intentions. The question is, Are the causes current or are we watching the trailing edge of a local retreat that our forebears set in motion with their naïve immigrant dreams of wealth, their belief that this land was infinitely and indestructibly abundant?

And how close did we come to losing even the more resilient species? The beaver, for example, though it is once again common throughout most of its range, was nearly extirpated from some areas of the continent earlier in the last century. In the Qu'Appelle and across most of the populated regions of Saskatchewan, beaver numbers began to fall sharply under the trapping pressure of homesteaders. By the 1930s, the populations were low enough to attract the notice of game managers at the Saskatchewan Department of Natural Resources. The department outlawed all trapping or shooting of beavers for fur, to give the species a chance to recover. As it happened, the head of the DNR at the time was Ernie Paynter, a Tantallon lad, the son of Hamona colony's W.C. Paynter. Ernie deputized people throughout the province's trapping regions to act as special conservation wardens who would monitor the beaver populations and enforce the ban on taking beaver. I suppose he might have thought he was co-opting a poacher, or perhaps he was not familiar with Jock's view of hunting regulations — nonetheless, Paynter appointed my grandfather as official Beaver Warden in the valley from Tantallon to Bear Creek. Jock rose to the occasion by enforcing the letter of the law upon all other local trappers, white and Indian, while allowing himself his usual latitude with the spirit of the law. Surely no one would mind the warden taking the odd beaver now and then?

This kind of irony — the poacher disguised as game protector —

confounds my attempts to simplify and summarize Jock McRae as a type. He becomes the old man in the chair again, smoking roll-your-owns, thinking his own thoughts; the father and grandfather who bore in his blood the imprint of glaciated, riverine landscapes, an affinity for hillsides that, along with the stories, survived his brief stand upon the Qu'Appelle's oak-treed, alluvial terrain. Influences as disparate as a valley in Caithness, wars in Europe, treaties at Fort Qu'Appelle, and legislators in Ottawa converged within his life and now, thirty years after his death, I am sitting above shale slides in the Calling River Valley, worrying about herons until the coyotes call out their evensong. This riverwatch, the hours I spend admiring birds, walking the bottoms of coulees, thinking or talking about this land, stem from the same ill-formed dreams, the same bastard aspirations of a man who knew simply that he wanted a bigger piece of the world than Caithness could offer. He drew pleasure and satisfaction from the river and from knowing that he was feeding his brood in the closest bargain possible between an immigrant landholder and a valley — no bailiff, no tenancy, and damn little else to claim a piece of him or stand in the way. Hauling Mrs. Hudasik's squatter shack from road allowance to road allowance whenever she needed it; primping his daughters for Christmas concerts by curling their hair with irons warmed in the lantern chimney; dancing with Millie like a ballroom dandy until the Luhtala boys had to pack up their guitars and fiddles and head home in the dark — all that was good in his life came from the same generous reservoir: these woods, this grass, this river.

But subsistence was not about virtue and did not come with ethics or a regard for the limits of an ecosystem. The ecologies of oxbow and riverbank below the shale slide — with their own nutrient gradients, salinity levels, vegetation communities, and trophic webs containing aquatic invertebrates, leopard frogs, beaver, mink, pintails, and herons — have somehow survived the onslaught of the hunter-farmers. The valley itself is just now recovering from the hunting and trapping pressures of the first half of the twentieth century. Black bear, elk, beaver, white-tailed deer, and other species are found near Tantallon today in numbers that have not been seen for a century. In the fall of '96, I heard elk bugling from a ravine near the Kallios', and Jerry says a bear damn near knocked on Bea's front door a couple of years back. Babes swears he has smelled bears when he has been picking berries — "They stink like an old boar." Two years ago, there was talk of a mountain lion taking a heifer just above the valley at Round Lake. Nature abhors a vacuum.

## Chapter Thirty-four

# GYPSIES

WITHIN THE LAST FEW YEARS the county has been very much infested by tinkers, and their number seems to be greatly on the increase. There are, between young and old, it is said nearly a hundred and forty of them in Caithness, composed of different bands or tribes, named the Macfees, the Newlands, the Johnstones, and the Williamsons. They have no particular place of abode, but roam about through the several parishes, following the profession of tinsmiths, but subsisting in a great measure by begging and stealing. They lie out all the year round, even in the roughest weather. . . . When inflamed by liquor, they very much resemble the lower orders of the Irish. From their personal appearance, they would seem to be of a mixed race. Some of them have the characteristics of the genuine gipsy. . . . They have a patois of their own, which they use when they find it convenient to do so. . . . About two years ago a benevolent scheme was set on foot to impart some religious instruction to these pariahs of society, and, if possible, to reclaim them from their wandering habits and dishonest practices. For this purpose a missionary was sent among them, but his labours were fruitless, and the scheme, which promised no success, was ultimately given up. Hugh Miller makes a striking remark that he never knew a gipsy that seemed to possess a moral sense. The Caithness gipsies apparently possess nothing of the kind, and, humanly speaking, it would seem as hopeless a task to civilize them as it is to convert the Jews.

— JAMES T. CALDER, SKETCH OF THE CIVIL AND
TRADITIONAL HISTORY OF CAITHNESS, 1887

THE STORM THAT USHERED the frogs and me to the edge of the Little Cutarm for my first night at Aunt Bea's became nasty halfway between midnight and dawn. Each thunderclap was louder and nearer than the last and Aunt Bea's small house shook like a tent beneath an artillery barrage. I could not sleep through the clamour. *Tales of Tantallon* had run its course, and so I grabbed another book, Annie Dillard's *Pilgrim at Tinker Creek*. The familiarity of the opening chapters did the job. I left Annie and consciousness sometime after she began talking about invisible clouds and meteor showers.

THE MORNING AND COWS. A warm wash of yellow light and the sound of cattle lowing draw me into the next day. The rain has stopped and the yard outside is aglow with shades of green sending light back to a clear sky.

Looking across the blend of tame and wild in Aunt Bea's overgrown garden, I see an arch of dark cumulus low in the sky — the night's storm clouds receding like a damp, grey sheepskin drawn away from the land. Into the pasture beside the garden, a single file of fifteen Herefords is arriving, the calves breaking into a lope as they near the gate. Bringing up the rear is a grey Simmental bull, balls and dewlap swaying with the effort of each step. The cattle probably took shelter from the storm on the wooded slopes that fall away from Aunt Bea's yard into the lap of the Qu'Appelle and Little Cutarm valleys.

I throw on some clothes and head out the door to have a look at the cattle and Aunt Bea's perennials. The garden is riotous with annual weeds filling in spaces between the stands of orange, blue, and burgundy of lily, delphinium, and columbine. Lamb's quarters and small-flowered mallow are doing most of the reclamation, with some assistance from mats of purslane. The dill, gone to seed, has joined with these other introduced species to blur the lines between wildness and domesticity.

Up to my chest in delphiniums, I watch a hummingbird gathering nectar at each blossom. A white-breasted nuthatch calls from the oak trees just beyond the lip of the valley. The garden, long-lived, long-tended, and now relinquished to time and nature, saturates the air with a melancholy that belongs here as though it had transpired this morning with other vapours from the undersides of the leaves.

Several cows have come up to the garden fence to hang their heads over the pickets and stare at the stranger in the garden. It is a familiar sort of attention, the kind any outsider will draw when he enters a small town pub or café. Even the cows know I am from away.

I head out the garden gate and along the barbed wire that keeps the cattle away from the rest of the yard. One swallow, then another, circles over the pasture and the scattered oak trees that the cattle have been using as scratching posts. My eyes follow the long, forked tails and the orange breasts of the barn swallows as they knife toward their "barn," the skeletal remains of a tiny house my grandfather built forty-some years ago for Eddie, his first grandson, Aunt Bea's eldest boy.

Eddie had just married. An eldest son of an eldest son, he was living in a house only a few steps away from the home where his mother had first raised him to her breast. On that day, nineteen years earlier, it was Evelyn's job to stay with Bea during the early labour so that she could go to the valley rim and wave a white flag when it was time for the two grandmothers to come and catch the baby. That is how close the households were: Eddie's and Aunt Bea's just above the valley edge, the two grandparents' farms below, all connected by footpaths, cowtrails, and car tracks.

The barn swallows are similarly inclined toward home. They stick to the same nest site, the same rafters of the same building, raising their broods year after year, generation after generation. "Site tenacity" the biologists call this, and the barn swallow is as good an example of the phenomenon as any. This common bird has survived beyond the tenure of the farming people whose barns first enabled it to expand its range throughout the continent. The barn swallow's heyday was the era of horse-powered agriculture, when long horse barns were a fixture on the prairie landscape. The working horses are gone, replaced by the same machinery that has depopulated the countryside. Most barns and houses stand empty, but as long as there are rafters, ledges, and sills to hold a mud-and-straw nest, the swallows will return each summer, tenacious as ever.

The swallows fly into the abandoned house, slipping between studs where walls once kept out cold, held up pictures. My attention shifts to a pair of boots among the debris scattered on the floor. No way of knowing for sure, but in this moment, this place, I believe they belonged to Eddie.

There is another term biologists use for site tenacity, a word straight from the core of our colonizing ethos, our European tradition of clinging for generations to a particular plot of land: *philopatry*, Greek and Latin syllables welded together to describe fidelity to the land of one's birth. It was philopatry that brought Odysseus back to the shores of Ithaca. The value runs deep in Western culture, and in many ways it is a good value; but I wonder if it does not need some adjusting if we are to apply it to landscapes as exacting and vulnerable as the Great Plains.

We have been aspiring to, and, I think, failing by a philopatry that honours the family that survives as long as possible on a single square of land. The ideal is so bound up with our belief in landownership that even after we have all moved away from "home," we feel guilty when the last quarter section passes into a stranger's hands.

This kind of philopatry is part of what draws me to the McRae homesite to look at the depression in the pasture just west of the Little Cutarm, part of what makes me regret that all the McRae land now belongs to others. But there is something askew in this model of inter-generational affinity for and ownership of a squared piece of the land surface. Its flip side is the European disregard for what has been the only sustainable lifeway on the Great Plains: pastoralism.

Missionaries and government officials thought the seasonal move-ment over vast stretches of the plains, as practised by the Cree and Assiniboine, was proof of their incivility and justification for the process of extinguishing Indian title. Civilized people stay put and grub out an existence from whatever scrap of land they can afford to rent or buy. Into the Touchwood Hills, a wooded upland in the northern reaches of the Qu'Appelle watershed, the Anglican Church sent forth Reverend Charles Pratt, half English, half Assiniboine, to bring the good word of settled agriculture and reservation life to his people. Pratt's schooling as a catechist convinced him that the Plains Indians were the ten lost tribes of Israel from the Old Testament and that their wandering way of life would come to a stop if he could convert them. In the early 1850s, Pratt established the valley's first mission where the Hudson's Bay Company a couple of years later erected Fort Qu'Appelle. Setting up in the

Touchwood Hills in 1858, Pratt tried to teach the local Cree that with the buffalo gone, gardening and the gospel would feed them body and soul.

In an old newspaper from the Touchwood Hills, I came across the reminiscences of Reverend Joseph Reader, one of the white missionaries who worked with Pratt in the 1870s and who helped to establish the infamous residential school on the Gordon Reserve. Both Pratt and Reader attended the Treaty Four signing in 1874 — Reader as a witness and Pratt as an interpreter for the Touchwood bands. Reverend Reader, like Pratt and Henry Youle Hind and anyone else keen on solving "the plight of the Plains Indian," equated the nomadic life with debauched heathenism and settled farm life with "God's Providence." It was the Crown, in Reader's estimation, that saved the red man from his own miserable existence with the terms of Treaty Four, the treaty that shunted the First Nations of the Qu'Appelle region onto small remnants of land in the valley and the Touchwood Hills:

*Her majesty's commissioners . . . convened this important gathering, which in God's providence, has resulted in opening up for settlement this vast tract of country surrendered, and in persuading the Indians to abandon a purely nomadic life, and to settle on the reserves which they themselves were allowed to choose. There they have been perseveringly taught and supervised by well-informed servants of the government, and have had in measure the golden opportunity of hearing the gospel of the grace of God. If they are not prosperous in the things of this life it is their own fault; and if they miss the opportunity of accepting God's unspeakable gift of His Son, the responsibility lies at their own door.[63]*

Unspeakable things happened at the Gordon Reserve residential school and at reserves throughout the region, but none of them were gifts, and the responsibility, we have learned, lies closer to other doors. The costs of "opening up for settlement this vast tract of country" have been high; and the European bias favouring agricultural site tenacity over pastoral lifeways has damaged our prairie culture and landscape beyond measure.

Looking to the fields on the far side of what remains of Eddie's nuptial home, I see wheat instead of prairie. Instead of sprawling pastures where wild and domestic grazers range outside small enclosed crops, cultivated fields roam from horizon to horizon and the pasturage is fenced on scraps of leftover land. The nearest buffalo are more than a hundred miles upstream in a provincial park compound. The nearest Indians are a fifteen-mile trip upstream at Ochapowace Reserve. They have a little more acreage per capita on their reserve than the buffalo have on theirs.

At the level of local culture, our ideal of philopatry failed in a few short decades. Like Aunt Bea's delphiniums and lilies, the ruins of Eddie's house in the pasture mark a specific horizon within the passing of that time. My mother, who looks at this small farmyard and remembers the day Sonny and Bertha got married, the day Eddie was born, the day she climbed the hill up from the McRae farm with Eddie on her back, and the day he carried his new bride into this house, also remembers the wandering people of earlier days. Warm August afternoons when a caravan of Indian or Métis families would stop to camp on the McRae land, watering their animals in the Little Cutarm, resting in the shade of the maples, and coming to the doorstep to trade a willow basket for a pound of butter. And she remembers that her mother called them gypsies.

Bittersweet memories all, from well-thumbed pages of the family ledger. Other memories, recalled only in silence and grief, are of the days when philopatry, the bond of father to son on the land, seemed all but cursed by nature. These are gaps in the McRae mythology, where love of father's land — an affection for pathways in the grass or a field of oats — was not enough to withstand fate, the forces of history, and the urge toward comfort and wealth.

No one will talk about family troubles, but I get a glimpse now and then of the ghosts that could explain exactly where fidelity to the land broke down. I see them in the eyes of my mother and her sisters when talk turns to the two events that in my dim understanding have come to mark the rough boundaries of the tragedy of the McRaes, a tragedy that has, I believe, much to do with failed philopatry. The first event was Sonny's death in 1949, and the second came two decades later — the night Eddie died in a car wreck near Esterhazy.

## Chapter Thirty-five

# FATHERS

THE UNWANTED INHERITANCE IS often the one that clings to our DNA, the tribal curse — a propensity for fibrous tumours or baldness, bad blood or soft teeth. Some of my amino acid troops no doubt take their marching orders from the McRae genetic regimen, but there is little in my physiology that brings Jock to mind, other than size-twelve feet and a stride made for wading creeks and stepping over fences.

Sutherland traits, on the other hand, are more obvious among the descendants of Jock and Millie — as plain as the red nose on our faces. A good half of us are afflicted with rosacea, a skin condition that is thought to be hereditary. I have it, one of my sisters has it, as well as several aunts, uncles, cousins, and second cousins: a ruddy nose and cheeks that at least in men can become swollen later in life, purplish on occasion and netted with spider blood vessels. Stress and liquor make the condition worse, giving rise eventually to the eggplant-on-the-face look made famous by W.C. Fields. Researchers have linked rosacea to stomach ulcers — another classic Sutherland trait and one that manifests itself any time a Sutherland under stress forgets the clan motto, *Sans Peur*. We are a fretful lot, family mottoes notwithstanding, and whenever we fret, our stomachs and our noses sympathize. My great-grandfather, Donald Sutherland, died young of a bad stomach. My mother has fought with ulcers most of her life. I acquired mine in my late twenties, and just last year cured it with a new bacteria-blasting therapy. The florid complexion remains, however, a superficial reminder of a visceral malaise.

Uncle Henry, or Sonny, was a Sutherland through and through, right down to the stomach. His gentle nature, soft-hearted ways, and urge to keep family peace did not come from his father. If not genetically from Millie, his temperament arose then from watching her protect her eight children as best she could from Jock's recklessness and intimidation. Having never known Sonny myself, I am left evaluating the testimony of his siblings, who all but canonized the firstborn McRae in the years following his death. Still, I am inclined to believe the stories of Sonny's goodness because I see it reflected in his two sons, Jerry and Robert. Much of this may be nurture and some, of course, accrues from their Kallio blood, but I imagine in these two cousins of mine, both good family men, the kind of man their father once was.

The day Sonny announced that he would be marrying a Kallio girl, there must have been reactions, both visceral and superficial, to the news. The McRaes and Kallios were friendly enough as neighbours — there were Sunday afternoon baseball games in summer and Saturday night steam baths in winter — but there was a cultural barrier between the two families that was as real as the river that divided their property. Immigrants from the British Isles placed themselves automatically at the top of homesteader society, with Slavic and Scandinavian settlers in a lower caste, somewhere just above the local Indians and Métis. To the McRaes, the Kallios were a peculiar bunch. Besides the steam bathing, the jumping in snow banks, and the strong coffee, they had strange religious practices. Jock called them holy rollers because he once peered through the window of their church and saw all the Finns "rollin' on the floor and moanin' like the divil, and the women with their skirts all up around their ears — it was a sight t' behold." To say nothing of the things they considered edible. Only a starving man or a Finn would relish the meat of an old boar. Old Charlie Kallio would call for Snooks, who ran a butcher and castration business on the side: "Snootz! Com fitz da boar!" A day or two after the boar was fixed, Millie would pause in her garden to sample the breeze. One whiff was enough: "By the gods, the Kallios are having boar for supper tonight!"

The Kallios responded to the McRae condescension with defensive-

ness and a Christian rectitude that afforded them a sort of moral supe-
riority. Charlie and his wife, Sanna, were staunch upholders of the
Lutheran way, and their daughters' purity was a matter of pride and
family honour. Dating, dancing, and smoking were forbidden. Most of
the Kallio girls managed to master all three by the age of fifteen. They
would wait until dark and then sneak out of their bedroom window on
the second floor, falling to the ground and scampering across the river
to the party at the McRaes' or one of the other local farmsteads. The
McRae boys didn't care if the Kallios were Finns or holy rollers, or the
devil incarnate, for that matter. I have no difficulty imagining Snooks,
Johnnie, Babes, and Sonny at those house dances, happy as frogs in a
downpour, happy just to hold onto the slender waist of someone from
the other side of the valley, someone blue-eyed, soft, and fragrant. Before
the thirties were out, the music, dancing, smoking, and drinking at those
parties filled the gap from Kallio to McRae with promises of marriage.

Aunt Bea's house — the place she came to as a bride in 1936 — is an
artifact of that phase in West Valley history. Like potsherds and burial
mounds, the sixty-year-old bedroom walls that surrounded me at night
bore tales that would not reveal themselves to clumsy speculation. I
waited for sleep, staring at the walls, thinking of the scrawl I once carved
into the soft wood of hidden places in the fixtures of the succession of
houses I lived in as a child. My own cryptography, messages for future
dwellers who I knew would come and go as we had come and gone from
bungalow to split level. I found no messages on Aunt Bea's walls those
nights, other than the graffiti from the previous New Year's snowmobile
party: "HAPPY NEW YEAR 1996." By daylight, though, questions came
to me as I was peeling potatoes in the kitchen or on my back soldering
copper pipes in the dirt crawl space below the house: *What did the Kallios
think of the marriage? How did old Charlie Kallio feel when he realized that one
of his daughters was going to marry a McRae?* His Bertha marrying a boy
from a rough Scots family, a family led by a man who was no better
than a half-breed, who made liquor, poached, and trapped instead of
working on his farm, who allowed dancing in his house and shirked
every moral and domestic duty of Christian man.

Or perhaps Charlie knew that Henry McRae was nothing like his
father. That Sonny would dedicate himself to stalwart, faithful hus-
bandry in his marriage and in his farming. In the late thirties and into

the forties, Bea and Sonny did well enough on their small rented acreage above Bruce's Point, raising three sons, healthy crops, a large garden, some pigs, cattle, chickens, and turkeys.

IT WAS TURKEY SHIPPING DAY in Tantallon, the day a grain crusher bit off half of Sonny's left hand.

The monsters that have been depopulating the countryside around Tantallon and throughout the Northern Great Plains since the 1930s have a hundred ways of getting rid of farmers. Pesticides and other toxic petrochemical-based substances are making cancer and immunodeficiency the common cold of rural life. If disease doesn't kill you or chase you off the land, there are always the macroeconomic forces directing the traffic of international trade. In bringing a global feast to the First World and local famine to the Third, our trade in food has made the farmer a liquid asset, a dispensable tool. But the old farmers in this part of the world see the lie and tell their sons and daughters there is no future on the land. Better to go to university, get a job designing pesticide-resistant canola or pushing loans for the Credit Union or poisons for Monsanto — that's where the money in agriculture is. Efficiency has made it so. Efficiency as defined not by nature but by financial institutions and by the agricultural multinationals that breed, patent, and treat the seed, manufacture the pesticides, and market the produce in a system that is converting everything and everyone from farm to table — soils, genes, domestic breeds, wildlife, farmers, researchers — into commodities that can be bought, sold, or rendered obsolete. Their work will be done perhaps on that not far-off day when efficiency is a Pentium processor and a few mouse-clicks that will let the tractor out of the Quonset and onto the levelled fields where it will run on Caterpillar tracks, seeding, spraying, and harvesting according to executable file commands. Meanwhile, though, the machines continue depopulating the quick and old-fashioned way.

Not long ago, the farmer worked with nothing more dangerous than the bull in his pasture. Then, as mechanization came to the countryside promising more results for less work, he switched to implements and fuels that quickly supplanted his own care, labour, and draft animals.

As an agricultural people, we began to accept farm technologies that could kill and maim our brothers, sons, fathers, and uncles. When we climbed aboard the sort of mechanical behemoths that tossed Allen Vance's life into the ravine, we gave our agriculture over to devices that can electrocute, dismember, crush, or flay an inattentive farmer hurrying to get the crop off before freeze-up. The machines we now rely upon have made short work of our first attempt at forming a post-indigenous rural culture. Our cities and cemeteries hold the refugees.

Efficiency? This is the efficiency that makes a man's own sons redundant, that devours neighbours and neighbourhoods. I have seen efficiency in the close lives of honey bees and clover and in the way an owl keeps her eggs warm against March's coldest nights — and it looks nothing like a four-wheel drive tractor hauling an air-seeder over battered and stripped prairie soil.

It was turkey shipping day. This from Evelyn, in a letter that explained her brother's death:

*December 6th, 1947, was Co-op Turkey Shipping Day in Tantallon. Everyone who had spring turkeys to kill and ship took them to Tantallon and they weighed, graded, priced, and packaged turkeys all day in the old Odd Fellows Hall. It's not there any more.*

*Lew and I had 19 birds that year, and we got all 19 A's — top grade. I must say they were beautiful birds, milk-fed. You could tell from the colour of their flesh. Charlie Kallio and I were on weighing duty. Everyone was in town for turkey day, all but Babes, Bertha, and Sonny — they had lost all their turkeys to the coyotes . . .*

A true efficiency on the farm would require and preserve neighbours. The first close neighbours the McRaes lost were the Hugh Irvines. Hugh, the brother spurned by Alex Irvine, had married a hardy Finn girl, Elizabeth Hudasik, who, with the birth of child number eight (she had ten), furnished West Valley with its local rendition of the plough-girl-gives-birth-in-the-furrow legend common throughout the Great Plains. It was a hot summer day and she was out behind the walking plough in a field near their shack. When her labour hit, she set the plough aside, walked over to the shady side of the building and began digging in the ground. Whether the heat and the contractions had made her delirious or she was simply following the instincts of a birthing mother, she scooped out a cool depression in the soil, lay down in it and delivered her child into the Qu'Appelle's fertile alluvium. To the McRaes, this story was amazing even in those years when childbirth heroics were common among farm women. Although they were good friends and often visited Elizabeth and her flock, the McRae children regarded the Hugh Irvines with a degree of pity and perhaps a little derision. Millie said they were "slovenish people," her term for anyone who kept a less-than-sparkling household.

The McRaes had regular first-hand encounters with Elizabeth's domestic standards. After a game of baseball the two families would pile into her kitchen for something to eat. Elizabeth would come in from working in the garden, wash her hands in a big enamel pan, fling the dirty water out a window, and then use the same pan, without so much as a wipe, to begin mixing a cake. In went handfuls and splashes of flour, lard, eggs, and milk. She would slide this, which always seemed to the McRae kids to be a magical concoction, into her wood stove, before whisking out the door and across the yard to the henhouse. A few minutes later Elizabeth would stride back into the kitchen holding up the corners of her apron, heavy with a couple dozen eggs, still warm and smelling of brood hens. These she dropped into a kettle of boiling water on the stove top. The cake, meanwhile, baked in the oven, sending its sweet golden smells into the room as the children ran in and out, bigger girls with baby sisters or brothers on their hips, a squabbling knot of boys overstrung and underfoot. Sometimes one of the Irvine girls would take the younger McRae girls into a hidden corner of the kitchen where loaves of bread had been laid out on the floor to cool. Without a word, the hostess, five or six years old, demonstrated how one warms one's bottom on a loaf of bread, inviting her guests to lift their skirts and do likewise, which they did with little persuasion and great satisfaction. The matter of whether any underclothes insulated this indulgence has not been entirely settled, but the bread by all accounts was tasty nonetheless, for it appeared on the table to be enjoyed along-side Elizabeth's cake and hard-boiled eggs.

When the eggs were done, she'd take them out of the kettle and toss in a couple of tea bags. Then the lot of them, anywhere from twelve to seventeen people, would sit down around a table of boiled eggs, fresh butter and slightly less-fresh bread, cake, and a steaming pot of what my uncle Johnnie had dubbed "henshit tea." Then came the flurry of hands reaching, grabbing, delivering fistfuls of food and cups of tea to mouths, emptying the table before Elizabeth had a chance to sit down. The kids would disappear into the yard, leaving a table covered by egg shells, empty cups, and crumbs. These meals, the McRaes will swear to this day, had something singularly nourishing and celebratory about them, in the way they were prepared, served, and eaten in the light and warmth of Elizabeth's "slovenish" kitchen.

Not long after Hugh was caught stealing grain from his brother's bins, he packed up Elizabeth and the children and left the country. The McRaes remember their sorrow as they watched the Irvines' wagon disappear around a bend in the valley road. The girls say they cried for days, mourning the loss of those Sunday afternoons and the henshit tea from a neighbour's hospitality.

It happened on turkey shipping day . . .

*Sonny had decided to crush some grain that day, and Babes was there helping. The crusher got plugged with grain. Sonny, with mitts on, put his hand in a ways to try and clear the auger. Bang!! His mitt caught and took his hand into the auger. He yanked his hand out of the mitt, but the damage had been done. Crushed hand, minus the ring finger — Babes found it later, still in the mitt, wedding ring still in place. Sonny went down to the house and fainted as he entered the door. Bertha saw what had happened, ripped a sheet apart and wrapped his hand. Sonny revived and he and Bertha walked down to Daddy's on the old trail. He took the car and drove himself into town. Doug Irvine took him to the hospital in Esterhazy. Dr. Medway fixed his hand, making it into a small hand without the ring or middle fingers.*

*Over the next three months, Sonny began having dizzy spells and memory failure. He'd be walking along and all of a sudden his eyes would quit tracking and he wouldn't know anyone or anything. Once he met Lew in town on a Saturday and just for a short while, a few seconds maybe, he didn't know his own brother-in-law and he couldn't speak a word. Just a few seconds and then he was OK again.*

*Sonny had quit smoking recently so we thought that might explain his spells. Everyone put it down to withdrawal and so he never went to the doctor.*

*Strange how his ulcerated stomach seemed to heal that summer. Sonny had always had such a terrible stomach and was rather thin and couldn't do heavy work, but that fall he was in such good health at threshing time he even pitched sheaves in the fields. But after Christmas, on January 11th, 1949, it was, he suddenly began throwing up blood. He was hemorrhaging from the stomach.*

Evelyn remembers that her mother once scolded their dog for howling at the sky. Millie held to a number of superstitions on the subject of death. One of them was that a dog howling at midday is an ill omen, a sign that someone near is dying. The first time, it was Oskar Kallio, Charlie's brother, dead at forty-five.

The day the air ambulance came for Sonny, Evelyn's dog would not stop its howling. The valley had been locked in an unrelenting arctic freeze for a week or more. Snow packed hard against buildings, barren skies a painful blue, the sun distant and cold as stars at night. To show the plane where to land, Jock lit two haystacks on fire on the big field above Bruce's Point. The heat streaked up into the cold emptiness of the sky; it could not touch the 36-below-zero air at ground level. The haystack beacons worked: the air ambulance flew above the valley, circled the field, and landed atop the snow-covered furrows Sonny had worked a few months before. Millie went aboard with Sonny as they rushed to the hospital in Regina. A couple of days later, after a transfusion — he had lost virtually all of his own blood — Sonny was strong enough to talk to his mother. He said something to her about being next in line for a shave and then lost consciousness.

The autopsy report said that Sonny had had a large blood clot for some time at the base of his heart. When his stomach hemorrhaged and his blood became low enough, the clot began breaking up. A large piece eventually made its way to his brain. It was likely that the original clot formed when the grain auger tore his hand up the year before. His blackouts and memory lapses could have been caused by smaller clots reaching his brain.

In Evelyn's recollection of the funeral, the family travels to the Valley View Cemetery in a closed sleigh with a heater. It is unbearably cold and windy. At the cemetery, Jock stands above the gathering on the mound of earth and snow next to the grave; his hat is in his hand, and he stares down at the coffin lowered into the ground. An icicle clings to the end of his nose and he looks old: every one of his sixty-five winters shows in the slouch of his shoulders and the lines on his brow.

Losing Sonny hit everyone hard. Aunt Bea more so than anyone, but if she faltered she did not show it. There were three boys and a farm to tend, and so grief joined itself to life. Evelyn, however, took ill. She had a severe cold at the funeral and the raw January wind blowing over the graves only made it worse. In a few weeks the cold became pleurisy. By May, the doctors were drawing tea-coloured fluid from her lungs: tuberculosis, they said. She would have to go to "Fort San," the TB sanitarium up-valley at Fort Qu'Appelle. She was pregnant with her third child by then and loath to leave her two babies and Lewis, fully expecting she might never return. The months passed slowly on her ward, and Evelyn became convinced that she and her unborn child were doomed. Moments after the birth, her baby daughter was taken away to a "preventorium" to ensure she did not have TB. For seven months, Evelyn was not allowed near her child and had to view her through a screen. "I was right squirrelly," Evelyn says now, thinking about her days at Fort San. Having her child whisked away at birth triggered post-partum depression and put her into a spiral that she did not come out of until 1952.

In April 1950, almost a year after her arrival at Fort San, Evelyn went back to the farm, but the doctors still would not release the baby. Three months later, she returned to bring her daughter home. Gradually, Evelyn regained her spirit, under the care of her mother and Lewis, a man of great equanimity, humour, and patience. By then she and Lewis had decided to give up farming and move into Tantallon, where they could run the local telephone office.

As for the rest of the McRaes, Jock and Babes kept busy helping Bea out with her farm. Snooks was in Rocanville, running a butcher shop, and Johnny had started his own cattle-and-grain farm southeast of Tantallon above Bear Creek. By the time Sonny died, the little girls, Opal, Doris, and Jeanne, were already young women living in Regina and Edmonton. The McRaes had gone from the valley like the Scattered Children of Kintail glorified in the clan song: "The red deer sleeps in sheltered nooks / Where homes were wont to be / . . . our restless feet have wondered far / And severed wide we be."

*Chapter Thirty-six*

# SONS

THE TWO GRANDMOTHERS, Millie and Sanna, held the promise of another generation in their hands the day Eddie was born. Evelyn was there at Sonny and Bertha's, helping Millie and Sanna and keeping the kitchen. The rest of the family waited downhill at the McRae farm. They watched and listened for a message from the top of Bruce's Point and when it came, they celebrated the good news that it was a big healthy boy, a first son of a first son who would grow up to take over the farm some day.

Eddie became at once Jock's pride and joy, the wild but soft-hearted kid who could do no wrong, but for whom wrong seemed to come as easy as a run down Henderson's Hill. Eddie was a Kallio by sinew and bone. He had a broad muscular frame, with a monumental head that rested on his shoulders like a block of chiselled fieldstone. His spirit, though, was a distillation of all that was reckless and hot-blooded in Jock McRae. Like his grandfather, he was cocksure, clever, and given a chance could charm his way out of responsibility for whatever trouble his own appetites and devilry had caused. Afterwards, whatever the transgression, there were always tears. Anger, belligerence, or delinquency followed by remorse, a pattern Jock had stuck to most of his life. With several aunties and four doting grandparents accommodating his shenanigans, forgiveness was always near at hand within the refuge of family. And so the apple of the old man's eye made it to manhood without having to leave boyhood.

When his father died, Eddie was just entering his teen years, getting big enough and smart enough to be dangerous. Always a lovable kid and now fatherless to boot, Eddie found that the community and his family cut him more slack than ever. At a time when he needed an older man to rein him in and bless him with guidance and discipline, he was let down by the men in his life. Jock let him go his own way and indulged the boy's mischief as he had always indulged his own. Eddie quit school, began running with the wildest kids in the area, and soon became more than Bertha could handle. I have talked to Tantallon people who remember Eddie as a teenager and a young man. It seems thirty-five years is enough to gloss over the misdeeds of a kid whose main problem was severe father hunger. Most prefer to recall his generosity first and then say things like, "Oh well, yes, he was a little wild, I guess." Or with a smile, "Eddie was a bit of a rangytang, all right," and then quickly point out that he was tender of heart and always sorry for his mistakes. Finally, and not without a little probing, come the stories that built his reputation as one of Tantallon's prominent ne'er-do-wells. "I guess there was his drivin'. He liked to tear up the roads a bit, probably drank a bit too much while he was behind the wheel. . . . One time he was barrelling down the valley road at sixty or seventy; it was night, dark as the inside of Toby's arse, and three jumpers came up on the road. Eddie grabbed his gun — he always had the 30.06 in the truck loaded and ready to go — and those deer were dead before the truck got a chance to slow down. He could shoot. Hell, you can't help but shoot good when you're huntin' all the time."

Most of the stories place Eddie within the influence of another local rangytang: the two of them shooting beaver on the river by moonlight; filling the freezers of Tantallon by jacklighting jumpers and hunting under permits taken out by people who needed meat but didn't hunt; raising hell in the Tantallon Hotel and taking a round out of the bar-keeper. Nothing done by halves. If you are going to drive, drive fast. Drink, drink hard. Hunt, anytime of the day or night or year. Fight, at the drop of a hat.

Eddie and his partner were pioneers of a sort, leading the first generation of farm boys who — unencumbered by chores and school, and

powered by easy liquor, too much weaponry, fast cars, and cheap gas —
managed to take rural delinquency beyond outhouse-tipping to a level
of mayhem that was a threat to community, nature, and self. A product
of his time and circumstances, Eddie embraced the opportunities of
postwar materialism in ways that were bound to offend the sensibilities of Tantallon's aging pioneers. So this is what the sod-busting and
stump-hauling and butter-churning has reared — hooligans roaring up
and down the valley in Chevs and Fords?

But the standards for acceptable behaviour were applied unevenly.
A man who uses a car like there is no tomorrow, who destroys valuable
property, or gets in a brawl now and then is regarded as irresponsible
and reckless. Another man who approaches his fields and his neighbour's land with the same rapacity is simply a good farmer. Maybe
farming is what a rangytang does when something forces him to settle
down. First your wild oats, then your tame.

For Eddie, the transition was supposed to have occurred when, still
a teenager, he did the honourable thing and married the girl who was
bearing his child. He took up farming, moved into the little house next
to his mother's, rented land, and helped Babes and Jock with the McRae
farms. He never let go of the drinking, fighting, and poaching, but his
remorse after each transgression increased. I remember him coming for
visits to our home in Esterhazy and the hushed adult discussions
between him and my mother. She was a sympathetic ear — he was the
boy she used to piggy-back up Bruce's Point to his mother's house. In
our living room he would cry like a child sometimes, sorry for the grief
and worry he caused his mother and family, sorry for losing his temper
again, sorry for beating the tar out of Archie Brown — even though the
mouthy bugger deserved what he got, and the fine from the RCMP was
worth it.

We were all shocked when Eddie died, but few were surprised that
it was in a car wreck. I remember that afterwards we went out to
the highway and looked. My father showed me the skid marks and the
approach that stopped Eddie's blue Travellall before it burst into
flames. Gary, Evelyn's oldest boy, was driving back to Tantallon after
seeing a movie in Esterhazy on the night it happened. He saw the RCMP
cars and stopped when he recognized the blue wreck in the ditch.

Everyone, the police in particular, knew Eddie and his truck, but the body was badly scorched, and Gary had to go the morgue and make it official: yes, that's my cousin, Eddie McRae.

Sometime before the accident, Babes had a nightmare about Eddie dying. It was during fall harvest. He and Eddie and Jock were racing to get everything into the bins before the weather turned. Babes was hauling grain in the truck, and Eddie was running the combine. After bringing in the last load for the night, Babes headed to Bertha's to get a few hours' sleep before the next work day dawned. It was well after dark, but the combine had lights so Eddie stayed out to get a few more bushels off the swaths.

Not long after falling asleep, Babes awoke in terror, hollering something about Eddie and the combine. Jock got up to see what was wrong.

"Eddie went through the combine! He's dead!"

Angry and scared, Jock shook Babes awake, told him he was a damned fool to have such dreams, and sent him out to fetch Eddie. "Go bring the lad in. He's done enough work for one day."

## Chapter Thirty-seven

# SWALLOWS AND NOMADS

*AUNT ALEXANDRA WAS of the opinion, obliquely expressed, that the longer a family had been squatting on one patch of land the finer it was.*

HARPER LEE, *TO KILL A MOCKINGBIRD*

IT WAS MAY 1968 WHEN Eddie died. I was ten years old. That summer was to be our last in Esterhazy. We moved across the province to Saskatoon, but it might as well have been across the continent. When my mother told Jock we were planning to leave, he wept for all that was gone and going.

The day my grandfather buried his eldest son, his grip loosened upon the hills, fields, and woods of the Little Cutarm; the day he buried the eldest son of that eldest son, the land at the mouth of the Little Cutarm fell away from his hands like the ashes of the dead. Something that could not be stopped with bluster and a show of arms had taken his progeny and the little world he had built; taken them and tossed them to the uncaring wind.

Within five months, we were gathered around another grave at the Valley View Cemetery, laying the old man to rest in the brown till above an unnamed stream that runs a mile and a half south, joining the Qu'Appelle near Henderson's Hill.

While I was in Little Tantallon in 1996, I spoke with Pearl Irvine, the wife of Doug Irvine, Alex's son. Doug is in a home now, she told me, and not doing all that well. Memories from the West Valley are at times more real than the walls of his room. She said that now and then when she is visiting, Doug's mind will clear for a moment — she sees a change in his eyes — and he will say, "I wonder what Jock McRae's been up to . . ."

I stare at the windblown remains of the house Jock had made as a wedding gift for Eddie, thinking about fidelity to places and how it applies in an age when people roam farther than ever from their homes in a modern rootlessness that is truly destructive of household, culture, and ecology.

Hearing the chitter of the barn swallows again, my thoughts turn to the other kind of fidelity to place, the tribal, gypsy regard for home practised by the bank swallows I have seen nesting at the submerged headwaters of the Qu'Appelle, at Ridge Creek, and at other tributaries throughout the watershed. *Riparia riparia* is a bird that is faithful to the river and its soft, eroding banks, the most ephemeral of habitats. Unlike the solitary barn swallow, the bank swallow nests in tightly synchronized colonies that change and move as the river gives and takes away. In science, such a lifeway is thought to be the opposite of philopatry. In life, though, much depends on the scale of what we are prepared to call "land of the father." Is it 160 acres square or is it a stretch of river valley, a range of hills, a watershed? The flaw in our settler version of philopatry is that we have been trying to impose a model of site tenacity that comes from another continent, that does not shape human culture against the demands and limitations of the local ecology.

This is a land meant for migrants, not settlers. We never really "settled" anyway. We arrived in a flood of immigration that poured out over the region like a great torrent of glacial meltwater, shaping the landscape to accommodate its flow. Colonies, villages, farms — human alluvium — deposited out of the flow for a short while, only to be swept up again in the next high water, the next movement to prosperity, better land, better jobs, a better El Dorado.

And for the brief periods of "settlement," we tillers of the soil did what the children of Cain have done all over the New World: we spurned the existing, proven lifeways of the land. These Indians are the lost tribes, we said, "purely nomadic," mere wanderers who must be shown the proper way to live — in settlements, with ploughs and farms, churches and schools.

Things might have been different, given a freer model of philopatry. Instead of forcing the Indians onto reserves and then surveying for land tenure and homesteading, we could have granted river valleys, whole watersheds to small bands of people — Indians, immigrants, or Métis — willing to live as semi-nomads. Each spring, the migrant tribes would leave the warmth of the southern plains or the shelter of the woods to return to their summer waterways, where they would hunt on the plains and grow food on the river bottoms. Yes, I know — only in our imaginations can we reconsider the moment when we chose the wrong path, when men like Hind forsook the wisdom and gifts of men like Mistickoos and dreamed instead of dams and floods; even so, I choose to think that our imaginations can redeem us.

The waters are ebbing now. As descendants of the flood, we can ask new questions: Is it more settled, more faithful to place and Creation, to move camp from summer to winter in a rhythm that has worked for millennia or to plunk a family down on a square acreage for one or two generations and then scatter all over the continent seeking new resources to mine, better places to settle? And we can try to recognize what is worth keeping from the flood, what will come to belong here, and what we must give up to be carried away in the river, the remnant of the deluge, that now moves across the floodplain of our history in this place.

If ever we should decide as a people that we want to live well and long in this land, to become like the Calling River, post-alluvial, "after the flood," a culture that meanders between the limits of its place in the landscape, always moving, changing, poetic and wise within natural boundaries — if we should ever come to such a turn, we will know where to begin: listen again to the voices of Mistickoos and the river; seek a new fidelity to landscape, watershed, and biome; leave site tenacity to the barn swallows; and look to the good sense of dwelling in close-knit, adaptive, and ephemeral communities that honour the ebb and flow of prairie waterways.

## Chapter Thirty-eight

# THIS GARDEN UNIVERSE

STEPPING BACK ACROSS THE BARBED WIRE and out of the pasture, I returned to Aunt Bea's yard. The sun was higher, suppressing birdsong already and invoking the mid-morning hum; the vibration of grass-bound insects now astir in the shimmering threshold between grass and sky. In a few steps I was in a rank patch of high brome grass. This, I remembered, is where the old pig corral used to be. The memories slowed my pace, had me stepping lightly, breathing through my mouth and listening for the snort of a rogue sow. As a boy, I always held my nose here. Grandpa's pig corral, across the driveway from Aunt Bea's garden, was unbearably smelly and it enclosed a band of the filthiest, godforsaken critters to see the light of day. Watching them through the slats in the corral, I was appalled and fascinated by them, could not take my eyes off their grey-pink corpulence. They were as amazing to me as my grandfather's long, tobacco-stained fingers, and somehow the life of those pigs and the sinuous power of those hands overlapped within the quiet watchfulness that formed my childhood memories of Aunt Bea's.

From the corral site I looked over at the garden and realized why it has always been surrounded by a strong, heavy-posted picket fence. That is just like Aunt Bea, I thought. Once would have been enough. She was not the kind to allow a man's stupidity and improvidence to cast her the victim's lot year after year. Pigs would never reach *her* lettuces, turnips, and delphiniums. Such a fenced garden is a refuge from the cloven-hooved side of nature, but it is at the same time a world beyond the rapacity in our lifeways, the short-sightedness in our agriculture. This, a sensible conscription of Creation with sensible boundaries, was where Aunt Bea cultivated her good cosmos — a unity that excluded grain augers, crop sprayers, hog factories, marketing boards, loan officers, and the countless compromises and abominations of our miscreant relationship with the land.

SEVERAL YEARS AGO I met one of Aunt Bea's nephews from her side of the family: the son of a Kallio girl who left home and headed for Toronto not long after my mother and her sisters made their way to cities in Saskatchewan and Alberta. His name is Brian Hoxha and he is a painter and print-maker. Though he grew up in Ontario and still lives in Toronto, as a boy Brian spent part of each summer in the Tantallon area visiting his western relatives. From the time he was six months old, his mother would bring him out here by train. The farm he came to know best belonged to his uncle Eino, Bea's brother. Eino's place is over the rim and downhill from Bea's, in the lee of the valley's northern slopes. Brian used to go for long walks with his uncle, learning the names and stories of West Valley and Valley View — the Hogsback, Henderson's Hill, Donald's Lake, the School Trail. He came to regard the hills and ravines of this area with an affection that matched his uncle's. Now Brian comes alone in his truck, loaded down with camping gear, oils and water-colours, and enough gessoed canvases for several weeks of field work. He paints stretches of valley from vantage points along its rim, upon its mid-slopes, or down along the bottoms. He comes every fall, timing his visit for the days when the trees release their underlying colours: the summer's trick unmasked to the bright truth of cadmium, ochre, and sienna. And, until recently, every fall he would spend a day painting Bea's garden in its failing glory at the end of the growing season.

The September I went out to watch Brian work, he told me that the previous year he had painted Aunt Bea's garden for the last time — "There's not much left to paint. It's amazing how it grew in so much in just one year."

When he says things like this, he lowers his head and then lifts it quickly to face you, frowning and smiling at the same time. He is blond, blue-eyed, and fair, about as fair as any Kallio I have seen, and he has their introspective intensity and mindfulness, a quiet circumspection that suits an artist who paints alone on wooded hillsides.

Some day, he told me, he will take all the watercolours and oil canvases he has done of the garden and put together a show. "I have a name for it," he said. "This Garden Universe Vibrates Complete."

As we hiked out to hillsides, sketching and scouting locations for him to do a full-sized oil, we spoke of Aunt Bea, her resolute spirit, and the high place she holds in our respective memories. He told me that in recent years, she would often run into the local black bear when she went out on her daily walks above Bruce's Point. After a moment of mutual recognition, the bear went on its way and Bea on hers, each undisturbed by the encounter.

When I asked him questions, Brian would pluck at a leaf of sage or bluestem, searching his mind for words to express his affection for the eastern Qu'Appelle. He said that he believes there are few places like it remaining anywhere. People who buy and show his paintings notice the difference between his Qu'Appelle work and his other landscapes. I see it too. A compassionate eye is behind the images on these canvases — no judgment or intellectualizing, no veneer of false nostalgia, but there is respect, forgiveness, reconciliation, and even love.

In landscape painting, as in all encounters with the land, there are many prospectors and few poets. There are those who will mine a place for its scenery or charm, for whatever they can gain or take away. There are others, the rare ones, who come to listen and learn and then respond out of the depth of their experience. Whatever they use is used with care for the whole; whatever they create, having come from integrity and respect, enriches the place like an honest song of praise. Our landscapes need honest poets and painters, and the eastern Qu'Appelle Valley needs Brian Hoxha.

Together we looked for fresh angles of familiar pieces of the valley. He took me out to a ridge to show me a view of one of his favourite landforms — Henderson's Hill — that I had never seen before. Then he opened his sketchbook at a leaf where he had drawn a composition of the painting he would make of the hill on a calmer day. Above the sketch, a few words scrawled in pencil said: "Three night birds trickled across the evening sky." It seemed as inscrutable as haiku at that moment but it set me to searching my own embittered heart for the compassion to forgive what has happened in the landscapes of my grandfather. A desire for such sentiment settled upon me and for the rest of our day together silenced the critic that usually sits atop my thoughts, pronouncing on the sacred and the profane.

ONCE BRIAN BEGINS A full-sized canvas he works steadily, furiously, until it is done. It usually takes five or six hours of standing on a side slope, peering around his field easel at the chosen field of landscape. When I asked him why he painted outdoors this way, he said that he liked being out on a sunny hillside on a fall day and then added, simply, "I like a charged painting." Later, as I watched him work, watched the canvas rock and shudder under the jab of his brush, I knew what he meant by the phrase. This is not parlour painting. At one point a large flying beetle became mired in a gob of cerulean on the upper right corner of the canvas. It wriggled its legs trying in vain to free itself from the slather. I mentioned this to Brian, and he said that he felt bad about killing bugs but sometimes he just leaves the little corpse on the canvas to become part of the surface relief.

It was a windy morning but Brian wanted to do a large canvas so we hiked into a relatively sheltered spot in the Little Cutarm valley just below the field west of Aunt Bea's farmyard — the field where an air ambulance once landed to take Sonny away to Regina. Dressed in a black and green mackinaw, jeans, and a broad-brimmed hat, he had strapped his Italian field easel, full of painting gear, to his back. Atop the easel was a bare stretched canvas, a frame of chalk white several feet across, broad enough to block my view of Brian from behind. As I followed this white rectangle down the cattle trails into the oaks and chokecherries of the Little Cutarm's eastern flank, I felt the same sense of comfort and curiosity, anticipation and trust that I have experienced on trips with field biologists or naturalists leading me to research sites on their home terrain. And the canvas swinging through openings on the trail, disappearing and reappearing from shadow, was a blank form that would return in six hours up the same path, with new data — not species density and richness, not soil types, plant specimens or tree cores, but a fresh record of an afternoon in the Little Cutarm, its light, colour, and shade, and one man's response to these.

After finding his spot, a clearing in the woods, Brian swiftly set up the easel, anchoring the canvas with bungee cords. Two of these he attached to the hillside by hooking their ends into a tangle of snowberry. I moved into the shade where I could see Brian's face and the backside of the canvas. The patch of ground he had chosen had a sharp slope and he was surrounded by tallgrasses — mostly big and little bluestem and sand reed grass.

A few squeezes of paint onto the palette and he was at work. The sun shining through the canvas showed a reverse monochrome image to me as he blocked in the composition with thinned oils. It was like watching Indonesian shadow puppets or a time-lapse sequence of cloth weaving itself from nothing. As layers of paint built up, blocking the sunlight from shining through the canvas, the image shifted in tones of grey. I could not see the brush or Brian's arm, only the increase of shadow from thicker and thicker layers of paint. It was pleasant, almost mesmerizing to watch hillsides and fields disappear under paint, and it put me into the same kind of trance I have experienced in staring at the flicker of a fire or the unrelenting roll of a river.

Later I opened my own bundle of watercolours and painted the terrace of hillside above the old McRae farm and stretching west to the Tinnish land. My effort was fussy and anemic, and the greens were all wrong, but I nevertheless enjoyed the feel of painting outdoors from life. My two-minute preliminary pencil sketch of the same stretch of land was more successful somehow. There is something about making a quick drawing while you look at the land that shifts your consciousness to a level nearer the place where passion, myth, and spirit reign. It is so easy to allow sight, in some ways our most superficial sense, to dominate our experience of landscape. The camera, and its capacity to readily reproduce images of animals and landscapes, has made our visual experience even more distanced and facile, summarizing the complexities of a place into views or scenes.

Watching an artist like Brian Hoxha paint is a fresh reminder that the land is more than an assemblage of views and we are more than viewers. I went around to the other side of the canvas to see the painting in progress. His hand, the left, moved in swift fluid strokes, pushing gobs of greyish blue-green into forms that were immediately recognizable as the ridges of hills on the far side of the Qu'Appelle. Bold, confident movement between palette and canvas; nothing tentative, nothing faint about this artist. When he decided to include an ash tree that had turned yellow ahead of its neighbours, he nailed it in six strokes of thick yellow-green, a dab or two of darker green, and four broad patches of orange-yellow.

The afternoon wore on and the sun began to warm the colours of the hillsides until the landscape took on the very tones of Brian's painting. Glancing from the easel to the land and back again quickly, I found it easy to daydream that the real valley and Brian's image had swapped places, that a transfusion had occurred, and further, to imagine a brush-wielding god afoot in the valley, painting a genesis in sudden, liquid strokes of light and colour.

When he was done, I said I liked the way he painted the valley's floodplain with the river a jagged blue tear through its midriff. He said nothing about the painting, and we talked a bit about his work in general as he packed things up. I could tell that he was not altogether satisfied with the day's work. He was too polite to say anything, but I felt I might have been the cause. Brian is someone who tromps through oak woods on hillsides, stopping to paint or sketch whenever and wherever it seems right. He depends on a certain intimacy between himself and a place, an intimacy easily compromised by the intrusion of a curious writer. This intimate regard for the places he paints almost always comes through in his Qu'Appelle work, wherein, no matter how bold the strokes or undomesticated the imagery, his respectful, confiding way with the valley lies plain for anyone to see. If this was missing from the painting I watched him make, I had only myself to blame.

The day was not yet over, so Brian and I headed down into the valley where his uncle Eino once farmed. Eino died in 1993, and Brian bought a half section of the farm — 320 acres of bluestem and spear grass pastures, oak woods, and a stretch of floodplain all on the north side of the valley. As we walked around the old yard site and into the empty barn, Brian surprised me by saying he had plans to move here someday soon. The first order of business, he said, would be a new roof on the barn. He had it all drafted out in his mind. With a skylight and some windows, it would make a fine studio. What about Toronto? I asked. He said he would keep his contacts in the east and spend part of the year there, but his home, at least in the warmer seasons, would be Eino's farm in West Valley. As he said this I remembered a postcard he sent me once, featuring a painting of the farm, composed from the west looking back toward Tantallon. Eino's Legacy, he called it.

As we left Eino's farm, Brian said he always ended a day of field work by watching the sun go down. He invited me to join him at one of his favourite sunset posts, a spot along the river where the old Kallio bridge used to be. I had been trying to locate the bridge site myself earlier in the summer and failed, so was glad of the chance to be guided there. When we arrived, the sun was already low enough to cast skeins of orange and cobalt upon the river's soft, early autumn flow. In the shadows, I could make out the remnant timbers on either bank, the river's testimony that no one has lived on this part of its south floodplain for many years — since the Kallios left.

Above the water's surface, into the air so fine, still, and resolute at day's end, a fish leapt. Then a sharp-shinned hawk flew in as we watched the western sky in silence. It landed close in a willow, watched us for a trice, and then flapped on downriver. We waited for the sun to drop its last span to the horizon, utter silence filling our ears. Then, as the sun grazed the valley rim, the call of something wild echoed from the hills above Charlie Kallio's homestead. It was a bull elk and its bugling at that moment was the sound of the Calling River Valley, a cry from a returning wildness, filling the breach left by Kallios, McRaes, and all the other ghosts and recriminations of West Valley's history.

As we walked out of the woods where we had spent the afternoon, Brian told me he sometimes wished he could "breathe this all in without exhaling." *This*, I understood, is the whole of the eastern Qu'Appelle: the valleys, the river, the skies, the big bluestem, the light and shade, the farms, the elk, the sharp-shinned hawk, and all that unites them here in life. His wish is the shaman's wish, the "dream of congruency" to which every dweller worthy of his place in the land aspires. In such a wish, I thought, there is hope for renewal.

And I thought about home and how to get there. Beyond Aunt Bea's garden universe, outside her picket fence where heedless men have had the run of the land, where our land-fetish had us clinging briefly to patches of prairie even as we inundated the sacred and the wild, drowning the very lifeways and traditions that kept the land sacred and wild. Beyond this boundary we, the survivors, now stand, watching, listening for signs of reconciliation and forgiveness, for the painters, poets, ecologists — anyone with the stories, imagination, and songs that will bring us home.

*Epilogue*

# FAIR DAY, TANTALLON

*UNTIL WE BECOME nomenclators of a place, we can never really enter it.*

— WILLIAM LEAST-HEAT MOON, *PRAIRYERTH*

A LANDSCAPE IN WHICH PEOPLE DWELL is a fully named place. Everything — hills, crossings, rivers, rocks, even the winds — has a name. Most are not on any maps, save those we carry in our heads. In West Valley most of the unmapped nomenclature speaks of possession: Donald's Lake, Bruce's Point, Lundy's Ravine, Henderson's Hill, the Christie Bridge, Kallio's Bridge, McRae's Crossing.

On one of my last days at Aunt Bea's, she came out from Esterhazy to see her old farmyard. As she guided me around the property, checking on the peonies and columbines, and lamenting the weeds, I did my best to get her talking about the names that enlivened the landscapes of her lifetime. I asked her about local place names. Within moments, we were talking about trails. She stood with me on the valley rim and pointed to the place where her parents once lived across the bottomlands. Told me about the trail she would take to get back home across the river for steam baths on Saturday nights; about her mother using the same trail to come visit her, in summertime picking berries all along the way. The trails, like the names, are falling out of use. The old road down to McRae's Crossing is used now only by cattle; the pathway following the valley rim to Bruce's Point is overgrown; children no longer run up the school path from the valley road to houses on the hills; and the old sleigh trail through the backwoods south to the valley bottom has not been graced by horse and cutter for more than thirty winters. But the pathways are still there. I have walked up and down each of them and seen the gullies, boulders, and rank growth that rush in upon their abandonment like cold air into an open room. It is these disused byways, more than the crumbling homes they intertwine, that will not let us forget what we have forsaken in vacating the landscapes of our grandparents.

This network of trails over the valley slopes is an artifact of a culture that was never quite in residence, never quite got around to naming the winds. I walk the hill paths now and feel the peculiar ache of having lost something I never really had. Though I am related to many of the path-makers, I am not one of them, nor will my children be. I do not know the bends in these paths, nor do I know where the straightest oaks are or where the cranberries grow any more than I know how to set my grandfather's mink traps or how to run his honey separator and the other tools that gather rust now in the shed next to Aunt Bea's.

I asked Aunt Bea about the abandoned CPR line at the foot of the hill — another neighbourhood trail gone trackless in recent years. She paused at the edge of her garden fence and told me she wonders these days if we aren't going backward instead of forward.

We just got started making the trails of a new culture here, naming the land, and turning space into place, when our civilizing ways moved us to a scale of commerce and trade that could only pull it all apart, undoing what had been built. The rails for the CPR line were torn up four or five years back. Aleck Mercer, Aunt Bea's neighbour in Little Tantallon, once worked on the Bear Creek section of the line, east up the tracks from Tantallon. He knew the section men who lived long ago at Bear Creek — men who lived like hermits and whose job it was to see that the rails were clear and the rail bed firm against undercutting springs and snowmelt. One man, he said, had the job of following each train as it passed through Bear Creek Canyon, extinguishing any fires started by fallen coal.

When the CPR declared the line redundant and the trains stopped running, local community clubs asked if the easement could be turned into a walking trail from Scissors Creek through the valley up the Little Cutarm all the way to Esterhazy. CPR management said no. They were not interested in trails or community projects. Before anyone could get a court order to stop them, CPR workers began dismantling trestles, tearing down fences, and burning bridges. According to Aleck, nothing was salvaged, not even the gigantic stringers that supported the valley-spanning trestles. The day they burnt that mountain of ties and timber, he said, you could feel the heat a mile away in Tantallon. Ninety years of corporate plunder and then the buggers leave, burning their bridges behind them. The gravel bed remains, but like the footpaths and sleigh trails of West Valley, it disappears a little more each summer beneath shrubs and encroaching weeds.

NO RAIL LINE AND NO grain elevators any more to take the produce of Tantallon to market, but at the end of each summer the village still puts on its annual Agricultural Fair. The old fairgrounds of my childhood, on the land the Tantallon Agricultural Society had to purchase from the CPR, have been converted into a campsite. Nowadays, the fair is held just behind the town rink on the east side of Main Street.

On the day of the eighty-fourth annual Tantallon Fair I sat down on the bleachers with my Uncle Babes and listened to a group of old-timers, mostly retired farmers and pensioned miners, talking as they watched the horse "showmanship and equitation."

"No Clydesdales?!"

"Nope. No one brought any heavy horses this year. All there is is these skinny little ponies."

"Well, that'll beat all. Fair's goin' to pot, has been for years."

"What's a fair without real horses?"

Now and then a younger woman walked by us on the way to the canteen, carrying a pie or cake.

"You gonna' walk right on by, honey, and not even give us a piece?"

A Hungarian farmer named Alfred, a local character decked out in a

Stetson, cowboy boots, and aviator sunglasses, joined our group. Alfred has a valley farm he calls The Ponderosa a few miles upstream of the mouth of the Little Cutarm. In between a discussion of who is dead and who is nearly dead and a reference to "pay day" (when the pension cheques arrive), Alfred slipped in a joke about how the Scot discovered the bagpipes in a pile of manure and has been trying to blow the shit out of them ever since. When talk turned to knee supports, I excused myself and headed to the horseshoe pitch where my cousin Jerry was in the finals. Now and then the crack of a baseball bat rang out from the ball diamond east of town, a circle worn into the native bottomland that once belonged to Alex Irvine: grama grass, Western wheat grass, sage, and yellow coneflower. People my own age, mostly potash miners, were playing in the Fair Day tournament. Later, after supper, there would be draft beer and rye-and-Cokes behind the Tantallon Hotel in the "beer garden" where the beer is beer and the garden is gravel.

After watching horseshoes, I walked into the rink to see the exhibits displayed on tables: garden vegetables, flowers, artwork, handwriting samples, baking, canning, crafts, and grain, each with its own hand-printed label announcing "Barley — Six Rows, Twelve Heads. Variety — 'Stander'" or "Single Petunia — One Colour, Three Blooms." Evelyn was there scrutinizing the produce. She had been a competitor, an exhibits judge, or both for more than sixty years. I asked her if she was coming to the community supper, a meal that I had great hopes for.

"Not bloody likely!" she said. "Do you know what they're serving? Kentucky Fried Chicken! If that's what those women call a community supper, no, I won't be going!"

When you have trussed as many turkeys and pinched as many perogies for Tantallon suppers as Evelyn has, you are entitled to some indignation at the younger generation. I went back to Bea's house disappointed, warmed up a can of beans, and sat on the doorstep trying to remember the Tantallon fairs of my boyhood. Instead, a fragment of birdsong from beyond the garden — a warbling vireo unable to resist the recrudescence of late summer — drew me back to the birds I had seen that morning alongside Donald's Lake.

ON THE MORNING OF FAIR DAY, I had gotten up at sunrise to look for early fall migrants at a pond down a short path running east of Aunt Bea's. Donald's Lake they call it, because it once belonged to Donald Coghill, a grandson of my great-grandfather. Before that it belonged to the Lamon family, so some local people call it Lamons' Lake.

Fall had arrived during the night on a northwest wind, and morning found the land draped in cold mists. I could see no more than fifty feet ahead as I walked the path from Aunt Bea's to the pond. A porcupine lumbered across the trail where it opened upon the clearing that encircles Donald's Lake. The maple and elm trees against the shore looked weary of their leaves. I imagined abscission layers forming between stems and leaves, stripping the green masks to reveal bright verities of orange and yellow. The fog was rising out of the valley and spilling down into the amphitheatre that embraces the pond. Shreds of mist passed before me, drifting through the space between the shoreline at my feet and a half-submerged stand of cattails three paces into the water. At the edge of visibility, where the lake and the fog blurred together, families of teal and ruddy duck silently paraded away from me and into the shroud of grey.

The lisping notes of migrant warblers rang loudly within the lake's bell of stillness: the contact notes of yellow and Tennessee warblers and red-eyed vireos, and then the hurried song of a Wilson's warbler from somewhere across the water. An oriole called nearby, and just overhead came the *eek* of a rose-breasted grosbeak in flight. A great horned owl hooted once, and everything in the world concentrated to a singular flow. Time slipped away from me. The fog increased, layers passing over the lake like Japanese panels, one behind the other. A muskrat broke the water into mercury-coloured circles at the edge of the cattails. Unseen waterbirds — grebes or coots — made splashy pattering sounds as they practised take-off manoeuvres.

The sounds of the songbirds intensified, thin piping whispers drawing nearer until out of the fog emerged a small, frenetic band of flycatchers, chickadees, and warblers, jumping excitedly from twig to twig in the willows right next to me. The birds, bright, fierce knots of life, hung upside down from branches like phosphorescent fruit. Unafraid or unseeing, they passed just above my head back and forth between two willow clumps. The wind shearing off one warbler's wing moved a strand of my hair. I imagined that the fog had made me invisible.

Then something emerged from the lake in front of me. It was the muskrat waddling up his trough of matted grass, stopping to shake like a water spaniel and splashing me with a spray of droplets. That done, he made his way slowly past me to the trail and then slipped into the mists.

The owl hooted another verse of its song. I looked out to Donald's Lake where the fog was now beginning to depart. In a few minutes the last wisps raced north off the pond, chased by a small gust of air blowing up from the valley's edge. The pond's surface rippled and danced in glistening shards of sunlight. The woods on the far side made their appearance, and Donald's Lake was once again the domain of sun and sky.

Turning away from the water's edge, I walked south along the wooded shoreline. It was still early and I wanted to see if the valley had given up its fog yet. Leopard frogs by the dozens jumped before my footsteps, escorting me through the high grass and across the narrow wheat field that separates the lake from the oak-fringed valley rim. Once I made the trees, I followed deer trails to a clearing atop a knoll that overlooks the S-bend that the Qu'Appelle takes from Bear Creek to the Little Cutarm. As far as I could see, several miles up and down the valley, it was draped in fog, brimming like a great river of mist running through the plains. I stood marvelling at the blue sunlit sky overhead and the clouded lowland at my feet. Somewhere below the blanket of grey, Tantallon was awakening to Fair Day. Horses were arriving in trailers, but there would be no heavy breeds. Women were primping gladiolas, polishing jars of cranberry jelly, and taking pies out of the oven as their children sat with bowls of Fruit Loops before televisions aglow with cartoons produced in Japan.

But the fog did not know these things. It was a cloud of unknowing that had been here many times before, over thousands of years, a recongregating of water molecules and dust particles traded between valley, river, and sky, temporarily concealing the valley and its dwellers from the scrutiny of time's passage. Beneath the mists, I thought, there could easily be other moments from other lives: a train loading alongside grain elevators; the clerks in front of Paynter's store setting out produce for the day; boys yipping in cannonball dives off the bridge; a mansion shaded by riverside elms; upriver, women washing clothes in the shallows, teenaged boys burying a still in a sandbar; farther upriver, a procession of mounted Cree warriors heading for Batoche; and farther yet, ten thousand buffalo grazing on big bluestem by restless waters flushed from uplands and from springs as far away as the valley's origins, where a stone buffalo watches over the shifts of a stream that flows east or west at its bidding.

When the fog lifts, these other lives will be gone, hidden in the clays and silts of the floodplain. Taking one last look at the river of mist, I left the clearing and headed back into the oak woods, down a game trail bound for the bottomlands. It was easy enough to conjure ghosts, to imagine myself a phantom, as I passed by twisted oaks with upper branches lost in the murk overhead and felt the roll of the season's first acorns underfoot: *A lot of mast on the ground. Should let the pigs out for a run. Where the hell are the partridge this morning? One of those bloody Finns has been up here again poachin'.*

As I came out of the woods and down upon the valley bottom at Eino Kallio's yard site, I felt as though I were accompanied by others, as though I were one step nearer the lives of the eastern Qu'Appelle. Returning to old pathways and stories will not deliver us out of the exile that we experience in our nostalgia and in our restless search for a way of dwelling here. Still, I believe that knowing the names, telling the stories, and walking the trails can draw us nearer the presences in a landscape, near enough for reconciliation to get a foothold.

A couple of discoveries, small blessings that came to me after I stepped onto the abandoned CPR line, made reconciliation seem all the more possible. Walking the trackless bed toward McRae's Crossing, I stooped to pick up a lump of coal dropped God knows how many decades ago from a steam train chugging its way to Hazelcliffe and Esterhazy. When I stood up again, I found myself facing, instead of the usual thistle and sweet clover that covers the rail bed, a healthy stand of big bluestem as high as my shoulders. A bobolink sang from the ditch. I walked into the grass in disbelief, pacing it off and looking for weeds. There were none. It was a solid easement of big bluestem 180 paces along the abandoned line. Two points for the natives: the ancient sequence survives here in the matrix of soil and seed.

I continued westward down the rail bed into the fog. The landscape was still hidden in mists. Fifty paces of rail bed was my horizon, but I knew the trail would eventually bisect the valley road where the train used to turn north up the Little Cutarm across the McRae land. As I came to the road, a white-tailed doe bounded out of the ditch and over the gravel surface. Once on the road, I made my way up-valley a short distance, watching for the Little Cutarm entering the Qu'Appelle from the north. Somewhere to my right was the three-corner field stretching below Bruce's Point. On my left, the old footpaths ran down to the washing place and to the Kallios' south of the river. Just as I began to wonder if I had somehow missed the creek in the fog, there it was, emerging from the mists like a stricken animal. I stared at the stream, watching its thin, yellow band of water trickle into the culverts at the road edge. As far as I could see upstream into the fog, the creek was flanked by bare mud pocked by hoofprints from the cattle that had trampled and eaten every shred of vegetation within thirty feet of its margins. The maple trees where "gypsies" once came to camp were dead snags, stripped of their bark and broken. A few weeks earlier, the creek had looked badly overgrazed, but the water was high enough and clean enough to hide the damage. Now there was only this wretched, urine-tinted livestock sewer at the bottom of a muddy ditch. My anger rising as I ran through a list of who and what to blame, I walked across to the south side of the road to see how the creek looked there.

The contrast staggered me; it was like turning a page or flipping a louvred image. Here, in an unfenced, ungrazed meadow, the creek was alive again. Not pristine — there were alien thistles, brome grass and other weeds — and although the water had to be the same the creek's surface was now a deep cobalt blue, tinted by the shadows of over-hanging bank vegetation. Cattails, sprays of sedge, and mounds of slough-grass covered the banks, shaping it from side to side with soft, meandering curves. A pool at the outlet of the culverts, the surface spat-tered yellows with emergent ranunculus and pondweed, spilled over stones and into an S-curve of creek that slipped from view behind bull-rushes half hidden in the fog.

Still watering the alluvium of these bottomlands and the lives we have left behind in sedimentary layers, Kiskipittonawe Sepesis survives. At my back was a culture and a history that rests now in layers of silt and mud; in front of me, the rank, promiscuous blend of native and immigrant vegetation doing all it could to purify the creek on its last stretch down to the Qu'Appelle. I decided to follow. For a moment, in the increasing light of that blessed morning, I was able to forgive and to hope.

# NOTES

1 Klaus Burmeister, "Folklore in the Intercultural Context: Legends of the Calling River," in *Culture, Education, and Ethnic Canadians*, conference proceedings, October 1 and 2, 1976, Regina, Sask.

2 Henry Youle Hind, *Narrative of the Canadian Red River Exploring Expedition of 1857 and of the Assiniboine and Saskatchewan Exploring Expedition of 1858*, Vol. 1 (Edmonton: Hurtig, 1971), 370.

3 Hind, *Narrative*.

4 Daniel Williams Harmon, *Sixteen Years in Indian Country* (Toronto: Macmillan, 1957), 76.

5 People of mixed aboriginal and non-aboriginal parentage did not refer to themselves as Métis until well into the twentieth century. In the nineteenth century they were known variously as mixed-bloods, half-breeds, the Bois Brule, or the *hivernants*. The name that perhaps captures the character of the mixed-blood people best was the one their half brothers, the Cree, devised: "Ootip ayim sowak," which translates roughly as "the people that own themselves" or "the people that nobody owns."

6 Avonlea Historical Committee, *Arrowheads to Wheatfields: Avonlea, Hearne and Districts* (Avonlea, Sask.: Avonlea Historical Committee, 1983), 5.

7 Wendell Berry advances this criticism of industrialized agriculture in *The Unsettling of America: Culture and Agriculture* (San Francisco: Sierra Club Books, 1977).

8 New York: Ballantine Books, 1966.

9 Carl Sauer, "Plants, Animals and Man," in *Selected Essays of Carl O. Sauer* (Berkeley, Calif.: Turtle Island Foundation, 1981), 290–91.

10 Ann Zwinger, "It Flows Along Forever," *Orion* (summer 1996): 32.

11 John Palliser, "Papers relative to the expedition by Captain Palliser of that portion of British North America which lies between the Northern Branch of the River Saskatchewan and the frontier of the United States; and between the Red River and Rocky Mountains," command paper presented to both Houses of Parliament by Command of Her Majesty: June 1859, p. 14.

12 Both of these quotations are from Hind, *Narrative*, Vol. 1, 269.

13 Later at the Red River where the overland portion of the expedition began, the paddlers were replaced by several half-breed hunters and guides.

14 Both of these quotations are from Hind, *Narrative*, Vol. 1, 329.

15 Herd law forced open-range ranchers to fence the prairie, making it safe for homesteaders to plough the grass under and raise crops.

16 This and the two subsequent quotations are from Hind, *Narrative*, Vol. 1, 360.

17 Hind, *Narrative*, Vol. 1, 359.

18 Ibid.,Vol. 2, 198–99 ff.

19 Toronto: McClelland & Stewart, 1992, 246.

20 Hind, *Narrative*, Vol. 1, 364.

21 W.O. Kupsch, "Largest Erratic in Saskatchewan?" *Blue Jay* 21, no. 1: 2–4.

22 All quotes are from a full transcript of the address carried in the *Moose Jaw Times* of May 28, 1959.

23 Museum Archaeological Files, Royal Saskatchewan Museum.

24 Ken Mitchell, "The Great Rock is Gone and No Cree Cries," *Maclean's*, February 1967, 4.

25 Museum Archaeological Files, Royal Saskatchewan Museum.

26 Mitchell, *Maclean's*.

27 Z.S. Pohorecky, "The Great Cree Stone," *Canadian Geographical Journal* 73, no. 3 (September 1966): 88–91.

28 Regina *Leader-Post*, December 2, 1966.

29 Museum Archaeological Files, Royal Saskatchewan Museum.

30 Birdie McLean, "Canadian Indian Statesman, Martyr, Poundmaker," *Northian: Journal of the Society for Indian and Northern Education* 5, no. 1 (winter 1971), 9–12.

31 Museum Archaeological Files, Royal Saskatchewan Museum.

32 As growers of tame grass monocultures, prairie farmers have never been fond of anything that eats grass intended for harvest. The smallest of grazers, the grasshopper, has inspired agri-scientists to develop some of the deadliest technologies used in the war on native grazers.

33 Fertilizer costs for a typical blend have risen from $279 per tonne in 1993 to $420 per tonne in 1996. Regina *Leader-Post*, December 5, 1998, p. 1.

34 John Macoun, *Manitoba and the Great North-West* (Guelph: World Publishing Company, 1882), 194.

35 Macoun, *Manitoba*, 194 ff.

36 Ibid., 72–73.

37 Ramsar is the name of a global treaty on wetland protection. It was

named for the city in Iran where the first Convention on Wetlands of International Importance was held, in 1971.

38 J. Kleine, Last Mountain Lake local histories, n.d., Archives of Saskatchewan.

39 *Silton Seasons* (Toronto: Doubleday, 1975), 12–13.

40 The citizens of one of the newest subdivisions recently banded together in civic action to kill the beavers in a lakeside pond that we often visit in the fall. It seems the beavers had not yet learned to distinguish between a native poplar and a pedigreed, nursery-reared, fluff-free hybrid growing on a suburban lawn.

41 It would be naïve to think that this contrast springs entirely from a difference in cultural regard for the land. Indian bands, like any modern people, are quite capable of exploiting and despoiling their resources, given sufficient economic incentive.

42 There are eighteen Indian reserves in the Qu'Appelle basin.

43 Hind, *Narrative*, Vol. 2, 131.

44 David Abram, *The Spell of the Sensuous* (New York: Vintage, 1997).

45 E. Manley Callin, *Birds of the Qu'Appelle, 1857–1979* (Regina: Saskatchewan Natural History Society, 1980), 93.

46 Callin, 102.

47 Callin, 94.

48 The Big Cutarm is the eastern counterpart to the Little Cutarm. One on either side of Tantallon, they both enter the valley from the north as major tributaries, among the last before the Qu'Appelle flows into the Assiniboine River at St. Lazare, Manitoba.

49 John McDougall, *Saddle, Sled, and Snowshoe: Pioneering on the Saskatchewan in the Sixties* (Toronto: William Briggs, 1886), 137.

50 Callin, 104.

51 Emigrants' ditty from Canadian Pacific Railway archives.

52 Wendell Berry, *The Hidden Wound* (San Francisco: North Point Press, 1989), 99.

53 Berry, 88, 99.

54 John Ruskin, *Seven Lamps of Architecture* (New York: Dover, 1989), 7.

55 See Alex McDonald's detailed summary of the Hamona experience, "Practical Utopians: Ed and Will Paynter and the Harmony Industrial Association," *Saskatchewan History* (Spring 1995), 13–26.

56 McDonald, 13.

57 Wolverine Hobby & Historical Society, *The Spy Hill Story* (Spy Hill: Wolverine Hobby & Historical Society, 1971), 418–19.

58 Gilbert Johnson, unpublished document on file at the Spy Hill Museum.

59  Edward Paynter to Harry J. Perrin, unpublished correspondence on file at the Spy Hill Museum.

60  Quoted from a letter from Ed Paynter to Lewis H. Thomas, February 3, 1951. The rest of this section is a patchwork of paraphrasing, factual record, and my own speculation with the odd phrase of Paynter's thrown in verbatim.

61  James T. Calder, *Sketch of the Civil and Traditional History of Caithness* (Wick, Scotland: William Rae, 1887), 42.

62  This is an imagined episode inspired by much staring at maps of Caithness and its River Thurso.

63  Rev. J. Reader, *Touchwood Times*, 1955, Jubilee Edition, p. 6. Reprinted from a 1920 edition.

# Selected Bibliography

Abram, David. *The Spell of the Sensuous*. New York: Vintage, 1997.

Avonlea Historical Committee. *Arrowheads to Wheatfields: Avonlea, Hearne and Districts*. Avonlea, Sask.: Avonlea Historical Committee, 1983.

Berry, Wendell. *The Unsettling of America: Culture and Agriculture*. San Francisco: Sierra Club Books, 1977.

Burmeister, Klaus. "Folklore in the Intercultural Context: Legends of the Calling River." In *Culture, Education, and Ethnic Canadians*, conference proceedings, October 1 and 2, 1976, Regina, Sask.

Callin, E. Manley, *Birds of the Qu'Appelle, 1857–1979*. Regina: Saskatchewan Natural History Society, 1980.

Harmon, Daniel Williams. *Sixteen Years in Indian Country*. Toronto: Macmillan, 1957.

Hind, Henry Youle. *Narrative of the Canadian Red River Exploring Expedition of 1857 and of the Assiniboine and Saskatchewan Exploring Expedition of 1858*, Vol. 1. Edmonton: Hurtig, 1971.

Kupsch, W.O. "Largest Erratic in Saskatchewan?" *Blue Jay* 21, no. 1: 2–4.

Leopold, Aldo. *A Sand County Almanac*. New York: Ballantine Books, 1966.

Lopez, Barry. *Arctic Dreams: Imagination and Desire in a Northern Landscape*. New York: Scribner, 1986.

Macoun, John. *Manitoba and the Great North-West*. Guelph: World Publishing Company, 1882.

McDonald, Alex. "Practical Utopians: Ed and Will Paynter and the Harmony Industrial Association." *Saskatchewan History* (Spring 1995): 13–26.

Pohorecky, Z.S. "The Great Cree Stone." *Canadian Geographical Journal* 73, no. 3 (September 1966): 88–91.

Sanders, Scott Russell. "Telling the Holy." *Orion* (Spring 1995).

Sauer, Carl. *Selected Essays of Carl O. Sauer*. Berkeley: Turtle Island Foundation, 1981.

Sealey, D. Bruce, and Antoine S. Lussier. *The Métis: Canada's Forgotten People*. Winnipeg: Pemmican Publications, 1983.

Spry, Irene, ed. *Papers of the Palliser Expedition, 1857–1860*. Toronto: Champlain Society, 1968.

Stegner, Wallace. *Wolf Willow: A History, a Story, and a Memory of the Last Plains Frontier*. New York: Viking Press, 1962.

Symons, R.D. *Silton Seasons*. Toronto: Doubleday, 1975.

Wolverine Hobby & Historical Society. *The Spy Hill Story*. Spy Hill: Wolverine Hobby & Historical Society, 1971.

Zwinger, Ann. "It Flows Along Forever," *Orion* (Summer 1996).

# Acknowledgments

Thıs book has taken me on a long walk through familiar and unfamiliar territory toward a country hidden by nostalgia, desire, and regret. The walking is over and now my thoughts turn to those who pointed me in the right direction, fed me, gave me shelter, wished me well. These are the people to whom I am indebted:

My parents, Norman and Jeanne Herriot, for telling me family stories and for knowing instinctively how important such stories are to the growing up of children. My life has been richer for having a mother who encouraged me to write and draw and a father who took me paddling down the South Saskatchewan in a canoe that I had watched him build in our garage the winter before.

The McRaes, all of my aunts and uncles, especially Aunt Evelyn, Uncle Babes, and Aunt Bea, for letting me listen to them and borrow their voices. They are rare and fine people and I am more than privileged to dwell in the shelter of such a family.

My wife, Karen, for showing me the innocence and loveliness in people, for teaching me that a good storyteller knows when to let Truth govern the true, for keeping all the plates spinning at home while I was away for weeks at a time, for putting up with my many faults, and for believing that all the hours at my desk would eventually come to good. Karen, you have made me grateful beyond telling.

The Saskatchewan Writers Guild and the City of Regina, for seeing fit to award me the 1996 City of Regina Writing Award, which allowed me the time to travel in the Qu'Appelle Basin for a summer, researching and writing as I went.

The staff at Stoddart Publishing, Don Bastian in particular, for their enthusiasm and diligence in taking my manuscript and making it into a book. Anne Holloway and Shaun Oakey, for their editorial touch, encouraging words, and thoughtful suggestions. My literary agent, Jan Whitford, for knowing just what to say to a skittish first-time author.

There are many others to thank for the hospitality, patience, assistance, and encouragement they offered: Paul Wilson, Peter Oliva, George Melnyk, Ken Mitchell, Sharon Butala, Robert Wright, John Dipple, Don Book, Lynden Penner, the late Zenon Pohorecky, Wes Fineday, Dr. Stuart Houston, Jack and Louise Sutherland, Tom Harrison, Les Hall, Florence Carrier, Velma Bear, Andy Goodfeather, Jack Semple, John Pollack, Gary and Sharon Tinnish, Jean Larose, Jerry McRae, and Brian Hoxha.

Finally, I reserve my deepest gratitude for the one person whose wisdom and generosity shaped this book from its early outlines to its final drafts. During my summer in the Qu'Appelle, the summer of 1996, I did a lot of walking, dreaming, napping, and praying. The first three led to the notes that became my first draft; the fourth, I believe, led to Myrna Kostash. Myrna, an internationally recognized author who has worked for many years at the vanguard of creative non-fiction in Canada, came to Regina that fall to serve as the public library's writer-in-residence (the first non-fiction writer ever to be appointed to the post). I began showing her draft outlines and chapters the week she took office. Suddenly I had the finest counsellor, advocate, and editor anyone writing this kind of book could wish for. Over the next two years, while researching and writing two of her own books and travelling to readings, lectures, and workshops around the globe, she gave far more time and thought to my manuscript than her schedule could afford. Long after her term as writer-in-residence expired and she moved back home to Edmonton, Myrna continued helping me with the manuscript, asking the tough questions, bringing me back down to earth, sharpening the focus of my rambling stories, and in a dozen other ways helping me to find my voice as a writer.

Myrna, I try not to imagine what my pile of notes would have come to without your guidance. You were a blessing to me, a generous spirit direct from whatever it is in life that makes us want to tell stories. Thank you.

While I share with Myrna and all the others named here the credit for anything good in this book, for the bad — anything that offends, misinforms, or disappoints — I take full and unqualified responsibility.

*Trevor Herriot*

# INDEX